KQP310 JOH

The Japanese Way of Justice

STUDIES ON LAW AND SOCIAL CONTROL
Donald Black, Series Editor

AUTHORITY WITHOUT POWER
Law and the Japanese Paradox
John Owen Haley

THE THERAPEUTIC CORPORATION
James Tucker

THE JAPANESE WAY OF JUSTICE
Prosecuting Crime in Japan
David T. Johnson

The Japanese Way of Justice

Prosecuting Crime in Japan

DAVID T. JOHNSON

OXFORD
UNIVERSITY PRESS

2002

OXFORD
UNIVERSITY PRESS

Oxford   New York
Athens   Auckland   Bangkok   Bogotá   Buenos Aires   Cape Town
Chennai   Dar es Salaam   Delhi   Florence   Hong Kong   Istanbul   Karachi
Kolkata   Kuala Lumpur   Madrid   Melbourne   Mexico City   Mumbai   Nairobi
Paris   São Paulo   Shanghai   Singapore   Taipei   Tokyo   Toronto   Warsaw

and associated companies in

Berlin   Ibadan

Library of Congress Cataloging-in-Publication Data

Johnson, David T. (David Ted)
    The Japanese way of justice : prosecuting crime in Japan / David T. Johnson.
       p.   cm. — (Studies on law and social control ; 3)
    Includes bibliographical references and index.
    ISBN 0-19-511986-X
    1. Public prosecutors — Japan.
    2. Prosecution — Japan.
    3. Criminal justice, Administration of — Japan.
    I. Title.
    II. Series.
    KNX4630.S73 J64   2001
    345.52′01 — dc21   00-069877

9 8 7 6 5 4 3 2 1

Printed in the United States of America
on acid-free paper

*To Mom and Dad and all my teachers,
with appreciation and admiration*

Preface

"The procuracy has more control over life, liberty, and reputation than any other organization in Japan." Ironically, this proposition elicits widespread agreement but few serious efforts to explore its causes, consequences, or significance. The irony makes the procuracy a little like the weather: everyone discusses it but no one does anything about it. This is the first book in English to analyze how Japan's two thousand prosecutors exercise their formidable powers. It paints an empirical sketch of prosecutors at work; the contexts in which they investigate, charge, and try cases; and the content of the decisions rendered. Since prosecutors wield vast discretion at every stage of the criminal process, and since criminal proceedings constitute one of the principal indicators of the character of a society, this study offers a window onto Japan. Because this book is comparative, chiefly with the United States, it also affords insights into American law and society.

The Japanese way of justice is in large part determined by the way prosecutors perform their jobs. If justice means taking into account the needs and circumstances of individual suspects, then prosecutors in Japan must receive higher marks than their American counterparts. If justice implies treating like cases alike, then the capacity of Japan's procuracy to do so is impressive indeed. If justice should promote healing, not just punishment, then Japanese prosecutors must be reckoned more restorative than prosecutors in the United States. And if justice depends on uncovering and clarifying the truth, then readers will see how fundamental this maxim is deemed to be in Japan. In these ways and more, the Japanese way of justice is uncommonly just.

Yet this account uncovers serious defects as well. In processing sex offenders, for example, Japanese prosecutors routinely discount and disregard the feelings of female victims. In their passion for preserving high conviction rates, prosecutors sacrifice the interests of victims who yearn to be heard in open court. In their insulation from political and public scrutiny, prosecutors seem unaccountable to legitimate authority and influence. And in their zeal to obtain the truth through confessions, some prosecutors plea-bargain, doctor dossiers, and conduct brutal interrogations, all actions that are illegal in Japan.

Japan is a long way from the United States. This book demonstrates that in many matters of criminal justice, the two nations are different worlds.

Author's Note

Except where common usage is otherwise, Japanese names are shown Japanese style: last name first.

Acknowledgments

Intellectual projects are never finished; one just stops. It is time to stop writing and start thanking the people who helped get me started, keep me going, and make me stop.

I have received invaluable support from many people. At Berkeley, where this project began, Malcolm Feeley, Franklin Zimring, Sheldon Messinger, Jerome Skolnick, and Gregory Noble provided the freedom I needed to discover what to say and the discipline I needed to turn discoveries into arguments. Mahalo. Other California help came from Andrew Barshay, Karen Chin, Gordon Hawkins, Rob Hennig, Sanford Kadish, Robert Kagan, Dong-no and Young-in Kim, Dan Krislov, Martin Krygier, Charles McClain, Margo Rodriguez, Edward Rubin, Tom Scanlon, Harry Scheiber, Martin Shapiro, Mike Smith, and Rod Watanabe. Pre-Berkeley, I thank Mary Brinton, Edward Laumann, Norval Morris, Gerald Suttles, and the late, great James S. Coleman at the University of Chicago, and Tom Correll and Paul Wiebe at Bethel College in St. Paul. Post-Berkeley, I thank Susan Pharr and Frank Schwartz at Harvard University; Patricia Steinhoff, Kiyoshi Ikeda, Eldon Wegner, Meda Chesney-Lind, Meiko Arai, and Georgia Niimoto at the University of Hawaii at Manoa; and Michael McCann, Marie Anchordoguy, Bryan Brown, and Dixielynn Gleason at the University of Washington. At Oxford University Press, Joan Bossert, Dedi Felman, and Lisa Stallings provided adroit editorial support. Many scholars gave helpful comments on earlier versions of this book, especially David Bayley, Donald Black, John O. Haley, Chalmers Johnson, David Nelken, J. Mark Ramseyer, and (in uncommonly generous ways) Daniel Foote. Thank you all.

I could not have started or stopped this project without generous financial support. The universities in Chicago and Berkeley gave me more money than I deserved. A Fulbright Graduate Research Fellowship, administered by the Japan-U.S. Educational Commission, enabled me to stay in Kobe long enough to get in and get along in the prosecutors office, and the United Nations Asia and Far East Institute for the Prevention of Crime and the Treatment of Offenders (UNAFEI) in Japan's Ministry of Justice provided an office, connections, and salary so that I could remain in Tokyo for fifteen more months of research. Thereafter, I received substantial (and serendipitous) support from the Boalt Hall School of Law's Earl Warren Legal Institute, directed by Franklin Zimring, and from Boalt Hall's Sho Sato U.S.-Japan Legal Studies Program, administered by Edward Rubin. Harvard University's Program on U.S.-Japan Relations made possible a stimulating year of postdoctoral study. The Abe Fellowship Program, the Social Science Research Council, the University of Hawaii at Manoa, and the University of Washington in Seattle also provided generous support. I am grateful to all of the above for helping fulfill the various requirements in my Maslowian hierarchy of needs.

A friend is someone who knows all about you and likes you just the same. To Richard Leo, my best friend, thank you for knowing, liking, listening, and critiquing. For education and entertainment of various and sundry kinds, and for helping me find and make meaning, I thank Adrienne Birch (Hawaii's top tita), Michael Beard, Tamami Cook, Laura Edles, Ariana Seldman, Mary Wittinger, and Yamamoto Jiro and his tattooed friends.

A host of people and organizations provided guidance during my stays in Japan, but I direct special thanks to Miyazawa Setsuo, professor of law at Waseda University. From inception to conclusion, Setsuo gave generously of his time, attention, and ideas. Like it or not, he is the godfather of this book, in more ways than one. I also thank the many Japanese reporters, scholars, and legal professionals who made my stays in their country often pleasant and always interesting: Ageishi Yoshiichi, Araki Jirō, Araki Nobuyoshi, Fujiwara Seigo, Hata Hiroto, Hayashi Mitsuo, Igarashi Futaba, Inoue Masahito, Irie Hiroshi, Kanda Kazunori, Kashimura Shiro, Kitamura Yoshinobu, Kobayashi Teruyoshi, Kobayashi Tetsuya, Kuramoto Teruyo, Mitsui Makoto, Miyamoto Masafumi, Miyauchi Tsutomu, Mori Katsuji, Murayama Masayuki, Nakatsukasa Masahiro, Ochiai Hiromitsu, Ōmori Reiko, Ōnuki Takeshi, Ōtani Mikiko, Ōtsuka Hiroshi, Sakamaki Tadashi, Shimizu Junichi, Shimizu Tateo, Shinomiya Satoru, Suami Takao, Sugawara Ikuo, Suzuki Yoshio, Takano Takashi, Tanase Takao, Tani Takashi, Tanji Hatsuhiko, Terasawa Yū, Tsuchimoto Takeshi, Wakamatsu Yoshiya, Yamaguchi Toshikazu, Yamashita Yukio, Yasuda Yoshiko, Yasunami Ryosuke, Yoneda Kenichi, who helped translate the survey, and countless others whose name cards I have misplaced or whose anonymity I have guaranteed. In America I thank criminal justice officials in Oakland, Minneapolis, San Diego, and Hawaii. You were as open and cooperative as I asked.

My biggest debt is to the many Japanese prosecutors I encountered, observed, interviewed, surveyed, learned from, and argued with during the thirty-three months in Japan when the basis for this book was conceived and constructed. The Japanese adage puts it better than I ever could: I cannot repay one ten-thousandth of this debt.

Finally, I am indebted to Ashgate Publishing Company and the Law & Society Association for permission to reproduce and adapt portions from the following of my articles: "Prosecutor Culture in Japan and the USA," in David Nelken, ed., *Contrasting Criminal Justice: Getting from Here to There* (Burlington, VT: Ashgate Publishing Company, 2000), pp. 157–204; "The Organization of Prosecution and the Possibility of Order," *Law & Society Review*, 32, no. 2 (1998): 247–308.

Honolulu, Hawaii   David T. Johnson
October 2000

Contents

The Japanese Way of Justice

Introduction

> The prosecutor has more control over life, liberty, and reputation than any other person in America. His discretion is tremendous. He can have citizens investigated and, if he is that kind of person, he can have this done to the tune of public statements and veiled or unveiled intimations. Or the prosecutor may choose a more subtle course and simply have a citizen's friends interviewed. The prosecutor can order arrests, present cases to the grand jury in secret session, and on the basis of his one-sided presentation of the facts, can cause the citizen to be indicted and held for trial. He may dismiss the case before trial, in which case the defense never has to be heard. Or he may go on with a public trial. If he obtains a conviction, the prosecutor can still make recommendations as to sentence, as to whether the prisoner should get probation or a suspended sentence. . . . If the prosecutor is obliged to choose his cases, it follows that he can choose his defendants. . . . [A] prosecutor stands a fair chance of finding at least a technical violation of some act on the part of almost anyone. . . . It is in this realm — in which the prosecutor picks some person whom he dislikes or desires to embarrass, or selects some group of unpopular persons and then looks for an offense — that the greatest danger of abuse of prosecuting power lies. It is here that law enforcement becomes personal.
>
> Robert Jackson, U.S. Attorney General and Supreme
> Court Justice, "The Federal Prosecutor"

> Japanese procurators . . . have considerably greater authority and discretion than has an American prosecuting attorney.
>
> Chalmers Johnson, *Conspiracy at Matsukawa*

Jackson and Johnson are right: American prosecutors have "tremendous discretion," yet the power of Japanese prosecutors is even more immense. Indeed, it is difficult to find a state agency — inside Japan or out — that wields as much power as Japan's procuracy. Commentators disagree about whether Japanese prosecutors exercise their powers for good or for ill. Some see them as a key to their country's crime control successes and as uncommonly able to rehabilitate offenders, restore victims, and do justice. Others behold obstinate, self-interested, selectively benevolent officials who, wanting to "play God," have appropriated powers properly possessed by judges

3

and used them to crush the rights of suspects, offenders, and victims. Unfortunately, there is no third school of thought populated by people who have studied the prosecutors whom others proclaim as achievers or subverters of justice. The purpose of this book is to draw an empirical sketch of Japanese prosecutors, the contexts in which they work, and the powers they individually and collectively exercise. Toward that end, this introduction explains and justifies the choice of prosecutors as a research subject, describes how I acquired evidence for my arguments, provides an overview of the criminal processes in Japan and the United States, and summarizes the book's main claims.

Why Japanese Prosecutors?

I spent much of the 1990s — including a thousand days in Japan — studying Japanese criminal justice. I focused on prosecutors because they make many of the most important decisions about who gets what in the Japanese way of justice, because they are a sorely neglected research site, and because I was able to gain intimate access to their work lives. Consider each reason in turn.

Contradictory Claims

Prosecutors in Japan often are regarded as significant actors, both in their capacity to control crime and in their ability to make just decisions. Daniel Foote (1992a), for example, believes "the objective of criminal justice in Japan, as in virtually every other nation, is maintaining order," and asserts that the "benevolent paternalism" of Japanese criminal justice works to control crime and maintain order, primarily by preventing recidivism through the rehabilitation and reintegration of offenders. On this view, since prosecutors "dominate" Japan's criminal process, both in precharge investigations and in the trials that follow, they are one key cause of the country's highly acclaimed crime control successes. John Owen Haley (1992) concurs, arguing that prosecutors play a "critical role" in a criminal justice system that attracts increasing attention from the West. The attention is deserved, Haley adds, because Japan's success in reducing crime is "its most spectacular postwar feat." Whereas American criminal justice is locked in a destructive "spiral of failure" which overemphasizes punishment and incapacitation, Japan's stress on the norms of "confession, repentance, and absolution" results in a remarkable "spiral of success." Similarly, William Clifford (1976) claims that Japan's "social miracle" of containing and even reducing crime in the postwar years is at least as profound an achievement as its more widely recognized economic miracle. As for the causes of that success, Clifford concludes that "in any society trying to deal with crime there must be a system or organization that can be trusted" to deal with it, and contends that in Japan "it is primarily the public prosecutors" who receive such trust. Satyanshu Mukherjee (1995) tries to "unravel the process" that has led to Japan's postwar crime control success. He finds that two primary causes are the ability of prosecutors to convict almost all offenders they charge, and the exceptional "efficiency" of a criminal justice system in which prosecutors play the pivotal role.

In short, prosecutors have been given much of the credit for Japan's considerable crime control successes. But pundits of the procuracy do not stop here, for many believe that prosecutors in Japan dispense an unusually high quality of justice. The best illustration is again Daniel Foote (1992a), the leading foreign authority on criminal justice in Japan. Although Foote acknowledges that there are "tradeoffs and drawbacks" in Japan's approach to criminal justice, for him the Japanese system has many "evident successes" besides crime control. He argues that the "benevolent paternalism" of Japanese criminal justice differs in three crucial respects from "crime control models" that prevail in the West and that stress the values of speed, finality, uniformity, and strict punishment. In Japan the speed of justice is less important than precisely and accurately discovering the facts and clarifying the truth. When efficiency and truth conflict, the latter predominates. In the same vein, dispositions in Japan do not become final until defense and prosecution have had one level of full review of both facts and law. If the system looks languid to outsiders, it may be because many Japanese "like it that way" (C. Johnson 1972). Most important, prosecutors, police, and judges consider each individual's personal circumstances in order to individualize justice and rehabilitate and reintegrate offenders. Thus, according to Foote, criminal justice officials in Japan eschew the uniformity of standards and procedures that characterize many Western systems of justice. In the end, the "benevolent paternalism" of Japanese justice reduces recidivism rates by reintegrating offenders, "satisfies victims" both materially and psychologically, and engenders "trust in [the system] among both the general public and offenders themselves" (1992a).

Other scholars agree that Japan's criminal process generates just decisions. John Owen Haley, for example, maintains that "the Japanese leitmotifs of confession, repentance, and absolution may provide insights for other industrial societies seeking to establish a more humane and just system of criminal justice" (1989), and thinks prosecutors deserve much of the credit for such achievements. B. J. George, Jr. (1984), has even higher praise, arguing that prosecutors in Japan "are committed to a standard of objectively fair administration of justice to a far greater extent than all but a handful of federal and state prosecutors in the United States. . . . In fair exercise of prosecutorial powers . . . Japan is both 'number one' and unique."[1] In sum, prosecutors in Japan are widely regarded as effective agents of crime control who are ex-

---

1. Many scholars have claimed that prosecutors in Japan are adroit at controlling crime and doing justice. For example, Ted Westermann and James Burfeind (1991:109) note that prosecutors in both Japan and the United States are given broad discretion but argue that "the reasons for dropping a case and the procedures for doing so are quite distinct in each country." The decision to prosecute or not is "markedly more discretionary in Japan" because prosecutors try to "promote individualized justice and provide incentives for rehabilitation." Unlike their American counterparts, Japanese prosecutors "often drop cases for reasons other than insufficient and faulty evidence," and their "benevolent and rehabilitative intent remains exceedingly strong." Malcolm Feeley (1985:602) believes the Japanese practice of dropping prosecution because the accused has made restitution "stands in sharp contrast with American practices." Marcia Goodman (1986) observes that American prosecutors have wide authority to decide whether or not to charge offenders, but contends that prosecutors in Japan possess even more discretion (because the law explicitly grants them the power to be lenient) and concludes that they generally exercise it fairly. See also Aoyagi (1981), Itoh (1987), E. Johnson (1996), Nomura (1991), Ota (1999), and Sasaki (2000).

ceptionally adept at reaching just dispositions. If these assessments are accurate, then Japan's procuracy is indeed extraordinary. Prosecutors in no other country have been so highly commended.[2]

However, Japanese prosecutors are considered extraordinary in less laudable ways as well. In his classic study of the *Conspiracy at Matsukawa*, Chalmers Johnson (1972) declares that Japan's procuracy is no longer as "fascist" as its prewar predecessor, but insists it is still "dangerous" because it combines the "power of prejudgment" with a rigidly bureaucratic and hierarchical structure. Johnson charges that even a quarter-century after postwar reforms, "in political cases or instances of a mistake by the procuracy," prosecutors' bureaucratic interests often "override their commitment to serve the public's interests," causing them to "obstinately" persist with charges that they ought to withdraw. Koyama Masaki (1991) concludes that the problems Johnson described remain all too evident. Prosecutors, Koyama claims, "seldom exercise their discretionary powers to withdraw charges," even when they should. Worse still, prosecutors "have often tried to conceal the problems of investigation," even though, as "quasi-judicial officers," they are obligated to investigate cases impartially.

The Dutch journalist Karel van Wolferen (1989) is an even sharper critic. In a book vilified in Japan but declared a "classic" by Western reviewers, he argues that Japanese prosecutors have "virtually unlimited discretion" to decide whether or not to indict, but he believes that there are serious problems in the way prosecutors exercise their powers. While acknowledging that prosecutors try to be "scrupulously fair" and that "their sense of duty to uphold the dignity of their office is beyond doubt," Van Wolferen claims prosecutors do "not accept being shown in the wrong." They are, he agrees with Chalmers Johnson, obstinate, stubborn, and intransigent. Furthermore, prosecutors "want to be God" and are "quite ready to tip the scales of justice out of social considerations." In Van Wolferen's view, because prosecutors are "beholden to the system" and "selectively benevolent," they discriminate against the "ideologically motivated" (especially leftists) and in favor of corrupt but conservative elites. Eamonn Fingleton (1995) joins the critics' chorus by declaring that prosecutors "have long displayed partisan behavior in attacking politicians who have tried to encroach on the Japanese bureaucracy's economic policymaking prerogatives." The procuracy's partisanship, he concludes, "has been a constant thread in Japanese administration going back to the 1910s if not earlier."

Many Japanese observers agree that prosecutors wield too much unchecked control over the criminal process, but two merit special mention. Ishimatsu Takeo (1989), a former High Court judge who presided over criminal trials for thirty years, believes prosecutorial dominance is so complete that "the real criminal trials" are conducted not by judges in open court but by prosecutors in the offices where charge decisions are made. According to Ishimatsu, court hearings are "empty

---

2. Their closest counterpart may be Dutch prosecutors, "a veritable cadre of thoroughly professional decision-makers" to whom David Downes (1988:13) attributes much of the credit for maintaining a "more humane" and "milder" penal estate than in England and other countries. On Dutch prosecutors, see also Peters (1992) and Fionda (1995).

shells," and the prosecutor-led criminal process "tends to lead to egregious trampling of human rights." Similarly, Hirano Ryūichi (1989), a former president of Tokyo University and the dean of Japanese criminal justice studies, argues that "the real substance of criminal procedure" and "the truly distinctive character" of Japan's criminal process lie in an inquisitorial investigative process that is dominated by police and prosecutors. Like Ishimatsu, Hirano regards trials as mere "ceremonies" for "ratifying" prosecutors' decisions, and arrives at the profoundly pessimistic conclusion that Japanese criminal justice is "abnormal," "diseased," and "really quite hopeless."[3]

A Neglected Research Site

In short, analysts agree that prosecutors play a pivotal role in Japan's criminal process, but advance sharply divergent views about the aims and effects of prosecutorial power. The variance in views is understandable considering that no one has systematically studied the institution about which these polarized pronouncements are made. The fact is, we know few facts about prosecution in Japan because no researcher has ever had regular, face-to-face contact with prosecutors through prolonged immersion in their work environment. In crucial respects prosecutors are not merely understudied, they are unstudied.[4] This lacuna is part of a bigger hole in Japanese studies, where the study of the state has been so neglected that few "elementary mappings" of its major agencies exist in English (C. Johnson 1995). Rarely, however, has the boldness of claims about Japan's bureaucracy so far outrun the corroborating evidence.

Disagreements about Japan's procuracy — is it "number one," or does it routinely trample human rights? — seem generated less by different readings of the evidence (the evidence is thin all around) than by authorial presuppositions. Many works rely on reports produced by prosecutors or other government representatives, sources possessing the capacity and the motivation to portray their system in flattering terms. On the other hand, the staunchest critics tend to ground their assessments in subjective moral intuitions rather than explicit comparative judgments about the

3. Other critical English-language works by Japanese authors have been written by Chiba University professor of law Murayama Masayuki and by Igarashi Futaba, a private attorney-at-law. Murayama (1992:233) believes Japanese prosecutors exercise such enormous powers that they "dominate the pre-trial stage in the criminal justice process." Igarashi (1984) has devoted much of her career to publicizing injustices and advocating reform of what is to her a badly defective criminal justice system.

4. Although the scholarly literature on American prosecutors is better, it is still not good. Indeed, Lawrence Sherman, president of the American Society of Criminology, has noted that one of the most fertile areas for research in the United States is prosecutorial discretion. Most criminal cases are handled outside the courtroom, but no one knows how prosecutors decide whom to prosecute, how effectively they make these decisions, how often they let risky people go, and so on. Sherman reports that the prosecutors he has approached have been "uniformly opposed" to allowing observation, let alone experimental study. "I've proposed repeatedly, and I've failed," he says. Researchers have a difficult time getting cooperation from the police, Sherman observes, but the prosecutors "are by far the worst." In his view, scientific scrutiny of the justice system has hardly begun. 'We're holding a tiny little cardboard match in the middle of a huge forest at night," Sherman states. "We're about where surgery was a century ago" (quoted in Gawande 2001:53). For criminal justice in Japan, make that two centuries.

character of Japanese criminal justice. Notably, no one has conducted field research inside Japan's procuracy.[5]

The Japanese-language literature is hardly better. Most is written by prosecutors themselves. Though instructive, these pieces, like the official sources relied on by many foreign writers, may present more *tatemae* (what prosecutors want you to believe) than *honne* (what is really true). The rest of the Japanese literature, produced largely by journalists, concentrates on a small group of prosecutors who work in Tokyo's Special Investigation Division (*tokusōbu*), the elite bureau that investigates and disposes of Japan's highest-profile white-collar crime cases. Though undeniably important, these prosecutors comprise less than 2 percent of the procuracy's total force of two thousand prosecutors (*kenji*) and assistant prosecutors (*fuku kenji*). Studying them reveals little about how crime is prosecuted in ordinary cases.[6]

Access

There are, therefore, compelling intellectual reasons to study Japanese prosecutors. They are powerful actors who have been the subject of much fanfare, both positive and negative, yet they have been almost completely ignored by social researchers, both native and foreign. I had an equally important practical reason for choosing this subject of study: I was able to gain unprecedented access to the world in which prosecutors work. Although getting in and getting along in the procuracy was difficult, in the end I gained and maintained sufficient access to gather evidence that can be used to adjudicate between the conflicting claims described above and to develop arguments not previously advanced. The next section describes how access and information were obtained.

Research Methods

Prosecutors make decisions, about what to do with suspects and offenders; how to deal with angry, fearful, and forgiving victims; how to present evidence in court; how to relate to bosses, subordinates, peers, police, attorneys, judges, the media, and the public; and a host of other matters. Understanding prosecutor decisions requires understanding prosecutor thought, a challenge best met by adopting the "naturalistic" penchant for intense, prolonged immersion in a research setting and direct observa-

---

5. For two months in 1978, Marcia Goodman (1986) observed trials and interviewed prosecutors, judges, and lawyers. She did not, however, observe prosecutors in the office settings where they perform their most important tasks.

6. Mitsui Makoto, professor of law at Kobe University, is one of only a handful of Japanese scholars who have studied prosecutor decision-making in routine cases. In a five-part series entitled "The Prosecutor's Discretion to Suspend Prosecution: Historical and Empirical Research," Mitsui analyzes procuracy and court records from one region for the period 1967–1968. He finds that in deciding whether or not to suspend charges, prosecutors emphasize "special prevention" factors for both property crimes and violent offenses (Mitsui 1970; see also Goodman 1986:37). Note, however, that Mitsui did not do field research or observe prosecutors working "on the job."

tion of the actors working there (Lofland and Lofland 1984). I employed the two main methods of the naturalistic research tradition: participant observation and in-depth, unstructured interviewing.[7] In total, I spent about two hundred days observing prosecutors at work and conducted approximately fifty in-depth prosecutor interviews. I interviewed a similar number of other officials — judges, lawyers, police, and prison officials — in Japan's criminal court communities, and had many conversations with former officials, including ex-prosecutors. Through these methods I gained access to prosecutors' deliberations, both private and collective, and insight into the decision-making core of their occupation.

I supplemented the naturalistic approach with other data-gathering techniques. I listened to countless hours of prosecutor lectures, presentations, and pronouncements; read numerous official handouts and reports (including many documents not intended for public consumption); studied scores of procuracy and court records, and dozens of articles and books on prosecution and related criminal justice subjects; worked for fifteen months as an employee in a branch of Japan's Ministry of Justice; and had a multitude of informal conversations with prosecutors, lawyers, legal apprentices, judges, police, prison officials, journalists, suspects, ex-cons, and members of the constituency prosecutors are legally charged to represent — the public. Using a snowball sample, I administered a survey to prosecutors consisting of 153 questions (see Appendix), from which I received 235 valid responses. The survey asked about life background, work objectives, the exercise of discretion, and other central aspects of the prosecutor's job. Results from the survey appear throughout the book, most prominently in chapter 3, "Prosecutor Culture."

I did field research in two main stages. The first, between August 1992 and February 1994, centered on Kobe, a city of 1.5 million in western Japan's largest megalopolis and home to one of the world's busiest harbors. Kobe is the site of one of the procuracy's fifty District Public Prosecutors Offices. Much of my research, especially in the beginning, took place in the office of Mr. Ono, Kobe's "instructing prosecutor" (*shidō gakari kenji*), the person in charge of the legal apprentices (*shihō shūshūsei*) who rotated in and out of the office at four-month intervals in preparation for future employment as prosecutors, judges, and private attorneys.

It took four months of forbearance to "get in" the Kobe office. Access was given on four conditions. First, in writing about the research, I was to hold in confidence the real names of all persons I encountered in the office. Second, I promised to submit one copy of my original research report (a dissertation) to the head of the office's General Affairs Bureau. Prosecutors insisted on this condition in order help me "avoid making errors about matters of fact" before wider publication, but agreed they could neither edit nor censor my work. After sending the report as promised, I received considerable feedback but few serious efforts to alter my views. Third, I agreed not to interfere with daily life in the office. This condition simply meant I should not bother busy prosecutors and should otherwise make myself as inconspicuous as possible. Last and most important, I was permitted to move freely in the offices where

7. Elsewhere I have described how I "got in" and "got along in" the prosecutors office (D. Johnson forthcoming). Here I present an abbreviated account.

Ono and the legal apprentices worked, but was to contact other prosecutors in the office through the instructing prosecutor. For the first few months this condition gave Ono control over the people I could contact and the information I could collect. As time progressed, however, having my own "handler" turned out to be as much a boon as a bane, for in addition to his official obligation to monitor my activities, Ono gradually acquired a personal obligation to help advance my research. Though I never gained complete freedom to roam the halls and offices at will, I eventually acquired substantial autonomy, a development Ono encouraged because it saved him considerable trouble.

Throughout the research in Kobe, getting close to prosecutors was my methodological migraine, an intense headache which recurred so regularly that even when I did not feel it I suffered from the knowledge that soon it would return. My difficulty getting along in the Kobe office can be illustrated by describing the process through which I conducted the survey. The original draft of the questionnaire was about 30 percent longer than the draft actually administered. Some sixty-four of the original questions were cut at the insistence of my Kobe handlers, and an additional ten were substantially rewritten at their "request." Hence, in order to get the survey into the field I was required to omit or change about one-third of the questions I wanted to ask. The cut content addressed issues that prosecutors deem sensitive, such as their extreme and growing reliance on confessions and the interrogations that induce them. Though I had better access to prosecutors than other researchers have had, I could not do all I wanted. Closed doors created curiosity about what lay behind the stages I was permitted to observe. I often acquired the interdicted information in other ways, and at least a few times the closed doors alerted me to important issues to which I otherwise would have remained oblivious.

The procuracy's efforts to police my research generated intriguing insights about the organization. When I gave my survey to Mr. Ono, for example, he asked for a floppy copy in addition to the paper version I originally submitted. Ono used his computer to create a giant grid consisting of my 227 "proposed questions" in the rows and the names of five prosecutors — Ono and four superiors — in the columns. He then gave copies of the grid to the other four prosecutors, as they had instructed. These five prosecutors then taught me a painfully thorough lesson about *kessai*, the system of "consultation and approval" that prosecutors in Japan routinely use to make decisions about whether to arrest and detain suspects, charge or appeal cases, and (as I learned) permit or forbid research. Each of the five prosecutors appraised every question in the matrix: an "O" meant the question could be asked, an "X" meant it should be axed, and a triangle meant further discussions (and perhaps revisions) were necessary. After several iterations of this process, and after executive prosecutors in Tokyo registered their approval, I was granted permission to proceed.

Although I was not privy to the survey deliberations, the decision rule seemed to be that one "X" was enough to kill a question. At any rate, the *kessai* process took eight months, by which time I had less than two months remaining to do the survey and follow-up interviews in Kobe. Administering the survey was simultaneously one of the most frustrating and most illuminating experiences I had in Japan. As documented throughout this book, *kessai* prosecutors perform critically important functions in the Japanese way of justice. They ensure that like cases are treated alike so as to achieve consistency. They educate young prosecutors about who is a "correctable" offender. They keep conviction rates high by reviewing the adequacy of evidence. They provide aid and support to prosecutors pursuing confessions. And (as I experienced) they perform political control functions in sensitive cases. These are lessons I would have learned less well were it not for the obstacles I encountered conducting the survey. If getting close was my methodological migraine, getting over the headaches brought more than just relief.

My research experience in Kobe contrasts sharply with parallel experiences in America. In Kobe, for example, getting in the prosecutors office took 120 days. In California it took about thirty minutes. In the summer after my first year in Japan I returned to Berkeley to do comparative research in Alameda County, a large urban prosecutors office centered in the city of Oakland. One of my professors called the district attorney to explain my research proposal. Two days later we visited the deputy chief. Unlike his Japanese counterparts, this American prosecutor showed little interest in me or my research. By the conclusion of our half-hour chat he had granted access to all people and practices in the office, including backstage activities such as plea-bargaining. In the weeks that followed I learned that other Alameda prosecutors were equally open, and in subsequent research in Minneapolis, San Diego, and Honolulu I encountered nothing like the barriers to entry and access that prosecutors posed in Japan. It is ironic that Japanese prosecutors are so closed when they, on the whole, have less to hide than prosecutors in America.[8] They apparently adopt the same stance as other bureaucrats in Japan: that one must "never reveal more than absolutely necessary" (Miyamoto 1994).[9]

The second phase of my research, from March 1994 through May 1995, took place in and around Tokyo, where I was employed as a researcher and editor at a branch of the Ministry of Justice called the United Nations Asia and Far East Insti-

---

8. There is a serious problem of prosecutor misconduct in the United States. For example, a *Chicago Tribune* study covering the period from 1963 through 1998 found 381 people whose homicide convictions were thrown out because prosecutors withheld evidence favorable to the defendant or knowingly used false evidence. The cases of those 381 defendants represent the floor of prosecutor misconduct, not the ceiling. The *Tribune* study covered only homicide cases, focused on only two kinds of misconduct, and had to rely on published appellate court opinions. Rulings at the trial court level rarely get published in legal databases. More fundamentally, prosecutor misconduct seldom comes to the attention of the defense, judge, or jury. It is, by definition, hidden (Armstrong 1999). A "significant minority" and growing number of American prosecutors engage in "win at all costs" misconduct (Moushey 1998). They do so in order to win and because they can; winning is rewarded and cheating goes unpunished. About 75 percent of prosecutor misconduct is called "harmless error" by American judges, and only six American prosecutors were criminally charged in the entire twentieth century. Two were convicted; each received a fine of $500. On the scope, causes, and consequences of prosecutor misconduct in the United States, see also Humes (1999) and Roberts and Stratton (2000).

Although prosecutors in Japan seem to engage in less misconduct than prosecutors in America, their problems are still serious (see chapters 6 and 8). However, this area is even more understudied in Japan than it is in the United States.

9. A similar irony holds for police in the two countries, with Japanese police more closed to outsiders even though they seem less apt than American police to engage in deviant acts (Bayley 1991:78). Other researchers have faced severe obstacles trying to administer surveys to Japanese police (Ames 1981:xiii) and prison inmates (Gerber and Weeks 1992).

tute for the Prevention of Crime and the Treatment of Offenders (UNAFEI for short). UNAFEI was established in 1961 by agreement between the United Nations and the government of Japan (Sasaki 2000). Its official purposes are to train personnel in criminal justice administration and to conduct studies about crime prevention and the treatment of offenders in order to "bring about sounder social development in Asia and the Pacific region." An officially unacknowledged but widely recognized function is to promote foreigners' understanding of and goodwill toward Japan. For UNAFEI's first five years the United Nations and the Japanese government shared equal administrative responsibility for the institute, but by 1970 the latter had assumed all administrative and financial duties, including payment for the transportation, lodging, and other expenses of the hundred or so foreign participants (mainly criminal justice officials) who attend the institute's training sessions each year. During my research all twenty-six members of the UNAFEI staff were employed by Japan's government. Of those, nine belonged to the "faculty" — the director and deputy director (both prosecutors), two additional prosecutors, one judge, and two persons each from corrections and probation. Thus, four of the staff's nine core members were prosecutors. Like the rest of the Ministry of Justice, of which it is part, UNAFEI is run by prosecutors, and because of its organizational and geographical proximity to elite prosecutors in Tokyo, the fifteen months I spent at UNAFEI resulted in far more exposure to executive and managing prosecutors than I was able to obtain in Kobe, where my research had focused on prosecutors engaged in the frontline activities of investigating, charging, and trying cases. The two stages of research thus complemented each other well.

An Overview of the Criminal Process

This book is comparative, chiefly between Japan and the United States. It skips or skims over other interesting parallels that could further illuminate what is distinctive and problematic about Japanese criminal justice. I limited the focus because I lack confidence in the quality of secondary sources for other countries and because I lack the requisite expertise to make broader comparisons. I, too, "have seen too many comparativists use bad secondary sources to rape Japanese law" for me to risk doing the same thing for, say, Germany or South Korea (Ramseyer and Nakazato 1999).

This book is also asymmetrically comparative in that it concentrates most on criminal justice in Japan. Although it has more to say *about* Japan, it has much to say *to* America about the character of its own criminal justice and the unarticulated, unexamined, and sometimes unsound assumptions that underlie it. Moreover, while this book focuses on prosecutors, one can no more study "just them" than one can study Hamlet or Genji exclusive of the other actors on their stages. It therefore explores the work world of Japanese prosecutors in relation to the system and society in which it is embedded.

The criminal processes in Japan and America differ in myriad ways. Postwar Occupation reforms were supposed to make Japan's inquisitorial system more adversarial, as in the United States, but there remain strong transwar continuities in Japanese criminal procedure, as the following two chapters explain. In order to locate prosecutors within the postwar criminal process and in order to introduce the distinctive, central roles they play in it, this section summarizes salient procedural differences between the United States and Japan. The focus is on formal differences defined by law. The gap between the "law on the books" and the "law in action" is a frequent topic in subsequent chapters, but since "law on the books" constrains, enables, and channels prosecutor behavior, the formal structure of the criminal process merits serious scrutiny.

America

It is tempting to suppose that generalizations cannot be made about "America" because the United States has thousands of different jurisdictions. Actually, however, there are "striking similarities in procedure" across the manifold American criminal justice systems (Eisenstein et al. 1988). At least six "common stages" for serious (felony) cases are shared by American jurisdictions.

1. Once a citizen complains, *arrest* initiates most criminal cases.
2. *A prosecutor makes an initial charge decision,* usually within twenty-four hours of arrest. Police interrogation of the suspect is completed between the time of arrest and the initial charge. Most interrogations are short, lasting less than two hours. In the vast majority of American jurisdictions, prosecutors do not interrogate suspects.
3. *Arraignment* before a judge or magistrate normally occurs within forty-eight hours of arrest. The court informs the defendant of the charge or charges, assigns a defense attorney if one has not already been obtained, and determines bail eligibility, type, and amount. The defendant enters an initial plea.
4. *A grand jury or "preliminary hearing"* (think of the latter as a "minitrial" before a judge or magistrate) *determines "probable cause,"* that is, whether there is sufficient reason to believe that the crime occurred and the defendant committed it. In California, preliminary hearings are held within ten working days of arraignment; in New York, grand jury hearings are held within six days.
5. *Guilt or innocence is determined* in a trial-level court, through a dismissal, a guilty plea, or a trial verdict rendered by a judge or jury. Hearings on motions challenging the evidence or raising other defenses take place between stages four and five.
6. *Sentence is imposed* on offenders in a separate hearing held after the trial verdict.

Japan

The contrasts between America and Japan are many and marked. Note especially the pivotal role prosecutors play in each stage of Japan's criminal process.

1. *The initiation of cases.* In Japan, police arrest fewer than 20 percent of all suspected Penal Code violators. This means that the vast majority of

cases involving identified suspects are sent to prosecutors for further processing without the suspect being arrested. Prosecutors can make arrests themselves but do so rarely, mainly in white-collar crime cases. Police consult with prosecutors about whether and when to arrest. The infrequency of arrest derives in large part from officials' desire to protect suspects from the stigma of arrest and from their belief that the failure to charge arrested suspects is impermissible.

2. *Transfer of cases to prosecutors.* Once a suspect is arrested, police have forty-eight hours to transfer the suspect and case to prosecutors if further detention is considered necessary. If a suspect is not arrested, investigations face no formal time constraints, though police must refer all cases above the "trivial" (*bizai*) level to prosecutors.

3. *Pre-charge detention and interrogation.* If prosecutors believe a suspect should be detained further, they must ask a judge, within twenty-four hours of receiving the case, to approve up to ten days of additional detention. They may later ask for another ten-day extension. Judges rarely reject these requests for detention. In all, police and prosecutors can detain a suspect for up to seventy-two hours before the suspect appears before a judge, and for up to twenty days afterward (twenty-five days for crimes such as insurrection). During the pre-charge period, interrogations are long, thorough, and intense. Police and prosecutors routinely interrogate suspects several times for hours each time.

4. *The prosecutor's charge decision.* In arrest cases the prosecutor must make a charge decision before the detention period expires — that is, within twenty-three days. Unlike America, in Japan there are no "initial charge decisions," no "arraignments," and no "probable cause hearings." The decision to charge is made solely by prosecutors and at one point in time. Suspects may not "plead guilty" after being charged, but they usually do confess. A suspect has a right to bail and to a state-appointed attorney only after the prosecutor has instituted charges.

5. *Two types of prosecution.* Prosecutors institute *summary prosecution* against most suspects accused of minor offenses. The defendant must consent to use of this procedure. The Summary Court examines only documentary and physical evidence submitted by the prosecutor and may impose on the defendant a fine not exceeding 500,000 yen ($4,167).[10] More than 90 percent of all cases are disposed of in this way. Serious cases are *formally prosecuted* and then tried in District or Summary Court.

6. *The one-phase trial.* A trial court consisting of one or three judges declares guilt or innocence and imposes sentence in the same proceeding; the verdict and sentence are not bifurcated, as in the United States. Except in Okinawa, Japan has had no jury trials since 1943. Trials convene discontinuously at a pace of about one session per month. The average

---

10. Unless otherwise indicated, this book uses an exchange rate of $1 = 120 yen.

trial takes a little more than three months to finish, and 94 percent of trials finish in six months or less. Trials are supposed to be adversarial. In practice, however, over 90 percent of defendants confess, and courts rely heavily on documentary evidence (dossiers) that prosecutors have submitted. Prosecutors can appeal any first-instance court decision, including acquittals.

In sum, prosecutors in Japan perform four major roles that American prosecutors either do not play or else perform in a markedly attenuated manner (Uviller 2000). First, Japanese prosecutors conduct pre-charge investigations and interrogations, both on their own initiative and in conjunction with the police. By comparison, American prosecutors seldom investigate or interrogate, except at the Federal level. Second, Japanese prosecutors have monopoly power to dispose of cases by making charge decisions, and may choose to drop any charge, no matter how serious the case or strong the evidence. In contrast, American prosecutors share the charge decision with other actors, including police (in rural jurisdictions especially), judges (in preliminary hearings), grand juries, and, albeit rarely, citizens (in "private prosecutions"). Third, Japanese prosecutors present the state's case at trial, recommend a proper judgment to the court, and appeal acquittals and sentencing decisions. In contrast, American prosecutors cannot appeal acquittals and can appeal sentences only in limited jurisdictions and restricted circumstances. Finally, Japanese prosecutors supervise the execution of sentences, ensuring that fines are paid and that correctional officials carry out all other punishments — including death sentences — imposed by the court. American prosecutors have few parallel powers to supervise the execution of sentences.

The scope of prosecutorial authority is vast in Japan. The evidence presented hereafter suggests that prosecutors use their power, for the most part, to generate justice of a quality that deserves more respect (and research attention) than it hitherto has received.

An Overview of the Book

This book unfolds in two installments. Part I, "The Contexts of Japanese Justice," assumes that a close-up of prosecutors is less instructive than a sketch that places them in broader perspective. It proceeds from the premise that prosecutors must be understood in relation to other features of their environment, and hence locates them in several overlapping contexts that permit exploration of the connections between Japanese criminal justice and significant social facts. Chapter 1 employs the widest lens. It considers the crime, caseload, political, and legal contexts of prosecution, and argues that these environmental factors make Japan almost "paradise for a prosecutor." Chapter 2 narrows the focus to consider prosecutor relations with police, judges, and defense attorneys in Japan's criminal court community. Since prosecutors wield considerable control in relation to each of these actors, this chapter may be read as another episode in the "paradise for a prosecutor" tale. Chapter 3 constricts the focus further, by describing and interpreting two core components of prosecutor culture: what prosecutors want (their "work objectives"), and what factors influence their decisions not to charge known offenders. This chapter explores the cultural context of prosecution, while the next chapter explores its organizational setting. Since prosecutors make decisions within the ambit of a special kind of organization, one must view their decisions within the context of that organization. Chapter 4 describes three key features of the prosecutors' organization: its national and hierarchical structure; its "core task," defined as "uncovering and constructing the truth," chiefly through confessions; and its division of labor between frontline operators, midlevel managers, and top-level executives. Like the other contexts depicted in part I, these organizational attributes shape the Japanese way of justice by channeling prosecutor practice in particular directions.

Part II, "The Content of Japanese Justice," examines the content or substance of prosecutor practice. It explains how prosecutors exercise and control their discretion and analyzes the consequences of their decisions and the quality of criminal justice thereby produced. Chapter 5 explores the subject of consistency. It argues that prosecutors in Japan harmonize two imperatives of justice that many Americans regard as always in tension and often incompatible: the need to individualize case dispositions (individualization), and the need to treat like cases alike (consistency). Students of criminal justice in Japan have long maintained that prosecutors aim for individualization, but few have recognized that they aspire to consistency with at least equal zeal. The procuracy's capacity to achieve both objectives is one of the country's most commendable accomplishments. Chapter 6 probes the place of "correction" in Japanese prosecution. It describes prosecutor efforts to determine which offenders are "correctable" and to "set right" those who are, and it explores prosecutors' imperfect attempts to repair harms done to victims, especially in sexual molestation cases. The word "corrections" is usually associated with postconviction stages of the criminal process. Chapter 6 reveals that, for better and for worse, the desire to "correct" can animate parts of the criminal process long before prisons and probation.

Chapter 7 locates Japan's famously and notoriously high conviction rate within the broader contexts of Japanese and comparative criminal justice in order to assess the veracity of conventional claims about the rate's meaning. It shows that the procuracy's conservative charging policy and hierarchical controls — the same controls that engender high levels of consistency — best explain the high rate of conviction. Chapter 7 also explores the effects of the policies which maintain the high rate: for suspects, victims, lawyers, judges, the public, and prosecutors themselves. The consequences are decidedly mixed. Ironically, a system that convicts almost all defendants is in many ways more protective of the accused's interests than are other systems with higher acquittal rates, but the same system requires prosecutors to rely heavily and increasingly on confessions for evidence. This is the subject of chapter 8. If conviction rates are the pride of Japan's procuracy, confessions are its cornerstone. Indeed, confessions are the basis for most of the major achievements in Japanese criminal justice, from consistency to correction to conviction. Some prosecutors fear the foundation is weakening, or even crumbling, as confessions become more difficult to obtain while techniques such as plea-bargaining remain illegal. Since the absence of a confession undermines other core commitments, especially the need to "uncover and clarify the truth" that is the imperative presupposed by the three other Cs, prosecutors feel powerful pressure to obtain thorough admissions of guilt.[11] In serious cases where the level of suspicion is high but suspects refuse to confess, prosecutors believe that they must charge and that they must have a confession before charging. Much of the most troubling prosecutor behavior, from plea-bargaining to doctoring dossiers to use of the third degree, arises from the system's inordinate reliance on admissions of guilt. As a result, confessions are both a pre-condition and a plague for criminal justice in Japan.

Chapter 8 concludes with a discussion of reforms that Japan should undertake in order to improve the quality of its criminal justice. In the end, however, I find that the Japanese way of justice is uncommonly just, in large part because prosecutors perform their jobs well. Unfortunately for Americans concerned about the quality of criminal justice in their own country, Japan is, in significant respects, not a feasible model for reform; too many differences separate the two countries. (Sometimes we can no more import our solutions than we can export our problems.) Yet even then — even when Japan makes a poor model for reform of American criminal justice — it remains a revealing mirror, if one takes the time to inspect the images that it reflects. I, for one, feel more disappointed than pleased when criminal justice patterns from my country are reflected in the mirror that is Japan. I expect some readers will see things differently; justice, like beauty, is at least partly in the eye of the beholder. But if justice means taking into account the special needs and circumstances of individuals, then Japanese prosecutors receive higher marks than their American counterparts. If justice means treating equals equally, then the ability of Japan's procuracy to do so is impressive. And if justice requires facts, then Americans would do well to recognize how seriously this maxim is taken in Japan.

Almost thirty years ago Chalmers Johnson (1972) concluded his massive study *Conspiracy at Matsukawa* — "the biggest *cause celebre* in the history of law suits in Japan" — by noting that even in a case which took fourteen years to acquit "twenty possibly innocent defendants" of murder, the outcome "was actually a victory for Japanese society and for Japanese justice." In the Matsukawa case, Johnson asserted, the Japanese "were well enough served by the [criminal justice] institutions they had created." They still are.

---

11. Although "truth" is a recurrent theme in this book, it is notoriously difficult to define. In criminal justice research, "truth" often refers to accurate accounts by competent people of what they genuinely believe from sensory experience, and to the honest production of papers and objects relevant to legal questions (Frankel 1978). This definition clarifies the meaning of "truth" but raises at least as many questions as it answers. How accurate are the accounts? How competent are the prosecutors? How genuine are their beliefs? How honest and complete is their production of relevant materials? These questions are explored in the chapters that follow.

PART I

THE CONTEXTS OF
JAPANESE JUSTICE

Paradise for a Prosecutor

Japan is a long way from the United States. With respect to law enforcement it is a different world.

David Bayley, *Forces of Order*

In prosecution as in policing, context matters immensely. David Bayley's (1991)
classic study of police behavior in Japan and the United States starts from the
premise that Japan is "heaven for a cop." Police in Japan confront little serious crime,
few guns or drugs, and an impressive quality of public order — contexts which make
their work less demanding and vastly less dangerous than police work in the United
States. Further, since Japanese police enjoy widespread public support and operate
in a "benign" political environment, they are able to perform their jobs "virtually
without stress" or serious misconduct. To Bayley, Japan is so thoroughly heaven for
a cop that "if Japanese and American police changed places, Americans would perform as efficiently as Japanese and Japanese police might come unhinged."[1]

The Japan that is heaven for a cop is equally paradise for a prosecutor. This
chapter describes five key contexts that facilitate prosecution in Japan: prosecutors
confront little serious crime, carry light caseloads, are insulated from public demands and political pressures, benefit from enabling laws of criminal procedure that
confer extensive powers to investigate crimes and dispose of cases, and try cases before judges instead of juries. The argument is comparative, usually with the United
States but occasionally with other countries as well. Scholars commonly claim that
American prosecutors "enjoy independence and discretionary privilege unmatched
in the world" (Albonetti 1987:292). That conventional wisdom is wrong. The United
States may not be hell for a prosecutor, but compared with Japan it is a long way
from heaven. In fact, the circumstances of work discussed in this chapter enable
Japanese prosecutors to perform their main duty — the processing of criminal suspects — more easily and effectively than prosecutors in the United States. Some prosecutors in Japan are reluctant to acknowledge this fact, because they keenly desire
to acquire powers they do not yet possess (such as the authority to grant immunity)

---

1. As described in chapter 8, heaven for police and prosecutors can be hell for suspects and offenders (Steinhoff 1993; Miyazawa 1992).

and because they believe such an admission would depreciate their accomplishments. More than thirty years ago, however, one iconoclastic prosecutor depicted
Japan as "the prosecutor kingdom" (Abe 1968:163). The label fits. This chapter explains why.

Little Crime

A prosecutor's main task is to process criminal suspects by charging and convicting
those who deserve punishment and screening out those who do not. For prosecutors
in Japan this task is facilitated by the low levels of crime in their society. Low crime
rates permit prosecutors to carefully consider each case they confront without being
distracted by the public demands and political pressures that consume the time and
channel the decisions of many of their American counterparts.

The best indicator of violence in a country is the incidence of homicide.[2] In 1992,
the United States had a homicide rate over nine times higher than Japan's: 9.3 per
100,000 population in the United States versus 1.0 in Japan. A World Health Organization study found that homicide rates in the United States were more than fifteen
times higher than in Japan: 18.5 per 100,000 population in the United States as against
only 1.2 in Japan. In fact, the WHO study, which summarizes data from twenty industrialized democracies, found only one country — England — with a homicide rate
as low as Japan's (Zimring and Hawkins 1997). Comparisons with Asian countries
yield similar conclusions, with Japan's closest Confucian competitors having homicide rates 60 percent (South Korea) and 80 percent (Hong Kong and Singapore)
higher than Japan. Homicide rates in the Philippines are almost triple those in the
United States and are thirty or more times higher than in Japan (Watanabe 1993:37).

---

2. See Mukherjee (1994–1995:11). The figures presented here are official crime statistics published
by the governments of the countries cited. Researchers have raised questions about inaccuracy, incom-
pleteness, and bias in official statistics. The two most common criticisms are that official statistics fail to
include unreported offenses (the problem of underreporting), and that different countries use different
indicators of crime (the problem of indicators). Dane Archer and Rosemary Gartner (1984:56) review
these methodological problems and conclude that "homicide data constitute a valid basis for comparative research on both the levels and trends of this violent crime." They add that "offense seriousness and
underreporting are inversely related — that is, most serious offenses [like murder and robbery] are reported." In short, in most cases official statistics on homicide and robbery are relatively accurate. One
must view with more suspicion, however, comparative statistics on property crime, though even here the
general point — that Japan has relatively little of it — can be confidently asserted.

Victimization surveys, in which persons are asked how and how often they have been victimized,
tell a similar story. In the International Crime Survey (ICS), researchers questioned from fifteen hundred
to two thousand respondents in each of fifteen countries in 1989 and in thirteen countries in 1992. Japan
was included in both waves. The authors of a recent ICS conclude that overall prevalence rates are positively related to degree of urbanization. Because of the greater supply of suitable targets and less informal social control, "city air" seems to breed crime in most countries — but Japan is a notable exception to
the rule (del Frate et al. 1993). Hence, with the exception of motorcycle and bicycle theft — of which
Japan has an abundance — and sexual assaults, Japanese are victimized infrequently.

Robbery, the most feared street crime in America, is an exceedingly rare event in Japan. For example, in 1991, for each robbery in Japan, the United States recorded 182, and for each robbery in Tokyo, New York had 462. Robbery rates for Australia, England, Germany, and Singapore do not approach those in the United States, but residents of those countries are still twenty to thirty times more likely to be held up than people living in Japan. Even South Korea, geographically and culturally Japan's closest neighbor, has robbery rates 6.5 times higher than Japan (Mukherjee 1994–1995:12).

Prosecutors also process relatively few property and drug crimes. In fact, the overall level of "serious" crime in Japan is four to eight times lower than in Western countries such as the United States, Canada, England, Germany, France, Sweden, Australia, and New Zealand. The gaps between Japanese and foreign rates may not be as great for property crimes like burglary, larceny, and motor vehicle theft, but the volume of such crimes in Japan still remains far below the levels in the industrialized democracies to which it is usually compared.[3]

Drug crimes in Japan and the United States are similarly incommensurable. Drug arrests in Japan were more common than ever in 1993, when the popular press warned that the nation had become a "drug heaven," but the United States still arrested over twenty times more drug offenders per capita (*Mainichi Daily News*, 12/4/94). Moreover, for each year since 1975, approximately 90 percent of all drug arrests in Japan have been for use or possession of stimulant drugs. Heroin and cocaine, which plague neighborhoods and crowd caseloads in the United States, are almost unheard-of in Japan.[4]

Light Caseloads

Street-level bureaucracies — schools, courts, police departments, and the like — typically provide fewer resources than necessary for workers to adequately perform their jobs (Lipsky 1980:29). Resource shortages characterize many American prosecutor offices too. Indeed, most accounts stress that American prosecutors are so overworked that they must routinely use their discretion to cut corners via plea-bargaining and other "shortcuts" so as to avoid the burdens of an adversarial trial (Allen 1996:29). Although this point has been contested, it remains the standard analysis of American prosecutors and has considerable basis in fact. For many American prosecutors, plea-bargaining is the Drano that keeps the system unclogged.

3. The Asia picture is different, for what distinguishes Japan from its Asian neighbors is not so much crime generally as violent crime. For example, Japan's larceny rate is about the same as that in Singapore but almost three times higher than in Hong Kong and five times higher than in South Korea (Watanabe 1993:37).

4. In the United States, at least 60 percent of all men arrested in 1988 had some illegal drug besides marijuana in their system. The corresponding figure for Japan is not available — why invest scarce resources researching an insignificant problem? — but most agree that compared with the United States, the number is "vanishingly small" (Bayley 1991:118).

Japanese criminal justice also relies heavily on prosecutor discretion and confessions rather than contested trials. Moreover, conventional accounts stress that prosecutors offices in Japan are understaffed, overworked, and hence institutionally incapable of processing all of their cases through the formal criminal process. On this view, prosecutors must rely on an informal second track of criminal justice which stresses the norms of confession, repentance, and absolution. The truth, however, is that Japanese prosecutors have relatively few cases to process. As a result, they are compelled to cut corners much less often than their American counterparts. Evidence for this claim comes from three primary sources: analysis of the data that underlie "institutional incapacity" assertions, caseload calculations for Japan's fifty district prosecutors offices, and my field observations and interviews.

Reconsidering "Institutional Incapacity"

It is widely believed that Japanese prosecutors are shorthanded and overworked.[5] One scholar argues that "with fewer than 2200 procurators to handle not only all criminal prosecutions but also administrative and civil litigation involving Japanese governmental entities, institutional incapacity is . . . [a] serious problem for Japan's criminal justice system." On this view, "demands on the procuracy increased" so much that "the total caseload" went from an average of 272.2 indictments per prosecutor in 1932 to 1,121.8 indictments per prosecutor in 1987. If that is so, then in 1987 prosecutors were over four times busier than their predecessors fifty-five years earlier, and "however insubstantial the number of criminal prosecutions . . . may be in Japan in comparison with the United States or other industrial democracies, there is no dearth of criminal cases . . . relative to Japan's judicial and prosecutorial capacity to handle those cases efficiently and effectively." The consequences of this "institutional incapacity" are said to be twofold: substantial delay in criminal trials, and "internal pressures to use extralegal mechanisms" in order to avoid prosecutions that would overburden the system (Haley 1991:123).

Claims of "institutional incapacity" rest on a tenuous empirical foundation. A close look at the evidence reveals that Japanese prosecutors are neither overburdened at present nor busier than they were in the prewar past.

In analyzing workload it is critical to distinguish between cases that can be handled perfunctorily by a prosecutor's assistant (*jimukan*) and cases that require substantial prosecutor time and effort. Over 80 percent of cases that came to the procuracy between 1982 and 1987 were routine traffic violations disposed of with a minimum of effort. In the vast majority, a prosecutor's assistant simply followed office guidelines ("speeding 20 kilometers per hour over the legal limit should be fined N yen"), and mailed the accused a notice declaring the fine and explaining the accused's right to dispute the disposition in Summary Court. Seeing little chance of a successful fight and wanting to minimize their process costs, almost all accused traffic offenders comply with the notices.

5. See Ramseyer and Nakazato (1999:181); T. Ōno (1992:63); Haley (1991:123); Nomura (1988:58); Kitajima (1980:100); and Abe (1968:169).

Since prosecutors' assistants handle most traffic violations, analyses that include traffic violations but exclude these assistants greatly overestimate workloads.[6] Moreover, even if contemporary prosecutors are busier than they used to be (below I provide reasons to think they are not), they may still have sufficient capacity to process their caseloads.[7] Longitudinal data about trends cannot be used to address contemporary questions about capacity.

Recalculating Caseloads

When prosecutor caseloads are recalculated, this time excluding both minor traffic cases and the assistants who handle them, the results differ dramatically from conclusions that "increased demands on the procuracy" have led to "institutional incapacity." As measured by indictments, prosecutors in 1987 were not four times busier than prosecutors in 1932. Rather, prosecutors in 1987 carried caseloads nearly three times lighter than their prewar predecessors (98 indictments per prosecutor for the modern period, versus 272 for the period 1932–1937). Indeed, prosecutors in the 1980s *processed* fewer total cases (250 cases processed per prosecutor per year, including suspended prosecutions and non-prosecutions) than prosecutors in the 1930s *indicted* cases (272). Simply put, prosecutors in the 1980s did not carry heavier caseloads than their forerunners did fifty years earlier. Nor do they today.

Similarly, when minor traffic cases are set aside, the data suggest that contemporary prosecutors are capable of processing their caseloads. From 1982 to 1987 the average prosecutor *indicted* 98.6 cases per year, eleven times fewer cases than previous methods have suggested. And during the same period each prosecutor *processed* about 250 cases per year, 4.5 times fewer total cases than previously reported. As shown below, this number approximates the figure one reaches by calculating caseloads with office-level instead of national-level data.

Of course, some cases require far more attention than others, as reflected in the distinction Japanese prosecutors make between *migara* and *zaitaku* cases. In *migara*

6. Some have recognized that Japanese prosecutors are "assisted by clerical, administrative, and investigatory staff" but have overlooked the significance of this fact when calculating caseloads (Haley 1991:218).

7. Prosecutors in the Ministry of Justice have lobbied repeatedly to increase the size of the procuracy beyond the 1,173 total that was fixed by law in 1972. Just as repeatedly, the guardians of the budget in the Ministry of Finance have refused those requests, arguing that the procuracy has sufficient capacity to carry out its duties. This changed, however, in 1996, when the procuracy was granted thirty-five new positions to process the high-profile Aum Shinrikyō sarin gas cases and to respond to public demand for more vigorous prosecution of corruption and other white-collar crimes (*Yomiuri Shimbun* 7/2/95). In April 2001, during Japan's "judicial reform" (*shihō kaikaku*) movement, Justice Ministry officials proposed that the number of prosecutors be increased by one thousand and the number of administrative assistants (*jimukan*) be increased by eleven hundred. The Justice Ministry plan called for establishing "specialist teams" of prosecutors in eight major cities, in order to deal with "new problems" such as computer offenses, medical malpractice, and other white-collar crimes. At about the same time, a Liberal Democratic Party research panel proposed doubling the number of prosecutors (*Asahi Shimbun* 4/18/01; *Mainichi Daily News* 4/19/01). These proposals were made despite a government restructuring plan that called for central government ministries and agencies to reduce personnel by 10 percent over ten years. If either proposal becomes law, the procuracy will markedly increase its capacity to process cases.

cases, police or prosecutors have made an arrest and detained a suspect during the period they investigate the alleged offense. For a variety of reasons, police and prosecutors are reluctant to arrest suspects unless they are confident the case will result in a charge and conviction for a serious crime. Thus, *migara* cases are the most important cases prosecutors handle. Furthermore, since by law suspects can be detained for only a limited time before being charged, prosecutors concentrate most of their resources on *migara* cases, in order to reach a decision about disposition before the clock runs out. In contrast, prosecutors dispose of *zaitaku* (at home) cases without arresting or detaining suspects. As a result, *zaitaku* investigations often drag on for weeks or even months, making them far less burdensome to prosecutors than *migara* cases.

As measured by *migara* and *zaitaku* caseloads, Japanese prosecutors are not especially busy. In 1992, the average district office prosecutor disposed of 51 *migara* cases and 146 *zaitaku* cases, about one *migara* and three *zaitaku* cases per prosecutor per week.[8] Of course, not all offices are equally busy. Indeed, executive prosecutors in the Ministry of Justice and the Supreme Prosecutors Office periodically equalize caseload distributions across offices by reapportioning prosecutors from less busy to more busy offices. In 1992, prosecutors in one of the busiest offices (Chiba, home to Narita airport and thus the site of many immigration offenses) handled an average of 78 *migara* and 176 *zaitaku* cases, while those in one of the least busy offices (rural Matsue in Shimane prefecture) processed only 25 and 110, respectively. In terms of serious (*migara*) cases, Chiba is three times busier than Matsue, but its prosecutors still dispose of only 1.5 such cases a week.[9]

By contrast, in 1994 American prosecutors working in "urban" jurisdictions processed an average of 360 cases, 80 of which were felonies.[10] For example, each prosecutor in the Hennepin County (Minneapolis) District Attorney's office processed an average of 148 adult felony cases, almost three felonies per prosecutor per week, nearly three times the Japanese average and twice the workload of prosecutors in even the busiest Japanese office.[11] In New York City, prosecutors handling misdemeanor arrests in the office of the Manhattan District Attorney routinely carry caseloads of between 150 and 200, and most felony assistants juggle twenty-five or more cases at a time (Heilbroner 1990:240). It appears that, in general, two types of

---

8. These caseloads are calculated by using *migara* and *zaitaku* figures for 1992, and Ministry of Justice figures for the number of prosecutors (*kenji*) and assistant prosecutors (*fuku kenji*) in each office. The data were obtained in July 1994 from the Hachioji branch of the Tokyo District Prosecutors Office.

9. In order to determine how to reapportion prosecutors to the fifty district prosecutors offices, in 1993–1994 the Ministry of Justice's Criminal Affairs Bureau calculated caseloads more precisely than I have been able to do with the available data. One official in charge of that project — a prosecutor — outlined the ministry's method but would not reveal data or results. When I showed him my own calculations, however, he said that though they were "rough" in places they were largely accurate.

10. U.S. Department of Justice, Bureau of Justice Statistics, October 1994 ("Prosecutors in State Courts, 1994"). "Urban" is defined as offices that serve a population of half a million or more. Since 1994, American prosecutor caseloads have declined because crime rates have decreased while the number of local prosecutors has increased. Even so, average urban American caseloads are still higher than in Japan (U.S. Department of Justice, Bureau of Justice Statistics, July 1998, "Prosecutors in State Courts, 1996").

11. Data provided by the Office of the Hennepin County Attorney, August 1995.

American prosecutor offices have caseloads lighter than their Japanese counterparts: local offices in sparsely populated rural areas, and federal offices that concentrate on serious cases, while leaving lesser but more numerous matters for local law enforcement agencies.

Field Observations and Interviews

The work experiences of prosecutors in Japan and my own observations in the field provide further evidence that Japanese prosecutors are less busy than is customarily supposed. A typical prosecutor's day is less full of official activity than previous accounts assume. Prosecutors made this point most directly in interviews. One twelve-year veteran of Japan's procuracy kept careful records of the number of cases he handled at each office in which worked. His busiest years were spent in the branch office at Kokura, a city on the southern island of Kyushu that is home to many *yakuza* gangsters. Kokura is widely regarded as one of the busiest offices in Japan. While there, he disposed of about 330 *migara* cases per year, and typically carried around ten *migara* cases at any one time. In contrast, in Fukuoka, a larger city also on Kyushu, this prosecutor handled about one hundred *migara* cases a year, while in Tokyo he processed only thirty in nine months.

Other prosecutors informed me that "70 to 80 percent of frontline prosecutors are not busy at all" and that "many are bored and would like more cases to handle." Once I asked a retired executive prosecutor to describe the most pressing problems facing today's procuracy. He expressed grave concern that the paucity of cases makes it difficult for frontline prosecutors to become skilled investigators. Another prosecutor used the following tripartite distinction to depict workload levels:

1. *Bored* prosecutors have between zero and three to four *migara* cases per week, are "idle" and even "lonely," and may feel that they are not regarded as important members of the organization.
2. *Comfortable* prosecutors have five to eight *migara* cases a week, a level most deem "just right." These prosecutors feel "useful" but not overworked.
3. *Busy* prosecutors have ten or more *migara* cases a week, work long hours, and may feel "overwhelmed." These prosecutors are "relatively few" in number.

Not only do Japanese prosecutors have few suspects to process, but those whom they do encounter have, on the average, a far more submissive stance to authority than Americans suspects do. The exceptions notwithstanding, Japanese suspects are more likely to admit guilt, repent, and accept responsibility, just as victims and witnesses tend to be more cooperative with law enforcement officials in Japan than in the United States (Bayley 1991:136). These differences in demeanor further facilitate the Japanese prosecutor's ability to obtain the information needed to process cases.

So, how busy are Japanese prosecutors? Whether the measure is cases indicted or total cases processed, whether one considers the question historically or comparatively, or whether one uses objective (caseload) or subjective (interview) standards, the conclusion is the same: Japan is paradise for a prosecutor because it has little serious crime and because its procuracy has enough people — some prosecutors say more than enough — to investigate, charge, and try criminal cases.[12] In this respect, Japanese prosecutors differ markedly from other street-level bureaucrats (Lipsky 1980).

Implications

Since Japanese prosecutors seldom feel pressured to "cut corners" the way American prosecutors do, they are able to devote much time and attention to each case they handle. This fact has several important consequences for the Japanese way of justice. Most centrally, the institutional capacity of Japanese prosecutors helps explain why they are able to construct meticulously detailed dossiers (*chōsho*) from suspects, victims, and witnesses before making a charge decision. To outsiders unfamiliar with Japanese criminal justice, the level of detail in the prosecution's investigation may seem baffling, breathtaking, or both. But thorough investigations and detailed deliberations are two of the most salient features of criminal justice in Japan, and both are concretely reflected in the length (and weight) of the state's dossiers. Prosecutors and police routinely produce several hundred pages of statements during the preindictment investigation, even in cases that seem thoroughly mundane. My notebooks are filled with comments about the prodigious production of dossiers: 250 pages taken from a businessman who confessed to fondling a girl on a train; nearly 500 pages from two juvenile boys suspected of vandalizing several vending machines; and over 1,200 pages of statements from and about a seventy-year-old man who denied attempting to steal four books from a book store. One primary source of this precision is the capacity of prosecutors to produce so much paper. The cause is no less important for being so basic: prosecutors are "precise" (*seimitsu*) because they can be.

The capacity to be precise also helps prosecutors achieve two imperatives of justice: the individualization of case decisions and the treatment of similar cases similarly. Since these subjects are treated more fully in chapters 5 and 6, here I merely suggest the connections. To individualize case decisions, a prosecutor must ascertain a wide array of relevant facts about the offense and the offender. To treat like cases

---

12. Prosecutors have raised three chief objections to this conclusion. Some argue that one cannot measure workloads by caseloads because prosecutors spend a lot of time consulting with police about pre-arrest investigations and other matters not reflected in case statistics. Such critics are right to point out the roughness of these workload measures, but compared to the energy prosecutors invest in *migara* cases, the time spent on pre-arrest consultations is usually inconsequential. Other critics note that prosecutors with the smallest caseloads are sometimes the busiest, especially the *tokusōbu* and *hombu gakari* prosecutors who handle, respectively, white-collar offenses and high-profile, "redball" crimes of violence. This objection is correct but insignificant, for such prosecutors account for only about 2 percent of the entire prosecutor force. The third set of critics notes that in most large district offices, prosecutors perform two distinct functions: some investigate and charge cases (*sōsa kenji*), and others try them in court (*kōhan kenji*). In contrast, in smaller offices a single case is generally charged and tried by the same prosecutor. My caseload estimates do not capture this difference in the organization of prosecution and therefore obscures variance across offices. Still, this distinction does not undermine my conclusions about the amount of work prosecutors in a single office perform or about the number of cases disposed of by an average prosecutor.

alike, a prosecutor must compare offenses and offenders across cases. Accurately ascertaining "the facts" and making the appropriate comparisons is possible — and is *only* possible — when prosecutors have sufficient time and resources to dig deeply into the case. Prosecutors in Japan routinely do.

Finally, in seeking to understand Japanese criminal justice, one must bear in mind the critical fact that generates countless criminal justice consequences: Japan has little serious crime. Many distinctives of the Japanese way of justice — such as the protection of prosecutors from political pressures — can be traced back to this bedrock reality.

Quiescent Politics

In the United States, chief prosecutors are almost always elected; in Japan they never are. This difference has important consequences for both prosecution systems. Most critically, as unelected, career bureaucrats working in a country where crime is not a chronic problem, Japanese prosecutors are insulated from many of the public pressures and political exigencies that shape prosecutor behavior in America. The result is that Japan's procuracy has solved one of the critical problems that confronts all organizations: how to acquire a reasonable degree of "autonomy" and external political support (Wilson 1989:26).

The Punitive Politics of Prosecution in the United States

American prosecutors are anchored in a contradiction. On the one hand, they are expected to be neutral, independent "ministers of justice," not simply advocates seeking conviction. As such, they are obligated to exonerate the innocent with the same vigor and determination that they pursue the guilty. On the other hand, the ability of American prosecutors to fulfill this obligation is undermined by the chief prosecutor's continuous, direct dependence on the electoral scrutiny of a public which fears crime and demands that officials get ever tougher with it. In order to gain or remain in office, American chief prosecutors must persuade the punitive public of the merits of their policies and the quality of their record.[13] Often this electoral imperative crowds out the prosecutor's commitment to the "minister of justice" role, a consequence some observers deem offensive or unethical.[14] Ironically, we "hold

---

13. Unfortunately, so few people have studied the electoral politics of American chief prosecutors that "surprisingly little is known about the average tenure or turnover of elected prosecutors" or about how they appeal to voters (Flemming et al. 1992:24). However, most observers agree that "much of a prosecutor's exercise of power is constrained by an external environment over which he has little control but to which he must respond" (Jacoby 1980:47, 276).

14. Francis Allen (1996:72), for example, recognizes that "community pressures, media publicity, and political influences may, on occasion, limit and direct prosecutorial action," but he stresses that such influences "may as often frustrate as advance rule-of-law values and sometimes represent precisely the sorts of interventions that prosecutors should be protected against." See also Blumberg (1979:122); Anderson (1995); Scheingold (1991:119); Burnham (1996:62, 386); Hagan (1994:139); and Donziger (1996:205).

our prosecutors politically accountable and then fault them for calculating the effects of their choices on their electability" (Uviller 1996:163).

Of course, accountability to the public constitutes the chief justification for the American prosecution system and is, in the eyes of some, an almost unqualified good (Pizzi 1993:1336; Blumberg 1979:ix). Nonetheless, electoral accountability has many unfortunate, unintended consequences. Public opinion research reveals that American voters know little about crime or criminal justice and are frequently hostile toward judges and prosecutors. In particular, many Americans believe prosecutors make so many concessions to offenders that "the bad guys" are neither charged nor punished as harshly as they deserve (McCoy 1993; Roberts 1992). Scholars have shown that American prosecutors actually concede little (Nardulli et al. 1988:245), but public misperceptions persist and continue to push prosecutors (and the rest of the criminal justice system) in an increasingly punitive direction (Mauer 1999). Many lament the results: large and growing racial disparities in arrests and incarceration (Mauer 1999),[15] badly overcrowded prisons (Zimring and Hawkins 1995b), scarce resources deflected away from more effective crime control policies (Hagan 1994), little discernible effect on the crime rate (Currie 1998), and countless miscarriages of justice (Moushey 1998; Armstrong 1999). In short, chief prosecutors are driven by electoral forces to favor their role as advocates seeking conviction over their role as ministers seeking justice.[16] Critics call this consequence "overzealousness" or "conviction psychology" and contend that it causes American prosecutors to prefer penal severity over other jurisprudential goals and to violate laws and professional codes of ethics with shocking regularity (Humes 1999; S. Fisher 1988).

The Quiescent Politics of Prosecution in Japan

In contrast to the punitive politics of American prosecution, the politics of prosecution in Japan could hardly be more quiescent. Since Japanese prosecutors are not elected and are largely impervious to public opinion, they are insulated from the punitive attitudes of the public whom they represent. The result, at least in the ordinary cases that make up the bulk of their criminal caseload, is autonomy to act as they see fit.

Japan is commonly depicted as culturally committed to an ethic of reintegrative shaming and as possessing an extraordinary penchant for repentance and reconciliation instead retribution or revenge (Braithwaite 1989:61). As we shall see later on, this is largely true of Japanese prosecutors. For the public more generally, it is also true for "everyday offenses" that do not rise to the level of criminal misconduct, but it is *not* an accurate description of public attitudes toward crime. Indeed, exper-

---

15. For instance, Michael Tonry (1994:475) argues that "it is difficult to imagine a persuasive ethical defense of promotion of [harsh drug and sanctioning] policies that were unlikely to achieve their ostensible goals but were foreseen to have an adverse disparate impact on Blacks."

16. Although the chief (district attorney) is the only elected prosecutor in American offices, the work of assistant prosecutors is "greatly affected" by the identity of the chief. Thus, electoral influences filter down through chiefs to their assistants (Flemming et al. 1992:76).

imental research shows that when judging serious crimes such as robbery, ordinary Japanese are at least as harsh as Americans, perhaps even more so, and that Japanese justify their choice of punishments with the same retributive, incapacitative, and general deterrent rationales that American respondents provide (Hamilton and Sanders 1992:157).[17] When researchers control for the severity of the offense and the prior record of the offender, the Japanese criminal justice system appears to send more people to prison than many Western democracies (though not the United States). In fact, "proportionately more offenders convicted of crimes such as larceny, which in many countries is considered to be a minor offence not warranting a prison term, are sent to prison in Japan than in other countries" (Mukherjee 1995:14). In short, among Japan's general populace one finds not the reintegrating and absolving qualities many liberals laud, but rather a strong impulse to punish crime severely, much as in the United States.

But there is a crucial difference: Japanese prosecutors confront little of the fear, fury, and wishful thinking that drive criminal policy in the United States, mainly because crime is not a serious "social problem" in Japan.[18] Instead, and with few exceptions, the Japanese media and public strongly support police and prosecutor actions (Miyazawa 1992:230; Ames 1981:72).[19] Moreover, even when segments of the public assert their punitive preferences, prosecutors can ignore demands considered unwarranted, unwise, or imprudent because they pay no electoral price for being nonresponsive.[20]

Implications

The quiescent politics of prosecution in Japan has at least three critical consequences for how prosecutors perform their jobs and thus for "who gets what" in the Japanese way of justice. First, political autonomy means prosecutors can consider

---

17. Hamilton and Sanders took large probability samples in one American and two Japanese cities, told respondents hypothetical stories ("vignettes" or "experiments in meaning") which depicted harmful behavior, and asked them to assess responsibility and punishment. Four "core stories" describe ordinary, noncriminal wrongs, and one of three "stranger stories" describes an armed robbery. Japanese judged the ordinary wrongdoers less harshly and more "reintegratively" than Americans did, but for the robbery the Japanese were consistently more punitive.

18. The 1992 International Crime Survey found that three times as many Americans as Japanese believed they were "very likely" to be burglarized in the coming year (6.7 percent vs. 2.2 percent). Moreover, while only 15.6 percent of Japanese said they "take care when going out in the evening" (the lowest percentage of the twenty countries surveyed), 32.6 percent of Americans admitted taking precautions (del Frate et al. 1993:39).

19. Public support for prosecutors is reflected in opinion polls which show that about three-quarters of Japanese adults "trust" or "somewhat trust" prosecutors (*Yomiuri Shimbun* survey, 12/16/98). The percentage of Americans expressing trust in prosecutors and other court officials is far lower (Flanagan and Longmire 1996:32, 46; Roberts and Stalans 1997:129). Americans have little confidence in prosecutors in part because they revile plea-bargaining, the core practice of most American prosecutors (McCoy 1993:64; Flanagan and Longmire 1996:54).

20. The chief exception is political corruption cases, in which public opinion does influence prosecutor behavior (D. Johnson 1997).

the full range of jurisprudential purposes when deciding how to treat offenders. For prosecutors, rehabilitation, reconciliation, and restitution are still legitimate aims, and in a wide variety of cases they pursue them (see chapter 6). In contrast, many American prosecution offices have abandoned all but the most harshly punitive rationales — retribution, deterrence, and incapacitation — because the political climate in which they operate does not permit consideration of the others.[21] As we have seen, public and electoral pressures and career concerns produce in many American prosecutors a "conviction psychology" that privileges their role as advocate seeking conviction over their role as officer of the court seeking justice. Insulated from external influences, the Japanese prosecutor strikes a different balance between these competing role demands, one which prescribes a broader definition of what a prosecutor should do and enables him or her to do it.

Second, Japan's quiescent political context permits prosecutors to concentrate on processing cases instead of attending to public opinion or electoral exigencies. Prosecutors' insulation from the media and public means they have few incentives to exaggerate their own or to claim credit for others' achievements, or to use criminal cases to shape public opinion or score electoral points (Stewart 1987:183; Scheingold 1984). Journalists in Japan rarely quote prosecutors by name or even rank, but simply refer to "an official in the prosecutors office" or "a certain prosecutor." This personal obscurity bothers few prosecutors (most seem oblivious to the alternative), for they gain no immediate career advantage by distinguishing themselves in the public's eye. And unlike American prosecutors who use the office as a stepping-stone to elected office or the bench (Blumberg 1979:122), Japanese prosecutors are rarely elected to political office after leaving the procuracy.

Since fame benefits them so little during their career or afterward, frontline prosecutors have little reason to seek it, and chief prosecutors have no reason to fear the threat of a "palace coup." The contrast with the United States is again apt. Incumbent chief prosecutors in America strive to achieve electoral invincibility, a goal which at times distracts them and their assistants from the business of criminal justice. To prevent internal opposition from threatening their bailiwick, some chiefs refuse to assign the most competent prosecutors to the most important cases. This has occurred regularly in the District Attorney's Office of Los Angeles County, sometimes with disastrous results (Taylor 1996:32). Coups, counterattacks, and preemptive strikes against ambitious subordinates are not part of the Japanese prosecutor's work environment. Absent such intrigue, prosecutors can — and do — concentrate more intently on their core tasks.

Third, across Japan's fifty district prosecutors offices there is little variation in either chief prosecutor style or organizational strategy. This uniformity is in large part a result of the procuracy's independence from external pressures. Generally speak-

---

21. One reflection of the demise of the "rehabilitative ideal" in the United States is the official policy of the ninety-four U.S. Attorney's Offices, which directs prosecutors to charge all "readily provable conduct," regardless of the effect on the offender's capacity to reform. See also Humes (1999) and Taylor (1996).

ing, Japanese prosecutors detect only small differences in personality from chief to chief and only slight changes in policy when the chief changes. Few prosecutors believe the identity of the chief makes much difference for what prosecutors do or what suspects get (Appendix, part 4:74). There is, in other words, considerable consistency in prosecutor policy and practice, both across offices and within the same office over time. Chief prosecutors in the United States, on the other hand, have highly diverse political styles which reflect their perceptions of their constituencies' demands. "Conservator" chiefs — almost the only style of leadership one sees in Japan — attempt to protect the status quo and hence engage at most in minor tinkering with office policy. In contrast, "insurgent" chiefs struggle to change the status quo, while "reformers" split the difference, pursuing incremental change through a cautious approach to policy reform (Flemming et al. 1992:37). Each leadership style shapes, in its own way, who gets what in the criminal process. Ultimately, the diversity of American leadership styles translates into highly divergent outcomes in different jurisdictions, even for cases that seem similar in all relevant respects. In Japan, the homogeneity of chief prosecutor styles helps make such inconsistencies much less common (see chapter 5).

One final but obvious qualification is in order: Japanese prosecutors are not completely insulated from public opinion or political exigencies. Indeed, some of the most important changes in Japan's postwar polity occurred precisely when the public demanded that prosecutors aggressively pursue allegations of high-level corruption (Mukaidani 1993a). Prosecutors in the "special investigation divisions" (*tokusōbu*) which target such corruption are commonly criticized for being beholden to party politicians (Tachibana 1993; Kubo 1989). Nonetheless, the influence of public opinion on even these prosecutors is "rather rare" and relatively weak, much as it has been on Japan's other elite bureaucrats (C. Johnson 1995:222). While the Japanese seem as uninformed about their prosecutors as Americans are about theirs, they are significantly less critical and completely unable to translate their misperceptions into votes. In short, and despite the exceptions, because Japan's procuracy is insulated from many of the political and public pressures that buffet American prosecutors, it has acquired sufficient freedom of action to define and pursue its tasks as it deems best.

Enabling Law

If prosecution is conceived as a system for turning case inputs into disposition outputs, then the previous sections show that Japanese prosecutors operate on markedly different inputs than their American counterparts do. Indeed, the crime, caseload, and political contexts provide Japanese prosecutors with an unusually enabling environment in which to make decisions that in the aggregate constitute the Japanese way of justice. This section extends the analysis by showing that prosecutors in Japan also possess an extraordinary array of legal tools for acquiring the information they need to make the decisions that convert criminal case inputs into criminal justice outputs.

Law and Lawmaking

Lawmaking may seem to be an area where, even in Japan, politics penetrates the procuracy. After all, Japan's Diet has formal authority to create, negate, and reform the laws that prosecutors must apply to particular cases. This logic does capture the American state of affairs. By circumscribing judicial discretion, for example, the sentencing guidelines passed by state legislatures and the U.S. Congress have greatly increased prosecutorial power over charges and sentences (Boerner 1995). Japan's constitution gives lawmaking authority exclusively to the elected members of the Diet, but in criminal law, no less than in other areas, "it is the bureaucrats who actually initiate and draft virtually all important legislation" and who "contribute significantly to the passage of bills within the Diet" (C. Johnson 1995:123). Since prosecutors hold almost all the key posts in the Ministry of Justice, the bureaucrats who possess the main lawmaking and law-revising powers are the same officials who apply those laws to suspects — the prosecutors.[22]

Though prosecutors possess the principal power to create and change criminal legislation, their power is constrained by the norm of unanimity, "the informal yet binding agreement that no legislative proposals will be forwarded to the cabinet without the unanimous consent of the bureaucrat leadership" of other ministries and organizations with an interest in the issue (Keehn 1990:1029). The norm of unanimity thus prevents prosecutors from changing most laws, no matter how mundane. Consider the following examples.

Since the end of the American-led Occupation in 1952, the Ministry of Justice's Criminal Affairs Bureau (CAB) has repeatedly been frustrated in its attempts to revise the Penal Code, Japan's primary source of criminal law. Among other things, CAB has wanted to extend the coverage of the Penal Code to include new forms of economic crime; narrow the code's broad and ambiguous wording; decrease the prescribed punishments for property crimes and increase the punishments for violent crimes; and modernize the code's hopelessly archaic language. Even though the ministry has committed significant human resources to these goals, all but the last have been frustrated by the norm of unanimity. One prosecutor who worked in CAB on such legislative reforms for twenty-two consecutive years (1954–1976) concedes that all his reform efforts came to naught. A few years before he was promoted from CAB to a position elsewhere in the ministry, this prosecutor led a reform team composed of six prosecutors who tried to introduce a bill to revise the Penal Code in some of the aforesaid ways. But the Bar Association, psychiatrists, and a group of young professors opposed provisions that would have created new economic crimes, and thereby thwarted the bill.

In the early 1980s the same prosecutor became director general of the Ministry of Justice's Bureau of Corrections. The bureau's chief objective was to revise Japan's

---

22. The most prestigious organ in the Ministry of Justice is the Criminal Affairs Bureau (*keijikyoku*, or CAB), whose Legislative Affairs Division is responsible for drafting and revising all legislation related to criminal law and the Code of Criminal Procedure. The chief of the CAB is always a prosecutor, as are the vast majority of key CAB personnel (interviews with CAB officials, November 1994).

Prison Law, a statute created in 1908, by more precisely defining the rights and duties of wardens, guards, and prisoners (legalization), by placing more stress on rehabilitation as one of the prison's missions and relaxing the mandatory work requirements for inmates (internationalization), and by modernizing the code's Meiji-era language (modernization). Once again, the procuracy's legislative goals were frustrated by the Bar Association, which felt the new bill would legitimate the controversial "substitute imprisonment system" that allows prosecutors to hold criminal suspects in police detention cells instead of official jails, and by the National Police Agency, which drafted its own separate bill in an effort to take control of the amendment process.

Prosecutors achieved their most notable legislative success in 1995, when the Legislative Affairs Deliberation Committee and the Diet finally approved CAB's proposal to modernize the Penal Code's archaic language (*Yomiuri Shimbun*, 2/14/95). CAB prosecutors had worked on this project for over four years before it was finally passed. Their goal sounds simple: to make the code's Meiji-era prose more comprehensible to a postwar populace that uses a markedly different system of writing. Prosecutors intended to update the language, not change the code's meaning. Nonetheless, since CAB prosecutors knew the norm of unanimity could shipwreck reform on the shoals of any one of countless nuances, they paid painstaking attention to seemingly picayune issues (which particle, *na* or *no*, should be used after an adjective?), frequently visited the Diet library to investigate historical matters they considered arcane or irrelevant, and engaged in numerous rounds of consultation and negotiation with the other interested ministries. This apparently simple reform exhausted the prosecutors who worked on it. When their efforts ultimately succeeded, they were greatly pleased.

One prosecutor in charge of updating the Penal Code's language occasionally becomes "envious" when he observes how easy it to create or reform law in Great Britain and the United States.[23] Usually, however, he favors the more prudent, time-consuming Japanese approach, because the political currents that generate change in other countries are "fickle" and because legislative reforms (such as the American movement to mandatory sentencing) often have harmful, unintended consequences.

Law and Crime-Making

Though the procuracy's capacity to shape legislation is sharply curtailed by the norm of unanimity, law still promotes prosecutor interests to a great extent, especially regarding ordinary street crimes. Law is thus a key feature of the prosecutor's work environment.

First of all, Japan's Code of Criminal Procedure confers vast power on investigators to acquire and control the information prosecutors need to perform their criti-

---

23. For example, between 1984 and 1992 the state of California created over a thousand new criminal laws.

cal task — the processing of suspects through the construction of "the truth." These legal rules give prosecutors an unparalleled capacity to "make" crimes out of cases. Previous work stresses five main features of Japan's "enabling legal environment":

1. Rules about *"voluntary investigation"* enable police and prosecutors to process over four-fifths of all suspects on an "at-home" basis and thereby avoid judicial scrutiny of their behavior.
2. Rules about the *admissibility of evidence* obtained from searches, seizures, and confessions strongly favor police and prosecutors over suspects and defendants.
3. Rules about *arrest* give police and prosecutors wide powers to apprehend suspects without a warrant.
4. Rules about *detention* give prosecutors "virtually guaranteed" powers to hold suspects after arrest, often in police station detention cells. Detained suspects have no legal right to bail or to state-appointed defense counsel until after prosecutors have filed charges.
5. Rules about *interrogation* give investigators authority to question suspects for up to twenty-three days on each single charge, and to paraphrase or summarize suspects' statements in their own words. The rules do not give defense counsel the right to be present at interrogations. Although suspects in custody have the right to remain silent, they also have a duty to endure questioning. Thus, police and prosecutors may continue interrogating even after suspects have declared their unwillingness to talk. Further, prosecutors possess power to designate the time, place, and length of meetings between defense attorneys and detained suspects.[24]

Though these rules are important, Japanese law enables prosecutors to "make" crime in other ways as well: it gives them monopoly power over the charge decision; it grants them discretion to withhold charges in any case and to withhold evidence from the defense in any case charged; it gives them a long time to investigate cases and make charge decisions; it permits them to compose dossiers in their own words and to use those dossiers at trial; and it allows them to appeal any unfavorable sentence or verdict, including acquittals.

---

24. For a more detailed discussion of Japan's enabling rules of criminal procedure, see the excellent study of Japanese police detectives by Miyazawa Setsuo (1992). Note also that Japanese prosecutors routinely (1) consult with police about arrest and search-and-seizure decisions, and (2) interrogate suspects and interview victims and witnesses during the pre-charge period. Except at the federal level, American prosecutors rarely do either. Thus, though Miyazawa focuses on Japanese detectives, his argument applies to prosecutors as well, either because the law directly enables prosecutors in the same way it enables police, or because the law enables police to pursue goals that prosecutors share. Note, too, that custodial suspects' "duty to endure questioning" generates conflicting opinions among Japanese scholars and legal professionals. Some believe that because the Code of Criminal Procedure contains no clear provision creating the duty and because the Supreme Court has not explicitly recognized it, the duty does not exist. In practice, however, prosecutors, police, and local courts assert the duty and act accordingly.

The Monopoly Power to Charge

Most fundamentally, Japanese law does not permit prosecution by the police, grand juries, preliminary hearings before a judge, or private prosecution, all but the last of which are commonly used in the United States in order to disperse and control the awesome power to charge. As a result, prosecutors in Japan have exclusive power to decide whether or not to institute charges, and courts may recognize no crime unless a prosecutor has first indicted a suspect.[25] This principle, called "the monopolization of prosecution power," concentrates more charging power in the prosecutor in Japan than in almost any other democratic country.[26]

The Power to Suspend Prosecution

At the same time, even if Japanese prosecutors possess sufficient evidence to win conviction at trial, they have discretion to divert offenders from the criminal process by not instituting formal charges. Article 248 of the Code of Criminal Procedure establishes the legal foundation for this power to "suspend" prosecution: "If, after considering the character, age, and situation of the offender, the gravity of the offence, the circumstances under which the offence was committed, and the conditions subsequent to the commission of the offence, prosecution is deemed unnecessary, prosecution need not be instituted." Thus, unlike Germany, Italy, Finland, Sweden, and other Civil Law countries where prosecutors are legally required to charge suspects if they have evidence to convict (the principle of mandatory prosecution), Japanese prosecutors completely control the input of cases into the criminal justice system (the principle of discretionary prosecution). In most years prosecutors use this discretion to discharge without prosecuting about 37 percent of all suspects whom they believe could be convicted.[27] The monopoly power to prosecute and the capacity to suspend prosecution are so central to Japanese criminal justice that many in the procuracy regard them as "the most important characteristics in the prosecution system" (Inagawa 1995:14; T. Ono 1992:68).

---

25. The sole but insignificant exception is a procedure known as "analogical institution of prosecution through judicial action" *(fushimpan seikyū)*. Some have argued that despite "the limited class of cases to which analogical institution of prosecution proceedings apply . . . the very existence of the statutory device no doubt fosters a quite careful attitude on the part of public prosecutors" (George 1984:420). This position exaggerates the importance of "analogical prosecution." First, the procedure applies only to a narrow range of crimes, mostly those involving abuse of official authority, as in police brutality. Second, the procedure is rarely used. Between 1949 and 1990, 10,800 complainants applied to have courts institute prosecution through this procedure, but judges brought charges in only sixteen cases, or about 1 in every 675. Of those sixteen cases, nine trials ended in conviction and suspended prison terms, four resulted in acquittal, and the remaining three were still being tried as of 1992 (T. Ono 1992:75). Third, prosecutors acknowledge that the procedure little affects their charge decisions (interviews with the author). For a description of a case in which this procedure did help to hold police accountable for brutality committed against an exuberant baseball fan, see Mikami and Morishita (1996).

26. The main exception may be South Korea (Moon 1995).

27. The 37 percent figure is for Penal Code offenses, excluding traffic crimes (Furuta 1995:4).

The Power of Time

The Code of Criminal Procedure gives Japanese prosecutors a long time to decide whether or not to charge a suspect with a crime, especially by American standards. Consider this contrast: after arrest, prosecutors in California have forty-eight hours to make the initial charge decision, while Japanese prosecutors have up to twenty-three days to detain and investigate suspects before deciding whether and what to charge.[28] For serious crimes, if twenty-three days seems insufficient then prosecutors may instruct the police to arrest the suspect for a more minor crime and use that detention period to interrogate the suspect for the serious offense. This practice, known as "pretextual detention," is illegal but common, in large part because courts seldom enforce the prohibition or exclude confessions thereby obtained (Ramseyer and Nakazato 1999:171).

Given this much time and relatively light caseloads, prosecutors in Japan can collect and collectively consider a great deal of information about the suspect, victim, and circumstances of the alleged offense before making what most observers consider "the most important decision that a prosecutor makes" (Abrams 1975:2).[29] Prosecutors use this time, as do police, mainly to gather evidence of guilt and information to determine an appropriate punishment. The sheer length of the investigation frequently favors the prosecution's interest in seeing that the guilty get their comeuppance. In some cases, however, time enables prosecutors to minimize the harm caused to suspects and their families through unnecessary or imprudent charges and to mitigate the real costs — financial, occupational, and reputational — that follow a criminal indictment. It is in this dual sense that time is power: to impose pain and to alleviate it. The lengthy pre-indictment period also helps prosecutors minimize the number of charges that end in acquittal. Since acquittals are widely believed to reflect the failures of individual prosecutors and of the procuracy as a whole, the power of time protects reputations as well.

28. In Japan the decision to charge is concentrated in one actor — the prosecutor — at one point in time. In contrast, the American system of prosecution is characterized by "multiple, redundant discretion," for at least three decision points "could properly be described as the 'charging' decision: booking, the filing of initial charges, and the filing of formal charges" (Walker 1993:87). Typically, police make the booking decision, prosecutors make the initial charge decision, and either a judge (at a preliminary hearing) or a grand jury makes the formal charge decision. Thus, California prosecutors have forty-eight hours to make the *initial charge* decision.

29. It seems no other prosecutors are required to make the charge decision as quickly as American prosecutors. Conversely, in few countries do prosecutors possess as much charging discretion or as much time to exercise it as in Japan. South Korea, where prosecutors have the monopoly power to prosecute and up to twenty-nine days to charge, is one of the few exceptions (Moon 1995:178). Even so, Japanese prosecutors claim that compared to prosecutors in France, Germany, and other Civil Law countries, they have little time to decide whether or not to charge (Fujinaga 1993:108). Such comparisons are misleading because Civil Law prosecutors play a less central role in the investigative process. The decision to charge may take longer in Civil Law countries than in Japan, but in most Civil Law countries an investigating judge (*juge d'instruction*) — not a prosecutor — conducts the pretrial investigation and decides whether there is sufficient evidence to charge. If there is, the investigating judge refers the case to a three-judge panel which assesses the evidence again. Only if the panel finds "reasonable cause" is the suspect formally charged and made to stand trial (Carbonneau 1995:314; Langbein and Weinreb 1978).

The Power to Compose Confessions

In Japan confessions are the king of evidence, and prosecutors are given wide legal latitude to compose them in their own words and to use them as evidence at trial, even if the confessor subsequently recants all or part of the confession.[30] As we have seen, the law gives investigators many tools to *extract* confessions: time, the single most effective instrument in their arsenal; a convenient place (police detention cells); control over meetings between suspects and defense counsel; and so on. But the law also enables prosecutors to *shape the form* of confessions (or denials, or anything in between) by permitting them to compose written summary statements (*kyō-jutsu chōsho*, or dossiers) of what the suspect says during interrogation. Thus, prosecutors are not required to record the suspect's words verbatim.[31] Critics of this practice and of the law which enables it argue that dossiers are really "the interrogator's essay, reflecting his interpretation of the suspect's statements, his choice of words, and his arrangement of the material" (Three Tokyo Bar Associations 1989:7). Critics further contend that prosecutors abuse this authority by adding to the dossiers words that were never spoken, and by omitting words that were, in order to strengthen the case against the suspect (Igarashi 1995:35). Prosecutors claim such abuses are rare, but as shown in chapter 8, the problem of illicit editorializing cannot be so easily dismissed. Dossiers are commonly doctored. Prosecutors defend the law and practice pragmatically. As one put it, "Suspects say many irrelevant things during interrogation. It would be undesirable and impossible to record everything they say for up to twenty-three days." This much is clear: prosecutors traffic in evidence, and most evidence consists of words. The authority to compose confessions in a prosecutor's own words, not the suspect's, is a power prosecutors find immensely useful. They are understandably, if unfortunately, loath to relinquish it.

The Power to Introduce Evidence at Trial

Japanese law permits prosecutors to use "composed confessions" at trial. In principle, of course, the Code of Criminal Procedure does not allow "hearsay" to be admitted as trial evidence (Article 320). However, broad exceptions to this rule enable prosecutors to enter as evidence many dossiers taken from suspects, victims, and witnesses during the investigation. Indeed, exceptions to the hearsay principle are so common that even some judges deplore the excesses. One judge, for example, laments that the fact-finding which should lie at the heart of court proceedings is conducted instead in interrogation rooms, where investigators compose statements, and in the court's chambers, where judges read them (Ishimatsu 1989:143). Many ob-

---

30. Three decades ago a scholar noted that the confession is "the decisive element of proof sought by every prosecutor before he takes a case into court and the single most important item determining the reception his efforts are likely to receive from most Japanese judges when he gets there" (C. Johnson 1972:149). The same is true today.

31. In contrast, interrogators in the United States and Germany are required to transcribe suspects' words verbatim. In many cases they also record interrogations on audio- or videotape (Leo and Ofshe 1998:494; Igarashi 1984:27). See also chapter 8.

servers agree. One scholar of criminal procedure claims that "the real substance of criminal procedure in Japan" and "the truly distinctive character of Japanese criminal procedure" lie not in the trial but in the investigative process and the police and prosecutors who dominate it (Hirano 1989:131). The appellations denouncing criminal trials for being merely paper proceedings are as numerous as they are colorful. "Trial by dossier," "formal ceremony," and "empty shell" are three of the most common.[32]

Prosecutors operating in less enabling legal environments may envy these broad exceptions to the hearsay rule, but to many Japanese prosecutors the exceptions feel burdensome. To be sure, with a little courtroom craftsmanship prosecutors can convince judges — the finders of fact in a Japanese trial — to consider as evidence statements not even written in the suspect's (or witness's) original words or which the suspect (or witness) may have repudiated as fabrications. Though prosecutors admit these allowances bolster the state's case at trial, they prefer to stress an undesirable, unintended consequence of their power to introduce evidence. Since the law and the judiciary regard prosecutor statements so highly, prosecutors take more statements, sometimes many more, than are necessary to convict — just in case a suspect or witness changes his or her story at trial. Ironically, light caseloads permit prosecutors to transform these "enabling" exceptions to the hearsay rule into onerous obligations. The transformations illustrate Parkinson's Law of Japanese Prosecution: the amount of time required to perform a task expands to fill the amount of time available to do it.

The Power to Withhold Evidence

Discovery law — or rather the lack of it — confers on prosecutors the converse power: they can create voluminous dossiers during investigations (and can encourage police to do likewise) because the law requires only limited disclosure to the defense. In fact, since prosecutors must disclose only statements that they introduce into evi-

---

32. Legal exceptions to the hearsay rule are as follows. First consider statements taken from victims and witnesses (*sankōnin*), not suspects. At trial, if the defense agrees to allow a prosecutor's statement to be admitted into evidence, the court may admit it (Code of Criminal Procedure, Article 326). If the defense does not agree, the prosecutor can call the victim or witness to testify. If the victim or witness gives trial testimony "contrary to or materially different from his previous statements," and if the court finds the previous statements more credible than the trial testimony, the court customarily admits the previous statements as evidence (CCP, Article 321). Thus, in some circumstances the law allows prosecutor statements to trump trial testimony. Police statements do not possess the same trump power, which is one of the chief reasons that prosecutors often duplicate police dossiers before trial.

The law regards statements taken from suspects differently than statements taken from victims or witnesses. As above, if the defense agrees to allow a suspect's statement into evidence, the court admits it (CCP, Article 326). However, if the defense does not agree, the prosecutor must show that the statement was taken "voluntarily." If the court rules that the prosecutor has demonstrated voluntariness, it can, and often does, admit the statement into evidence. Thus, the law on the books treats identically all statements taken from suspects, whether obtained by police or by prosecutors. In practice, however, since judges applying the law to particular cases tend to regard prosecutor dossiers more highly than police dossiers, they admit the former more often than the latter.

dence at trial, they need not worry that multiple statements taken from the same source might be contradictory, nor that certain statements could reveal weaknesses in the state's case.[33]

This is less the case in America, where prosecutors bemoan their obligations to disclose evidence to the defense. Indeed, the U.S. Supreme Court's "Brady doctrine" declares that "suppression by the prosecution of evidence favorable to an accused . . . violates due process" (Stewart 1987:208). As a result, veteran American prosecutors routinely inform their rookie colleagues that "at the start of a criminal trial you absolutely must give the defense a copy of every document concerning the case signed or written by every witness, police officer, or detective. Failure to turn over material results in an automatic mistrial. Remember, an *automatic mistrial*" (Heilbroner 1990:42). Assembling and disclosing such material, a formidable task for American prosecutors, costs Japanese prosecutors little in the way of time or trial advantage. Hence, Japan's narrow rules of discovery, like the broad exceptions to the hearsay rule, greatly enhance prosecutors' control over information that is vital to the performance of their core chore — the processing of suspects.[34]

The Power to Appeal

Finally, Japanese law gives prosecutors wide latitude to appeal unfavorable court decisions. Like defendants, prosecutors have the right to appeal the sentence and the verdict twice: first to one of eight High Courts, and then again to the Supreme Court if the lower court decision contradicts the Constitution or Supreme Court precedent. But prosecutors are careful about what they appeal. In 1993, for example, they filed only 163 appeals with the High Courts. In the same year High Courts decided 3,387 criminal case appeals (*Kensatsu Tōkei Nempō* 1993:423). Thus, criminal defendants were about twenty times more likely than prosecutors to appeal lower court decisions. Considering Japan's high conviction rate, this is unsurprising. Since prosecutors are careful about what they appeal, it is also not surprising that their appeals prevail more often than appeals from the defense. Indeed, in the ten years between 1982 and 1991, prosecutors reversed an average of 75 percent of the cases they ap-

---

33. The author of a highly respected text on Japanese criminal procedure describes Japan's discovery law as follows: "After institution of prosecution, the [defense] attorney can copy and inspect documents and other evidence relating to the prosecution in the precincts of the court. However, he must obtain the permission of the presiding judge before he can copy evidence." Thus, "under the present law, the defense cannot examine documents and evidentiary matter in the hands of the public prosecutor. . . . The practical importance of the right to inspect and copy evidence and documents has declined in comparison to the old [prewar] law [of criminal procedure]. . . . Practicing lawyers have been pressing for legislation [to create broader discovery rights], and there seems to be good reason for it" (Dando 1965:110, 550, 555). Courts may direct prosecutors to disclose evidence to the defense, but they rarely do so (George 1990:96; Mitsui et al. 1988:515).

34. These discovery rules benefit prosecutors at the cost of considerable injustice, as in the postwar Matsukawa case (C. Johnson 1972) and four death penalty retrial acquittals (Foote 1992b:72). All of these miscarriages resulted, at least in part, from prosecutors' failure to disclose potentially exonerating evidence to the defense.

pealed to the High Courts, while defendants succeeded in less than 17 percent of their appeals (Ishimatsu 1993:202).

No Juries

The enabling legal environment has one other feature of crucial importance, for Japanese prosecutors do not have to deal with an institution many American prosecutors find perversely unpredictable: juries. After briefly reviewing the history of Japan's prewar jury, this section explains how postwar prosecutors benefit from the absence of the "inscrutable black box" that is the lay jury (Abramson 1994:212).

The Rise and Demise of the Japanese Jury

Japanese prosecutors have not always been so fortunate. Between 1928 and 1943 the Jury Act provided a right to jury trial in a limited range of criminal cases, and in the first several years of that period juries proved to be a moderately popular choice for defendants.[35] In 1929, the peak year, 143 criminal defendants chose to be tried by jury. However, by 1942 the popularity of jury trials had declined dramatically, with only two jury trials in the entire year. In the following year the Jury Act was "suspended as a wartime measure" (Lempert 1992:37).[36] It has not been revived, despite many efforts to do so (Shinomiya 2001).

The jury's decline and demise have been explained in various ways. Most scholars note that defendants who chose a jury trial gave up their right to appeal jury errors of fact, thus foreclosing an avenue which could reverse convictions or reduce sentences. Under this condition, few defendants found jury trials attractive. Other analysts stress other contributing causes: that juries were merely impotent ornaments of democratic legitimacy because judges could reject their verdicts; that Japan's national character prefers hierarchy, and so Japanese seek professional rather than peer decision-making; that defendants feared juries would be more severe than judges; that jury trials were expensive and difficult to administer; and that defense attorneys did not like dealing with the unfamiliar procedures that jury trials required (Tanaka 1976:483; Lempert 1992:38).

---

35. Japan's Jury Act (*Baishin Hō*) was passed in 1923 but did not take effect until 1928. The jury system it established was influenced by the Anglo-American model but "differed in important particulars." First, defendants had a right to jury trial only in a narrow range of cases. Bench trials remained the rule for most cases. Second, juries returned not general verdicts but rather special verdicts about particular questions of fact. Third, all jurors did not have to agree on a verdict; only a majority did. Finally, jury verdicts were not binding. If a judge did not like a jury's verdict, he could empanel successive juries to hear the case de novo until one found the facts that would permit the "proper" outcome (Lempert 1992).

36. Okinawa, which was ceded to U.S. control after World War II, had criminal jury trials from March 1963 (and in civil cases from May 1964) until May 1972, when the prefecture was reincorporated into Japan (Nihon Bengoshi Rengōkai 1992:8). Besides Japan, Germany, Pakistan, and India have abolished or suspended jury systems. In Britain, the cradle of the modern jury, the jury system "has been slowly disintegrating, so that today only 1 percent of civil trials and 5 percent of criminal trials are decided by juries" (Adler 1994:xvi).

But the most intriguing account of the jury's decline comes from a study of the criminal court in Sendai, several hundred miles north of Tokyo. Between 1928 and 1943 the Sendai court received 206 cases eligible for jury trial.[37] In ninety-one of those cases the defendant confessed, and in ninety-six others the prosecutor withdrew the indictment. Of the sixteen defendants who were tried by jury, ten were acquitted, an acquittal rate of 62 percent. Another three defendants were found guilty of a lesser charge, so fully thirteen of the sixteen defendants (81 percent) who received jury trials were either fully or partially acquitted. The author of this study (formerly an assistant judge in Sendai) believes prosecutors favored suspending the Jury Act because juries reached so many unfavorable verdicts (Hayashi 1987:17). Others contend that judges also "disliked trial by jury," perhaps for the same reason (Tanaka 1976:491). As we shall see, whether disdain for jury verdicts helped cause its demise or not, it is easy to see why Japanese prosecutors were hardly jury enthusiasts.

An Insignificant Absence: Grand Juries
and Ham Sandwiches

American prosecutors face two types of jury: grand and trial. Grand juries function in about half of American jurisdictions (all federal districts and twenty-three states), and vary in size. The federal grand jury, for example, is a lay body consisting of between sixteen and twenty-three members. The democratic vision for the grand jury is clear: it hears evidence of criminal activity presented by the prosecution and determines whether the government's evidence is sufficient to justify bringing formal charges. In principle, the grand jury serves as a legal shield protecting criminal suspects from the potentially repressive state as embodied in the prosecutor. In fact, however, because it has subpoena power to compel testimony from uncooperative witnesses, the grand jury has, with only limited exceptions, "a right to every person's evidence" (Katzmann 1991:105). Moreover, the grand jury usually investigates "only those whom the prosecutor wants investigated and indicts those he wants indicted" (Blumberg 1979:139). These two facts—the grand jury's subpoena power and the prosecutor's control over the grand jury—mean that in practice the grand jury is less a constraint on prosecutorial power (a shield) than it is an effective weapon in the prosecutor's arsenal (a sword). Indeed, from overture to finale, grand jury hearings are completely run by the prosecutor. Defense counsel is not even present during the proceedings, and the prosecutor need not present evidence favorable to the accused. Grand juries are so thoroughly under the prosecutor's control that many prosecutors boast they can get them to do their bidding, whatever it might be—even to "indict a ham sandwich" (Heilbroner 1990:245). Because the grand jury barely constrains American prosecutors, its absence in Japan avails prosecutors little (Uviller 2000:1705).

37. In the entire country between 1928 and 1943, a total of 484 cases were tried by jury, of which 230 were homicide and 214 were arson cases. Of the 484 total cases, 81 resulted in acquittal, for a national acquittal rate of 17 percent—approximately the same acquittal rate that obtains in most American jurisdictions today (Nomura 1992a:248).

A Significant Absence: Trial Juries
and Unpredictability

But Japanese prosecutors never face trial juries either, and this absence makes an immense difference in how they perform their jobs. Most important, prosecutors can more reliably predict the consequences of charge decisions without juries than with them. As a result, prosecutors in Japan control not only the inputs into the criminal process but also, to a large extent, the outputs as well.

American prosecutors wield their discretion in the shadow of the jury. Since they dispose of the vast majority of criminal cases through plea-bargaining, few cases actually result in trial by jury.[38] Nevertheless, because jury trials require intense preparation, and because jury trial outcomes are difficult to predict, the jury's presence, in fact or in possibility, affects nearly everything American prosecutors do, from pre-arrest to post-conviction (Frohmann 1992). As one American prosecutor told me, "juries have a hugely important influence on what we do, not just at trial but all along the road to trial too." Further, since prosecutors have a strong preference for avoiding uncertainty, their charge decisions are "significantly influenced by the uncertainty of the assessment of the prosecutorial merit of a case, which is the probability of conviction" (Albonetti 1987:310). American prosecutors cannot reliably predict that probability. To them, juries often seem to render "shoddy," "bizarre," and "patently stupid" verdicts (Heilbroner 1990:118; Adler 1994:xv).

Research reveals that prosecutors are right to regard juries as unpredictable. In their classic study *The American Jury* (1966), Harry Kalven, Jr., and Hans Zeisel studied disagreements between judges and juries in criminal cases. For 3,576 trials in which juries reached a verdict, judges disclosed in questionnaires the decisions they would have reached if they had been responsible for the verdicts. The main findings are as valid today as when they first were published (Hans and Vidmar 1986:116):

> Judge and jury agreed on a verdict in only about 78 percent of criminal trials. In 22 percent of criminal trials — almost one in four — the judge disagreed with the jury's result.

> When judge and jury disagreed, the jury was seven times more likely to be more lenient than the judge, either acquitting where the judge would have convicted or convicting on a lesser charge where the judge would have convicted on a greater one.

> Thus, in each one hundred cases, the judge and jury had twenty-two disagreements. Of those, the jury was more lenient than the judge in nineteen, while the judge was more lenient than the jury in three.

---

38. One study of twenty-seven U.S. cities found that on the average only 5 percent of charged cases resulted in a jury trial. The percentage of filed cases resulting in trial by jury ranged from 1 percent (Pueblo, Colorado) to 15 percent (Seattle). The more serious the charge, the greater the likelihood of trial. In Los Angeles, for example, 29 percent of homicide indictments went to trial, as did 20 percent of sexual assaults and 12 percent of robberies, but only 5 percent of larceny indictments ended in trial by jury (U.S. Department of Justice 1988:84).

Many observers — and prosecutors in particular — regard verdict disagreements as jury mistakes, but Kalven and Zeisel do not. They found that when the nature of the evidence was taken into account, the judge and jury disagreed in about 40 percent of the cases the judge described as "close" on the evidence, but disagreed "in only about 9% of the cases the judge described as clear." Thus, judges thought juries were clearly wrong in about one case in eleven.

Is that a lot? To some American students of the jury it is not, but to the Japanese prosecutors and judges I have asked it unquestionably is (Lempert 1992:54). Still, no matter how one assesses judge-jury disagreements, one fact is beyond dispute: for American prosecutors, jury unpredictability is a regular, inevitable, and sometimes ruinous occupational hazard.[39] Indeed, whether the jury is frequently irrational and incompetent, as its critics claim (Pizzi 1999:203), or, as its defenders argue, "the most potent and ingenious vehicle for self-rule ever invented," its significance for prosecutors is impossible to overlook.[40] The jury vexes, perplexes, and consumes the attention of American prosecutors more than any other feature of their occupational environment.[41]

Without juries, prosecutors in Japan operate in a far more predictable environment. Most fundamentally, since judicial decisions vary less than jury decisions do, Japanese prosecutors can more accurately foresee the probability of conviction than American prosecutors can (Ramseyer and Nakazato 1999:180). If a Japanese prosecutor believes the court might acquit or convict on a reduced charge, she (or her supervisors) can withhold or adjust the charge accordingly. Simply put, no jury means more certainty, and more certainty means fewer "mistaken" prosecutions. This predictability is one of the main reasons for Japan's high conviction rates (see chapter 7).

At the same time, predictability creates incentives for prosecutors and suspects to settle cases before trial, a fact many observers overlook. One scholar correctly notes that "the criminal process in Japan in effect moves along two parallel tracks," the first of which utilizes "formal institutional processes similar to most contemporary legal systems," and the second of which stresses cultural factors (such as repentance, confession, and absolution) and the informal settlement of cases. This ac-

39. Of course, juries may also help prosecutors by shielding them from outside political pressure (Lempert 1992; Arnold 1935) and, through "trial tariffs," by increasing their leverage in plea-bargaining (Littrell 1979; Langbein 1978).

40. Tell American prosecutors that acquittal rates in Japanese criminal trials are lower than in the United States, and their first reply is apt to be a query: Does Japan have juries? On discovering it does not, most American prosecutors will respond with an "Oh, well, that explains it" certainty that shows they are convinced this difference makes all the difference. Jury unpredictability also makes American prosecutors reluctant to let juries be the measure of their performance. As one prosecutor declared, "Juries are just so crazy that they'd make me nuts, too, if I took what they do too seriously." Another explained that a jury acquittal can mean only one of two things: either the jury irrationally "let off" a factually guilty defendant, or else it acquitted the guilty for understandable but unfortunate reasons.

41. In order to manage jury unpredictability, prosecutors and defense attorneys stress the critical importance of picking a "good jury." Neither side wants conscientious jurors; they want favorable jurors, and try hard to get them. American prosecutors often told me that selecting a good jury is the most important part of trying a case. Academic research and the growing use of jury consultants suggest such views are widespread (Hans and Vidmar 1986:63).

count further notes that for the decision to charge, "two determinative elements" are the attitude of the offender and the victim's willingness to pardon (Haley 1991:125).

While the suspect's and victim's attitudes are important, so are the opportunities and incentives they and the prosecutor face. Without a jury, all the parties to a case can foresee the likely outcome of a trial, as to both verdict and sentence. If a defense attorney predicts his client will be convicted and sentenced to prison for, say, auto theft, he can advise the thief to beg, borrow, or withdraw the money needed to settle the case privately with the victim (*jidan suru*). Likewise, if the victim expects that the sentence will be either unacceptably short or, as often happens, suspended, she may agree to write a "letter of forgiveness" (*tangansho*) to the prosecutor in return for compensation from the thief. Most important, if the prosecutor believes the thief is unlikely to offend again, or that charging him would serve neither the public interest nor the thief's rehabilitation, or that trying the case is simply not worth the trouble, she may encourage or even pressure the victim and offender to agree on a settlement so that she can suspend prosecution. In short, Japanese prosecutors work in the shadow of a trial court just as their American counterparts do. But since the shadow cast by Japan's courts is not darkened by jury uncertainty, prosecutors, offenders, and victims can clearly see the advantages and disadvantages of repenting, confessing, absolving, and settling. In this way, the cultural imperatives that motivate the "second track of Japanese criminal justice" have deep structural roots.

The predictability provided by bench trials also enables prosecutors to protect their individual and organizational reputations. As we have seen, Japanese prosecutors enjoy widespread public support. One key cause is the absence of juries: without them, prosecutors are able to minimize acquittals by dropping charges and encouraging informal settlements. Since acquittals are regarded as a disgrace (*shittai*) by prosecutors, the mass media, and "the great majority of the Japanese people," the procuracy can manage the public's perception and enhance its own legitimacy by strictly controlling the number of "dangerous" cases which go to trial (Hirano 1989:130).

Quality control is further enabled because, unlike juries, judges must justify their decisions in writing. Japanese judges write extremely detailed or "precise" (*seimitsu*) sentences. Even in simple cases where the defendant completely confesses, judges may write eight or ten pages explaining the decision. In complicated or contested cases they routinely write book-length manuscripts. Precise sentences make prosecutors uneasy, for those that find fault with the state's case bring disrepute to both the prosecutors in charge and to the procuracy as an organization. In order to avoid judicial disapprobation, prosecutors conduct extensive interviews with offenders, victims, and witnesses, thus creating their own "precise" (and often redundant) statements to submit as evidence at trial.[42] In the absence of juries, judicial sentences thus help explain one of the chief distinctives of Japanese criminal justice — its detailed and precise decision-making (Nomura 1994:143; Ishimatsu 1989:143).

42. More often, prosecutors direct police to do the interviews and interrogations and to compose the dossiers. Then they check the police work (Nomura 1988:58).

Finally, the vast majority of Japan's criminal trials do not resemble fights, battles, or sporting events, as the adversarial logic of its laws seems to prescribe, but rather "ceremonies" or "empty shells," devoid of even minor disagreements. In fact, the most important event in many criminal trials is the prosecutor's presentation to the court of the dossiers which were prepared during the pretrial investigation. Despite the legal norm asserting that court "judgments shall be rendered on the basis of oral proceedings," dossiers form the basis for most court decisions (Ishimatsu 1989). If, as in the United States, trial attorneys in Japan had to convince lay jurors of the merits of their respective positions, Japanese trials could not be the tedious, paper-processing sessions they so often are today. This fact has led some scholars to advocate a return to the jury system, and even the Supreme Court has taken sufficient interest in the issue to send judges abroad in order to learn how laypersons elsewhere participate in trial decision-making (Maruta 1990). Most observers believe a return to the jury system is unlikely, much to the pleasure of the Japanese prosecutors who profit from the predictability of the present system.[43]

Conclusion

Five features of the prosecutor's work environment—low crime rates, light caseloads, quiescent politics, enabling law, and the absence of juries—make Japan paradise for a prosecutor. These features provide prosecutors with the tools necessary to do their job: time, autonomy, power, public support, and predictability. These contexts of justice influence the content of justice by shaping prosecutor behavior.

Since prosecutors in Japan are bureaucrats as well as legal professionals, it is unsurprising that the Japan that is paradise for prosecutors was bliss for other bureau-

43. As of 2001, although Japan was still "the only advanced nation that [did] not involve the public in its judicial process," change seemed in the offing (*Asahi Shimbun* 2/1/01). The Council on Reform of the Judicial System, a panel of government advisers, had reached a general agreement that citizens should be involved in the court process in trials involving serious offenses such as murder, but disagreement remained about the exact form that public participation should take. The Japan Federation of Bar Associations favored reintroducing a jury system whereby jurors selected from the public at large would deliver verdicts independent of judges. In contrast, the Supreme Court proposed giving citizens a chance to express opinions to judges but not the right to be involved in arriving at verdicts. The Ministry of Justice—the prosecutors—took an intermediate position, opposing a jury system but allowing citizens to discuss cases with judges and to decide verdicts and sentences together (as occurs in certain cases in Denmark, Sweden, Germany, and France). According to council insiders, prosecutors took a "go along" approach. Since some kind of lay participation was likely to be implemented, resistance to all reform was deemed futile and unwise. Not surprisingly, prosecutors elected to support a form of reform that would not undermine predictability or their control over case outcomes. They thus proposed that the "ideal balance" would be for two citizens to join three judges in select court cases. Prosecutors maintained that a jury system is not "what the public wants" because it "would be virtually impossible for citizens forming the jury to evaluate evidence and explain in detail reasons for reaching their verdict by themselves" (*Asahi Shimbun* 1/6/01). Actually, opinion polls taken one month prior revealed that the public was evenly divided between favoring a system in which lay juries and judges jointly try cases and favoring the kind of jury system used in the United States (*Yomiuri Shimbun* 12/1/00).

crats during most of the postwar period. In a seminal essay published in 1975, Chalmers Johnson asked, "Who governs Japan?" Though Johnson claimed scholars, himself included, were "not yet prepared to answer" the question, he concluded that while "the bureaucracy does not rule in a vacuum in Japan . . . it does hold an ascendent position." In the intervening years many scholars have challenged, revised, and elaborated Johnson's claim, but he remains convinced of the primacy of bureaucratic power in Japan:

> Who governs is Japan's elite state bureaucracy. It is recruited from the top ranks of the best law schools in the country; appointment is made on the basis of legally binding national examinations — the prime minister can appoint only about twenty ministers and agency chiefs — and is unaffected by election results. The bureaucracy drafts virtually all laws, ordinances, orders, regulations, and licenses that govern society. It also has extensive extra-legal powers of "administrative guidance" and is comparatively unrestrained in any way, both in theory and in practice, by the judicial system. To find a comparable official elite in the United States, one would have to turn to those who staffed the E-Ring of the Pentagon, or the Central Intelligence Agency at the height of the Cold War. (1995:13)

If Johnson is correct (and many believe he is),[44] then this chapter reports one part of a much bigger story about the power and place of bureaucrats in postwar Japan. I must add, however, that if finding a "comparable official elite" in the United States requires turning to the Pentagon or CIA of bygone years (as Johnson suggests), then finding a comparable prosecutorial elite is impossible. There is none.

Finally, this account of the contexts of prosecution must be qualified in at least three ways. First, Japanese law has two distinct faces. For ordinary crimes like larceny and assault, the law is highly enabling of prosecutor interests, but for corruption and other white-collar offenses, the law disables prosecutor interests by forbidding or restricting practices that prosecutors in other countries — especially the United States — consider essential. The most important of these practices are subpoenas, wiretaps, undercover operations, and grants of immunity. In cases where American prosecutors utilize these powers, Japanese prosecutors do not possess equivalent authority (D. Johnson 1997). Restricting such practices may be tantamount to tolerating the kinds of offenses, like corruption, that these practices are designed to uncover and that seem to constitute one of Japan's biggest crime problems. Nonetheless, in the bulk of ordinary criminal cases — the kinds that occupy the attention of the vast majority of Japanese prosecutors and of this writer as well — the enabling face of Japanese law gives prosecutors an extraordinary capacity to obtain information, "make" cases, and process suspects. To me, the enabling face is the more striking visage of Japan's Janus-faced law.

Second, there are problems in paradise, as subsequent chapters suggest. The thousand days I spent in Japan were, by most reports, the most turbulent period for the procuracy since the early postwar years of occupation and reform. There were widespread allegations that prosecutors gave special treatment to elite politicians im-

---

44. See Upham (1987), Van Wolferen (1989), Keehn (1990), Fingleton (1995), and Woodall (1996). Others disagree; see, for example, Curtis (1988), Curtis (1999), and Ramseyer and Rosenbluth (1993).

plicated in corruption (Mukaidani 1993a). There were revelations of prosecutor brutality against criminal suspects and witnesses (see chapter 8). There were reports of prosecutors engaging in illicit sex in unseemly places (*Shūkan Shinchō* 5/26/94). A veteran prosecutor was demoted for sexually harassing a female reporter (*Japan Times* 1/12/94). A prosecutor's assistant was fired from his job and charged with embezzling $50,000 from the procuracy (*Yomiuri Shimbun* 12/2/94). And, most tragically, there was a prosecutor—a husband and father of two children—who hanged himself in his office, implicating by his exit a supervising prosecutor who had a notorious reputation for denouncing his subordinates without cause (*Shūkan Bunshu* 10/13/94). The procuracy was shaken by these events to varying degrees, but the structural pillars depicted in this chapter show few serious signs of toppling, slipping, or eroding. In short, and despite these problems, Japan remains a propitious place to prosecute most kinds of crime. It seems likely to remain so for a long time to come.

Last, if American prosecutors could somehow enter the work world of Japanese prosecutors, most would not call it paradise. Americans, and American legal professionals especially, strongly value autonomy, and Japan's procuracy may be too encompassing—too much like a "total institution"—to satisfy the American craving to be let alone (Goffman 1961:6). Indeed, during the 1980s Japan's procuracy had difficulty recruiting and keeping people on the job because even many Japanese believed the organization was too all-enveloping. Still, if Japan is paradise for a prosecutor one would expect that fact to be reflected in prosecutors' attitudes. It is. Three of my survey questions tapped prosecutors' job satisfaction. Their answers reveal a widespread feeling of fulfillment with their work. The items inquired about the past, present, and future, and the results are as follows:

I am glad I became a prosecutor.
— 206 agreed or strongly agreed (87.7 percent)
— 3 disagreed or strongly disagreed (1.3 percent)
— 26 could not say either way (11.1 percent)

I am very satisfied with my job as a prosecutor.
— 188 agreed or strongly agreed (80.3 percent)
— 9 disagreed or strongly agreed (3.8 percent)
— 37 could not say either way (15.8 percent)

I will remain a prosecutor until I retire.
— 168 agreed or strongly agreed (72.4 percent)
— 16 disagreed or strongly disagreed (6.9 percent)
— 48 could not say either way (20.7 percent)

Webster's defines paradise as "a state of good fortune or happiness." Whether applied to the objective circumstances of prosecution or to the subjective perceptions of a large majority of Japanese prosecutors, the label fits. The next chapter, on prosecutors' relationships with other actors in the criminal court community—police, judges, and defense attorneys—can be considered another episode in the paradise for a prosecutor tale.

2

Prosecutors and the Criminal Court Community

The crucial elements [of a criminal court community] are common work-place and interdependence.

> James Eisenstein, Roy Flemming, and Peter Nardulli,
> *The Contours of Justice*

The prosecutor is relatively passive in the criminal process.

> Malcolm Feeley, *The Process Is the Punishment*

This chapter uses the concept of the criminal court community to explore the role of the Japanese prosecutor vis-à-vis police, judges, and defense attorneys. It shows how the prosecutor in Japan controls the criminal process and thereby governs the criminal court community in ways that are impossible in the United States. Nominally, Japan has an adversarial system in which the prosecution and defense are equal and opposing parties whose clash is umpired by a passive judge. In fact, however, prosecutors dominate defense attorneys to an extent seldom seen in other democracies. Moreover, while prosecutors sometimes delegate and defer to police, they possess a high level of control in the cases that matter most. Within the criminal court community, only judges restrain prosecutor power in any significant way, yet even they seem reluctant to interfere with prosecutors' prerogatives, especially their discretion to charge.

In studies of American criminal justice, the metaphor of the criminal court community has often been used to illuminate the organizational interdependencies that lie at the heart of the criminal process.[1] Such research reaches disparate conclusions about the place of prosecutors in American criminal court communities. Some studies find that prosecutors dominate American criminal courts because they

---

1. The core elements of a criminal court community are interdependence and common workplace. That is, members of a criminal court community depend upon and influence each other, in large part because their work environments overlap (Eisenstein et al. 1988:24)

control the flow of cases in the system, own the potent symbols of "law and order" politics, have independent power bases, and can mobilize the prosecutor organization in the pursuit of office policies (Flemming et al. 1992:20). Other studies find that because prosecutors do little more than "ratify" police decisions, police are the pivotal actors in American criminal courts (Feeley and Lazerson 1983; Littrell 1979). A third school contends that few broad generalizations can be made about who wields authority because the different actors influence each other in different ways at different stages of the criminal process (G. F. Cole 1970). Though their descriptive conclusions differ, all of these studies agree that a focus on interorganizational relations is indispensable for understanding who gets what in the criminal process.

In contrast, the concept of the criminal court community has rarely been used to examine criminal justice in Japan.[2] This is unfortunate, for Japanese prosecutors, police, judges, and defense lawyers manifest interdependencies as strong as those that bind their American counterparts, and with equally important consequences. The three sections is this chapter show that prosecutors in Japan interact with police, judges, and defense attorneys in many of the same ways prosecutors do in the American system. However, the Japanese patterns suggest a clearer conclusion about the overall balance of power, for prosecutors in Japan exercise influence to an extent seldom seen elsewhere.

Prosecutors and Police

Prosecutors and police hold similar expectations for each other in Japan and the United States. In both nations, prosecutors want police to provide them with sufficient evidence to convict offenders who deserve punishment and with sufficient conformity to law to keep the state's case uncontaminated by due process problems. Conversely, police in both countries want prosecutors to charge offenders who "ought" to be charged. Cops everywhere, it seems, disdain prosecutors too timorous to charge anything but clear winners (or "layups," as American police scornfully put it).

However, three important differences overshadow these cross-cultural similarities and thus demonstrate that theories about criminal courts derived from the American experience fit the Japanese case poorly: Japanese prosecutors actively participate in investigations instead of relying on the police for case information; Japanese prosecutors strongly and routinely direct police investigations; and Japanese prosecutors interact with police repeatedly during the pre-charge investigation. Together, these three differences constitute the most important pattern of police-prosecutor relations: prosecutors are often proactive, not passively reactive, in their dealings with the police.

2. The most notable exception is Miyazawa Setsuo's (1992) study of Japanese detectives. Other works on the Japanese police say little about their relationship to prosecutors (Bayley 1991; Parker 1984; Ames 1981). Similarly, studies of the Japanese courts stress doctrinal developments (Beer 1984) or the courts' connections to politics (Ramseyer and Rosenbluth 1992; Danelski 1984), but largely ignore their connections to prosecutors or defense attorneys.

Prosecutors Investigate Crimes

First of all, Japanese police have less control over the power to investigate crimes and to control information than do American police, and Japanese prosecutors have more control than do American prosecutors. To be sure, the Code of Criminal Procedure gives police in Japan primary responsibility for investigations, but it also confers on prosecutors a complementary authority to investigate any case, either by supplementing police investigations with their own inquiries or else by initiating investigations on their own.[3] Although budget and personnel constraints compel prosecutors to rely on the police to conduct most investigations, prosecutors regularly utilize their own investigative powers, even in cases Americans would regard as petty. Indeed, my research confirms reports that front-line prosecutors spend most of their work time (perhaps 60 percent) investigating cases — that is, interrogating suspects, interviewing victims and other witnesses, and examining physical evidence (Parker 1984:107). Of course, some American prosecutors also investigate cases. Federal prosecutors do (Stewart 1987), as do white-collar-crime prosecutors (Katz 1979). These, however, are exceptions to the U.S. rule. Unlike Japan, in the American offices where most street crimes are charged, prosecutors conduct few interviews (especially prior to the charge decision) and even fewer interrogations.[4]

Two key consequences follow from the fact that prosecutors investigate cases directly. First, since these investigations occur prior to the charge decision, prosecutors possess a deeper knowledge of the evidence when that all-important decision is made. As a result, they can anticipate evidentiary problems and either mitigate them before charging or else not charge at all. Either way, the reality of routine prosecu-

3. The most important laws defining the powers to investigate and the police-prosecutor relationship are found in Articles 189–194 of the Code of Criminal Procedure. Article 189 appears to give police primary authority to conduct investigations. It states that when an offense has been committed, a police officer *shall* investigate. In contrast, Article 191 says that prosecutors *can* investigate. Police and prosecutors agree about these provisions in three respects: that the difference in verbs is significant (prosecutors told me the "shall" in Article 189 really means "must," and the "can" in Article 191 means "may"); that the law gives police primary authority to investigate crimes; and that prosecutors do possess their own authority to investigate crimes. However, prosecutors and police disagree about two important matters: how much prosecutors should investigate crimes, and the scope of the prosecutor power to direct police investigations. As explained in the text, prosecutors investigate many crimes and routinely direct police investigations.

4. One exception is the "felony review system" developed by former Cook County (Chicago) District Attorney Richard Daley in the 1980s. Under this system, about forty assistant district attorneys are assigned to one of several felony review units for a period of one to two years. Depending on the case, these prosecutors either supervise police interrogations directly, by attending the interrogation sessions, or else conduct the interrogations themselves. Daley's stated reasons for initiating the reform were to lend greater credibility (and therefore evidentiary value) to suspects' statements, and to give prosecutors a clearer sense of what evidentiary problems a case has before making the decision to charge. Prior to the reform suspects often alleged, and judges and juries believed, that police coerced, manipulated, or fabricated suspects' statements. Some argue that Daley's real motivation was more political than substantive — to create forty new patronage positions. In the first several months following the reform, police resisted and resented the change, but most now embrace it for the same reasons Daley says motivated the reform (interview with former Cook County assistant district attorney, August 1995).

tor investigations helps explain Japan's low acquittal rates (see chapter 7). Second, since prosecutors acquire information about the suspect's attitude and life environment, they can make informed decisions about the suspect's potential for reform. In this way, prosecutor investigations help explain the rehabilitative character of Japanese criminal justice (see chapter 6).

Prosecutors Direct Police Investigations

Law and custom combine to give prosecutors wide powers to direct police investigations. Article 193 of the Code of Criminal Procedure grants them authority to give "necessary general suggestions" and "general instructions" to police and to "cause police to assist" in investigations *conducted by the prosecutors themselves*. Police and prosecutors disagree about how to interpret the italicized phrase, wherein lies a major source of friction between them. Police tend to interpret these words as referring only to investigations that prosecutors have independently initiated (*dokuji sōsa*), while prosecutors construe them more broadly to cover all investigations, whether initiated by prosecutors or by police (*dokuji sōsa* and *kakunin sōsa*). These disagreements were especially strong in the first two decades or so after the new CCP was enacted in 1947. Though they have abated some they are still intense (Kameyama 1999).

No matter how much police resent and resist perceived prosecutor intrusions onto their turf, the main facts are unmistakable: prosecutors routinely direct investigations, and police habitually comply (George 1984:54; Araki 1985:609). In my own survey of 235 prosecutors, 86 percent agreed or strongly agreed that "generally police follow my instructions closely" (Appendix, part 4:53). In fourteen months of fieldwork I saw little evidence to the contrary. If police do not comply with prosecutor instructions, prosecutors can initiate a formal process through which uncooperative police may be disciplined or even removed from office (CCP: Article 194). Prosecutors rarely use that authority because they rarely need to. At times, however, they do pressure police to cooperate, customarily by telephoning the offending officer's superior in order to cajole and complain. But this informal pressure is seldom necessary. More than half the prosecutors surveyed said that police do not just passively comply with prosecutor directives but "frequently ask for advice about how to deal with cases and suspects" (Appendix, part 4:54).[5]

---

5. Prosecutors directed police long before the current laws (or current prosecutors) came into existence. Indeed, one scholar uses just four words to succinctly summarize the prewar relationship: "prosecutors dominated the police" (Mitchell 1976:35). When Itoh Shigeki became Prosecutor General in 1986, he was the first person without any prewar prosecutor experience to rise to the top of the hierarchy. As in the rest of Japan's bureaucracy, prosecutor promotions are based largely on seniority, so Itoh's ascent meant that for the first time in its history the procuracy lacked personnel with prewar experience. Between the war's end in 1945 and Itoh's rise to the top, prewar prosecutors had over forty years to educate their postwar subordinates about how to relate to the police. Many did so with enthusiastic concern for maintaining the prewar patterns of interaction (interviews with retired prosecutors). Early in his career Itoh argued that prosecutors should delegate more investigative authority to the police, but his proposal died when it ran into opposition from others in the organization (Itoh 1963).

Prosecutors and Police Have Time to Interact

As explained in chapter 1, the law gives prosecutors and police a long time — up to twenty-three days — to investigate cases before a charge decision is made. Prosecutors do not always use all the available time, but difficult cases receive at least several days of intensive police and prosecutor attention. Furthermore, prosecutors and police routinely consult about when to make an arrest so that the legal clock does not start ticking too soon. In contrast, most U.S. prosecutors have only forty-eight hours after arrest to decide whether or not to charge, and many of those I observed tried to make the decision in less than half that time. American police, therefore, rarely have more than a few hours to interrogate suspects or talk to victims and witnesses before they must transfer the case to a prosecutor so that an initial charge decision can be made (Leo 1996).

These time differences are profoundly significant. Most obviously, Japanese prosecutors possess vastly more case-relevant information when they make charge decisions than do American prosecutors, in large part because the law gives them sufficient time to acquire it. Of course, the necessary converse is that Japanese suspects can be held in legal limbo, unsure whether they will be charged or not, far longer than their American counterparts. Crucially, Japanese prosecutors and police can and do discuss the state of the evidence, thoroughly and repeatedly. Unlike the United States, where legal time limits force police to give prosecutors take-it-or-leave-it arrest reports, the first post-arrest contact between Japanese police and prosecutors is not the last. Instead, it is the beginning of a sequence of connected encounters — something much closer to a relationship than the simple exchange which characterizes many police-prosecutor encounters in the United States. During these repeated interactions, Japanese prosecutors tell police what additional information is required to make a sound charge decision and to convict at trial. They routinely get what they ask for.

In sum, these three differences enable Japan's prosecutors to be more independent of police than are their American counterparts. Prosecutors in Japan do not merely ratify police decisions (Feeley and Lazerson 1983), nor does the Japanese style of justice inexorably push the responsibility for deciding case dispositions to the lowest level — the police — of the criminal justice system (Littrell 1979). Instead, over the course of an investigation prosecutors solicit and obtain from police a great deal of information useful for the charge decision, and they supplement that information with evidence they gather themselves. In these ways, prosecutors continue to be the dominant partner in their relationship with police, much as they were in prewar years (Mitchell 1976:35).[6]

Still, prosecutors are not completely independent of police influence, nor do

---

6. Prosecutors most command and control the police in cases that garner the most public attention: corruption scandals and other high-profile "redball" crimes especially. Police resent the controls as onerous and intrusive, and critics claim the arrangement makes for ineffective crime control, but the pattern persists. Prosecutor control of police, and thus transwar continuity, is especially strong in the Tokyo region. In the Kansai region of Osaka, Kyoto, and Kobe, the delegation motif is more pronounced. For a description of transwar continuities in Japanese policing, see Aldous (1997).

they dominate all encounters with the police, nor do they relate to the police in the same way in all cases. In fact, prosecutors also delegate and defer to the police, sometimes in extraordinary ways. It is to these variations on the theme of prosecutor power that I now turn.

Delegation

In many cases prosecutors delegate authority for making case dispositions to the police and loosely review the police decisions. The law allows police to drop "trivial" (*bizai*) cases from the criminal process only when prosecutors explicitly authorize them to do so. Article 246 of the Code of Criminal Procedure states that when a police officer has investigated a crime, "he shall send the case together with the documents and pieces of evidence to a public prosecutor," except for cases "specially designated by a public prosecutor." Prosecutors — typically the deputy chiefs (*jiseki kenji*) of the fifty District Prosecutors' Offices — designate those special cases by sending to police chiefs in their respective jurisdictions standards that define which cases may be dropped.

The decision to drop such cases is called *bizai shobun*, "disposition of trivial crimes." As the appellation suggests, the designated crimes are minor, mainly thefts and assaults. The standards vary from district to district, but prosecutor executives supervise the District offices to ensure that variations remain satisfactorily small. In the early 1990s deputy chief prosecutors instructed police to drop theft cases on three conditions: if the value of the stolen goods was less than 10,000 yen (about $85); if the offender had a fixed residence (this standard disqualifies transients, many of whom are foreigners); and if the offender repented. At the end of each month police managers send summary reports of the trivial cases they have dropped to the relevant District Office, where prosecutors review the general trends. When prosecutors perceive irregularities in the reports, they direct the responsible police managers to reform the practice of *bizai shobun*, the reports, or both.

Prosecutors admit that "police have considerable discretion over what to treat as minor" (Foote 1992a:342). Indeed, that is the way prosecutors want it. And prosecutors know that police stretch the standards (often by relaxing the 10,000 yen cap in order to fit stolen bicycles and mopeds under the ceiling), though they insist worrisome abuses are rare and deviations from the guidelines seldom depart from their own definition of a "minor" case. Conventional accounts of *bizai shobun* stress the practice's rehabilitative and reintegrative aims, and many police and prosecutors do speak and act consistently with that claim. But one primary purpose and function of *bizai shobun* is to maintain the efficiency of criminal justice administration, chiefly by relieving police and prosecutors of the responsibility for carefully investigating or trying the 40 percent of Penal Code offenders disposed of in this manner. In this way delegation serves the interest of prosecutors and police.

Deference

Prosecutors also defer to the police, most conspicuously when deciding whether to suspend prosecution in cases with "borderline" evidence, and when confronting instances of demonstrable police misconduct. Consider each type in turn.

As described in chapter 1, prosecutors have complete discretion to decide whether or not to charge a suspect with a crime. Two cardinal considerations determine whether they charge: the adequacy of the evidence and the desirability of prosecution. Even if prosecutors believe there is sufficient evidence to convict an offender, they may still withhold charges if, for other reasons, they deem prosecution "unnecessary" (CCP: Article 248). All charge decisions must be justified in writing and formally recorded in one of several categories. Cases not prosecuted despite solid evidence of guilt are placed in the "suspension of prosecution" (*kiso yūyo*) category. In recent years about 40 percent of all adult Penal Code cases have been so designated, making suspension of prosecution an extremely important prosecutor power. Prosecutors maintain that the primary reason for suspending prosecution is to protect suspects from the stigma that results from indictment, and thereby to encourage rehabilitation.

Although prosecutors often do suspend prosecution in order to foster rehabilitation, prosecutor pronouncements exaggerate the importance of that objective. In fact, prosecutors sometimes suspend prosecution less to rehabilitate offenders than to maintain harmonious relations with police. They typically report charge decisions to the police, especially in serious cases. In my survey, about 54 percent of prosecutor respondents said that "I usually try to convince the police of the appropriateness of a disposition before making that disposition." Only 21 percent said they do not, while the remaining 25 percent said it depends on the case and on the police. Convincing police that there is insufficient evidence to convict can be difficult and unpleasant, because "failure is impermissible" for the Japanese detective and because a detective's sense of personal and professional worth is closely tied to his performance in clearing cases (Miyazawa 1992:x). In short, police do not like to be told their investigations have yielded "insufficient evidence" to charge, and prosecutor statements to that effect generate police resentment and resistance.

When the evidence is borderline, prosecutors face a difficult choice: they can drop the case by declaring there is insufficient evidence to convict, thereby risking police displeasure and noncooperation in future investigations, or they can suspend prosecution even though the law and office guidelines direct prosecutors to do so only when they have sufficient evidence to convict. Notwithstanding those directives, there are strong incentives for prosecutors to choose the latter horn of the dilemma. Suspending prosecution in borderline cases not only lubricates relations between police and frontline prosecutors, it also improves procuracy statistics and hence provides prosecutor executives with useful "evidence" of the organization's interest in rehabilitating suspects, evidence they unremittingly use for public relations purposes.

Several kinds of evidence show that prosecutors suspend prosecution in order to curry police favor. First, I directly observed it on two separate occasions, both theft cases. The prosecutors in charge of the cases decided to suspend prosecution even though throughout their respective investigations they spoke clearly and frequently about the cases' evidentiary inadequacies. In each case, two supervising prosecutors (*kessaikan*) approved the decision, and in at least one a superior encouraged the ultimate disposition.

In addition, the jargon-filled argot of Japan's criminal court communities has a label for the practice of suspending prosecution when the evidence is insufficient to charge or convict. The "insufficiency of evidence" disposition is called *kengi fujūbun*, and "suspension of prosecution" is called *kiso yūyo*. The two categories merge when prosecutors conjugate their labels to create the phrase *kenpu teki kiso yūyo*, literally translated as "insufficient evidence suspension of prosecution". This phrase is found nowhere in official statistics or categories, nor does one read it in prosecutor essays or scholarly articles on the subject. Its absence from scholarly writings stems from reliance on formal statements of office policy and practice, pronouncements which reveal little about suspension of prosecution dispositions. Inside the office, however, one hears it uttered often.

Legal apprentices (*shihō shūshūsei*) who train in the Prosecutors Office complain about *kenpu teki kiso yūyo*, though not always loudly or directly enough for their supervising prosecutors to hear. Many of these legal apprentices believe prosecutors should more rigorously observe the procuracy's own policies for making disposition decisions, since recording a case as a "suspended prosecution" can hurt suspects if the disposition becomes known to employers or family members who recognize that the decision means "guilty but forgiven." Further, the direct effect on a suspect's self-evaluation may be severe. Most significantly, because a suspended prosecution is regarded as "a suspect's first bite at the apple of lenience," it can generate harsher prosecutorial treatment if the suspect is rearrested (Foote 1986:103; Goodman 1986). In this way, suspending prosecution can unfairly stigmatize suspects and violate their due process rights.

Finally, prosecutors acknowledged in interviews that they suspend prosecutions more than the rules allow. One, a prosecutor for six years, said that *kenpu teki kiso yūyo* dispositions are "extremely common." Police, he explained, inspect the outcomes of cases they send to the prosecutors office. If cases are not charged because of "insufficient evidence" (especially *migara* cases where police have arrested a suspect), "the police look bad and relations with prosecutors go to pot."

The motif of prosecutor deference is seen even more vividly by examining how prosecutors respond to alleged instances of police misconduct. In the most illuminating example, Itoh Shigeki, Japan's most famous postwar Prosecutor General and widely revered as the "god of prosecutors," spoke unambiguously about the procuracy's need to maintain good relations with the police. Known as "the JCP wiretap case," this incident began when members of the Kanagawa police force were found to have illegally wiretapped the phone of Ogata Yasuo, a Diet member and leader of the Japan Communist Party. Although prosecutors appeared to have enough evidence to charge and convict a number of police, including some high-ranking officers, they chose instead to suspend prosecution of the two low-level suspects (a sergeant and a patrolman) with the dirtiest hands. In his memoirs, Itoh acknowledged that "it is unjust to punish only those at the bottom" of the police hierarchy, but he noted that if prosecutors had traced police responsibility to the top of the police organization "the entire police force, not just the section directly involved in the scandal, will resist." In such a confrontation, Itoh continued, "there seems to be no guarantee that we will win. Even if we do, ill feelings will remain on both sides and it will be difficult to maintain social order" (Itoh 1992:137).

In Itoh's view, this ending to the case — no criminal charges filed despite strong evidence of widespread illegal police behavior — "was best for the nation" (Itoh 1992:137; Miyazawa 1989:21). Perhaps. If more vigorous pursuit of police misconduct had created the negative fallout Itoh predicted, there would have been a price to pay in future investigations, for police and prosecutors *and* for the public. However, sacrificing one pillar of the rule of law — the ideal of equality under the law — was a heavy price to pay. In the interest of maintaining harmonious relations with the police, prosecutors seem willing to pay that price. Indeed, there is evidence that prosecutors regularly indulge police misconduct, especially in cases where police beat or mistreat suspects during interrogation (T. Ōno 1992; Ochiai 2000).

Emotional Landscapes

The interactions between police and prosecutors generate and reflect a wide range of emotions. As in most relationships, the sentiments in this one are asymmetric. The main emotional patterns correspond to the relational patterns described above. Most notably, prosecutors are more satisfied than police with the state of the relationship.

As discussed above, prosecutors want two things from police — information (obtained through aggressive investigations) and restraint (or conformity to due process). But prosecutors do not demand equal measures of both, and when the two imperatives conflict the need for information usually prevails. Prosecutors demand, excuse, and ignore aggressive police action because such police behavior helps them perform their core task — discovering the substantive truth of a case — and because judges do little to control police or prosecutor investigations (Miyazawa 1992:217; Ramseyer and Nakazato 1999:170).

Because police generally give prosecutors the information they want, prosecutors are pleased with the state of the relationship. Indeed, in my survey the great majority of prosecutors report that the police follow their instructions well and that their relations with police are "excellent" (Appendix, part 4:52–53). My fieldwork adds flesh to these survey results, for I seldom observed in Japan something that is ubiquitous in the United States: prosecutors insulting, belittling, and disparaging the intelligence and competence of the police who send them cases. Of course, American prosecutors rarely do this when the police are present, but when police are out of earshot their scorn is clear-cut and cutting. Their obloquies range from clever quips ("Let's just say his bulb doesn't burn too bright"), to sweeping criticisms ("Most of what they send me is total garbage"), to crude character attacks ("He's a stupid, incompetent piece of shit"). I do not provide corresponding critiques from Japanese prosecutors because I heard nothing remotely similar. If "conflict and animosity" are the norm in American police-prosecutor relations, such feelings are far less evident among prosecutors in Japan (McDonald 1982; Jacoby 1980).

In contrast, the emotional landscapes of Japanese police are replete with crags of frustration and resentment. In interviews, police acknowledged numerous "problem areas" in the relationship. Most police discontent arises from concern about "the three Ts": timidity, turf, and trust.

Many police say their biggest frustration is that prosecutors are too timid to charge cases that should be tried. Prosecutors, they say, are overly concerned with the remote possibility of acquittal, in part because "they are harshly criticized [by the public and other prosecutors] if they lose." Although this kind of complaint is commonly heard from American police, too, another form of timidity may be more distinctively Japanese: the reluctance of prosecutors to let police even try to make cases for fear that they will end in non-prosecution or acquittal anyway. As noted above, police routinely consult prosecutors about whether and when to make arrests, especially in potentially high-profile cases. This gives prosecutors the chance to direct police attention toward some crimes and away from others. According to police, prosecutors often demand near perfect evidence before allowing arrest. In other cases prosecutors simply instruct police not to pursue certain leads, before the question of arrest even arises. Some police say the second form of timidity (quashing cases before arrest) is more common than the first (non-charges). A former executive of the Tokyo Metropolitan Police Department told me that prosecutor reluctance to pursue potential cases was his biggest occupational frustration.

Police direct their second major grievance at perceived prosecutor intrusions on their autonomy, or "turf." Another retired police executive criticized prosecutor trespasses onto police turf through an elaborate metaphor which likens Japanese criminal justice to a version of capitalism found more commonly in economics textbooks than in Japanese reality. Putting aside the question of the metaphor's accuracy as a description of capitalism, the criminal justice system, I was told, should work as follows:

> Police are like manufacturers; they make cases by investigating bad acts. The prosecutor, as middleman or marketer, must ultimately satisfy the end consumer, or judge. In order to be successful manufacturers, police must make a good product and respond to the consumer's needs. However, as in the real business world, the manufacturer and the marketer should be independent. Hence, commands from the marketer-prosecutor about how to make cases are unreasonable. Prosecutors do not know how to make cases themselves — that is the police's area of expertise — so the worst problems occur when prosecutors direct police investigations. Unfortunately, this happens often. Police need to be careful so that prosecutor interventions do not get out of hand. We must prepare ourselves in order to avoid reversion to the prewar pattern in which prosecutors dominated us. (Interview, April 1995)

Although other police I interviewed did not construct this elaborate a metaphor, many did stress precisely the same point. One said that "the best prosecutors do their job [charging cases] and allow police to do theirs [investigation]. The worst are those who interfere." Another explained that he most resents executive prosecutors who intervene in big investigations because they are out of touch with frontline developments. Indeed, there is much police dissatisfaction over prosecutors' tendency to "take over" big cases that the police have initiated.[7] The following quotation colorfully captures their discontent:

> Don't tell them, but prosecutors force us [the police] to do the dull cases and try to take the redball ones for themselves. Of course, in the beginning of most cases prosecutors take no interest in what we are doing, but if a police investigation starts to look promising they swoop in and steal it away. If we oppose them there will be hell

---

7. The Japanese word for "takeover" is *yokodori* (literally "taking from the side"). The verb connotes meanings such as "snatching," "seizing," "expropriating," or even "stealing," and it is in this disparaging sense that police and other critics use the word (Hatano 1994b:55; T. Ōno 1992:146; Kubo 1989:150).

to pay later on, so we just do what they say. What? Discipline or dismissal? No, that's not the issue. What worries us is that next time we send an ordinary case to the prosecutors they will bounce it back to us saying something lame like "there's not enough evidence" or "your investigation is inadequate." Anyway, those guys have the power to charge, not us, so if they get bent out of shape we're really up a creek. (Kubo 1989:149)

The last major source of police resentment is prosecutors' refusal to trust police enough to permit their participation in major investigations, especially in corruption cases. Prosecutors have both principled and self-interested reasons for "taking away" from the police cases which seem likely to attract intense public interest.[8] In fact, prosecutors took away many of the cases that eventually became huge scandals, including the Lockheed, Recruit, and Sagawa cases, three of the biggest corruption scandals in the last fifty years. To the police, one of the worst instances of prosecutor distrust occurred when prosecutors arrested former Prime Minister Tanaka in 1976. Fearing a leak, prosecutors did not inform top police executives until after the arrest. Tsuchida Kuniho, then the chief of the Tokyo Metropolitan Police Department, was practicing *kendō* (Japanese fencing) when informed of the arrest. On hearing the news he erupted in a fury one seldom sees in Japan, shouting, "Those SOBs shut us out!" and shattering his bamboo sword against the floor of the *dōjō* where he trained (T. Ōno 1992:155).[9]

In sum, evidence of police frustration over "the three Ts" weakens claims that the relationship between police and prosecutors is one of cooperation between equals, not of police subordination.[10] However, these frictions should not be exag-

---

8. Prosecutors have long argued that only they possess the knowledge and training required to deal with the legal, economic, and accounting problems that corruption cases entail. Prosecutors also point out that since many retired police populate the world of electoral politics, old-boy connections can derail corruption investigations by the police. While these are legitimate worries, prosecutors' concerns about organizational autonomy and individual ambition seem equally important reasons for their reluctance to give police much of a role in corruption investigations. That traditional reluctance is being increasingly challenged by outside observers (Tachibana 1993), police (Hatano 1994b), and even prosecutors themselves (Kameyama 1999).

9. Police-prosecutor discord has other roots in addition to their conflicting desires to "own" big cases and take credit for investigative successes. Education is one. A study conducted in the 1970s reports that only three of forty-four detectives had any junior college or college experience (Miyazawa 1992:41). In contrast, all prosecutors have college degrees, as do most assistant prosecutors. Prosecutors also have passed Japan's notoriously difficult bar exam, one of the most demanding qualifying tests in the world. At the highest personnel levels one finds other police-prosecutor differences. The great majority of police officials in the National Police Agency, as in most of Japan's other elite ministries, are graduates of prestigious Tokyo University, while managers and executives in the procuracy come from a much wider range of colleges and universities. In fact, though a large majority of postwar Prosecutors General have graduated from Tokyo University's Law Faculty, other executive positions have been filled by graduates of a far wider range of schools (Narushima and Uehara 1989). Finally, prosecutors earn substantially higher incomes than their police counterparts. These differences in background, educational credentials, and pay exacerbate the conflicts over turf and the ownership of high-profile cases.

10. Article 192 of the Code of Criminal Procedure states that "there shall be mutual cooperation and coordination on the part of public prosecutors and . . . judicial police officials regarding criminal investigation" (George 1984:420).

gerated, for descriptions of the emotional currents depend on the point of comparison. Prosecutors and police are not — emphatically not — the equal partners prescribed by law and presumed by scholars, but their relationship is just as surely more harmonious than what one observes in most American criminal court communities. Even as police describe the various "problem areas" in their relationships, many stress that, for the most part, they get along with prosecutors well. The key, many stress, is respect. As one put it, "If prosecutors respect us, we get along fine. But if they do not trust us, or criticize our performance, or make unreasonable demands, or take cases away, then we get angry. Generally, though, they respect us and we get along fine."

Prosecutors and Judges

By law, judges are supposed to check prosecutors' decisions to arrest, detain, charge, and punish, and prosecutors are supposed to anticipate and respond to judicial review. This, anyway, is the legal logic for how prosecutors and judges should relate, and it is what one hears from carriers of the *tatemae* torch (what most prosecutors want you to believe). In important respects, however, the legal prescription fails to fit reality. By digging beneath the surface of the official view, one finds evidence that many prosecutor practices are little restrained by judges.

Postwar Reforms and Transwar Continuities

Prior to Occupation reforms, Japan's Supreme Court was not a separate branch of government but a "semi-independent" organ in the Ministry of Justice. Then as now, the ministry was run by prosecutors, who "controlled all budgetary and administrative matters of the judiciary, including the appointment, promotion, transfer, supervision, and dismissal of judges and court officials" (Luney 1990:137). Prosecutors frequently used these levers to pressure judges, thereby breaching again and again the principle of judicial independence. From arrest through investigation to trial, judges did little to restrain prosecutors (Mitchell 1976:35). Postwar reforms recast the legal relationship between prosecutors and judges, giving the latter independence and power they did not previously possess. But judges seldom use their newfound powers to check prosecutor behavior. Whether during investigation, at trial, or concerning the charge decision, prosecutors get what they want from judges with notably few exceptions.

In order to perform effectively, prosecutors (and police) need judges to provide at least three things during the pretrial period: arrest warrants, detention warrants, and "good" bail decisions. First consider arrest. The law permits prosecutors, prosecutors' assistant officers, and police supervisors to apply for arrest warrants (CCP: Article 199). Compared to their counterparts in other countries, Japanese investigators do so sparingly, typically arresting only 25 to 30 percent of all criminal suspects. Further, "in serious or complicated cases . . . it is also customary for police officers to consult with a public prosecutor" before making an arrest, in order to avoid arbitrary arrest and the unnecessary stigmatization of suspects (Horiuchi 1994:2). However, when investigators do want to make an arrest, they find judges extremely coopera-tive. In 1987, for example, courts refused only 115 of 141,766 requests for an arrest war-rant, or about one refusal for every 1,233 requests (Igarashi 1989:5). In more recent years the ratio has not changed appreciably.

Next consider detention. In 1992 prosecutors requested detention in 88.6 per-cent of all cases where an arrest was made. Judges refused only 110 of 77,545 deten-tion requests, about one in every 705. Equally important, the judge invariably agrees with the prosecutor's request as to place of detention. This means investigators can (and routinely do) detain suspects in police holding cells (*daiyō kangoku* or *ryūchijo*) instead of official detention centers, thereby increasing the convenience of the in-vestigation and, according to critics of the system, encouraging widespread coercion and other abuses of authority (Igarashi 1984).

Finally, consider bail. Suspects have no legal right to bail until after indictment, whereupon they may apply to a local court for release. When an application is filed, the court sends the prosecutor a form on which to express a bail opinion. By law, judges must grant bail as a matter of right. However, since the Code of Criminal Procedure carves out broad exceptions to the rule, in practice bail is granted only to suspects who are expected to uphold their confession through trial (Satsumae 1982). Suspects who insist on their innocence stand only a tiny chance of being released (Igarashi 1989:6).[11] Simply put, suspects who do not confess do not get bail. In 1988, for instance, over 90 percent of defendants confessed, but only about 22 percent of all arrested and detained suspects were granted bail. In short, if arrested, you are likely to be detained, and if detained, you are unlikely to get bail, even if you confess.

At trial and on appeal, prosecutors also appear to get what they want from judges: evidence admitted, defendants convicted, and punishments imposed. Pros-ecutor evidence, especially the suspect's confession, is seldom excluded from trial (Miyazawa 1992). This helps prosecutors win convictions in the vast majority of cases. For example, in the six-year period between 1987 and 1992, District Court ac-quittal rates never strayed far from zero, ranging from 0.09 percent in 1987 to 0.38 percent in 1991.[12] Thus, even in an unusually "good" year for defendants, only one in 265 cases ended in acquittal. Typically the proportion is closer to one in 800.

Judges not only convict what prosecutors charge, they also impose sentences prosecutors seem to like. Prosecutors in Japan have the legal right to appeal any ver-dict or sentence but they rarely use it. In 1992, District and Summary Courts judged 55,487 criminal defendants (first-instance verdicts). Prosecutors appealed to a High Court in only 93 cases — about one in every 597 first-instance outcomes. In the same year the country's eight High Courts reversed twenty-nine of thirty-six acquittals

---

11. In fourteen months in Kobe, I learned of only one case where a judge granted bail despite a pros-ecutor's opposition. In that case a physician submitted an affidavit to the court stating that the detainee's poor health would worsen if he was not released.

12. In fact, the 1991 rate is the highest in years, largely because an election law case in Osaka resulted in 122 simultaneous acquittals — more acquittals in one case than in the whole country in most single years (see chapter 7).

(80.6 percent) prosecutors had appealed, and increased the severity of sentence in thirty-three of fifty-six (58.9 percent) other prosecutor appeals.[13]

In most countries, including Japan and the United States, the discretion to charge is the prosecutor's most important power and the main reason "the prosecutor has more control over life, liberty, and reputation than any other person" (Jackson 1940:18). Apart from their everyday review of cases at trial, judges in Japan rarely check the procuracy's authority to charge. The most significant judicial attempts to control prosecutor discretion occurred in the late 1970s when High Courts ruled in two separate cases that prosecutors had abused their discretion to charge. In both cases, however, the Supreme Court reversed the High Courts, thereby affording prosecutors almost complete insulation from judicial scrutiny of their charging decisions.

The first case arose out of the infamous Minamata pollution scandal on the southern island of Kyushu. Throughout the 1950s and 1960s the Chisso Chemical Company released industrial effluents in the water around the town of Minamata. Mercury in the effluents brought illness and disease to many people, although the causal connection was not made clear (or publicly acknowledged by Chisso or the government) until years after the first victims had alleged it. Through sit-ins and demonstrations at the Chisso headquarters in Tokyo, some of the victims pressured the firm's executives to apologize and provide compensation. In response, Chisso used employees and gangsters to keep the demonstrating victims away from company executives. Over a twenty-two-month period, confrontations between these groups resulted in fights and injuries on both sides, but prosecutors decided to charge only two men, both protesters. The surname of one defendant — Kawamoto — became the case's identifying tag. Kawamoto's "outraged defense counsel called for the case to be dismissed as an abuse of prosecutorial discretion," but the Tokyo District Court rejected the defense claims, convicted Kawamoto, and, perhaps revealing its ambivalence about the case, imposed an unusually light sentence — a 50,000 yen fine, suspended for one year.

In 1977 the Tokyo High Court "asserted its power to review the exercise of prosecutorial discretion and to grant relief from" an improper indictment. It reversed the District Court and dismissed the prosecution's case against Kawamoto. On appeal to the Supreme Court, prosecutors lost the battle but won the war. In its 1980 decision, Japan's highest court held that "justice did not require that the High Court's decision be reversed and the District Court's decision be reinstated." It thus protected Kawamoto against the stigma of conviction. At the same time, however, and more important for prosecutors, the Supreme Court ruled that Kawamoto's prosecution was "not improper" and that courts could invalidate only "extreme deviations" from the "proper" exercise of discretion (Goodman 1986:69; Upham 1980).

In 1980, the same year as the Supreme Court's Kawamoto decision, the Hiroshima High Court dismissed an indictment against another defendant. Again, how-

---

13. See the Annual Report of Statistics on Prosecution for 1992. Of course, prosecutors do not appeal all unsatisfactory verdicts or sentences, only those deemed likely to succeed. Thus, prosecutors dislike more court decisions than is reflected in the number of appeals. Even so, it strains credulity to suppose that appeals constitute only the tip of an iceberg of prosecutor dissatisfaction.

ever, the Supreme Court reversed the High Court, ruling that the prosecution need not be declared invalid simply because similar offenders had been accorded more lenient treatment in the past. Mr. Fukumoto, the defendant in this case, had been charged with violating the Public Election Law by accepting money and gifts from a candidate in a local mayoral election. At the first-instance trial in District Court, Fukumoto argued that prosecutors had abused their discretion by charging him but not the mayor or other high-status offenders. The District Court rejected Fukumoto's claim, found him guilty, and fined him 120,000 yen. On appeal, the High Court found that "the police investigation did discriminate in favor of the socially prominent," and then ruled that it violated due process for prosecutors to indict Fukumoto based on the results of the unconstitutional police investigation. But the Supreme Court "rejected nearly every one of the High Court's findings." Since then, prosecutors' discretion to charge has never been significantly challenged. Judicial review, which once seemed a promising means of checking prosecutor power, no longer elicits the same expectations (Goodman 1986:76).[14]

For a narrow range of statutorily defined crimes, judges possess legal authority to overrule prosecutors' non-charge decisions, but they rarely use this power either. As mentioned in chapter 1, the sole and insignificant exception to prosecutors' monopoly charging power is "analogical institution of prosecution through judicial action" (*fushimpan seikyū* or *junkiso tetsuzuki*).[15] Under the Japanese procedure, if accusers or complainants are dissatisfied with a prosecutor's decision not to charge, they may ask a District Court to institute prosecution. The purpose of the procedure, which applies to only a handful of crimes involving abuse of official authority, is to prod prosecutors into charging suspects — especially police, prison, and other government officials — they might otherwise be reluctant to charge. Many commentators argue that the procedure serves its purpose well (George 1984:68; Nomura 1994:161).

In reality, however, judges seldom exercise their power to institute prosecution on their own. Between 1949 and 1990, 10,800 accusers and complainants applied to judges to bring charges in this way. In only sixteen cases — one in every 675 — did a judge decide to indict. Critics infer two conclusions from these statistics: that prosecutors are inappropriately lenient toward police and other officials who abuse their authority, and that judges are extremely reluctant to participate in a charging process they deem the proper domain of prosecutors (T. Ōno 1992:75; Nomura 1994:161).

Agents of the Judges?

Thus, there is much evidence consistent with the claim that postwar prosecutors operate in the comfortable shadow of a compliant judiciary, just as they did in the pre-

---

14. The procuracy's own internal controls on the discretion to charge are far more effective than the judicial controls described here (see chapter 4).

15. This procedure was adapted from German law when Japan's new Code of Criminal Procedure was enacted in 1946. Today, law in both countries enables courts to compel prosecution in certain cases. However, in the German procedure (*Klageerzwingungsverfahren*) a court can only order a prosecutor to charge a case, while Japanese courts may institute prosecution directly, bypassing the prosecutor completely.

war era. Indeed, one is tempted to summarize their postwar relationship in the same words — "prosecutors dominate judges" — that scholars have used to characterize the state of this matter in the 1950s (Mitchell 1976:35). That conclusion, however, would misrepresent reality, for while the primacy of the procuracy is a principal melody, other motifs must not be ignored.

To begin with, judges have "the last word" within the legal domain (Haley 1998: 212). From arrest to detention, bail, charge, verdict, and sentence, judges make the final decisions. Though they routinely agree with prosecutors, it can be difficult to tell if they are following or leading.

Prosecutors reject assertions that they dominate judges. In interviews and essays, prosecutors argue not that they have commanding influence over judges but that they understand the judiciary so well they can calculate decisions to elicit agreement instead of opposition (Suzuki et al. 1981:50). There is qualified support for this assertion. In some cases prosecutors do not ask judges to sign detention warrants or deny bail precisely because they know such requests would be refused. These cases, where prosecutors forgo action on the basis of such predictions, go unreflected in official statistics about arrest warrant refusals or acquittal rates and thus render such statistics misleadingly incomplete. The prosecutors' argument is like the principal-agent claims American scholars have made about other sectors of "Japan's political marketplace." Just as the appearance of bureaucratic dominance in, say, the political economy is consistent with an interpretation that bureaucrats "faithfully implement [politicians'] policy preferences," so the appearance of prosecutor dominance may sometimes reflect prosecutors' ability to accurately predict and faithfully implement judicial preferences (Ramseyer and Rosenbluth 1993:12).

A range of evidence supports this principal-agent interpretation. First, prosecutors know judges well, better than most American prosecutors know their legal siblings on the bench. After passing the bar exam but before becoming full-fledged legal professionals, prosecutors and judges (and lawyers) go through the same legal apprenticeship. During this period, all future prosecutors spend four months training in a criminal court (and four more in a civil court), so by the time of their appointment to the procuracy they already have a good understanding of the norms which govern judicial behavior and the "going rates" which prevail in the criminal court community. Those understandings deepen through frequent interaction with judges after becoming a prosecutor, both in the workaday world of the criminal court and, especially in small, rural jurisdictions, through informal associations (*tsukiai*) after hours.

Prosecutors' ability to predict judicial behavior is further enhanced by the system of personnel exchanges between the judiciary and the procuracy (*hanken kōryū*). Every year since 1948, prosecutors and judges have traded places. Since transfers are temporary, the vast majority of judges and prosecutors return to their home office after two to three years. Between 1948 and 1994, 850 exchanges took place. At present, between ten and fifteen people make the shift each year (Nomura 1994:31). Most judges who enter the procuracy do so as *sōmu kenji*, or prosecutors who represent the state in civil and administrative lawsuits. Prosecutors who move to the bench typically hear either criminal cases or civil cases to which the state is a party. Not surprisingly, the Japan Bar Federation has long opposed this personnel exchange system, arguing that it is one of the principal reasons that private citizens rarely prevail in suits against the state. The expressed purpose of the exchange is twofold: to strengthen the state's attorneys in civil and administrative cases, and to educate judges about how the bureaucracy and the procuracy work so that when they return to the bench they can more adeptly adjudicate cases involving those actors. By all accounts the exchange system produces the intended effects, but it also affords prosecutors a participant's-eye view of the criminal court's backstage activities. Such experiences influence what prosecutors anticipate from judges and what, therefore, they seek from their former colleagues on the bench after they return to the procuracy.

Prosecutors' efforts to predict judicial behavior and respond accordingly are most evident when they calculate sentence requests (*kyūkei*). In addition to making the charge decision, investigative prosecutors (*sōsa kenji*) also make a precise recommendation about how much punishment indicted defendants deserve (e.g., "three years and six months imprisonment at hard labor"). The trial prosecutor (*kōhan kenji*) reviews the recommendation, adjusts it if it seems inappropriately heavy or light, and reads it to the court at the conclusion of the trial. In all but the most trivial cases, sentence requests are the product of extensive prosecutor research into prior judicial decisions. That research has been facilitated by the advent of computers which, at the tap of a few experienced fingers, can select a range of similar cases and present detailed data about the facts in them, including whether the defendant confessed, showed remorse, made restitution, had a prior criminal history, and so on. Prosecutors also use the computer to generate records of the sentence requested and the sentence actually imposed. They study these precedents carefully because they know judges will do the same during deliberations.

Prosecutors usually add to the sentence request about 20 percent more time than the precedents seem to warrant on their face, in order to compensate for the fact that judges routinely discount sentence requests by about that much (Nomura 1994:37) and to allow judges to maintain the appearance that they are not blindly conforming to prosecutor preferences.[16] Court observers have long noted that judges routinely "discount" prosecutors' sentence requests by a predictable amount, and many take it as evidence that prosecutors play the tune to which judges dance (Nomura 1994). Knowledge of the processes through which sentence requests get made suggests a more complicated metaphor: judges and prosecutors play the same song in different keys, each dancing in step with the other.

"The Punishment Problem"

But prosecutors and judges sometimes get out of step. When they do, private grievances can get transformed into public issues that reveal tensions beneath the surface of this outwardly placid relationship. This is what happened in "the punishment problem," a public disagreement between prosecutors and judges that captured the

---

16. When I asked one prosecutor why he felt the need to request a stiffer sentence than what the judicial precedents seemed to suggest, he sardonically said that "we have to let judges do something."

public's attention and revealed strains in the criminal court community as few other incidents have.

On March 26, 1986, Ishihara Kazuhiko — a sixty-year-old native of Tokyo and graduate of Tokyo University, the Superintending Prosecutor of the Osaka High Public Prosecutors Office, and the number three prosecutor in the national hierarchy — held a press conference for reporters covering criminal justice in the Osaka region. The press conference itself was unexceptional, for Ishihara met monthly with journalists to explain new case developments. As the chief executive prosecutor in the Osaka jurisdiction he not only oversaw appeals to the Osaka High Court but also supervised the entire Kansai region, an area which includes six District Prosecutors Offices, about three hundred prosecutors and assistant prosecutors, and over twenty million people. At this day's press conference, however, Ishihara made an extraordinary pronouncement. Citing statistics, he sternly rebuked Osaka judges for imposing sentences which were too lenient, far more lenient than those imposed by judges in Tokyo.

Prosecutors had long been aware that judges in Kansai were more lenient than judges elsewhere. Theories explaining why often circulated through the office grapevine and dominated party conversations. However, before Ishihara, no prosecutor had ever spoken about the "punishment problem" (*ryōkei mondai*) on the record. Many prosecutors remained silent out of respect for the independence of the judiciary and concern that direct criticism would only exacerbate the situation. Other would-be critics restrained themselves because, as natives of Osaka or the surrounding Kansai region, they felt a loyalty to the region and, more instrumentally, because criticism of the courts would hurt their legal business when they left the procuracy to practice private law in Kansai. As a native of Tokyo, Ishihara felt neither loyalty to the region nor concern about his post-prosecutor career. Before making the original pronouncement, Ishihara consulted with the six District Office chief prosecutors in his jurisdiction, obtaining the full support of each. However, he chose not to consult with the Supreme Prosecutors Office out of concern that this controversy might cause his superiors "trouble" or, even worse, elicit opposition or veto. However, after making his statements, which he repeated in more elaborated forms on several occasions, Ishihara did receive a letter of support from Prosecutor General Itoh Shigeki, commending him for his action.

Ishihara's core complaint was that sentences imposed by Kansai courts were too lenient, especially in comparison to what Tokyo courts were doing. Following his first press conference, executive prosecutors established a special research team in the Ministry of Justice's Research and Training Institute in order to document the disparities more precisely. The research team released several interim reports before announcing its most detailed findings in November 1986. The disparities were clear and, in some cases, even bigger than critics had supposed. For example, the rate at which courts suspended sentences of imprisonment was only 50.4 percent in Tokyo and 55.8 percent for the nation as a whole, but was 58.5 percent in Kobe (part of the Kansai region) and 61 percent in Osaka. Moreover, judges in Osaka were 50 percent less likely than Tokyo judges to put offenders on probation when they did suspend execution of sentence (8.0 percent vs. 11.9 percent), and judges in Kobe and Osaka gave offenders "overlapping" or "double" suspended sentences far more often than Tokyo judges (5.3 percent, 2.4 percent, and 1.3 percent, respectively).

The research team also studied how closely judicial sentences matched prosecutor sentence requests in murder cases. It divided sentences and sentence requests into seven ranks, with divisions made at three, five, seven, ten, twelve, fifteen, and twenty years of imprisonment. In the five years between 1979 and 1984, the Tokyo District Court agreed with the prosecutor request or imposed a sentence only one rank lighter in 90.0 percent of all murder cases; the corresponding figure for the Osaka District Court was 68.6 percent. Thus, the Osaka District Court imposed a sentence two or more ranks lighter than the prosecution's sentence request over three times more often than the Tokyo District Court (31.4 percent vs. 10.0 percent). In addition, between 1978 and 1985, the Osaka High Court was almost four times less likely to impose a sentence of death on convicted murderers than was the Tokyo High Court: two death sentences out of 1,680 murder convictions (0.12 percent) in Osaka, versus ten death sentences out of 2,295 murder convictions (0.44 percent) in Tokyo.

Sentence disparities were not the only regional difference that concerned prosecutors. Acquittal rates are famously low in Japan, but here, too, prosecutors uncovered significant variation across jurisdictions. In 1984 the Osaka District Court acquitted 0.46 percent of all suspects, over three times the rate for the Tokyo District Court (0.14 percent) and more than double the national rate (0.21 percent). In addition, prosecutors showed that Osaka trials lasted substantially longer than Tokyo trials, with over twice as many Osaka trials as Tokyo trials lasting three years or more (0.99 percent vs. 0.45 percent). Further, when prosecutors appealed first-instance sentences, those in Tokyo fared much better than their colleagues in Osaka. Between 1979 and 1984, 79.1 percent of prosecutor appeals to the Tokyo High Court resulted in heavier sentences for the defendant, while only 57.6 percent of prosecutor appeals to the Osaka High Court so prevailed. The average for the nation's eight High Courts was 70.9 percent. Conversely, defendants in Osaka gained lighter sentences in 27.3 percent of their appeals, compared to only 21.2 percent in Tokyo (Nomura 1988:174).[17]

Ishihara's criticisms attracted more attention than he anticipated. The day after his first volley, all of Japan's national newspapers ran headlines emphatically reproducing Ishihara's point: "We Cannot Overlook Kansai's Lenient Punishments" (*Asahi*); "Osaka Sentences Are Too Sweet" (*Sankei*); "Kinki [another name for the Kansai region] Punishments Are Too Light" (*Mainichi*); and "The Punishments of the Osaka Courts Are Too Lenient" (*Nikkei*). Predictably, weekly magazines reported the "punishment problem" more sensationally: "If You're Going to Commit Murder, Do It in Osaka" (*Shūkan Shinchō*) and "Osaka Prosecutors Can't Stand It Anymore: The '30% Kansai Discount' on Sentences" (*Shūkan Asahi*). In an interview eight years later (May 1994), Ishihara told me that "the great majority of Japan-

17. Courts are not the only government organs which appear to be more lenient in Kansai than in Tokyo. Applications for visa renewals are sometimes rejected by the Tokyo Immigration Office but later approved by the Osaka Immigration Office's Kobe branch (*Yomiuri Shimbun* 10/25/94).

ese" agreed with his claim that if Osaka punishments were more lenient than punishments in Tokyo, then they ought to be raised to match the Tokyo norms.

Not everyone was pleased with Ishihara's analysis. Leftist radicals and rightist gangsters threatened to kill him. Fearing for his safety, Ishihara had police escorts pick him up at home each morning, accompany him to all public appearances, and drop him off at home each night. In addition, lawyers harshly denounced Ishihara in newspaper editorials and magazine articles, though Ishihara says many lawyers in the Osaka region told him privately that they welcomed his criticisms because evidence of significant criminal wrongdoing (like a long prison sentence) gives them greater leverage in civil settlements. The Japanese bar's official response was unambiguously critical. The Osaka Bar Federation produced a massive rejoinder (272 single-spaced pages), published in two parts one and two years, respectively, after Ishihara's original press conference. The bar's response recapitulates his criticisms and the prosecution's supporting statistics and counters point by point many of the procuracy's claims about disparity. Most notably, it alleges that Ishihara's aim was not merely to generate discussion about the issue of disparity in criminal punishments, but to "accelerate the wrecking of criminal trials," a pointed reference to the "hollowing out" of Japanese criminal trials into "empty rituals" for "ratifying" the prosecution's investigation.

The judiciary's response was less confrontational. Indeed, one searches the newspapers in vain for responses from judges. It is tempting to invoke the "transwar continuity" thesis of prosecutor dominance in order to explain why the judiciary did not publicly stand up to the procuracy — judges did not lash back because they knew they could not win a direct confrontation. However, Ishihara provides a more subtle three-part explanation for the silence of the judges. Some judges, he surmises, including executive judges in the Supreme Court's General Secretariat, were afraid they would lose a public confrontation with prosecutors because the facts were not on their side. Other judges confided to Ishihara privately that they agreed with his position and were grateful he raised the issue, even though none could say so publicly for fear of criticism from their colleagues and concern over adverse career consequences. According to Ishihara, however, most judges simply employed a strategy familiar to all Japanese bureaucrats: they ignored the procuracy's attacks — literally "killed them with silence" (*mokusatsu shita*)[18] — in the hope that the controversy would die down and the situation would return to normal. Another authority quoted in Japan's largest daily newspaper interpreted the judicial response in the same way: "Osaka judges are not so weak as to be swayed by Ishihara's speech. They have decided to adopt the attitude that they will kill the issue with silence" (*Yomiuri Shimbun* 6/17/86). Looking back at what happened since he first raised the "punishment problem," even Ishihara admits that this was "the unfortunate result."

---

18. The most famous use of this phrase occurred in July 1945 when the Allied Powers presented the Japanese government with the Potsdam Declaration demanding Japan's unconditional surrender. Some historians believe the Prime Minister's remark that Japan would "kill it with silence" prolonged the war and led to much unnecessary suffering.

Perhaps the closest thing to a direct judicial rebuttal was a series of newspaper editorials written by retired judges. In a column published a month after Ishihara's original statement, a retired judge of the Osaka High Court offered a five-part refutation:

1. The prosecution's criticisms are based on shoddy research which does not sufficiently disaggregate crime by type of offense.
2. Since judges should assess punishment on a case-by-case basis, even real statistical disparities are irrelevant.
3. Rather than assuming Tokyo is the standard to which Osaka should conform, one
   could just as reasonably conclude that Tokyo punishments are too severe and so
   should be adjusted to fit the Osaka norms.
4. The criticisms are inappropriate because they undermine public confidence in
   the courts.
5. The criticisms are "an improper interference with the independence of the judiciary." (*Asahi Shimbun* 4/29/86)

The first point lacks much merit. The prosecutors' research may be unsophisticated
but its main conclusions have not been refuted by any of the critics. The former
judge's fifth point is logically his least compelling — independence matters of course,
but so does accountability — yet it was strongly stressed by lawyers and judges alike.
The fact that they seem concerned about the judiciary's ability to resist prosecutor
encroachments may reflect how little time has passed since judges were thoroughly
under the procuracy's thumb and how tenuous their current independence is (Y. Yamamoto 1994; Miyazawa 1994a).

The "punishment problem" teaches three important lessons about criminal justice in Japan. First, the regional disparities in punishment counsel caution in general-
izing about "Japanese" criminal justice. As scholars have demonstrated for the United
States, so for Japan: the topography of criminal justice "does not resemble a uniform
plane." Rather, justice is "contoured" and differences abound, especially in judicial
decision-making (Eisenstein et al. 1988:290). Of course, there is far less legal pluralism
in Japan than across the fifty United States, and there is more consistency in Japan's
procuracy than in its judiciary (as shown in chapter 5). Moreover, in prosecution as in
policing, differences along most dimensions of comparison are greater between the
United States and Japan than between any two American offices (Bayley 1991:xi). This
is why it is possible to generalize about a "Japanese way of justice." Nevertheless, there
is enough criminal justice variation in Japan to warrant more scholarly attention than
it has so far received (D. Johnson and Miyazawa 1994:680). Indeed, the language of
criminal court insiders reveals that disparities in punitiveness exist not only across geographical regions but even across different benches in the same Japanese courthouse.
Japan's criminal courts are divided into sections (*bu*). Those with punitive and lenient
tendencies are called "hell sections" (*jigokubu*) and "heaven sections" (*gorakubu*),
respectively (Nomura 1994:36). Judges are understandably reluctant to acknowledge
such disparities, but increased research efforts to gain access to courtrooms could uncover more of the reality of diversity lying beneath the principle of uniformity.

Second, the "punishment problem" suggests that prosecutors neither control
judges as they did in the prewar years nor to the extent that a cursory reading of statistical evidence might lead one to conclude. Prosecutors did not dominate judges
before Ishihara's criticisms — thus the pronouncements — and they have not done so

since. When Ishihara retired from the procuracy in 1987, he encouraged prosecutors to continue publicizing the regional disparities in order to pressure Kansai courts to change. Seven years later he told me that the debate had died when he left office, leaving few lasting effects on criminal court outcomes.

Finally, the Ishihara case poses a challenge to accounts — including my own — that regard Japanese prosecutors as deeply concerned about the rehabilitation and reintegration of offenders. The strongest of these accounts claims that in order to correct offenders, Japanese officials have "in effect abandoned the most coercive of all legitimate instruments of state control" — punishment (Haley 1991:138). Almost a year after Ishihara first made the "punishment problem" a public issue, Prosecutor General Itoh Shigeki tried to justify the procuracy's criticisms in similarly benevolent terms. Itoh declared that "compared to other regions in the country, punishments in Osaka are too light. If punishments are too lenient, I fear efforts to rehabilitate and reform offenders will become futile. That is why I want to rectify the situation" (*Yomiuri Shimbun* 2/18/87). The unstated but unmistakable premise underlying Itoh's remarks is that more punishment rehabilitates better than less. That premise is questionable on at least two grounds: it is inconsistent with research findings about the relationship between punishment and rehabilitation (Walker 1994:207), and it contradicts prosecutors' own studies that show less intrusive sanctions are more likely to lead to reform (Foote 1992a:364).

Prior to Itoh's statement, the procuracy stressed the needs to punish crime severely and to eliminate regional disparities. Those claims elicited active resistance from the bar and passive resistance from the bench. Itoh then modified the procuracy's rhetoric, presumably in order to convert bar and bench resistance into support for change. Yet Ishihara's original pronouncements and subsequent procuracy efforts to substantiate his claims reflected almost no evidence of prosecutor concern for rehabilitation, reintegration, or correction. Far from having abandoned the criminal sanction, prosecutors seemed intent on imposing more punishment on more people. The main aim of the pain was to create greater consistency across similar cases in different jurisdictions. The procuracy's interest in increasing Kansai punishments went beyond the merely rhetorical. Following Ishihara's March 1986 pronouncement, the six District Prosecutors Offices in the Kansai region raised the recommended sentences for a number of offenses, including crimes by gangsters, stimulant drug offenses, gun crimes, and negligence resulting in injury or death (*Yomiuri Shimbun* 12/9/86; *Asahi Shimbun* 3/20/87). But judges do have the last word. In 1994 I attended a lecture by the director of the Trial Division of the Kobe District Prosecutors Office. He spent more than half of his ninety-minute talk documenting, through statistics and stories, persistent disparities between the Osaka and Tokyo regions. In his view, Kansai courts remained unacceptably lenient, and he, like many of his colleagues, saw little the procuracy could do to change that lamentable fact.

Prosecutors and Defense Attorneys

In relation to police, prosecutors exercise considerable but incomplete control over key criminal justice decisions, while in relation to judges, prosecutor power is constrained by the fact that judges rule last. In relations with defense attorneys, their apparent adversaries, prosecutors possess almost total control, much as they have since 1876, when defense lawyers first appeared in Japan's criminal court communities.

In principle, defense attorneys stand in the position of greatest opposition to prosecutors. That, at least, is the role they have been assigned in Japan's ostensibly adversarial system. In reality, however, defense attorneys do little to influence how prosecutors investigate, dispose of, or try cases. Throughout the criminal process, from arrest through investigation to indictment, trial, and sentence, three factors — law, tradition, and the demographics and economics of the bar — severely restrict what defense attorneys can do for suspects and defendants. The ironic result is that prosecutors dominate precisely the actor whom law ordains as the principal check on the state's power to punish.

The More Things Change . . .

The transwar continuities are profound. Richard Mitchell notes that in prewar Japan "a [defense] attorney's traditional role was to humbly point out extenuating circumstances, beg leniency, and promise no future violations" (Mitchell 1992:71). Further, before it was revised in 1949, the Lawyers Law "placed control over the bar in the hands of the procuracy" (Rabinowitz 1956:70). The chiefs of the various District Prosecutors Offices possessed authority to supervise the bar associations in their respective jurisdictions and frequently attended bar meetings in order to do just that (Nomura 1992a:74). Moreover, the Justice Minister, who was almost always a prosecutor, could invalidate official bar decisions (Mitchell 1976:34). To prevent the bar from becoming dangerously cohesive and powerful, the procuracy even forbade the many local bar associations from uniting to form a national bar (Nomura 1992a:75). Although postwar reforms took away the procuracy's legal powers to supervise the bar and invalidate its decisions, they left prosecutors with an abundance of other legal means by which to prevent criminal defense attorneys from playing a significant role in the criminal process (Rabinowitz 1956:76).

Of course, one can exaggerate the extent to which Japanese prosecutors dominate defense attorneys, for even in the United States prosecutors wield wide powers in the criminal court community, and many defense attorneys remain "at best a potential silent partner or ally of the bench" in struggles for status and influence (Flemming et al. 1992:162). In both Japan and the United States the prosecutor has the upper hand. For a defense attorney, however, the hand of the Japanese prosecutor exercises more complete control over the criminal process than does even the hand of the most powerful American prosecutor. The comparative differences are stark.

Criminal Defense in Postwar Japan

Unlike most industrialized democracies, Japan does not have an organized defense bar composed of lawyers who specialize solely or mostly in criminal defense work. With few exceptions, all of the country's eighteen thousand attorneys earn the bulk of their income from civil cases. Lawyers who do criminal defense tend to dabble in it, except for a small group consisting largely of (to be blunt) old, languid lawyers.

In a pioneering empirical study of criminal defense activity in Japan, Hata Hiroto (1993) interviewed sixty-three lawyers about their criminal defense work (thirty-eight in Kobe, eight in Osaka, and seventeen in Fukuoka). The results of Hata's study overestimate lawyer involvement in defense work because his sample purposefully excludes the many lawyers who do only civil or administrative work. Even so, Hata found that the thirty-eight Kobe lawyers had an average criminal caseload of 5.5 cases, to which they devoted an average of 21 percent of their work time and from which they earned about 20 percent of their income. If one excludes from consideration the three attorneys in the sample who worked full-time on criminal cases (all were former prosecutors and over seventy years of age), the Kobe attorneys spent about 14 percent of their work time on criminal cases.[19] Similarly, if one excludes three attorneys who had exceptionally heavy criminal caseloads (twenty, thirty, and thirty-four, respectively), the average criminal caseload per defense attorney declines to about 3.5, a figure close to the median criminal caseload (three cases per attorney) uncovered by a much larger national survey of 1,772 lawyers. In contrast, the Kobe lawyers in Hata's study had an average civil caseload of 20.5 and an average "negotiation" caseload (advising clients about business deals, investments, and the like) of 11.4. Thus, even when analysis is restricted to the select group of private attorneys who actually do defense work, only about one-tenth of all cases they handle are criminal (3.5 out of 35.4).

Hata's study distinguishes six types of attorneys who perform defense work. The six categories are defined primarily by how much work time a lawyer devotes to criminal cases and by whether the lawyer is privately retained or is provided at state expense. In the first two categories — "criminal defense experts," retained privately or publicly — there are seven lawyers. Of the seven, five are over seventy years of age and one is in his sixties, while four are former prosecutors and one is a former judge. Put differently, all the lawyers in Hata's study who were over age seventy specialized in criminal defense work. Of the remaining fifty-eight lawyers in the sample, only two specialized in criminal defense work (and one of those was in his sixties).

Why do older lawyers concentrate on criminal defense while younger lawyers avoid it? Young and middle-aged lawyers find criminal work unattractive because law and prosecutors do not allow them to vigorously defend their clients; because despite their youth they subscribe to traditional attitudes about the defense attorney's role, which prescribe a "go along" instead of a "go for it" style; and because defending criminal cases pays less than other work. On the other hand, older lawyers are attracted to criminal defense work because that is where their comparative advantage lies (Hata 1998). In most criminal cases they can do about as much for the accused as can their more energetic, mentally agile juniors. Which is to say, not much.

Law's Limits

Defense attorney activities during the pre-charge period are sharply curtailed by the following legal restrictions:

---

19. Another sociolegal scholar has estimated that a typical Japanese attorney carries a caseload that is 5 to 10 percent criminal matters (Rokumoto 1988).

Suspects have no right to bail before indictment. Suspects who assert innocence are almost always denied bail.

Lawyers are not permitted to be present during interrogation. While suspects may exercise their right to remain silent, they also have a duty to listen to as many questions as the interrogator wants to ask.

Before indictment there is no system of court-appointed counsel. Thus, suspects who cannot afford an attorney may have to wait as long as twenty-three days until one is appointed. Fewer than 10 percent of suspects secure lawyers during the investigative stage.[20]

Prosecutors have authority to restrict the accused's access to legal counsel by designating the date, place, and time of interview "when it is necessary for the investigation." When clients do not confess, prosecutors typically limit access to a few short visits over the course of the investigation.

Prosecutors, police, and prison guards may censor written communications between the accused and defense counsel.

In short, during investigations, law is the prosecutor's most important ally. By making skillful use of it, the prosecutor can prevent defense counsel from performing a meaningful role during the most critical stage of the criminal process. Once indicted, the defendant's situation improves, for then the state assigns counsel to indigent defendants and prosecutors allow counsel greater access to the accused. However, by this time there is precious little even a Japanese Johnnie Cochran can do. The real substance of criminal procedure in Japan happens during the investigation, and prosecutors and police are given extraordinarily wide powers during that period. In ninety cases out of a hundred, suspects never meet an attorney during the investigation, and in most of the remainder, defense attorneys are forced to follow a legal script which makes them little more than bit players (Murayama 1992; Igarashi 1989).

The defense lawyer's position scarcely improves at trial. Exceptions to the hearsay rule are so frequent that the crucial evidence in most cases comes not from witnesses or from oral arguments made in open court, but from dossiers constructed during an investigation in which defense attorney activities were tightly (and legally) restricted. As we have seen, in American criminal justice juries cast a shadow of unpredictability over all stages in the pretrial process. In Japan the most important arrow of influence points in the opposite direction. Prosecutors' near complete control over the investigation casts a long shadow over all subsequent stages, rendering trials mere ceremonies instead of the fact-finding institution prescribed by law.

Crucially, defendants in Japan have narrow rights to "discovery," that is, to examine the evidence prosecutors have collected during the investigation (including potentially exculpatory evidence). In fact, defense attorneys can compel disclosure only with a court order, which judicial precedents permit "only under very narrow circumstances" (Foote 1992a:382). Without meaningful discovery rights, defendants

---

20. As described below, the introduction of the "duty counsel system" (*tōban bengoshi seido*) has improved the situation somewhat.

are reliant on the goodwill of prosecutors to disclose evidence that might exonerate the defendant or mitigate guilt (Nomura 1988:180). It does not take a malevolent imputation of ill will to suppose that prosecutors' interest in gaining a conviction sometimes supersedes their desire to do justice, especially in cases where disclosure may hurt the state's case. Indeed, many of the worst miscarriages of justice have occurred when prosecutors did the self-interested but legal thing by withholding exculpatory evidence from the defense (Foote 1993c). Much of the drama in the famous Matsukawa conspiracy case, the biggest cause célèbre in the annals of Japanese crime, was generated because throughout the fourteen years the case was in the courts, "unbelievably important new clues kept turning up in procuracy warehouses" (C. Johnson 1972:43). Ironically, since defense counsel had better discovery rights in the prewar years, here we see transwar continuity with a vengeance (Nomura 1988:179).

The legally ordained impotence of defense lawyers places prosecutors in a position of "absolute and incommensurable advantage" (Nomura 1988:180). Though an account of relations between prosecution and defense could stop here, this one will not, for defense lawyers' role perceptions and the economics of criminal defense further serve prosecutor interests.

The Defense Attorney's Role

Defense attorneys in Japan perceive their role differently than American defense lawyers do. Their greatest concern "is that innocent individuals not be mistakenly convicted" (Foote 1992a:381), and in this regard one finds nothing distinctively Japanese. However, the concern to prevent miscarriages of justice is unaccompanied by the view, common among American lawyers, that "the system itself is so biased or so uncommitted to rehabilitation that defense counsel should try to win an acquittal any way possible" (Foote 1992a:381).

With few exceptions, defense attorneys in Japan believe they should relate to prosecutors as cooperatively and constructively as possible. In fact, one of the most comprehensive surveys of lawyers ever conducted found that over 60 percent of respondents (1,071 out of 1,772) said they "had *never* [my emphasis] actively recommended that a suspect or defendant exercise the right to remain silent" (Japan Federation of Bar Associations Survey 11/14/91). Given the many legal levers for extracting confessions from suspects, and given how infrequently defense lawyers counsel a strategy of silence, the fact that 92 percent of all defendants confess is hardly surprising.

American defense attorneys would be surprised, however, by the kind of assistance some Japanese attorneys give their nonconfessing clients. In 1993 I followed a rape case in Kobe from arrest through conviction and sentencing. The defense counsel's behavior in the case was a dramatic departure from the role prescribed by adversarial scripts. The defendant, a Japanese "punk" (*chimpira*) in his early twenties who had several run-ins with the law while a juvenile, was accused of violently raping a female acquaintance three times in an eight-hour span. He did not confess, despite mountains of evidence against him: the victim's tearful, compelling testimony; hospital photographs of her bruises and contusions; two independent eyewitness accounts; and the victim's speedy report of the rapes to medical and police authorities. The defendant admitted the sex but claimed it was consensual. Nothing besides the defendant's story corroborated his version of the events. Thus, if defense counsel had wanted to vigorously defend his client, he had little choice but to try to discredit the victim's testimony. There appeared to be ample room to do so. The defense counsel could have asked why the victim let a remote acquaintance into her apartment, and then into her bedroom, at 2 o'clock in the morning, or why she had not cried out to alert people in the neighboring room, or why she had left the sleeping defendant a note on the kitchen chalkboard explaining why she left the apartment and where she had gone. The note seemed a particularly good defense target. It was written in a cordial tone that seemed, at least on its face, incongruous with the horrors she described to police, prosecutors, and now the court. It was signed "bye-bye."

Instead of challenging the victim's testimony, however, the defense attorney asked her two or three perfunctory questions and then put his own client on the stand. Asked to explain what had happened, the defendant offered his version of the events, stating that the victim had seemed to welcome and enjoy the sex; that his threats merely reflected his swaggering style and were intended to impress, not frighten her; and that he had beaten her because she deserved it for her "cheekiness." When the defendant finished his five-minute summary, it quickly became evident that I was not the only person in the courtroom who found his tale incredible. The defense attorney's first follow-up question was as blunt a departure from the partisan role as one can imagine. "Who are you trying to kid?" the attorney scolded. "Do you really think anyone is going to believe that story? I don't. Do you think the judges are convinced? Come on. That's really far-fetched. At least try to tell the judges a better story than that."

Unpersuaded by his advocate, the defendant offered a feeble rejoinder but made little effort to change his story. To no one's surprise, save perhaps the defendant himself, the three-judge panel found him guilty of rape and sentenced him to three years and six months imprisonment.[21]

If it had happened in the United States, this case may have ended in a mistrial or reversal on the grounds of "ineffective assistance of counsel." Neither occurred here. Instead, in post-trial interviews the trial prosecutor, one of the three judges, and several attending legal apprentices confessed that they found nothing troublesome about the defense lawyer's behavior. (I was unable to interview the defense lawyer.) True, the judge explained, the defense was not especially vigorous, but that was probably a calculated choice aimed at getting the defendant to abandon his implausible story and display remorse to the judges who would decide his fate. When I asked the trial prosecutor if, maybe, the defense lawyer had performed part of the prosecutor's role for him, he said he did not see things quite that way, but that the defense attorney had indeed made his job easier. A few of the attending legal apprentices, who in less than a year would be playing for real the roles they now were trying on and trying out, were more critical of the defense attorney's actions, but none condemned his behavior in the way most American law students would.

---

21. Contrast the attitude of the Japanese defense lawyer with the view of American lawyer and law professor Alan Dershowitz. Dershowitz proclaims that "I have only one agenda: I want to win. . . . It is the job of the defense attorney — especially when representing the guilty — to prevent, by all lawful means, the 'whole truth' from coming out" (Dershowitz 1982:xv).

I have described this case in detail because it vividly illustrates how differently many Japanese defense attorneys view their roles.[22] Rather than seeing themselves as partisan, adversarial advocates whose chief duty is to obtain the most lenient treatment possible for their clients, Japanese lawyers often seem just as concerned to "make sure that all relevant facts concerning the suspect, including the suspect's factual guilt, [are] brought to light, thereby enabling the state to determine the sanction that would best serve the interests of the suspect and society as a whole" (Foote 1992a:381). Of course, Japan has its own small supply of adversarial lawyers, many of whom prosecutors disdain as "radical leftists." And Japanese evaluations of nonadversarial lawyers are not uniformly benign. While many legal professionals believe cooperative, constructive, conciliatory strategies better serve the interest of justice than do the more combative styles found in the United States, at least a few agree with the assessment of a farm boy from New Zealand who found himself arrested (and ultimately convicted and deported) for possession and distribution of marijuana. Because the suspect knew little Japanese, I was asked to translate during the prosecutor's interrogations. During a lull in one session I asked the soon-to-be charged youth what he thought of his defense attorney. His attorney was one of the most highly respected defense lawyers in a city of 1.5 million people. "My lawyer," said the Kiwi accused, "is as good as tits on a bull."

Policing the Lawyers

Prosecutors routinely police defense lawyers to ensure that their behavior does not depart too far from the norms of constructive, cooperative engagement. One prominent instance occurred in 1977 when defendants and their attorneys were adopting unorthodox adversarial tactics in several high-profile trials (including the Dhaka hijack case). Some defense attorneys did not show up for hearings, others came late, and a few defendants "fired" their lawyers in midtrial in order to slow down the proceedings and draw attention to their cases (as the Aum Shinrikyō guru Asahara Shōko did before his murder trial began in 1996). In short, the public witnessed unusually uncooperative, disruptive criminal defense tactics.

Prosecutors in the Ministry of Justice took it upon themselves to remedy the situation by introducing a bill in the Diet that allowed defendants to be tried without a defense attorney present.[23] Through the media, they made numerous appeals to

22. Although the case described here is admittedly an extreme instance of Japan's nonadversarial ethic, one need observe only a few Japanese trials to discern the main pattern. For example, in an assault case a lawyer defended a man until shortly after indictment, whereupon a different lawyer took over the case (it is unclear why) and the first lawyer became a witness for the prosecution. The first lawyer, a former prosecutor, provided seriously incriminating testimony against the defendant. This case had the unintended but salubrious consequence of heightening public interest in questions concerning the defense attorney's proper role (Nomura 1992a:42).

23. This seemed to contravene Article 37 of the Constitution, which guarantees the accused "the assistance of competent counsel . . . at all times." The Ministry of Justice bill proposal would have allowed a trial to proceed without a defense lawyer present if the defendant fired the lawyer or the lawyer quit during the trial; if either the defendant or the lawyer failed to appear at trial; or if the lawyer excused himself from the trial after being ordered by the court to maintain better courtroom decorum (Zaikai Tenbō 1979).

the public to support the bill and condemn the deviant defense tactics. One high-level prosecutor dubbed the lawyers "radical law-jacks," and the Ministry of Justice conducted an opinion poll which showed that 88 percent of the public approved the ministry bill. Even many top judges expressed support for the bill. Early in the controversy the bar federation did little to aid the rogue attorneys, but when prosecutors claimed that the bar was yielding to the violent governance of a handful of radical attorneys and that two-thirds of lawyers supported the Ministry of Justice position, the bar broke its silence and lashed back at the ministry. Ultimately, though the ministry's bill failed in the face of resistance from the bar and opposition parties, the procuracy's efforts succeeded. Defense attorney "misconduct" nearly ceased when the bar enacted reforms to curb the controversial behavior (Zaikai Tenbō 1979:58).

In recent years the intensity and frequency of prosecutor criticism has increased, partly because of the advent of more vigorously adversarial defense lawyering among a small group of attorneys who have joined Japan's Miranda Association. Founded in 1992, the Miranda Association is committed to protecting and furthering the rights of criminal suspects, much as the U.S. Supreme Court's 1966 *Miranda* decision aimed to do. Attorneys in the association employ three main strategies: they advise suspects to refuse to be interrogated; they advise suspects to refuse to sign or stamp any dossier made during interrogation; and, if dossiers are made, they resist their introduction as evidence at trial (Miranda no Kai 1997:6). It has to be said, however, that the Miranda Association is a marginal movement, even among attorneys. In December 2000 I attended a meeting of the association in Tokyo. The main subject of conversation was why the organization had failed to recruit and influence more than a handful of attorneys.

Departures from standard defense practice infuriate prosecutors. In 1994, for example, Prosecutor General Yoshinaga Yūsuke told one of Japan's major legal periodicals that he was deeply troubled by defense attorneys who "ignore the spirit of the Code of Criminal Procedure, willfully distort the law, and advise suspects not to sign dossiers regardless of their content" (*Shūkan Hōritsu Shimbun* 6/3/94). Lawyers in Shizuoka prefecture — the birthplace of the Miranda Assocation — protested Yoshinaga's criticisms at a press conference where they announced they had sent an open letter to Yoshinaga demanding responses to two questions: In what ways do defense lawyers "distort" the law? and why not introduce a discovery system for dossiers? (*Mainichi Shimbun* 11/8/94). Predictably, Yoshinaga had no response.

In 1995, the deputy chief prosecutor of the Tokyo District Prosecutors Office expressed more specifically what troubles prosecutors about the Miranda strategies. He argued that by advising clients to refuse to cooperate with investigators, defense lawyers were "going too far" and even "violating the law." Suspects do have a right to remain silent, the deputy chief noted, but they do not have a right to refuse to be interrogated. Defense lawyers were "ignoring public safety" by adopting unethical and illegal strategies. For prosecutors, these deviations from the normal — and normative — defense lawyer's role "cannot be acknowledged" as legitimate. Miranda lawyers dispute each of these allegations, but prosecutors assiduously police them and publicize departures from the traditional norms of defense lawyering (Miranda no Kai 1997:61). The most problematic policing occurred in 1998 and 1999, when Yasuda Yoshihiro, a prominent Miranda lawyer, was arrested for allegedly obstructing justice by conspiring with his client to hide millions of dollars in rental income. Yasuda remained in jail for over a year, Tokyo courts having repeatedly denied bail at prosecutors' request. By singling out Yasuda, who also headed the defense team for Aum guru and defendant Asahara Shōko, prosecutors sent a message to defense lawyers contemplating combative tactics in more ordinary cases (Fox 1999). They also illustrated the adage that the certainties of one age can become the problems of the next.

The Economics of Criminal Defense

The size, constitution, and distribution of Japan's legal profession discourage vigorous defense advocacy and hence further enable prosecutors to control the criminal process. Though it is slowly growing, Japan's bar is small, made up of only about eighteen thousand attorneys. By comparison, the United States has nearly one million registered attorneys. Even if one adds to the Japanese total the estimated 110,000 others who do licensed legal work (judicial and administrative scriveners, notaries public, and patent and tax accountants), Japan has at least three times fewer legal professionals per capita than does the United States. Each year, only about a thousand who take the bar exam pass it, though the quota increased to fifteen hundred in 2001 and may reach three thousand or more by 2005. Since 1990 the bar pass rate has hovered around 3 percent. In contrast, in 1991 over forty-three thousand persons were newly admitted to the various American bars, and state bar pass rates ranged from 40 to 80 percent.

About half of Japanese attorneys engage in solo practice. Most of the rest work in small offices of two to five partners (Rokumoto 1988). A high percentage of Japanese lawyers are motivated to take the bar by the desire for a job that provides both security and autonomy (most company and government jobs offer only the former). Once they enter the profession, most lawyers aim to practice independently (Haley 1991:111). Lawyers are heavily concentrated in urban areas: 48 percent work in Tokyo, 60 percent in Tokyo and Osaka, and 80 percent in the ten largest prefectures. This leaves rural people with little access to lawyers and few means to exercise their rights (Rokumoto 1988). Indeed, a 1993 survey found that 56 percent of all the cities, wards, towns, and villages in Japan have not even a single lawyer's office (*Asahi Shimbun* 11/24/93). About two-thirds of all defendants do not hire their own lawyer but are provided with a state-assigned attorney (Nomura 1992a:61). Comparable national figures for the United States are not available, but a research project that analyzed nine medium-sized criminal court communities in three states (Michigan, Pennsylvania, and Illinois) found that 57 percent of all felony cases were handled by either public defenders or attorneys paid by the county or court (Flemming et al. 1992:136). It thus appears that at least as many defense lawyers are provided by the government in Japan as in the United States.

Still, the comparative differences overwhelm this similarity. For one, Japan has no analogue to the public defender institutions found in many U.S. jurisdictions, and almost no attorneys engaged in full-time public defense work. As we have seen, the few who are so engaged tend to be elderly lawyers, usually former prosecutors, and "new leftists" committed to progressive social change. In addition, the Japanese state assigns counsel to indigent defenders only after indictment, by which time prosecutors have gathered so much information that typically there is little even the most zealous, skilled attorneys can do except try to mitigate the severity of sentence. At most trials this is done by asking the defendant questions to elicit demonstrations of remorse, and by questioning relatives, friends, and employers about their capacity and willingness to "supervise" the defendant if the court suspends sentence. State-assigned counsel in Japan are not known for being the zealous, adversarial, and combative advocates many of their Americans counterparts are (McIntyre 1987:171). In the trials I observed, most defenses could only be called perfunctory. Some were so incomplete (as in the rape case described above) that if judged by American standards they could constitute malpractice. In death penalty cases, state-assigned counsel have even told courts that "because the defendant's behavior was brutal, the death penalty is necessary" and "the death penalty is appropriate; there is no reason to appeal" (Nomura 1992a:61).[24]

Although state-assigned counsel do the bulk of defense work in Japan, most of the work they do is not criminal defense. They, after all, are not criminal defense specialists. More important, since state-assigned work is generally not well compensated, it is often an unwelcome addition to one's workload. Defending members of Japan's Mafia (*yakuza* or *bōryokudan*) and conservative politicians ensnared in corruption scandals does pay well, normally bringing in between 1 million and 10 million yen ($8,000 to $80,000) just as a retainer. In other cases, privately retained attorneys typically receive retainers of between 150,000 and 300,000 yen ($1,200 to $2,400), over and above which they may earn additional remuneration for success at obtaining bail, a suspended prosecution, a suspended sentence, or an acquittal. The minimum fee for privately retaining counsel at a District Court varies from 200,000 yen ($1,600) to 500,000 yen ($4,000), depending on the outcome of the trial. In contrast, the going rate for state-assigned counsel who must appear in court three times over the course of a trial (about the average trial length) is only 65,000 yen ($520).

Thus, a small slice of private defense work pays handsomely, most private work pays adequately though not as well as civil case opportunities, and publicly assigned work pays poorly (Murayama 1992:244). As a result, the attorneys who do publicly assigned work — fully two-thirds of the defense work in the country — tend to be either young, unestablished lawyers or "old age attorneys." The two groups share the com-

24. Defense lawyers first began appearing in criminal courts in 1876. Thereafter only the state could assign counsel for the defense. When the forerunner to today's Code of Criminal Procedure was enacted in 1880, defendants obtained for the first time the right to select their own attorney. A 1924 law further reinforced the state-assigned counsel system, but simultaneously conferred power on legal apprentices (at that time this meant only prosecutors and judges in training, not lawyers-to-be) to defend the accused in court. Even if a defendant hired his or her own attorney, the law allowed courts to trump that choice and assign an attorney of its own choosing instead. In this way, defense lawyers "were forced to play a role which stressed administrative convenience more than protecting the rights of defendants." With the passage of the new Code of Criminal Procedure in 1949, the system of state-assigned counsel took its present form. Today, defendants who cannot hire their own attorney must petition the court to assign one. The court then asks the relevant bar association to recommend an attorney. Once the bar makes its recommendation, the court issues an order to the recommended attorney to take up the case (Nomura 1992a:59).

mon inability to generate other kinds of more remunerative work (Nomura 1992a:62). Between these groups the large middle of the bar avoids state-assigned defense work because, quite simply, they have better things to do.

Japanese lawyers have lamented their "detachment from criminal defense work" for years, but until recently they have done little to solve or even explain the problems they claim to deplore. But there are exceptions. One of the country's most aggressive, effective lawyers (and later a Supreme Court justice) has traced the declining appeal of defense work to three ultimate causes. First, after the trials of student radicals in the 1960s, judicial attitudes changed so that judges now pay less attention to defense arguments in court and more attention to the efficient administration of trial proceedings. Second, perfunctory mini-defenses have spread from the growing mass of traffic offense trials, where they may be fitting, to other trials where vigorous defenses are still appropriate. Third, the mass media's strong support for the prosecution has discouraged lawyers from undertaking criminal defense work or using aggressive defenses (M. Ōno and Watanabe 1989:48). While these three factors surely help to explain the steady drift of the Japanese bar away from criminal defense work, any account of the present situation must stress two more proximate causes as well. First, prosecutors so dominate the pre-indictment stage that in most cases there is little defense lawyers can do except show up in court and plead for mercy. For many lawyers this is a job "not worth performing." As we have seen, the second cause reflects a more tangible problem: all but a few criminal cases pay poorly in comparison to other work opportunities.[25]

Recent reforms, such as the Miranda strategies, have increased the quantity and vigor of criminal defense work, but the changes are hardly sufficient to alter the conclusions just drawn. In 1989 the Japan Federation of Bar Associations published a report strongly criticizing lawyers for their "detachment" from defense work, and in 1990 it created a Criminal Defense Center to support defense lawyers. Around the same time (in Kobe it began in 1992), prefectural bar associations throughout the country began establishing "duty counsel systems" (*tōban bengoshi seido*) to provide legal advice to indigent suspects before indictment. The state does not provide counsel for the accused until after prosecutors have filed formal charges. The bar, recognizing that suspects are most in need of legal advice before that point, created duty counsel systems to fill the void. Each participating lawyer is asked to be on call a few days a year for eight or ten hours each day. When a detained suspect requests help, one of the "on call" lawyers goes to the detention site to explain criminal procedure and the suspect's legal rights and to advise the suspect about defense strategies. While this is an improvement over the previous system, only the first meeting is free of charge. Suspects who want continued advice must pay the going rate, 200,000 yen

25. As of the mid-1990s, the minimum retainer in civil cases was 100,000 yen ($800). Standard rates for compensation depended on the amount recovered. Rates began at 15 pecent of total awards less than 500,000 yen ($4,000), and declined in eight steps to 2 percent of total awards exceeding 1 billion yen ($8 million). Thus, if a plaintiff recovered 3 million yen ($24,000), the attorney received 335,000 yen ($2,680) plus at least the 100,000 yen ($800) retainer. For an account of how much Japanese lawyers get paid for each of thirty-three typical legal disputes (almost all civil), see *Shūkan Yomiuri* 7/10/94.

($1,600) for a retainer and another 200,000 yen as compensation if the suspect is not formally charged.

Japan also has a meager system for legal aid which enables only a small number of criminal suspects to borrow money in order to obtain a lawyer's assistance prior to indictment. The suspect's employment status and job type are irrelevant; only suspects who have been arrested and detained and who deny the charges against them are eligible, and even they must pay back whatever money they are loaned. In 1992, most legal aid associations loaned individual suspects a maximum of 60,000 yen ($480) for retainer and 10,000 yen ($80) for other legal expenses. Compared to other industrialized nations, the Japanese government provides paltry funding for its legal aid associations. For example, with an economy far smaller than Japan's, the British government (in 1992) gave the equivalent of 156 billion yen to its legal aid associations (about $1.25 billion). In contrast, the Japanese state (in 1994) provided slightly more than one-thousandth that amount (200 million yen, about $1.6 million). The total budget for Japan's fifty legal aid associations was more than that—about 1.4 billion yen—because private contributors provided six times more than the government did, but Japan's legal aid associations have still faced chronic budget shortfalls. Significantly, the vast majority of legal aid money is used to help litigants in civil cases, not criminal suspects or defendants. In fact, in the nine months between April 1 and December 31, 1991, Japan's legal aid associations gave financial assistance to only 207 suspects nationwide (Murayama 1992). In the same period prosecutors disposed of over 1.6 million cases. Thus, only about one in 60,000 criminal suspects received legal aid. This system of legal aid does little to balance the scales of advantage in Japan's criminal process.

Cooperation and Contention

Considering how little defense lawyers can do to influence case outcomes, it is unremarkable that many are dissatisfied with the status quo. In a 1991 survey of the nation's 14,452 lawyers (of whom 1,772 responded), the Japan Federation of Bar Associations found that over one-third of all respondents believed "Japanese criminal trials are quite hopeless," almost two and one-half times the percentage who disagreed with that statement. In the same survey, over three-quarters of all respondents said they believed it is "necessary to reform criminal trials."[26]

What is remarkable is how little lawyer dissatisfaction gets directed at prosecutors. In the same survey fully 58 percent of all respondents said they had never—not even once—thought a prosecutor's decision to charge was "inappropriate," while over 96 percent thought so three times or less in their entire legal career. Lawyers' evaluations of prosecutors' non-charge decisions are similarly supportive. About two-thirds of all respondents stated that they have never considered "inappropriate" a prosecutor's decision not to charge a suspect, while over 98 percent had thought so only three times or fewer. Lawyers are more critical of judges. More than half be-

---

26. For a more detailed description of the survey results, see the 1991 Japan Federation of Bar Associations report, "*Keiji Saiban no Kasseika o Motomete" ni Kansuru Zenkaiin Ankēto Kekka Hōkokusho.*"

lieved that judges have made mistaken or inappropriate findings of fact at trial, and over two-thirds think judges have imposed inappropriate sentences. Moreover, 70 percent of lawyers thought judges are "too severe" toward the bail requests of suspects and defendants who do not confess, and nearly 90 percent thought they are "usually" too severe.

Lawyers acknowledge that they seldom challenge police or prosecutors by adopting confrontational strategies. Two-thirds of all lawyers had never "actively suggested" that a suspect or defendant exercise the right to remain silent, and almost 95 percent had never even asked to attend a suspect's interrogation. Furthermore, over three-quarters of responding lawyers had never asked a judge to order prosecutors to disclose evidence, while close to two-thirds said they had never objected when prosecutors moved to introduce as evidence at trial — as they often do — a statement taken during the investigation period from someone other than the suspect (that is, when prosecutors have tried to obtain an exception to the hearsay rule).

Against these currents of harmony and cooperation there flow lesser currents of conflict and contention. The most long-standing, significant controversy concerns the scope of the defense lawyers' right to meet with suspects during the pre-charge investigation period and the corollary authority of prosecutors to restrict those meetings. Article 34 of the Constitution and Article 39 of the Code of Criminal Procedure would appear to give lawyers wide scope to meet with clients during the detention period. However, a clause in the latter gives prosecutors authority to "designate the date, place, and time of interview . . . when it is necessary for the investigation." This has precipitated many disputes about lawyer-client meetings. Lawyers argue that prosecutors use this provision as a shield to restrict access to suspects, especially in cases where the investigators' success in obtaining a confession is likely to make or break the state's case. Until recently, attorneys were allowed only one meeting while the suspect was in police custody and two to five meetings during the twenty days of prosecutor custody. The average meeting lasted only about fifteen minutes. Access to legal counsel is still "wholly at the discretion of the police and prosecutors." At least in this respect, the prosecutor's authority to set conditions on these meetings leaves Japan "a far cry from the American practice" (Bayley 1991:146).

In recent years prosecutors "have loosened somewhat the limitations on preindictment meetings between suspects and counsel," usually when doing so poses little risk to their ability to make a case (Foote 1992a:382). Wakamatsu Yoshiya (1990:ii), a lawyer and the author or editor of three of the most widely read books on this subject, has noted that "little by little we have begun to see signs that there might be a breakthrough in the obstructions placed on the right to meet with suspects." Wakamatsu attributes improved access to three major influences: the international attention and criticism the problem has attracted; the efforts of the bar to loosen the restrictions; and reform movements inside the Ministry of Justice and procuracy. The last influence seems most significant. In 1988 the Ministry of Justice and the Japan Federation of Bar Associations agreed that prosecutors would not use their authority to restrict the length or number of meetings "uniformly" (Nomura 1994:150). In effect, prosecutors promised to use their "designation powers" more flexibly. While most observers acknowledge a shift toward greater freedom of access for defense counsel, critics still charge that if the client continues to refuse to confess during the twenty-three-day period of pre-indictment detention, lawyers are, on the average, limited to three visits of fifteen minutes each (Igarashi 1989:5).

Despite these circumscribed reforms, prosecutors remain so sensitive about the subject of lawyer-suspect meetings that they would not permit me to include a survey question asking if they agreed that "defense attorneys should be given greater access to their clients during the investigation period." I was informed that since the 1988 agreement between the Ministry of Justice and the bar had solved the problem, the premise of my question was misguided. In place of the original question I was urged to ask whether "defense attorneys should meet more often with their clients during the investigation period." Like many other "suggestions" regarding the survey, this was an offer I could not refuse — not, at least, if I wanted to ask *something* about the issue. The prosecutors' proposed query — which carefully omitted any reference to prosecutor restrictions on defense counsel meetings with suspects — became survey question 45. Only 37 of 235 prosecutor respondents (16 percent) agreed with it. In the same vein, precisely zero prosecutors agreed that "suspects should be permitted to have a defense attorney present during interrogation" (question 44). Responses to both questions show how staunchly unwilling prosecutors are to relinquish the advantages that the current system provides.

Prosecutors' sensitivities became even more apparent when they insisted I delete from the questionnaire an item asking if "a defense attorney should advise a client to tell the truth to police and prosecutors, even if the client has committed the offense." Even though 60 percent of defense lawyers in Japan have *never* advised clients to the contrary, prosecutors seemed eager to avoid the kind of bar backlash which has occurred when they express normally unexpressed grievances, or when they reprove lawyers for deviating from standard operating procedures in the criminal court community.

In fact, few things pique more prosecutor anger than defense lawyers who depart from established criminal court routines. I once observed a usually unflappable prosecutor become apoplectic when a defense lawyer asked to attend the interrogation of his client. After curtly turning down the telephoning mendicant, the prosecutor exploded in a tirade, impugning everything from the offending lawyer's common sense to his rural origins. Statistics show the lawyer had broken a nearly sacrosanct norm. In the bar survey of 1,772 lawyers, only 83 (5 percent) had *ever* asked to attend the interrogation of an adult suspect. Since the respondents are categorized by number of years of experience, it is possible to estimate the total number of years all respondents had worked as lawyers (approximately 23,386 years). One can also estimate the total number of such requests responding lawyers had ever made (111). Dividing the second number into the first yields an estimate of "number of years experience as a lawyer" per "request to attend interrogation." On the average, one request is made for every 210 years of lawyer experience. Assuming an average career length of thirty-five years, that comes out to one request for every six lawyer lives, or nearly seven times less frequently than the average lawyer obtains an acquittal (once every thirty-one years). Of the 111 requests to attend interrogation, one-third were approved. These survey questions seem to reveal two lessons about defense lawyering in Japan: "ask and you might be given" and "don't ask."

One final example illustrates the strong prosecutor disdain for adversarial defense lawyers. In February 1995, the Ministry of Justice sponsored two public lectures, one by an American prosecutor and the other by a judge from Singapore. The annual lectures, among the ministry's most important public events, were attended by hundreds of Japanese government officials, legal professionals, legal apprentices, and prominent citizens. During the intermission between lectures I met a veteran defense lawyer well known for her aggressive, uncooperative defense work. Coincidentally, a few days before the lectures I had shown two of her essays to a prosecutor who had scornfully dismissed her as a "lunatic leftist" for, among other things, advocating that defense lawyers oppose efforts to use hearsay evidence at trial and for counseling suspects not to confess. While I was talking to this lawyer, the prosecutor happened to come by and join our conversation. Having never met the lawyer he remained — for a while anyway — oblivious to her identity, so the three of us chatted about the just-finished lecture on undercover investigations in the United States. When I finally introduced the defense lawyer's name, the prosecutor mumbled a curt greeting ("yoroshiku") and made an abrupt, unapologetic beeline for another conversational partner. The prosecutor's behavior was unambiguously rude and, it seemed, intentionally so.

I next met the shunned attorney just before giving a talk to some lawyers and professors at one of the Tokyo bar associations. Curious about the earlier event, I asked her if prosecutors routinely treat her with such open disdain. Swelling with pride, she acknowledged that they do. Moments later, when she introduced me to the audience, she could hardly contain her delight as she described my question and the incident that prompted it. To this lawyer (who later joined the Miranda Association) the prosecutor's response was mainly a source of mirth and pride. She was, she said, used to it. But to my prosecutor friend this lawyer was so far outside the cooperative mainstream that he felt no compunction about violating elementary norms of civility. I did not ask him about the incident but I did ask a mutual friend and judge for his reflections about it. The judge believed that the prosecutor shunned the lawyer because he feared being regarded as "polluted" if seen by his peers in the presence of a "radical."

Conclusion

Students of American criminal justice paint two contrasting portraits of the role of defense lawyers in the criminal process. The first suggests that for most defense lawyers, "getting along means going along" with the established routines in the criminal court community. Several factors — social and professional ties with prosecutors and judges, concerns to maintain credible reputations, and economics — combine to "mute the adversarial urges" of many defense lawyers (Flemming et al. 1992:163). In contrast, the second portrait depicts American defense lawyers as intensely zealous advocates who put practical flesh on the normative bones of the adversarial ideal. Empirical research has revealed strongly adversarial advocacy in a wide range of criminal defense contexts. Indeed, from Chicago's combative public defenders who suffer unfairly from the "stigma of ineptitude" (McIntyre 1987:3) to New York City's elite white-collar-crime bar where defense strategies are "highly and intensively adversarial" (Mann 1985:229), many American lawyers present vigorous defenses.

In comparison with either the adversarial "ideal" or the American reality, Japanese defense attorneys play a markedly different role. Their criminal court communities have established routines from which they rarely deviate, and "getting along" is less a matter of "going along" than it is of being compelled to go along. The laws of criminal procedure so advantage the prosecution that there is little else defense attorneys can do. There are lawyers who adopt adversarial defense tactics like those used in the United States, and their numbers are increasing, but they are so few and their strategies are so ineffective that they constitute little more than an anomalous blip on the predominant pattern of defense attorney cooperation.

A popular adage among Japanese prosecutors lists their "enemies" in order of importance: "first the bar, second the socialists and communists, no third, no fourth, and fifth the newspapers" (Setō 1983). This maxim suggests that though the press is not an especially mettlesome watchdog, lawyers may be a more significant opponent than my account suggests. The Japanese bar, acting collectively and in concert with other organized groups, has managed to thwart prosecutor-inspired efforts to reform laws and to increase the severity of punishments in the Osaka region. In addition, because a disproportionate number of "left-liberal" lawyers staff its key committees, the bar's collective decisions are more progressive than the sentiments of the "average" lawyer (Haley 1998:51). Nonetheless, the bar's influence does not alter three critical facts about defense lawyering in Japan: suspects seldom enjoy a lawyer's help prior to indictment; even when a suspect does secure a lawyer before indictment, there is little the lawyer can do to assist her client; and once prosecutors have indicted a suspect it is, in the words of one defense attorney, "all over except the trial ceremony."

Will attempts to shift the balance of advantage in the criminal process have the intended effect? Perhaps. The bar's concern about the "separation of lawyers from criminal defense work" has prompted efforts to reverse or slow the slide. In all likelihood, however, recent reforms — like the "duty counsel system" and the Miranda Association — will produce only marginal changes in the criminal court community's deeply rooted routines. Similarly, even if the size of the bar doubled by 2010, the increase would, by itself, be unlikely to alter the economics of defense lawyering significantly enough to attract or enable more vigorously adversarial lawyers (Miyazawa 1999). In short, the current system places so much power in the procuracy's hands that only a colossal abrogation of those prerogatives seems likely to produce significant change in the balance of advantage. If anything, Japan's enabling law is likely to grow more enabling as investigators acquire powers (such as the authority to wiretap) they have not previously possessed.

In 1923 Judge Learned Hand, a distinguished American jurist, decried his country's criminal procedure for giving the accused "every advantage." Hand overstated his case and may even be flat wrong (Goldstein 1960:1152; Gershman 1992:393), but his view — or one much like it — remains shared by many practitioners, scholars, and citizens (Rothwax 1996; Pizzi 1999).

One seldom hears Hand-like arguments in Japan, and for good reason: they would be utterly unconvincing. Evaluations of Japanese criminal justice are split between those who believe the existing system works admirably well (Ota 1999) and those who find it "hopeless" and "diseased" (Hirano 1999), but there is little disagreement about the limited role defense attorneys play. As one of Japan's few zealous defense attorneys has shown, scholars, judges, prosecutors, and attorneys unite in concluding that defense lawyers have little effect on case dispositions (Wakamatsu 1990:152). The division of control over information which is fundamental to the adversarial ideal is, in Japan's ostensibly adversarial system, concentrated in the hands of the same people — prosecutors — who control so much else in the criminal court community. If prosecutors used that information to single-mindedly indict, convict, and punish offenders, then the established processes would seem to work to the serious disadvantage of criminal suspects and to the overwhelming advantage of the state. The next chapter shows, however, that prosecutors seek more than mere punishment. In fact, they use their powers to pursue a wide range of jurisprudential objectives, some of which serve the interests of offenders.

3

Prosecutor Culture

The intent of all my work . . . has been to display and analyze the different assumptions and intentions the Japanese bring to public life, compared to the Americans, and to uncover the likely consequences of these Japanese orientations.

Chalmers Johnson, *Japan: Who Governs?*

Culture is to an organization what personality is to an individual.

James Q. Wilson, *Bureaucracy*

No question has more engaged students of Japan than the obvious one: How different is this, the first major industrial society to emerge outside the Western tradition? Likewise, no question has bred more, or more rancorous, disagreement. For every scholar who believes there is no need to invoke "the peculiarities of Japanese culture" in order to understand the essence of Japanese law or politics, another can be heard contending for the converse. This book addresses a parallel question about Japanese prosecutors — How different are they? — and this chapter concentrates on two core qualities of Japan's prosecutor culture: prosecutor preferences, or what prosecutors want, and prosecutor beliefs about the factors that influence their discretion. It shows that prosecutors in Japan and the United States have markedly different work objectives and, in important respects, hold different beliefs about how to exercise the discretion to charge.

I describe and interpret key aspects of Japan's legal culture by analyzing evidence — primarily survey evidence — collected between 1992 and 1995. The meaning of the concept of *legal culture* is far from settled. I use the term to denote ideas, values, expectations, and attitudes toward law and legal institutions (Friedman 1975). By analogy, *prosecutor culture* refers to prosecutors' mental and emotional products — the ideas, values, expectations, and attitudes they have about criminal law, behavior, and justice. I say little about the "external" or "public" legal culture of Japan and instead focus on the "internal" legal culture of prosecutors, for three reasons: because prosecutor attitudes and values are poorly documented even though they are often invoked as explanations and justifications; because the culture of legal professionals has large effects on the operation of a criminal justice system (Rutherford

1993); and because, as a practical matter, I cannot say something about everything.[1] In analyzing Japan's prosecutor culture, I make frequent comparisons with prosecutors in other nations, chiefly the United States. I compare because it is impossible to understand prosecution in one country or culture without seeing how it differs from prosecution elsewhere (Lipset 1996:17). Studies of Japan's prosecutor culture "cannot but be comparative," and only through comparison can its specific properties be recognized or assessed (Guarnieri 1997).[2]

The chapter unfolds as follows. In the next section I provide background information on the gender, age, education, family history, and job assignments of Japanese prosecutors. After that, I focus on two key features of their occupational culture. First I examine "what prosecutors want," both in becoming prosecutors and in performing their jobs. Then I explore what prosecutors believe about how they should exercise their discretion to charge. The final section poses important but unanswered questions about prosecutor culture in Japan.

Who Are the Prosecutors?

I surveyed 235 Japanese prosecutors and assistant prosecutors about a variety of work-related attitudes and behaviors. In all, I asked 153 questions about their background, work objectives, exercise of discretion, and other aspects of the prosecutor's job (see Appendix). All respondents completed the questionnaire outside my presence. I heeded the advice of professional survey designers to search for questions on my topic that have been asked by other researchers, and I adopted many items from surveys of American prosecutors, adapting them where appropriate to fit the Japanese context (Sudman and Bradburn 1982:14).

As explained in the introduction to this book, the original draft of the questionnaire was almost 30 percent longer than the version actually administered, but sixty-four of the original questions were cut at the insistence of my prosecutor handlers,

---

1. If what distinguishes social research from journalism is the systematic analysis of large amounts of purposefully collected evidence, then much of the work on Japan's legal culture, and especially the part pertaining to criminal justice, seems more like journalism than social research (Ragin 1994:8). Most scholarly works either assume or argue that Japan possesses a unique legal culture that is extraordinarily efficacious (Haley 1991:129; Bayley 1991:189; Foote 1992a:321; Upham 1989:7; Braithwaite 1989:49; Westermann and Burfeind 1991:109; Wagatsuma and Rosett 1986:461; Ames 1981:228; Parker 1984:120; Thornton and Endo 1992:28; E. Johnson 1996:8). However, the most rigorous attempt to compare legal cultures in Japan and the United States finds that, at least with respect to serious crime, the two countries share more legal culture than prevailing accounts suppose (Hamilton and Sanders 1992:157).

2. Even in Western countries little is known about the beliefs and sentiments that influence criminal justice practitioners—especially prosecutors. Considering the importance of their work, it is unfortunate that this remains uncharted territory. Nevertheless, the paucity of comparative data is a baseline fact that limits the kinds of comparisons one can perform. Fortunately, Lauren Rayment (1999), a student at the University of Washington Law School, was able to administer to Seattle prosecutors an English version of the survey instrument I administered in Japan. Her research has greatly facilitated my efforts to analyze Japan's prosecutor culture in comparative perspective.

and another ten were substantially revised at their behest. Thus, in order to get the questionnaire into the field, I was required to omit or change nearly one-third of the survey items I wanted to ask. The cut and altered items fall into several identifiable types: questions about other members of the criminal court community, whether defense attorneys, judges, police, or prosecutor bosses; items asking for evaluations of the procuracy's performance; and queries about prosecutor practices that have been criticized in the past (such as their alleged overreliance on confessions or refusal to acknowledge mistakes).

The questionnaire was first administered in January 1994 to forty prosecutors (*kenji*) and assistant prosecutors (*fuku kenji*) in the Kobe District Prosecutors Office. Then I used a snowball sampling technique to generate an additional 195 responses from twenty-four other District Prosecutors Offices. In all, I received responses from prosecutors working in half of the fifty District Prosecutors Offices and in the Ministry of Justice. Like the procuracy itself, the 235 respondents were spread unevenly throughout the archipelago: 12 in Hokkaido (5 percent), 158 in Honshu (67 percent), 19 in Shikoku (8 percent), 33 in Kyushu (14 percent), and 5 in the Ministry of Justice (2 percent). (Eight respondents did not provide their office location.) Nearly half of the responses ($n = 113$) came from three large urban offices: Kobe, Tokyo, and Yokohama.

A Man's World

My respondents were overwhelmingly (94.5 percent) male, as is the procuracy. When I began the survey only about 50 of Japan's 1,130 prosecutors were female, or about 4.4 percent (Satō 1993:33). Since then, the percentage of female prosecutors has increased steadily. In 1995 the percentage of new prosecutors who were female exceeded the percentage of new private attorneys who were female, and the percentage of new female judges was nearly twice as high as either.[3] Even with the increase, however, women still constitute less than 10 percent of the total prosecutor force. Japan's procuracy is very much a man's world, a fact many prosecutors admit

---

3. In recent years the number of women recruits has been increasing. For example, in April 1995 the Ministry of Justice announced that eighty-six people were appointed as new prosecutors that year, the largest number ever. Of the eighty-six, sixteen (19 percent) were women, also the largest number ever. These increases have been attributed to Japan's protracted economic recession, which makes the security of a prosecutor position more appealing to many new legal professionals; to bar examination reforms that expanded the number of bar-passers from five hundred to a thousand (and to fifteen hundred in 2001); and to increases in the percentage of female bar-passers. In 1995, 633 people graduated from the Legal Research and Training Institute of the Supreme Court after passing the bar exam and completing a two-year apprenticeship. Fourteen percent of the new graduates became prosecutors. By comparison, in the same year ninety-nine people (16 percent) were appointed to the judiciary, of whom thirty-four were women. Of the other 453 graduates who became private attorneys, 78 (17 percent) were women (*Yomiuri Shimbun* 3/6/95). The percentage of female bar-passers has increased steadily between the 1950s and 1990s. In the 1950s women constituted 3 percent of all bar-passers. The figure rose to 5 percent between 1965 and 1975, and to about 10 percent by the mid-1980s. From 1987 to 1991 the percentage ranged from 12 to 15, and in each of the three years from 1992 through 1994, about 20 percent of all bar-passers were female (Oki et al. 1995:22). By comparison, in 1960 women represented about a third of French *stagiaires* and a quarter of *avocats* in Paris and its suburbs, and in Italy in 1966 women constituted about 4 percent of all lawyers.

and more than a few celebrate. I interviewed six of the fifteen female respondents in my survey. All spoke impassively about the problems they encountered in an over-whelmingly male office even though all described being given case and job assign-ments that might invite charges of invidious discrimination if they occurred in the United States. Only one admitted that gender discrimination "may be a problem." The others stolidly stated that their male bosses "were just like that" or else seemed resigned to the fact that "there is no use complaining."

Women prosecutors are seldom assigned to positions in either of the two launch-ing pads for prosecutor elites — the Special Investigation Division (SID) of the Tokyo District Prosecutors Office and the Criminal Affairs Bureau (CAB) of the Ministry of Justice. Only since 1990 have women been admitted to the ranks of the SID's "elite troops," and then only on what several prosecutors described as a "token" basis — one at a time (out of an SID force that varies from thirty to forty). Similarly, while I was doing research in Tokyo, the sole female prosecutor in the CAB told me she was just the second woman ever to work there, in the ministry's most elite bureau. She vaguely explained that CAB's first female prosecutor had "not worked out very well." Female prosecutors are also treated differently outside the "elite career courses." One former elite prosecutor, now a member of the upper house of the Diet, correctly notes that many women prosecutors are assigned to trial work instead of investigations. The managers and executives who make such assignments say that "trial work suits women best because trials are the face of the procuracy," but the truth is that many believe "investigations are too difficult for women to perform" (Satō 1993:33). Since most tri-als are more akin to ceremonies than to adversarial battles, it is difficult to avoid the conclusion that in Japan's procuracy women are status inferiors, much as they are in other large Japanese organizations (Tashima 1998).

Age

The prosecutors in my sample spanned four decades in age, ranging from twenty-four to sixty-three years of age, with a mean age of forty-one years. Five in six re-spondents were below age fifty, and 102 of the 235 were in their thirties. Rookie pros-ecutors tend to be about two years younger than new judges and two years older than new lawyers. In 1995, the average age of the new prosecutors was 29.3 years; while the corresponding figures for new judges and new lawyers were 27.4 years and 31.1 years, respectively.

Education

Compared to the diverse college and law school backgrounds of their American counterparts, prosecutors in Japan receive strikingly similar educations. All 149 pros-ecutors had undergraduate degrees, as did over half of the eighty-six assistant prose-cutors. They came from a wide range of colleges — forty-five in all — but more than half were from only four universities: Chuo (forty-six), Waseda (twenty-six), Tokyo (twenty), and Kyoto (twelve). Thus, prosecutors are heavily concentrated in the schools that have long been regarded as the main feeders for the judiciary, the pri-vate bar, and the procuracy, not to mention the rest of the elite bureaucracy and the world of big business. The larger number of Chuo and Waseda graduates is in part a function of the large number of law graduates these two colleges produce.

Educational homogeneity extends to area of study as well. In the survey, 181 of the 197 college graduates — nearly 92 percent — majored in law at college. No other major had more than five prosecutor graduates. Unlike the United States, where legal education is primarily post-baccalaureate, legal education in Japan is mainly undergraduate, as it was for all of the law graduates in the survey. One result is that, as a group, the bar-passers who embark on the legal apprenticeship that precedes their choice of legal profession have received comparatively narrow educations and hardly any of the practical legal training that most American law students acquire at law school. Their educational focus is further narrowed by the difficulty of the Japanese bar exam, one of the most difficult credentialing exams in the world. In 1987 the bar pass rate was just under 2 percent; by 1994 it had skyrocketed to 3 percent. In order to pass the exam, nearly half of aspiring legal professionals take it six times or more (Ōki et al. 1995:21). It is offered only once a year. Most aspirants devote themselves to full-time study during these years, often attending special cram schools which charge $1,000 to $5,000 a year for tuition. Among other purposes, the two-year legal apprenticeship for bar-passers (reduced to eighteen months in 1999) aims to broaden their knowledge of the world after the long, cloistered period of narrowly legal study, and to impart some of the skills necessary for their subsequent legal careers.[4]

Family Background

Prosecutors' fathers and mothers have decidedly different occupational backgrounds. Over three-quarters of all mothers worked primarily as housewives; not one was a legal professional. In contrast, prosecutors' fathers were about evenly distributed among four of the survey's five occupational categories: public officials, company employees, self-employed, and "other." Only 4 percent of prosecutor respondents reported that their father is or was a legal professional, far lower than the 19 percent reported in a survey of private practitioners in the former West Germany (Abel and Lewis 1988:37). It seems that, like many other entrance exams in Japan, the bar exam is a relatively open, meritocractic screening procedure, at least compared to the screening systems used in some other industrialized democracies (Rohlen 1983:61).

Job Assignments

The largest proportion of prosecutors (114) worked in small District Offices or in branches that employ a continuous or "vertical" prosecution system in which the

---

4. In Japan, prosecutors and other elite bureaucrats share many common qualities. They are predominantly law graduates chosen from among the educated elite who wield great power while working as generalists in organizations that stress seniority and consensual decision-making. Prosecutors and other administrative elites also tend to retire early and get re-employed. Japan "shares many attributes of its bureaucracy" with Britain, France, and West Germany, but not with the United States (Koh 1989:252). In several respects, Japan's prosecutor culture appears to most closely resemble prosecutor culture in France (Frase 1990; Guarnieri 1997; Carbonneau 1995).

same prosecutor handles a case from the pre-charge investigation through trial. About an equal number worked in larger District Offices that have bureaus. In these offices, cases are prosecuted "horizontally," so that an investigative prosecutor transfers cases to a trial prosecutor immediately after the case is charged. In descending order of frequency, the other prosecutor respondents worked in general affairs bureaus (fifteen), the Special Investigation Division in Tokyo (four), and the traffic (four) and public security (two) bureaus. Prosecutors in the larger District Offices perform a wide range of more particular roles, the great majority as frontline "operators," investigating and processing cases. Only fourteen prosecutor respondents came from the management ranks. As a consequence, the survey results are biased toward the culture of frontline prosecutors, not managers or executives.

Work Hours

Finally, prosecutors report working an average of fifty hours a week. The range is wide, running from twenty-nine hours a week on the low end to one hundred hours a week on the high. The distribution of hours worked is bimodal: fifty-two respondents said they worked forty hours a week and the same number said they worked fifty (the survey question was open-ended). Thus, while a few prosecutors report that they are extraordinarily busy, most do not. This is further evidence that, as documented in chapter 1, most prosecutors do not suffer from the press of heavy caseloads or "institutional incapacity."

What Do Prosecutors Want?

Prosecutor preferences are a core component of prosecutor culture. Unfortunately, what prosecutors want and why they want it are sorely neglected questions in the sociology of criminal justice. Typically, even scholars who attend to what prosecutors want do so not by trying to measure, describe, interpret, or explain their preferences, but by postulating them a priori, as if they were as self-evident as the Euclidean axiom that "two points determine a line." This approach has rendered our knowledge of prosecutor culture badly deficient.[5]

The prevailing postulate about prosecutor preferences—or at least American prosecutors' preferences—states that they aim to "maximize the expected number of convictions weighted by their respective sentences, subject to a constraint on the resources or budget available to the office" (Landes 1971:61; see also Forst and Brosi 1977). This claim stands on no confirmatory evidence. It rests instead on "logical" inferences about what prosecutors must want in an adversarial system of criminal justice and, perhaps more important, on its consistency with other assumptions in the rational choice tradition. Corollary formulations of prosecutor preferences totter on equally weak empirical foundations: prosecutors want to maximize the gross number of convictions (Chambliss and Seidman 1984; Neubauer 1974); prosecutors

5. Not just for prosecutors but for criminal justice more generally, "a profound lack of clarity of definition and of adequate measurement of objectives abounds" (Gottfredson and Gottfredson 1988:vi).

are preoccupied with their record of punishment and are in the business of producing favorable statistics (Reiss 1975; Sutherland and Cressey 1978); and, as an organization, a prosecution office's dominant goal is a high conviction record (Stanko 1981).

Other views posit different preferences in a similarly axiomatic style. Pressed by
a heavy volume of cases, prosecutors want to process them efficiently in order to
"keep the cases moving" (Blumberg 1979; Utz 1984). Prosecutors want "not so much
to win as not to lose" (Kaplan 1965; Skolnick 1967). Prosecutors, enmeshed as they
are in relationships with police, judges, defense attorneys, and political elites, want
to accommodate each of their major "clients" (G. F. Cole 1970). U.S. Supreme
Court Justice Robert Jackson's (1940:19) claim that "the duty of the prosecutor is not
to win a case but to see that justice is done" has often been invoked as the normative
standard to which prosecutors should aspire, but it is rarely regarded as what prosecutors actually want. In only a handful of works are prosecutors portrayed as intent
on doing justice, and even then the point is seldom stated or demonstrated explicitly
(Carter 1974; Littrell 1979; Mather 1979; Feeley 1992b; Tevlin 1993).

What prosecutors in Japan want also is poorly documented. Indeed, extant claims
totter on even weaker empirical foundations than do corollary claims about American
prosecutors. Most commentators posit a strong prosecutor interest in rehabilitating offenders and reintegrating them into their communities (Foote 1992a; Haley 1991; Bayley 1991; Braithwaite 1989; Parker 1984; Itoh 1982; Aoyagi 1986). In the absence of supporting evidence, however, there is much room for disagreement (Miyazawa 1995;
Peters 1992). Ironically, historical works provide better evidence of what prosecutors
wanted in the past than do contemporary works about what they want now. These histories regard the prewar procuracy as a central agent of state control that utilized reintegrative strategies in order to "solve the crucial problem of maintaining the integration of Japanese society during the dual crises of political modernization and
impending war" (Steinhoff 1991:6; see also Ogino 2000; Mitchell 1992; Tipton 1990).

The following sections attempt to establish what contemporary Japanese prosecutors want. In the process, it interrogates the prevailing but unsubstantiated claims
that what they want is distinctly rehabilitative and thus distinctively Japanese. In
order to assess how different Japanese prosecutor preferences are, I compare them
with what is known about American prosecutor preferences. I present the evidence
in two installments, by describing the reasons for becoming a prosecutor in the first
place, and then, and in more detail, by portraying prosecutors' work objectives.

Reasons for Becoming a Prosecutor

Prosecutors enter their profession for a wide variety of reasons, but a content analysis[6] of their stated motivations reveals five main (and overlapping) inducements: the
desire to do justice; the appeal of investigations; the fit between job and personality;
the influence of "significant others"; and the attraction to authority.[7]

---

6. The main premise of content analysis is that the many words of a text can be classified into far
fewer content categories (Weber 1985:9).

7. I employed a number of research methods in order to learn why people became prosecutors. First,
the survey included an open-ended question asking each respondent his or her "motives for becoming a

THE DESIRE TO DO JUSTICE

By far the most frequently mentioned reason for becoming a prosecutor is the desire to do justice ($n = 84$). Many prosecutors employed the identical phrase for wanting to "realize justice" (*seigi no jitsugen*). For some this means protecting the rights of victims and society, while for others it means securing justice (and help) for criminal suspects and offenders. As one respondent wrote, "Since prosecutors wield so much control in the criminal process, and at early stages in the process, they are in a privileged position to protect suspects' rights. Isn't preventing abuses of rights in the first place at least as important as trying to identify abuses after the fact and seeking remedies for them [as defense attorneys do]?" Another prosecutor stated that "of all the legal professions, only prosecutors are in a position to cry with victims and get mad at offenders. We can do both." Still another said that "compared to judges and defense lawyers, prosecutors can do more to help offenders reform and to restore relationships between offenders and their victims."

THE APPEAL OF INVESTIGATIONS

A smaller subgroup ($n = 21$) emphasized investigation work as the primary motive. For those in this category, investigations are interesting because they reveal the character of people better than trials do, and because they teach truths about the world one otherwise could not know. Most prosecutors discover that investigation is an interesting aspect of the prosecutor job during their legal apprenticeships. One explained that he became a prosecutor because investigations make the job "stink of humanity." Other prosecutors span the first two categories by linking their desire to do justice to their capacity to discover the truth during the pre-indictment investigation. As one observed, "If you want to do justice, you have to know what happened. Investigations enable us to know."

THE FIT BETWEEN JOB AND PERSONALITY

A third category of respondents ($n = 32$) became prosecutors because the job fits their character better than other jobs do. Most in this category framed their decision narrowly, as a choice between becoming a judge, a private attorney, or a prosecutor, but in fact many prosecutors make the decision to become a prosecutor in stages. First one resolves to take the formidable bar exam, often in order to acquire the security and autonomy that come with being a lawyer (Haley 1998:53). Only after pass-

---

prosecutor" (Appendix, part 1:11). I received 193 valid responses, ranging in length from a few words to several carefully crafted paragraphs. In follow-up interviews with respondents I probed for more detailed descriptions of their career choices. In addition, I spent hundreds of hours working and relaxing with the legal apprentices who were then in the process of deciding whether to become private attorneys, judges, or prosecutors. Finally, I searched autobiographical accounts for descriptions of prosecutors' reasons for joining the procuracy (Bessho 1983; Idei 1986; Imai 1999; Inoue 1989; Itoh 1982, 1987, 1988; Kawai 1979; M. Satō 1993; Shimizu 1998; Yasuhara 1985). For the classic account of why American prosecutors enter the profession and how they adapt after doing so, see Heumann (1981).

ing the bar do many aspirants give serious thought to which legal profession is most suitable. For some, a judge's job is too passive. As one put it, "Reading documents all day long [as judges do] without encountering any 'raw humans' is too tedious." For others, the profits that private attorneys must pursue make that alternative the source of so much stress, insecurity, and potential failure that they reckon it a "disgusting occupation." In this way, the perceived drawbacks of becoming a judge or lawyer push some people away from those legal professions. Simultaneously, opportunities to "actively make cases" by conducting investigations and exercising discretion pull them toward the procuracy.

THE INFLUENCE OF "SIGNIFICANT OTHERS"

The motives of this group ($n = 23$) are distinctly other-directed. These prosecutors were encouraged by people they liked, trusted, or respected to pursue the prosecutor path. Many administrative assistants (*jimukan*) become assistant prosecutors (*fuku kenji*) because their supervisors urge them to take the requisite exams. Likewise, many prosecutors (*kenji*) were strongly influenced to become prosecutors by a teacher or supervising prosecutor during their training as legal apprentices. More broadly, some prosecutors say they were swayed by parents or relatives already in the procuracy or by college "seniors" who had preceded them on the same course. In one account, a thirty-seven-year-old prosecutor who had been in the procuracy for seven years explained that as the eldest son in his family, Japanese custom calls for him to take care of his parents in their old age, something he could not do as a prosecutor because of the frequent job transfers. Fortunately for this prosecutor (he liked his job a lot), his parents did not oppose his desire to become a prosecutor because they could rely on a younger child for support if necessary. Thus parental permission, together with his girlfriend's resistance to marrying a private attorney, led him into the prosecutor profession.

THE ATTRACTION TO AUTHORITY

Finally, some prosecutors ($n = 7$) stressed their desire to wield the vast power inherent in the prosecutor role. These people said they wanted to become the "fulcrum" or "pivot point" of the criminal justice system, as prosecutors are widely and accurately held to be. Some emphasized the legal authority prosecutors have to suspend prosecution, even in cases where there is sufficient evidence to charge and convict. As one prosecutor put it, this authority is a "flexible power which judges do not possess. It can be used, of course, to benefit suspects, but at the same time, if it is applied unfairly one will inevitably be criticized. Thus, prosecutors must exercise this power with great care."

These five categories are neither mutually exclusive, nor do they exhaust the wide range of motives for entering the procuracy. Indeed, prosecutors often gave multiple, overlapping reasons for joining the profession. Nonetheless, even the most intricate stories tend to get spun around these main motivations. Above all, in choosing to become prosecutors, men and women select a profession they find "meaningful" because it confers both the obligation and the power to "do the right thing," something many believe defense lawyers cannot as routinely do. The vast majority of prosecutors seem content with their choice: nearly nine in ten said they are glad they became a prosecutor, and three in four said they will remain a prosecutor until they retire.[8]

Prosecutor Work Objectives

Now consider what prosecutors aim to achieve *after* entering the procuracy. Part 2 of the survey presented respondents with seventeen potential work objectives. For each objective, respondents were asked to circle one of four answers in order to "indicate how important you believe it is to try to achieve this objective when disposing of cases." The four responses were (1) not an objective, (2) not a very important objective, (3) an important objective, and (4) a very important objective. I generated the list of objectives from the scholarly literature on prosecutors, from several months of field observations prior to constructing the questionnaire, and from a pre-test of the survey. The following analysis is based on the percentage of prosecutors who regarded each work objective as either "important" or "very important." Table 3.1 ranks the objectives from most important to least important and juxtaposes the results of the same survey administered to Seattle prosecutors in 1999.

Most strikingly, table 3.1 shows that *many* work objectives are salient to prosecutors in both Japan and the United States. Indeed, thirteen of the seventeen objectives were considered important or very important by two-thirds or more of all Japanese prosecutors, and nine of the seventeen were important or very important to at least two-thirds of Seattle prosecutors. This finding belies the common assertion that prosecutors pursue a single objective, such as maximizing convictions or sentences or some product of the two. Moreover, prosecutors in both countries say they want least what pundits of the procuracy presume they want most.[9] Table 3.1 further shows that most objectives (twelve of seventeen) are more important to Japanese prosecutors than to American prosecutors, by an average of about 10 percent per objective. This is evidence that prosecutors in Japan view their role more broadly than do prosecutors in the United States.

8. In the 1980s more prosecutors seemed discontent with their jobs. In an article titled "The Prosecutor Crisis," one magazine reported that about fifty prosecutors were quitting the procuracy each year, mainly out of dissatisfaction with the office's personnel and transfer decisions and its rigidly bureaucratic character (*Sunday Mainichi* 4/26/87). Similarly, in 1989 the Tokyo Bar Federation reported the results of a survey administered to 144 former prosecutors who quit the procuracy and joined the private bar in the previous two decades. The fifty-six respondents answered eleven questions about their perceptions of the procuracy and their reasons for leaving it. Many expressed discontent over transfers, personnel decisions, and the bureaucratic work environment.

9. In his study of a large prosecutors office in California, Lief Carter asked prosecutors to rate the importance of nine work goals and to evaluate how well the office accomplished each. Carter does not provide a summary of the survey results. He says, however, that the three most important objectives for the California prosecutors were (1) maintaining a high level of professional legal performance; (2) separating the innocent from the guilty; and (3) striking a fair balance between the conflicting interests and desires of victims, police, judges, defense counsel, and the public. Although I borrowed from Carter's survey to construct my questionnaire, many objectives that are important to Japanese prosecutors—such as "clarifying the truth"—are not found in his study (Carter 1974:179, 195).

TABLE 3.1 Prosecutor objectives in Japan and the United States

Objective	Japan		Seattle	
	Rank	Percent	Rank	Percent
Discovering the truth	1	99.6	2	96.5
"Proper" charge decisions	2	97.9	4	94.7
Invoking remorse in offenders	3	92.7	16	8.8
Rehabilitating and reintegrating offenders	4	91.5	12	28.1
Protecting the public	5	91.1	1	98.2
Treating like cases alike	6	90.7	6	78.9
Respecting rights of suspects	7	83.9	2	96.5
Reducing the crime rate	8	83.8	10	59.6
Giving offenders the punishment they deserve	9	82.5	5	93.0
Maintaining good relations with the police	10	80.8	8	73.7
Having public understand that office is responding properly to crime	11	77.4	7	75.7
Repairing relations between offender and victim	12	67.6	17	0.0
Disposing efficiently of as many cases as possible	13	65.5	11	33.3
Maintaining reputation of office	14	36.6	9	68.4
Invoking public condemnation of the crime	15	28.6	15	14.0
Maximizing punishment	16	21.9	13	15.8
Prosecuting and convicting as many cases as possible	17	8.6	13	15.8

Sources: Author's (1994–1995) survey of 235 Japanese prosecutors; Rayment's (1999) survey of fifty-seven American prosecutors from the King County Prosecutor's Office in Seattle, Washington.

I have grouped the objectives into four categories based on the aggregate percentage of Japanese prosecutors who found them important or very important: cardinal objectives (ranks 1 and 2), primary objectives (ranks 3 to 6), secondary objectives (ranks 7 to 13), and tertiary objectives (ranks 14 to 17).[10]

CARDINAL OBJECTIVES

The two cardinal objectives—"discovering the truth about a case" (99.6 percent) and "making a proper charge decision" (97.9 percent)—are important to virtually all Japanese prosecutors. Indeed, only one regarded the former, and only five the latter, as "not very important," while no one considered either "not an objective." Discovering the truth is such an important purpose that it constitutes the "core task" for Japan's frontline prosecutors (see chapter 4).

Though the vast majority of Seattle prosecutors also deemed truth an important objective, commitment to this aim runs deeper in Japan, and in different grooves, for a variety of reasons. First, American prosecutors play a more limited role in the investigations, where facts are initially uncovered and truth is first constructed. Their pre-charge assessments of truth are largely shaped by police reports, not by firsthand exposure to witnesses and suspects. After the charge decision, American prosecutors

10. The original version of the questionnaire asked prosecutors to evaluate how well they achieved the various work objectives, but prosecutors cut that section before allowing the survey to be administered. One said they wanted to avoid the public criticism that would result if word got around that prosecutors believe some objectives are not realized.

routinely "settle the facts" in plea negotiations, frequently torturing truth in the process (Utz 1978). If the facts are not settled via plea-bargaining, American prosecutors then confront the sporting logic of the adversary system, which assumes that truth will emerge as the by-product of vigorously partisan advocacy. On this view, a true result does not depend on the truth-seeking of the advocates. The stress on winning often obscures and distorts the truth (Pizzi 1999; Amar 1997). Indeed, the adversary ethic even spills over into the pretrial investigation to distort fact-finding there (McCoy 1996). Japan differs in each of these respects, rendering its prosecutors preoccupied with "the truth" to an extent the survey results cannot reveal.

The cardinal importance of truth may be the core characteristic of Japan's prosecutor culture. Prosecutors in Japan are not content merely to discover the "rough truth," as happens in the United States (Heilbroner 1990), or to fix their account of the truth in imprecise language, as commentators such as Kawashima Takeyoshi (1979) suppose. Kawashima, an eminent sociologist of law, argued that Japanese words, meanings, and reasoning are inherently indefinite, unfixed, imprecise, indeterminate, vague, and ambiguous. This non-Western, "Japanese way of thinking," Kawashima claimed, permeates the legal process at all levels. Watch a Japanese prosecutor prepare dossiers during a criminal investigation, however, and one must greet Kawashima's claims with disbelief. With few exceptions, the prosecutor's dossiers record the official version of the facts—the truth as the prosecutor discerns and constructs it—with painstaking precision. Even in a simple case of bike theft where the suspect confesses fully, prosecutors commonly produce written accounts of the crime that exceed fifty pages. For more complicated cases the dossiers, stacked one on top of another, look like an unbound version of the *Encyclopedia Britannica*. In short, Japanese prosecutors not only aim to uncover the truth of the cases they process, they construct and convey the facts more "precisely" than their peers in other dossier-producing countries.[11]

Discovering the truth is linked symbiotically with the other cardinal objective, "making proper charge decisions" (or, as the survey item put it, "not prosecuting the innocent and prosecuting and convicting only those who have really committed crimes"). The symbiosis is straightforward: discovering the truth is necessary in order to make good charge decisions, and making good charge decisions can be done only after constructing an accurate account of what the physical evidence shows and what competent people genuinely believe happened (Frankel 1978:73). Thus, the quality of criminal justice depends on the quality of the charge decision, and the quality of the charge decision depends on how well investigators have ascertained the truth. In this sense, justice is truth in action, and the pursuit of truth is the first hallmark of Japan's prosecutor culture.

PRIMARY OBJECTIVES

Each of the four primary objectives is important to at least 90 percent of Japanese prosecutors. The first two, "invoking remorse in the offender" and "rehabilitating and reintegrating the offender," stand in the same mutually dependent relationship

11. Of course, the process used to uncover and construct the truth also intrudes more deeply on suspect's autonomy, and sometimes tortures the truth in the process (see chapter 8).

as do the two cardinal objectives. Prosecutors aim to invoke remorse in offenders because they believe penitence is the essential first step on the road to reform. In their view, rehabilitation requires repentance.

The pursuit of rehabilitation through remorse distinguishes Japanese from American prosecutors even more sharply than does the stress on truth. The contrast is truly stark. In Japan, more than 90 percent of prosecutors regard remorse as important; in Seattle, less than 9 percent do. In part this difference reflects the fact that American prosecutors do not confront suspects and defendants until late in the criminal process, so they have few opportunities to invoke contrition. But there is more to it than that. Over three times as many Japanese prosecutors say they aim for rehabilitation and reintegration. American prosecutors are largely unconcerned with these aims, except perhaps for juvenile offenders. The "decline of the rehabilitative ideal" so evident in the United States (Allen 1981) and Great Britain (Rutherford 1993) has no parallel in Japan. This could be because Japan's Confucian past continues to influence contemporary legal culture. The Confucian tradition assumes original virtue and the perfectibility of people rather than, as in some Judeo-Christian traditions, original sin and immutable character (R. J. Smith 1983). The different assumptions may generate different beliefs and behaviors: in America, a set of prosecutor preferences pessimistic, or at best agnostic, about the possibility of rehabilitating offenders; in Japan, systemic efforts to reform the remorseful. Of course, prosecutor culture is embedded in circumstances that further facilitate reform. Japan's less adversary criminal process, light caseloads, enabling laws, political insulation, and absence of juries all help prosecutors pursue ends besides "protecting the public" and "giving offenders their just deserts," two of the aims that stand atop American prosecutors' hierarchy of objectives. The following case illustrates the resolutely rehabilitative ethos of the Japanese way of justice. Chapter 6 explores the subject in much more depth.

A forty-five-year-old defendant was on trial for violently raping a female acquaintance twice in the same day. The defendant was "rabble," neither well integrated into mainstream society nor the holder of conventional values and beliefs (Irwin 1985). He was dirty, unkempt, uneducated, and unemployed. Most Japanese probably considered him irksome, offensive, and threatening too. He had a long history of felony convictions, including two prison terms for rape. Years earlier he had lost much of his right arm in a prison factory accident, and he frequently used the stump to gesture as he spoke. As is customary in Japan, the trial was straightforward. Police and prosecutors had secured several mutually corroborating confessions from the defendant and had recorded them in dossier which they submitted to the court. Since the defense did not oppose the prosecutor's motion to introduce these documents as evidence, the court's verdict and sentence were based mainly on the dossiers. The prosecutor also submitted the victim's statement in written form, thus making it unnecessary for her to appear in court. Since there was no disagreement about what the defendant did, the trial focused on what he deserved as punishment. The prosecutor called no witnesses, choosing instead to simply, even perfunctorily, remind the three-judge court of the defendant's prior record and the seriousness of the present offenses. The defense attorney, a state-appointed lawyer who appeared to be at least a few years on the Bob Hope side of seventy, called only one witness — his client.

The defense attorney first tried to get the defendant to show that he was sorry for what he had done. At this he succeeded. On cue, the defendant proclaimed his heartfelt sorrow for the pain he had caused the victim and announced his intention never to do such a thing again. However, the lawyer's attempts to have his client tell the court how, exactly, he would try to reform generated only incomprehensible mumbling and vague promises that the defendant would "do his best." At this point the defense attorney decided to expound the rehabilitative effects of haiku poetry.

"Have you ever written haiku poetry?" the lawyer asked.

"Never have," replied the confessed rapist.

"You should," retorted the lawyer. "I write haiku often, and there's nothing like it for focusing the mind and purifying the spirit."

"I see."

"Have you ever heard of Basho?" queried the attorney. "He's a famous haiku poet you know."

"I've never heard of him."

"Well you should read him, and you should write your own haiku too. I think it would do you some good. Basho wrote this haiku. It's famous. 'An old pond/A frog jumps in/Plop.' Pretty good, huh? Haven't you ever heard this poem?"

"No I haven't," replied the defendant.

"Well, I think you should begin studying haiku poetry. Something like this could really help you reform your ways."

"Yes," responded the defendant, "I'll try it. Thank you."

When the defense attorney recited Basho's famous frog poem (the best-known verse in haiku history), I struggled, unsuccessfully, to smother a snicker. The defendant was clearly the kind of person James Q. Wilson (1983:260) had in mind when he declared that "wicked people exist." Like Wilson, I believed that all that could be done with some such people was to set them apart from the innocent. He was, I was sure, completely beyond hope. To treat him otherwise would "make sport of the innocent and encourage the calculators." Could this defense lawyer be serious?

He could. More remarkably still, the prosecutor agreed with him. After this trial session ended I found the prosecutor and the three legal apprentices who had observed the trial, reminded them of the defense attorney's exhortations, and asked what they thought. Unlike me, all found the defense attorney's remarks perfectly appropriate, and all shared the belief that, with effort, the defendant could be restored to something approximating his original virtue. "Why not?" the prosecutor responded to my incredulous inquiry. "Maybe haiku poetry could help the defendant turn his life around."

"Treating like cases alike," another primary prosecutor objective, has often been considered a goal American prosecutors cannot and therefore should not try to achieve. Lief Carter (1974), for example, argues that the American ideal of justice embodies two mutually incompatible ideals: individualization and uniformity (or "treating likes alike"). Carter believes that a "bureaucratic model of management" is necessary in order to achieve uniformity, but contends that that model does not fit the nature of the prosecutor's job. Hence, prosecutors should seek to individualize case dispositions without worrying about uniformity, as they did in the California office he studied. Similarly, descriptions of Japanese criminal justice assert that prosecutors emphasize "individualized determinations based on careful considerations of the individual's personal circumstances" but give little regard to uniformity (Foote 1992a:341). In short, scholarship in both countries reaches the same conclusion: that prosecutors do little, and care little, about treating like cases alike.

This orthodoxy, at least as it applies to prosecutors in Japan, is wrong. In fact, "treating like cases alike" is an important objective for Japanese prosecutors. Only two prosecutors out of 235 said it is "not an objective," and these respondents were not simply reciting *tatemae*, or the officially accepted view. Treating likes alike is clearly their real intention too. Survey responses about *kessai* consultations with superiors (Appendix, part 4:33, 34, 35, 36, 37, 38, 72, 95) and office precedents and guidelines (Appendix, part 4:70, 71, 73, 78, 80) also suggest that the organization's structure and standard operating procedures are dedicated to the ideal of "treating likes alike." My own observations lead to the same conclusion, as chapter 5 explains in detail. The consistency objective is so primary that it must be considered, along with the commitments to truth and correction, as a principal hallmark of the Japanese way of justice.

SECONDARY OBJECTIVES

Seven objectives were deemed significant by four to five of every six prosecutors. Most notably, "repairing relations between offender and victim" was important to two-thirds of all Japanese prosecutors; in Seattle it was important to no one. This big gap reflects deep differences in the two countries' thinking about crime and criminal justice. For the most part, American prosecutors construe crime as a matter of lawbreaking and criminal justice as a matter of crime control and just deserts. This conception ignores dimensions widely recognized in Japan — that crime harms victims, relationships, and communities, and that prosecutors can help repair such injuries. Of course, even the most determined Japanese prosecutor can do little to mend relations unless the victim and offender are similarly motivated. However, without the desire to repair relationships, any healing which does occur will be as rare as it is serendipitous (see chapter 6). Among other causes, prosecutors' reluctance to pursue this objective lies behind the recent movement toward "restorative justice" — justice that promotes healing — not only in the United States but in many other countries as well (Umbreit 1998). If the movement continues to gain momentum, Japan's prosecutorial penchant for repairing relationships may presage change in other criminal justice systems (Haley 1999).

The significance ascribed to the final secondary objective — "disposing efficiently of as many cases as possible" — suggests that even though prosecutors have light caseloads, they still consider efficiency an important aim.[12] Interviews helped reveal why the value matters. The eight High Prosecutors Offices review the District

12. Though Japanese prosecutors operate under some pressure to produce favorable office statistics, police operate under more. One prosecutor told me the following story about the extraordinary lengths to which police will go in order to produce good statistics. The story gives new meaning to the subtitle of Miyazawa Setsuo's (1992) excellent book on Japanese detectives — *A Study on Making Crime*.

Police stations in Japan compete twice a year to see which can seize the most guns and drugs or arrest the most organized crime members (*bōryokudan*). These competitions (called *gekkan*) help determine who gets promoted, at both the frontline and the managerial levels. In Tokyo a former member of a *bōryokudan* (call him B) found himself in front of my prosecutor informant being grilled about how and where he had acquired the gun for possession of which he had been arrested. After several hours of intense interrogation and confusing, contradictory statements, B finally told the prosecutor that the police

Offices in their respective jurisdictions at the end of each year. As a result, frontline prosecutors feel pressure during the last weeks of December to dispose of cases that have been on the books for a long time (particularly "at-home" cases in which the suspect has not been arrested). Several prosecutors reported that pressure to "clear the books" for the new year was greater in the past than at present, but even today managers and executives try to ensure that office statistics reflect well on their individual and office performances.

TERTIARY OBJECTIVES

Only one of the four goals in this category was regarded by more than a third of prosecutors as either important or very important ("maintaining and improving the reputation of the prosecutors office"), and even then the level of support barely exceeded one-third. Commitment to this objective might have been stronger if I had been able to sample prosecutor executives more broadly, for one key executive task is to promote the procuracy's legitimacy by protecting its reputation. Nevertheless, Japanese prosecutors seem less concerned with the reputation of the office than others have claimed (Van Wolferen 1989:220), in part because it already enjoys widespread public support, and also because prosecutors' job security does not depend, either directly or indirectly, on electoral scrutiny. Almost twice as many Seattle prosecutors, whose boss is elected, believed that maintaining the office reputation was an important work purpose.

One objective — "invoking condemnation in the public for the crime and criminal" — was included in the survey because John Braithwaite's (1989) theory of "reintegrative shaming" argues that it is an important criminal justice objective in Japan and because Braithwaite urges researchers to test his theory with data. The weak level of support (28.6 percent) suggests that "invoking the public's condemnation" is

---

had ordered him to bring a gun into the police station by the end of the month (also the end of the *gekkan* competition period), had threatened him with arrest for an unrelated assault if he did not comply, and had promised him summary prosecution (and thus a light fine) if he cooperated. B told the police he did not have a gun to bring in, but the police were adamant. They reminded B that the gun he had brought to them five years earlier did not even shoot, and they warned him that he had better not repeat the same mistake. B consulted with his fiancée and employer about what to do. The latter urged B not to cooperate with the police, but the police pressure persisted and a day before the *gekkan* period ended B bought a model gun from a friend, borrowed a drill, and attempted to modify the model so it could shoot bullets. His fiancée and employer joined him in the project, and after modifying the gun they held a small going-away party for B, drinking and toasting until the early hours of the last day of the *gekkan*. B's comrades urged him to take care of his health during what they expected to be an uneventful ten-day detention. They also offered to help B pay the fine the police had promised he would receive.

Early on the morning of the last day of the month, B turned the gun and himself in to the police. After the prosecutor confirmed B's story in interviews with B's employer and fiancée, he had another prosecutor interview the relevant policeman. The cop admitted pressuring B to bring in a gun, but said he had not ordered B to *manufacture* one. In the end, B's prosecution was suspended, so neither he nor his comrades in arms had to pay a fine. The responsible police officer (a detective in the organized crime branch) was forced to resign. He was neither arrested nor prosecuted, though he could have been (for being an accomplice). The prosecutor said that serious cases of *gekkan*-induced misconduct are rare, but that less serious abuses abound. Most commonly, police compel *bōryokudan* members to bring in guns or drugs by threatening to arrest their wives or bosses.

not an important prosecutor objective, even in Japan. Braithwaite defines the key concept in his theory, shaming, as "all social processes of expressing disapproval which have the intention or effect of invoking remorse in the person being shamed and/or condemnation by others who become aware of the shaming" (1989:100). Since the first method of shaming, "invoking remorse in the offender," is a primary prosecutor objective, my survey provides partial support for the claim that Japanese criminal justice promotes shaming processes. However, the second method of shaming — invoking public condemnation for the crime — appears hardly important at all. Indeed, prosecutor commitment to this work objective was so weak that when I was trying to gain approval to administer the survey, prosecutors reviewing the item had difficulty understanding what it meant. Upon finally comprehending what the question is designed to measure, one prosecutor quizzically asked, "Why would we want to do that?" He went on to explain that because people already condemn crime strongly, there is no need to further incite them.

The last two work objectives in table 3.1 express the prevailing view about what American prosecutors want even though they seldom are sought by either the Japanese or the Americans. The first, "maximizing the punishment imposed on criminals," was considered important by only one in five Japanese respondents and "very important" by a trifling 1 percent. The second, "prosecuting and convicting as many cases as I can," proved even less popular. Indeed, it is by far the least important of all seventeen objectives. One cannot draw an accurate picture of prosecutor preferences by using assumptions and stereotypes from the prevailing accounts of what prosecutors want. Japanese prosecutors are not the princes of punishment their American counterparts are so often characterized and caricatured as being. The survey suggests that neither are the Americans.

The objective of this section on objectives has been to summarize the preferences held by prosecutors in Japan. Though the picture resembles a rough sketch more than a high-quality close-up, it is still an improvement over the assumptions that in the past have often substituted for data. Additional research must be done in order to portray prosecutor preferences more adequately. We still know little about this critical corner of legal culture.

Suspension of Prosecution and the Exercise of Discretion

The second core element of prosecutor culture consists of attitudes and beliefs about how prosecutors exercise discretion. In this section I examine how prosecutors think about their authority to suspend prosecution, one of their most important discretionary powers.[13] The argument develops in three parts. The story in part one reveals

---

13. As described in chapter 2, prosecutors can divert offenders from the criminal process even when there is sufficient evidence to convict at trial, no matter the severity of the offense (Code of Criminal Procedure, Article 248). This practice is known as suspension of prosecution (*kiso yūyo*). In many countries, including Austria, Finland, Germany, Ireland, Italy, Poland, Spain, Sri Lanka, Sweden, and Turkey, prosecutors do not have comparable discretion to withhold charges (Tak 1986:33). For insightful comparisons of prosecutorial discretion in sentencing, see Fionda (1995).

how prosecutors in Japan perceive the "risks" of discretion. Then I summarize the suspension of prosecution doctrine so that, in the last part, I can examine prosecutors' beliefs about how to exercise the discretion conferred by that doctrine.

"Prosecutors Mature by Being Deceived": A Homily about Risk

The most widely read essay ever written by a Japanese prosecutor is probably Itoh Shigeki's (1982) "A Prosecutor Gets Tricked" ("Damasareru Kenji"), a three-page discourse which introduces a book of essays by the same title. That book was followed five years later by a similar book of essays entitled *Mata Damasareru Kenji* (A Prosecutor Gets Tricked Again). The verb in the titles — *damasareru* — is what the Japanese call a "suffering passive." It connotes a range of related meanings: to be tricked, cheated, deceived, suckered, made a fool of. All imply that the prosecutor has been had.

In the lead essay, Itoh tells the tale of a burglary case he handled in 1949 at the Tokyo District Prosecutors Office. It was his first day on the job. The suspect, a middle-aged man, had just confessed to a burglary when a woman carrying an infant on her back papoose-style rushed into Itoh's office to reproach the man for his crime. "How could you do such a thing?" the woman bawled. "Aren't you ashamed for the baby?" From the way the suspect and woman interacted Itoh inferred, reasonably enough, that they were husband and wife and that the baby was their child, an impression further reinforced when the man tearfully swore he would not "cause you guys any more trouble." Itoh had been instructed that this kind of case calls for a suspended prosecution, so he obtained the approval of his superiors, warned the man not to slip up again, and released him without filing any criminal charges.

Two days later Itoh observed the same man entering the office of a veteran prosecutor — in handcuffs. The prosecutor informed Itoh that the man headed a gang of thieves who had committed over two hundred burglaries in the area, and that shortly after Itoh had released him he was arrested for a related crime. Perplexed by this sequence of events, Itoh telephoned the cop in charge, who told Itoh that for the second offense he had brought the thief to a different prosecutor because "a rookie just can't cut it in a case like this." Itoh also learned that the thief's wife and child were nothing of the kind. In fact, the woman was an acquaintance of the gang and had been paid to put on a performance designed to deceive Itoh into suspending prosecution.

Itoh concludes the story with a maxim that is widely repeated in prosecutor circles: "Prosecutors mature by being suckered and suckered again." To Itoh and, as we shall see, to most Japanese prosecutors, the main aim of suspending prosecution is to help reform offenders and reintegrate them into society. In so aiming, prosecutors are occasionally tricked by performances of the kind that bamboozled Itoh. Even then, however, prosecutors believe that some such tricksters return to society and, as Itoh puts it, "reform perfectly." More important, the reverse error — wrongly prosecuting a case that should not be charged — is considered much the graver mistake, so much so that even for a rookie prosecutor it is, in Itoh's words, "absolutely unforgivable."

Itoh's homily teaches two truths about prosecutor culture in Japan. First, it exemplifies the strong commitment that prosecutors have to learn from their mistakes so as not to repeat them. Prosecutors may "mature by being deceived," but since maturity is not a quality the inexperienced naturally possess, mistakes are to be anticipated and, if at all possible, avoided. One sees evidence of the procuracy's organized hunt for mistakes wherever one looks: in the ubiquitous guidelines for charge and sentence decisions; in the two or three levels of *kessai* consultations required for all major discretionary decisions; in the yearly after-the-fact audits of case dispositions; and, perhaps most strikingly, in the great lengths to which prosecutors go in order to avoid making, or being perceived to make, mistakes. Like elite bureaucrats in other Japanese ministries, prosecutors are judged on the basis of "the demerit principle" (Miyamoto 1994:122). Since mistakes generate criticism, undesirable job and case assignments, and other negative career repercussions, prosecutors are extraordinarily prudent (Tōjō 1968:62).

But not all mistakes are equally grave, and herein lies the second and more important lesson to be learned from "A Prosecutor Gets Tricked." Stated broadly, prosecutors confront two types of risk when deciding whether or not to charge a case: they may choose not to charge an offender who then reoffends (a *type I risk*), and they may charge someone who is subsequently found not to deserve criminal punishment (a *type II risk*). A prosecutor takes a type I risk when, as Itoh did, he decides not to charge an offender who then goes on to commit additional and avoidable harm. Conversely, a prosecutor takes a type II risk when he charges a suspect who does not deserve to be punished. The accused may deserve no criminal punishment either because there is reasonable doubt about whether he really committed an offense or because punishment will not achieve any legitimate jurisprudential purpose (such as rehabilitation or deterrence).

A second Itoh essay stands in counterpoint to the first and helps clarify the relationship between the two risks. This chapter, which concludes Itoh's 1982 book and may be the second most famous piece written by a prosecutor, is entitled "Prosecutors Do Not Let the Wicked Sleep." As the title suggests, the essay exhorts prosecutors to aggressively investigate and prosecute criminal behavior. Thus, while the first piece implores prosecutors to seek the reform of offenders through suspended prosecutions, even at the cost of being deceived, this piece entreats them to "cry together with victims" and to deal sternly with offenders. The policies advocated in the two essays, like the purposes of punishment more generally, may not be reconciled — or reconcilable — in particular cases. When it is impossible for prosecutors to pursue both aims simultaneously, they tend to favor the teachings of the first Itoh essay over the second. They prefer, in other words, to err on the side of less punishment rather than more.

All cultures are biased toward some risks and against others. Since no person or group can attend equally to all hazards, some order of priority must be established among them (Douglas 1986). The culture of Japanese prosecutors is biased toward type I risks of the kind Itoh took in the burglary case — suspending prosecution even when there is enough evidence to convict and punish an offender. American prosecutor culture is more inclined to take type II risks, pursuing conviction and punishment even when there are doubts about the probability of gaining conviction. Why the difference?

Consider the United States first. Though the label differs, American prosecutors also possess authority to suspend prosecution. They are reluctant to use it, however, in part because their political permeability leaves them vulnerable to public criticism if a released suspect reoffends. Chief prosecutors are elected, and the electorate often demands that offenders be punished harshly. The ghosts of Willie Horton and Richard Allen Davis (among a host of other release risks who failed) remind American prosecutors of the punitiveness of public opinion and of the price to be paid for disregarding it. In short, and in general, the cost of a reoffense — a type I failure — figures more prominently in prosecutor calculus in the United States than in Japan. Prosecutors in Japan incur few costs when a type I risk fails, for crime is less a public problem there, and public criticism of prosecutors for not being "punitive enough" is less commonly heard.[14]

In contrast, the cost of an acquittal — a type II failure — weighs more heavily in the calculus of Japanese prosecutors, for they are harshly criticized — by the public and by the organization — for acquittals. Indeed, even partial acquittals in minor theft or assault cases generate media headlines and public fury about the procuracy's "sloppy investigations," "reckless practices," and "fascist intentions" (Hatano 1994b). This criticism of type II mistakes helps maintain Japan's "high-precision" criminal justice system, in which few criminal indictments end in acquittal. As chapter 7 describes, critics allege that Japanese prosecutors are "cherry-picking airtight cases." To be sure, in choosing to charge only cases that are certain to end in conviction, prosecutors do their utmost to avoid type II mistakes. However, if prosecutors are "cherry-picking" cases it is partly because Japanese people prefer cherries to lemons. Significantly, when the public seems willing to accept the risk of an acquittal — in corruption cases involving Diet politicians — the postwar acquittal rate is 45 percent (Nomura 1994:55). Thus, prosecutors' preference for type I risks grows out of Japan's general legal culture, just as prosecutor culture in the United States rests on broader cultural foundations.

Suspension of Prosecution

The authority to suspend prosecution is widely regarded, by prosecutors and outsiders alike, as one of the most important features of Japanese criminal justice. Judged by how much prosecutors talk about it and how much suspects are affected by it, suspension of prosecution may be the procuracy's most significant practice.

Japanese writers commonly claim suspension of prosecution is a uniquely Japanese practice that harmonizes with other qualities of Japanese culture (Aoyagi 1986:194). The first half of this claim is wrong. American prosecutors possess similar discretion to divert offenders from the criminal process even in cases where there is

---

14. One notable exception occurred in the Urawa case of 1948, when a Diet judiciary committee alleged that excessively lenient practices in the procuracy and judiciary "reflected the remnants of 'feudal' attitudes unfit for a democracy." Prosecutors and judges resisted this intrusion on their autonomy, and prevailed. The Diet investigation ended, and there have been few repetitions (Haley 1998:81, 105). Beginning the late 1990s, however, politicans and the public began to push for increased punishment for a variety of offenses, including drunk-driving, negligent homicide, and crimes committed by juveniles. The pursuit of stricter punishments was in large part motivated by grievances from victims and their families and the attendant media publicity (*Yomiuri Shimbun* 12/2/00).

enough evidence to convict. Prosecutors in many other countries — Denmark, France, Great Britain, Holland, Norway, and South Korea, just to name a few — do too (Tak 1986:33). In this respect there is nothing uniquely Japanese about the power to suspend prosecution. However, the practice does fit well with other features of Japanese culture, especially the propensity for wrongdoers to confess (Wagatsuma and Rosett 1986) and the disposition to believe that people are "perfectible" through social engineering (R. Smith 1983).

Though the doctrine was not codified in law until 1922, prosecutions have been suspended in Japan since the 1880s (Foote 1992a:347). In the early years, however, prosecutors employed the practice primarily to mitigate prison overcrowding and reduce demands on an overburdened national budget. By the early 1900s the formal justification had shifted to stress reforming offenders and ensuring their reintegration into the community (Aoyagi 1986:194). It continues to be justified in rehabilitative terms today (Inagawa 1995). In practice, too, one important factor influencing this decision is the likelihood of rehabilitation (Mitsui 1974a).

In recent years prosecutors have disposed of between 30 and 40 percent of their caseloads by suspending prosecution. For a variety of reasons, this figure has declined since the prewar years, when more than half of all criminal cases were so disposed (Aoyagi 1986:195), but the still high percentage reflects how significant the practice remains. Any account of prosecutor culture must consider prosecutor beliefs and attitudes about it. Unfortunately, aside from Mitsui Makoto's unduly neglected research in the 1970s, no one has tried to measure the factors that motivate prosecutors to suspend prosecution. Part 3 of my survey was designed to do that. It is a means of exploring another important but neglected portion of Japan's prosecutor culture.

Part 3 of the survey had two sections. Section 1 asked prosecutors to indicate how strongly they agree or disagree with ten statements about suspension of prosecution. The answer scale ranged from (5) "strongly agree" to (1) "strongly disagree," with the midpoint meaning that respondents "cannot say either way." Section 2 asked prosecutors to indicate the importance of each of eighteen factors in determining whether or not to suspend prosecution "when you are investigating a case and think that suspending prosecution is a possible disposition for the case." This section had three possible answers: (3) "an important factor"; (2) "depending on the case, sometimes important and sometimes not"; and (1) "not an important factor."

The original draft of the survey included a detailed hypothetical case similar to those used by W. Boyd Littrell (1979) in his study of New Jersey prosecutors. The hypothetical would have enabled me to analyze prosecutor responses to the same set of case facts. Unfortunately, prosecutors would not permit the questionnaire to be administered in a form that included the hypothetical. They feared (they said) two deleterious consequences: that the published results would encourage the calculators to take as many bites from the apple of leniency as the survey evidence seems to allow (a deterrence concern), and that the results would be interpreted as an official statement of procuracy policy which might give defense lawyers a new resource for arguing that indictments were unfair. One wonders, of course, whether prosecutors' opposition also stemmed from the desire to keep their practices insulated from external scrutiny and criticism. Whatever the reasons, the data were generated by a question that left room for prosecutors to imagine differently the particular case circumstances shaping their suspension of prosecution decisions.

Prosecutors regard this decision as an important, difficult, and rewarding part of their job. Almost all respondents (98 percent) agreed or strongly agreed that "the decision whether or not to suspend prosecution is one of the most important judgments a prosecutor makes." Only one disagreed. Almost three-quarters of prosecutors believed the suspension of prosecution decision is "difficult" to make, and nearly three in five said such judgments are "one of the most rewarding, meaningful parts of my job." Indeed, most prosecutors who have written memoirs give primacy of place to decisions to suspend prosecution and to the effects of such decisions on themselves and on offenders (Aoyagi 1986; Bessho 1983; Itoh 1982; Kawai 1979; Satō 1993; Yasuhara 1985).

The aim of the suspension of prosecution system is, as Itoh Shigeki (1987:188) notes, "to prevent offenders from reoffending by rehabilitating and reintegrating them into society without stamping them with a branding iron." For nearly ninety years this aim has been the official justification for the practice, and the vast majority of prosecutors believe it often realizes this aim. In fact, more than four out of five prosecutors agreed or strongly agreed that "in some cases suspending prosecution better helps to rehabilitate and reintegrate offenders than does prosecution."

At the same time, however, suspension of prosecution is also applied for less legitimate reasons. Prosecutors under pressure to dispose of cases efficiently sometimes take a procedural shortcut, suspending prosecution even in cases where there is insufficient evidence to convict. As explained in chapter 2, these shortcuts violate office policy, which allows prosecutors to suspend charges only when there is sufficient evidence to convict. Prosecutors suspend charges in order to curry police favor, but survey and interview results suggest they seldom do so out of efficiency considerations. Prosecutors were almost evenly divided about whether "compared to prosecuting a case, suspending prosecution saves time and effort." Nearly half said it depends on the case (46 percent) and the remaining half was about equally split between those who agreed (30 percent) and those who disagreed (23 percent). One prosecutor told me that "suspending prosecution does save time when the choice [to suspend or not] is clear, but in many cases the choice is hard. Then I have to acquire a great deal of information in order to make a good judgment and convince my superiors of my decision. That takes time." Only 6 percent of prosecutors agreed that "I sometimes suspend prosecution in order to save my time and effort for other cases," whereas about four in five said they do not. Prosecutors explain that they cannot suspend charges merely to conserve resources because they must justify their decisions in writing and, more important, in *kessai* consultations with as many as three senior prosecutors. Whether or not to suspend prosecution is a primary topic in such consultations, with almost four in five prosecutors saying that "at *kessai* I frequently discuss [the issue]."

Finally, the survey asked two questions about the conditions imposed on offenders whose prosecutions are suspended. Nearly four in five respondents said that before suspending prosecution they usually make the offender promise to do some things after the case is suspended, such as "maintain good conduct" or "make reparations" (*jidan*) to the victim. In many of the interrogations and interviews I observed, prosecutors exhorted suspects to reform and make reparations, and exacted promises accordingly. However, prosecutors rarely obtain information about an offender's behavior following the suspension of prosecution decision. Hence, they are largely unable to monitor compliance with the pre-disposition promises. Of course, since suspended prosecutions are recorded by the organization, if a forgiven offender re-offends, the prosecutor in charge of the case often learns of the earlier disposition.

Prosecutor Beliefs about Exercising Discretion

Engraved in stone on the Department of Justice building in Washington, D.C., is the adage "Where law ends tyranny begins." In truth, where law ends discretion begins, and how it is exercised means either reasonableness or caprice, justice or injustice (Davis 1969:3). In Japan, the discretion to suspend prosecution is the most momentous power prosecutors wield. This section describes prosecutors' beliefs about the factors that influence this critical discretionary choice.

Charging decisions are complex. Table 3.2 shows that prosecutors believe a wide range of factors influences their suspension of prosecution decisions. In fact, the most striking feature of this table is how few conditions are considered unimportant. Of the eighteen factors listed, only the last three were deemed unimportant by a quarter or more of the prosecutors, while twelve of the eighteen were considered important by at least 25 percent.

But some factors are clearly more important than others. The first seven factors can be considered primary, for two reasons. First, from 70 to 90 percent of all respondents regarded these factors as important, a range far higher than the corresponding percentages for the other eleven factors. Indeed, one sees a clear break in level of importance between the seventh and eighth factors ("prior record," at 70 percent, is considered important by 50 percent more prosecutors than "future effects of prosecution on suspect," at 47 percent). In addition, almost no one regarded the primary factors as unimportant. In fact, for six of the seven primary factors, not even one prosecutor answered "unimportant," while for the seventh ("whether suspect repents") only one prosecutor so answered. For these reasons, the following analysis focuses on the primary factors.

Extant accounts of criminal justice in Japan stress that several distinctively "Japanese" considerations influence prosecutor decisions, yet the first two primary factors, three of the first four, and four of the seven are case characteristics considered important in most criminal justice systems in the world, including the United States. These are, in other words, universal primary factors. For example, American prosecutors' decisions are greatly influenced by "seriousness of the offense" and "prior record" (Gottfredson and Gottfredson 1988:132). These considerations correspond to "damage done by the offense" and "prior record" (ranks 1 and 7 in table 3.2). Likewise, the other "universal primary factor" — suspect's motive — is a key index of the suspect's mental state at the time of the offense, and therefore is an important indicator of culpability, in the United States no less than Japan. In fact, research shows that when judging responsibility and punishment for non-serious wrongs, the offender's state of mind influences Americans more than Japanese, but that when the offense is serious, people in the two countries make similar use of information about the offender's mental state (Hamil-

TABLE 3.2 Prosecutor beliefs about factors influencing suspension of prosecution decisions

Rank	Factor	Percentages[a]		
1	Damage done by the offense	90	10	0
2	Likelihood of reoffending	90	10	0
3	Whether suspect repents	80	20	0
4	Suspect's motive	76	24	0
5	Whether suspect compensates victim	76	24	0
6	Victim's feelings about punishment	71	29	0
7	Prior record	70	30	0
8	Future effects of prosecution on suspect	47	51	2
9	Legally prescribed punishment	45	49	6
10	Suspect's prior relationship with victim	34	65	1
11	Suspect's age	32	65	3
12	Suspect's demeanor during interrogation	29	55	16
13	Suspect's family ties	24	66	10
14	Public opinion	20	72	8
15	Suspect's social status	19	73	8
16	Suspect's cooperativeness with police and prosecutors	10	51	39
17	Suspect's marital status	3	69	28
18	Police opinion	3	44	54

Source: Author's survey of 235 Japanese prosecutors (1994–1995).
[a]The three figures in this column reflect, respectively, the percentage of prosecutors who regarded the factor as "important," "sometimes important and sometimes not," and "not important." For example, "damage done by the offense" was considered important by 90 percent of prosecutors, sometimes important by 10 percent, and unimportant by no one. The percentages have been rounded to the nearest whole number.

ton and Sanders 1992:183). Elsewhere in my survey, 93 percent of Japanese prosecutors agreed or strongly agreed that "the most important single consideration in determining the sentence to impose should be the nature and gravity of the offense," and 78 percent said that "most people charged with serious crimes should be punished whether or not the punishment benefits the criminal" (Appendix, part 4:9,1).

In sum, most of the primary factors influencing suspension of prosecution decisions in Japan — and the most important factors at that — are not uniquely Japanese but are relevant considerations in discretionary prosecution systems around the world. Prosecutors in Japan strongly believe that punishment is an appropriate response for many criminal offenders.

At the same time, the belief in punishment coexists with a strong commitment to norms that do appear to be distinctively Japanese. For instance, Japan's system of criminal justice is said to emphasize "the importance of individualized determinations based on careful consideration of the individual's personal circumstances" (Foote 1992a:341). Consistent with this claim, 96 percent of Japanese prosecutors believe "it is important to individualize treatment of each suspect" (Appendix, part 4:30). Similarly, 80 percent of prosecutors regard the suspect's repentance, or lack thereof, as important. Offenders often make restitution (*jidan* or *higai benshō*) to victims in order to repair harms and demonstrate the sincerity of their remorse. About 76 percent of prosecutors believe restitution has an important influence on suspension of prosecution decisions. Finally, "the victim's feelings about punishment" are deemed important by 71 percent of prosecutors.[15] The question, then, is not whether repentance, confession, and absolution are important to Japanese prosecutors, for clearly they are, but whether in the service of rehabilitation and reintegration Japanese prosecutors are more influenced by these norms than their American counterparts. They are.

Repentance and Rehabilitation in Japan and the United States

That Japanese prosecutors remain committed to a rehabilitative ideal is less remarkable than the extent to which American prosecutors have forsworn it. In the words of one California prosecutor (a "politically correct" liberal Democrat, active in the gay and lesbian rights movement, and living in Berkeley, widely considered one of the nation's most progressive cities), "It is not the prosecutor's job to help suspects." Prior to trial, of course, American prosecutors have little contact with suspects and therefore few opportunities to assess their attitudes. The Berkeley prosecutor said increased contact with suspects might be "fun" and probably would help her "understand the streets better," but she still does not desire it. "I don't want to be swayed by emotional arguments," she said. "Everyone looks pathetic and sympathetic behind bars [after arrest]. My job is to give offenders the punishment they deserve, and hearing their sad stories just gets in the way."

Another California prosecutor, a twenty-year veteran and the boss of an urban branch office, declared that "since the legislature is out of the business of rehabilitation, we should be too. Our role is not to rehabilitate. The even hand of justice must not be swayed by concerns for the individual circumstances of particular cases. . . . To be professional, we must avoid all favoritism and inconsistency." Ironically, this prosecutor invoked the fear of "inconsistency" as a reason for forsaking rehabilitative concerns even though American prosecutors make far less consistent decisions than the Japanese prosecutors who have not forsworn rehabilitation. This is the theme of chapter 5.

The same prosecutor further explained that disregard for the rehabilitation of offenders is official policy. Whenever a criminal suspect is booked by the police but not charged by a prosecutor, the prosecutor must report the "reject reasons" to the Department of Justice. There are eleven categories of T-reasons (as they are known in the office), each with two to twelve subcategories. They are printed and distributed to all prosecutors. The main reject categories are as follows:

T1 — Lack of Corpus (insufficient evidence to prove crime occurred, etc.)
T2 — Lack of Sufficient Evidence (witness not credible, etc.)
T3 — Inadmissible Search and Seizure (questionable probable cause for arrest, etc.)
T4 — Victim Unavailable/Declines to Testify (victim requests no prosecution, etc.)

---

15. Prosecutors regard the victim's attitude as a slightly stronger influence on the charging decision than the suspect's attitude, though whether or not restitution has been made appears to be more important than either (Appendix, part 4:22–24).

T5 — Witness Unavailable/Declines to Testify (witness privilege, etc.)
T6 — Combined with Other Counts/Cases (more/less severe charge filed)
T7 — Interest of Justice (nature of offense, relationship of the parties, etc.)
T8 — Other (other due process or jurisdictional considerations, etc.)
T9 — Prosecutor Prefiling Deferral (district/city attorney hearing, etc.)
U2 — Referred to Out-of-State Jurisdiction (U.S. Attorney General, etc.)
U3 — Deferred for Revocation of Parole/Probation

Most of these reject reasons concern questions of evidence or point to prosecution alternatives other than charging the count police booked. The T7 category — "Interest of Justice" — may seem to reflect rehabilitation as a legitimate reason for not filing criminal charges. Wrong. Nowhere among T7's dozen subcategories is the notion that withholding charges (the American analogue to suspended prosecution) can promote rehabilitation and thus serve justice. Likewise, the American Bar Association "Standards Relating to the Prosecution Function" begin from the premise that prosecutors should charge if there is enough evidence to convict. The Standards list factors a prosecutor may properly consider in determining whether or not to charge, but conspicuously absent from the list is the attitude of the offender. At the federal level, too, Department of Justice policy instructs prosecutors to charge all "readily provable" offenses, regardless of the effect on the offender's rehabilitation (Katzmann 1991:128). In practice and policy, rehabilitation is as anathema to American prosecutors as campaign finance reform is to American politicians.

Of course, American offenders are less inclined to display remorse — a probable prerequisite to rehabilitation — than are offenders in Japan. As another California prosecutor told me, even if office policy allowed her to take offenders' attitudes into account, it would make little difference anyway because they rarely repent. Instead, she explained, American suspects and offenders are more inclined to shout obscenities at prosecutors and judges or wear shorts, caps, and even "fuck the police" T-shirts to court. "These people don't *want* to be rehabilitated," she exclaimed. Thirty minutes of observing courtrooms in Japan and the United States is enough time to notice the radical differences in defendant demeanor between the two countries. Japanese defendants are almost unfailingly polite, deferent, and respectful, while American defendants routinely display a "defiant individualism that confronts authority and power with few indications of deference, fear, or remorse" (Sanchez-Jankowski 1991:26). Through friends and relatives, the defiant attitude even gets physically inscribed on courtroom walls and chairs. My own quick count in a California courtroom found that one preferred graffito fits in the "fuck the prosecutor" genre.[16]

16. David Heilbroner (1990:14) recounts a case which vividly illustrates the propensity of American offenders to deny wrongdoing and defy authority, even when literally caught in the act. In Manhattan, where Heilbroner worked as an assistant district attorney, kids often "slip a folded piece of paper into the [subway] token slot so the token won't go into the token box. After a passenger loses a token and walks away, the kids come back, suck it out of the slot, and sell it for a buck on the street." One token booth clerk became so frustrated with these "stuff 'n' suckers" that she smeared Krazy Glue on the token slot. The next person to try it found his lips bonded to the turnstile. The first police officer on the scene called a medical technician, who injected a saline solution between the turnstile metal and the perpetrator's lips. The saline dissolved the glue and the token-sucker was arrested. His first words to the arresting officer? "Listen man, I wasn't sucking tokens."

Minnesota prosecutors shared these attitudes about the irrelevance of remorse and repentance. One said that in dealing with juveniles contrition and a willingness to get treatment are important considerations but that he has "a whole different attitude with adults," which he summarized as "Tough shit! You should have been remorseful before committing the crime." When I pointed out that, actually, an offender could be remorseful only about past wrongdoing, the prosecutor elaborated. "I am hard-core with adults — tough but fair. I am into fairness, not excuses. You couldn't be that remorseful if you did it." One of his colleagues seemed to agree. "In intentional crimes," this former public defender declared, "no contrition is possible. In this job you have to be cynical of human nature because everyone acts out of self-interest. Many suspects believe manufacturing remorse will get them something. I seldom see real contrition."

Thus, American prosecutors resist allowing evidence of remorse to influence charge decisions. Indeed, they seem to resist even *seeing* evidence of remorse. But American prosecutors do use an offender's "bad attitude" to justify extra severe treatment. Prosecutors in some California offices call such considerations "asshole enhancements." In one case a young man was arrested for possessing a single rock of crack cocaine. The prosecutor raised her original plea bargain offer (by two years) and bail request (doubled) because the offender cursed at his public defender, was unruly during the preliminary hearing, and generally behaved "like a jerk" during the pretrial period. In short, while a suspect's attitude causes American prosecutors to increase but not mitigate punishment, in Japan it does both.

I routinely observed prosecutors in Kobe take suspects' attitude into account when deciding whether to suspend prosecution. In many instances they were not content simply to hear formulaic expressions of remorse, but probed suspects at length to discern the depth, direction, and sincerity of contrition. They must have judged wrongly on many occasions, but as Itoh's homily about risk suggests, the fear of misjudging does little to dissuade them from earnestly seeking to know how offenders really feel about their crimes. As in Itoh's story, some offenders act, pretending to feel remorse when they do not. This possibility leaves few prosecutors as cynical about offenders or as skeptical about rehabilitation as their American counterparts are. For prosecutors in Japan, "correction" is pursued no less by them than by corrections officials.

The converse is also true: a suspect's defiant, noncompliant, or unrepentant attitude prompts prosecutors in Japan to be more punitive, at least in certain cases (see factor 16). Japanese prosecutors have their own version of the American "asshole enhancement," albeit less colorfully captured as a "denial tariff" or *hininryō*. When a suspect insists on innocence despite evidence to the contrary, prosecutors may charge cases they otherwise would not — or, more commonly, push for a more severe sentence at trial. One prosecutor imposed the first type of "denial tariff" on a middle-aged British man arrested for selling hashish. I translated during the interrogations. In the early stages the prosecutor wanted to suspend prosecution because the amount of hashish was small, the suspect had no prior record, and prosecution would have disrupted the Japanese family into which the suspect had married. In order to get prosecution suspended the suspect had only to acknowledge his wrong and promise not to possess, use, or sell illegal drugs anymore. The suspect elected not to confess, despite the prosecutor's repeated entreaties that repentance would be in his own best interests. Over several days of interrogation the prosecutor's attitude evolved from the original desire to forgive the suspect in order to encourage reform, into the conviction that charging and imprisoning the suspect was necessary to "teach him a lesson." The prosecutor charged. Such responses to non-remorse are routine. Indeed, four in five prosecutors recognize the denial tariff by agreeing that lack of remorse "influences the sentence we recommend" (part 4:88).

There is one last notable fact about how prosecutors exercise the discretion to charge: they give careful consideration to the victim's injuries, feelings, and prior relationship with the offender. This regard for the victim sets the Japanese way of justice apart. Prosecutors believe it is important, where possible, to restore victims who have been harmed by crime, and they expect offenders to show concrete evidence of repentance by financially contributing to that restoration (factor 5). These norms reflect deep assumptions: that crime harms more than just a state interest and that criminal justice should promote healing. The latter premise is controversial, at least in the United States, but it is a guiding principle for Japan's procuracy. As one prosecutor put it, "If it doesn't hurt the offender, why not help the victim?"[17]

I have shown that prosecutors in Japan often aim to repair relations between victims and offenders, and that this purpose distinguishes their work objectives from prosecutors in the United States. Of course, relations can be repaired only when there was a relationship in the first place. Almost all Japanese prosecutors regard "prior relationship" as an important influence in at least some cases (factor 10). It is important because prosecutors, like judges deciding divorce and labor relations disputes, believe "community" should be confirmed (Haley 1998:123).[18]

Finally, in deciding whether to charge, Japan's prosecutors consider the victim's feelings about punishment (factor 6). Indeed, not a single prosecutor deemed this factor unimportant. Victims are routinely asked what they think should happen to their offender, and the difference between a demand for severe punishment and a request for leniency can spell the difference between a criminal charge and a suspended prosecution. Since defense lawyers know this, they urge their clients to compensate the victim in exchange for an agreement to ask the prosecutor to "go easier" on the suspect. Many Japanese are dismayed by what they see as an American indifference to victims. Once, in open court, a judge asked me if I had seen the Ameri-

17. Restitution is occasionally coerced from offenders, and offenders with money can sometimes "buy" more leniency than offenders without. These and other rejoinders to the prosecutor's rhetorical question are explored in chapter 6. Whether prosecutors *should* concern themselves with victims' attitudes and desires is a contested issue. Some scholars and victims' rights advocates say of course (Umbreit 1998). Others disagree, arguing that the effort to reconcile victims and offenders harms victims by denying them the vindication of a public finding of the offender's guilt, and hurts offenders by relying on arbitrary criteria, eliminating procedural protections, and allowing the victim to exploit public authority for private gain (Weisberg 1995).

18. For example, employers in Japan "have not been permitted to discharge employees for bad attitude, poor performance, and even theft in cases where the employee shows remorse, offers to make reparation, accepts the company's authority, and, in the view of the judges, is likely to avoid such behavior in the future" (Haley 1998:137). The judicial concern to "confirm community" can also be seen in family, landlord-tenant, and contract law.

can movie *The Accused* on television the previous evening (I had). In the film the character played by Jodie Foster is raped and the prosecutor disposes of the case without consulting her. While waiting for a witness to enter his courtroom, the Japanese judge asked me how often such disregard for victims occurs in the United States. I mumbled something incoherent, and an hour or so later had lunch with the judge to discuss the issue.

The truth is, American police, prosecutors, and judges often take victims' wishes into account when deciding how to dispose of cases (Vera 1981; Stanko 1981; Zeisel 1982; Kerstetter 1990; Frohmann 1992). Reports from Germany and France suggest many European prosecutors do likewise (Blankenburg et al. 1990). But, at least compared to the American prosecutors offices I have observed in California, Minnesota, and Hawaii, Japan's prosecutors are uncommonly likely to do so. The victim's desire, and the offender's effort (if not success) at "making the victim whole" are often taken into account. Often, not always. Chapter 6 explains how prosecutors attempt to "correct" victims' desires when they do not suit case processing "needs." Though this occurs most commonly in sex crimes, in recent years several traffic crime cases have drawn public attention when prosecutors failed to inform victims that the offenders would not be criminally charged (Morita 1994; *Asahi Shimbun* 1/25/99). Nationwide, all offices had norms requiring prosecutors to consult victims *before* a charge decision is made, but only about three-quarters of offices had standard operating procedures for informing victims after the fact. The outcry following the traffic cases prompted the Justice Ministry to implement notification policies in the remaining offices and to create new positions in urban offices for responding to victims' inquiries.

Conclusion

There are striking but unappreciated similarities in the considerations that influence charge decisions in Japan and the United States. Several primary factors are the same in both countries, especially the seriousness of the offense and the likelihood of re-offending. Likewise, the inclinations to be more severe toward defiant offenders and to consider the victim's attitude and relationship to the offender are relevant case characteristics in both countries, albeit in varying degrees. However, one big difference sharply distinguishes American and Japanese charge decisions: Americans prosecutors are deeply distrustful — even cynical — of virtually all displays of remorse, while Japanese prosecutors try hard to elicit contrition and believe that genuine repentance leads to reform. The Japanese penchant should not be overstated, of course, for prosecutors do — and must — scrutinize confessions for sincerity. As seen in Itoh Shigeki's homily, many prosecutors learn the hard way that offenders can act insincerely in the effort to obtain lenient treatment. Still, prosecutors in Japan believe one of their chief duties is to discern which offenders are really repentant and which are not, and they are empowered to do so by a number of work contexts: the long pre-charge investigation period; the legal levers for acquiring information; the nonadversarial nature of the criminal process; and the propensity of offenders to acknowledge wrongdoing. Thus, there is a close fit between the cultural imperatives that animate prosecutors and the structural realities that make possible their attainment.

The other nucleus of prosecutor culture — work objectives — also varies markedly between Japan and the United States. Discovering the truth, invoking remorse, rehabilitating offenders, treating likes alike, and repairing relations between offenders and victims appear more primary to prosecutors in Japan than in America. Conversely, American prosecutors seem more inclined to stress "crime control" objectives such as protecting the public and giving offenders their just deserts. The low priority American prosecutors give to rehabilitation is especially interesting when it is juxtaposed with the reverence they express for respecting suspects' rights. Their respect for due process may reflect the fact that American judges are more likely than Japanese courts to exclude evidence gained in violation of legal entitlements (Ramseyer and Nakazato 1999:168). In a sense, American prosecutors care about the rights of suspects because they have to: they cannot convict otherwise. But to Japanese prosecutors it is an odd coupling of objectives — rights matter, but rehabilitation does not. It seems American prosecutors, like American police, conceive their roles more narrowly than their counterparts in Japan, while Japanese prosecutors, in seeking to rehabilitate offenders and repair relationships between offenders and victims, penetrate the parties and the community in ways deemed inappropriate or unnecessary in the United States (Bayley 1991:80).[19] One condition enabling this penetration is the permeability of the boundary between public authorities and private citizens that has long characterized Japanese society (Garon 1997).

I have not addressed many interesting questions about prosecutor culture, questions that deserve more attention than scholars have given them heretofore. Where, for example, does prosecutor culture come from, and how can one explain the emergence of cultural norms such as the need to "discover the truth," the importance of an offender's attitude, or the imperative to treat like cases alike? How does the "internal culture" of prosecutors relate to the broader "external cultures" of Japanese society? Are there identifiable subcultures within Japan's procuracy or criminal court communities? What are the strengths and weaknesses of Japan's prosecutor culture? Are criminal trials in Japan as compelling a cultural form as in the United States, where great moral, social, and political dramas are acted out on the trial stage? Or is Japanese culture so little beset by conflicting social values — freedom vs. order, group allegiance vs. individual autonomy, equality of opportunity vs. equality of outcome — that trials are a less revealing symbolic venue than they are in America?

One final question, concerning the causal efficacy of prosecutor culture, cannot go unaddressed. Do prosecutors' stated commitments to "discover the truth about cases," "invoke remorse in offenders," and "treat likes alike" actually influence how they dispose of cases and treat offenders? The sociologist Paul Lazarsfeld advised that "if you want to know why people do something, ask them!" Though the

---

19. This does not mean the American prosecutor plays a narrow role. Indeed, in plea-bargaining, the routine dispositive device in American criminal procedure, tremendous power is concentrated in the prosecutor's hands because she simultaneously functions as advocate seeking conviction, jury finding the facts, and judge imposing sentence (Langbein 1978). For Japanese prosecutors, however, one must add to these roles a helping function which is in some respects analogous to the role played by social workers or physicians.

research for this chapter has followed that suggestion, other research has reached the decidedly non-Lazarsfeldian conclusion that the impact of prosecutor attitudes on prosecutor behavior "is marginal at best, nil for the most part." This conclusion led the trio who conducted the research to move beyond "the tip of the proverbial iceberg" — beliefs and attitudes — to explore the iceberg's "structure and contours" (Nardulli et al. 1988:360). The remaining chapters of this book explore the iceberg's base — the structure and contours of Japan's procuracy — and the content of the decisions prosecutors generate. In the meantime, however, it must be said that prosecutor culture influences the Japanese way of justice by shaping how cases get processed and suspects are treated.

The difference that culture makes may at times seem small in comparison to structural influences (such as the absence of juries), and parts of prosecutor culture surely arise from structures that create and maintain them (as when prosecutors' orientations to risk reflect political realities in the wider society). Nevertheless, prosecutors' assumptions, attitudes, and emotions do affect the content of criminal justice. The aim to elicit remorse, for example, motivates prosecutors to pursue not merely a confession but the right kind of confession. Obtaining it can mean the difference between a suspended prosecution and a criminal conviction. Similarly, the imperative to treat like cases alike means, among other things, that frontline charge decisions must be reviewed and approved by two or more prosecutor superiors, so as to ensure that justice not only aspires to but achieves a high level of consistency. Even when it seems impossible to demonstrate the causal efficacy of prosecutors' culture, it is clear that their beliefs, attitudes, and values justify important practices. The *kessai* system of consultation and review, for example, figures prominently in all the remaining chapters. It rests on a foundation of cultural presumptions: that hierarchy works, that organization matters, and that decisions should, where possible, be made collectively. In short, prosecutor culture matters as both cause and justification. It is created and continuously re-created, and it counts.

4

The Organization
of Prosecution

The rationalization and bureaucratization of the penal process has undoubtedly been the most important development to have taken place in
penality in the nineteenth and twentieth centuries.

David Garland, *Punishment and Modern Society*

Organization matters.

James W. Wilson, *Bureaucracy*

B ecause prosecutors make decisions within the scope of an organization, one
should study their decision-making within that context. In Japan, prosecution
has three key organizational features: a national and hierarchical structure; a core
task defined as "uncovering and constructing the truth"; and a division of roles
among operators, managers, and executives. Operators perform the procuracy's core
task, the construction of truth through the composition of dossiers. Managers coordinate and control operators. This is a critical function because an organization is,
at root, a system of consciously coordinated activities. Executives secure autonomy
and resources for the organization so that operators and managers can perform their
roles effectively. On the surface, the organizations of prosecution in Japan and in
America may look much alike: they are bureaucratic; they distinguish between operator, manager, and executive roles; they function as criminal justice gatekeepers;
they promote workers on the basis of some combination of merit and seniority; and
they confront analogous problems of compliance, resources, and autonomy. However, these surface similarities must not obscure deep differences in how core tasks
are defined, mission is cultivated, operators are controlled, and autonomy is gained.
In the end, the procuracy's organizational features shape Japanese criminal justice
by channeling prosecutor practice in specific ways.

Structure

The United States has some three thousand discrete prosecutors offices, each with its
own chief, structure, policy, and practice (Flemming et al. 1992:24). Japan has one:

a national, centralized, hierarchical, career procuracy whose structure corresponds to that of the judiciary.

Formally the procuracy is just one organ among many in the Ministry of Justice, but in reality prosecutors function as the ministry's head, directing almost all of its principal activities. The titular boss of the ministry is the Minister of Justice, a cabinet member who, with few exceptions, is an elected politician. As in Japan's other ministries, however, the minister does not run the department whose portfolio he holds, and the parliamentary vice minister, always an elected official and formally this agency's number two person, wields even less power. Instead, the minister reigns while the prosecutors rule. In fact, prosecutors rule so thoroughly that many cannot even recall their current boss's name. Most dismiss the minister as "utterly irrelevant," except perhaps in corruption cases involving high-level politicians. Like the postwar Emperor, the minister mainly exercises symbolic authority.

Government charts and other expressions of "official reality" do not reveal that prosecutors monopolize all key posts in the Ministry of Justice. In other elite ministries the administrative vice minister is the top career official, but not here. Instead, he — the top positions have always been held by men — is "only No. 5" in the hierarchy, below the Prosecutor General, the Superintending Prosecutors of Tokyo and Osaka, and the Deputy Prosecutor General (Omiya 1994:116). These top five posts are always filled by prosecutors, as are the leadership positions in the Secretariat and the Criminal Affairs Bureau, the ministry's two most important organs. Elsewhere in the ministry, prosecutors occupy almost all positions of section chief or higher. In 1993, for example, they held twenty-nine of the top thirty-two positions in the Criminal Affairs Bureau, widely recognized as the ministry's most powerful and prestigious bureau. In short, prosecutors run the Ministry of Justice (Nomura 1994:29).

The Supreme Public Prosecutors Office stands at the apex of the procuracy proper, above the 8 High, 50 District, and 453 Local Offices. The eight High Offices form a status hierarchy that all prosecutors recognize. At the top stands Tokyo, followed by Osaka, Nagoya, Hiroshima, Fukuoka, Sendai, Sapporo, and Takamatsu. Tokyo, with approximately forty-five prosecutors, is the largest High Office; the other seven have from four to thirteen prosecutors each.

The fifty District Offices are located in the forty-seven seats of prefectural government and in three additional cities on the northern island of Hokkaido. The District Offices are responsible for investigating, charging, and trying all cases in the first instance except those reserved by law for Summary Courts (offenses punishable by fine or other light punishment), Family Courts (offenses harmful to the welfare of juveniles), and High Courts (crimes of insurrection). Of the fifty District Offices, thirty-seven lack specialized divisions and are staffed by only five or six prosecutors (*kenji*) and assistant prosecutors (*fuku kenji*). The other thirteen offices have specialized divisions, so that one prosecutor investigates and charges a case and another tries it in court. The fifty District Offices have 203 branches geographically located to handle cases that cannot be processed efficiently in the headquarters. Only the Tokyo, Osaka, and Nagoya District Offices have Special Investigation Divisions, home to the "elite troops" charged with prosecuting Japan's highest-profile crimes.

At the bottom of the hierarchy are 453 Local Prosecutors Offices, staffed exclusively by assistant prosecutors, not prosecutors who have passed the bar. These Local Offices correspond to Summary Courts, which by law cannot impose punishments greater than three years' imprisonment. Thus, local prosecutors charge only relatively minor offenses such as habitual gambling, theft, and buying or selling stolen property. More serious cases are transferred to a District Office or one of its branches.

These office levels — supreme, high, district, and local — are tied together, both in theory and in reality, by "the principle of prosecutor unity," one of the most important of all facts about the organization of prosecution in Japan. This precept holds that "the procuracy is a national, united, hierarchical structure in which superiors command and subordinates obey and all prosecutors form one body" (Nomura 1978a:126).

The principle of prosecutor unity is rooted in provisions of the Public Prosecutors Office Law that give the various office heads, and all prosecutor managers, authority to direct their subordinates in any work-related area, whether investigation, indictment, or trial. While the Minister of Justice (not a prosecutor) is the formal head of the procuracy, the same law restricts, in theory at least, his ability to control prosecutors by conferring power to direct only the Prosecutor General in respect to "particular cases." However, since the principle of prosecutor unity also gives the Prosecutor General power to direct all prosecutors in all matters, whether general or specific, it is legally possible for the Minister of Justice, through the Prosecutor General, to influence any case outcome.[1]

The principle of prosecutor unity stands in tension with another provision of the Public Prosecutors Office Law, the "principle of prosecutor independence." This tenet states that each individual prosecutor is an "independent government agency" with power to institute prosecution and perform other functions authorized by law. The principle of prosecutor independence thus distinguishes prosecutors from employees in other administrative agencies who function merely as "support organs" for the minister in whose name they act. Prosecutors have two forms of legal protection for their independence. The first gives them "guaranteed status." Hence, no prosecutor can be fired, suspended, or given a pay cut except in narrowly defined circumstances and through specific legal procedures. The second form of protection derives from the restriction on the Minister of Justice's authority to direct and manage prosecutors, as described above.

In reality, however, the principle of prosecutor independence "lies buried in oblivion" beneath the principle of prosecutor unity and the corollary demand for obedience to superiors. As a prominent law professor and longtime student of the procuracy has noted, "the independence of prosecutors is merely nominal because, as a

1. Since 1945, a Minister of Justice has openly used "the power to direct and manage" the Prosecutor General in only one case, the shipbuilding scandal of 1954. Justice Minister Inukai, a member of Prime Minister Yoshida Shigeru's cabinet, directed the Prosecutor General to delay the arrest of the Secretary General of the Liberal Democratic Party Secretary, Sato Eisaku, ostensibly because the Diet was deliberating two bills concerning the status of Japan's Self-Defense Forces. Prosecutors and the public so strongly condemned this political move to protect a member of the LDP elite that Inukai was forced to resign. The investigation of Sato, however, lost momentum, and he was neither arrested nor charged. Ten years later, in 1964, Sato became Prime Minister, and in 1974 he won the Nobel Peace Prize for his anti-nuclear diplomacy (Nomura 1988:95). It is difficult to discern how subsequent Ministers of Justice have used their authority behind the scenes to influence case outcomes. Many prosecutors deny it happens, as do most members of the LDP, but journalists and academics hold a range of opinions on the issue (Mukaidani 1993a; D. Johnson 1997).

matter of fact, prosecutors are not allowed to independently exercise authority" (I. Matsumoto 1981:310). Kawai Nobutarō, one of the most esteemed prosecutors in Japanese history, confirms that view. Writing in Japan's equivalent of the *Atlantic Monthly*, Kawai describes "the iron principle of the organization," that "those above command and those below obey." His analogy is as apt today as when he penned it in 1954.

> The law says that in the procuracy those above command and those below obey. We call this "the unity of prosecutors" [literally "the one body of prosecutors"]. I am sorry to employ such a plebeian example, but if we compare a criminal investigation to basic construction work, then the frontline investigating prosecutor is like a human wheelbarrow used for flattening the earth. The managing prosecutor wields a stick to direct the frontline prosecutor to "carry mud here" and "place a brick there," and then goes off to the next construction site to do more of the same. The human wheelbarrow works very hard to carry dirt and pound cement as directed. The only job left to the human wheelbarrow is to decide how to pound the concrete and to what depth. (quoted in Kubo 1989:134)

The next sections explain in more detail (and less metaphorically) how the prosecutor "wheelbarrows" define and perform their roles and tasks. Throughout the analysis that follows, the "principle of unity" will be evident in prosecutors' beliefs and behavior. The procuracy's strong solidarity and hierarchy have been criticized for undermining the principle of prosecutor independence and for making decision-making in corruption scandals vulnerable to political pressures (D. Johnson 1997). The "iron principle of the organization" does have costs, both for individual prosecutors and for particular case outcomes.[2] Some of the costs are explored in chapter 8, where the organization's solidarity can be seen facilitating cover-ups of egregious prosecutor misconduct, much as cohesion and "the code of silence" do in police departments worldwide (Chevigny 1995). In the Japanese context, however, "unity" has important merits too, as when it helps prosecutors achieve consistency across cases (chapter 5) and minimize acquittals at trial (chapter 7).

Roles and Tasks

Prosecutors in Japan perform three major roles, as operators, managers, and executives. *Operators* investigate, indict, and try cases. These frontline workers perform the organization's core tasks: processing suspects by "clarifying the truth" about alleged

---

2. Among other costs, prosecutors who oppose their superiors may be "eliminated" from the organization, as happened to Abe Haruo, an ex-prosecutor and ex-con. Born in 1920, the second son of a Hokkaido judge, Abe traveled the "elite course" for much of his career. He graduated from Tokyo University's Law Faculty in 1943, joined the procuracy in 1951, and was sent to Harvard for additional study. On returning to Japan he was assigned to several important prosecutor posts. However, Abe's unusual penchant for openly criticizing the organization resulted in a series of undesirable transfers and job assignments. Disgruntled with this treatment, Abe quit to become a private lawyer. In the early 1980s he was convicted of criminal extortion and attempted extortion while representing plaintiffs in the Japan Automobile User Union case. He was sentenced to two years' imprisonment, suspended for four years. Some commentators believe prosecutors unfairly targeted Abe in order to stymie Japan's nascent "consumers' movement" (Kubo 1989:97).

bad acts, determining legal guilt or innocence, and specifying appropriate sanctions. *Managers* monitor and coordinate the work of operators in order to attain organizational goals, and *executives* have special responsibility for securing organizational autonomy and maintaining public support.[3] Consider each in turn.

Operators: Uncovering and Constructing the Truth

Operators[4] do the work that justifies the procuracy's existence. They perform its core task, the work that enables the organization to manage its most critical environmental problem (Wilson 1989:33). For prosecutors, the central problem is the historian's challenge: determining what happened, or who did what to whom and why. The bad acts from which most crimes are made consist of events that have already occurred. Since the past does not exist and cannot be directly perceived, prosecutors come to know it not through immediate observation but by collecting and interpreting evidence (Littrell 1979:47). Thus, the prosecutor's core task is to clarify and construct the truth about allegedly bad conduct — to recover bad acts from their ambiguous past by finding a coherent story in them or imposing one on them so that sound charge decisions can be made. Of course, operators perform many other tasks as well, like deciding whether and what to charge, presenting the state's case at trial, supervising the execution of sentences, and so on. But their central task, the fundamental work on which all other work depends, and the job prosecutors themselves regard as their primary duty, is to explicate the facts of cases by acquiring and organizing evidence during the pre-indictment investigation.

As described in chapter 3, prosecutors believe their core task is to "clarify the truth" about alleged criminal acts. In the survey, 216 out of 235 prosecutors (92 percent) ranked "explicating the truth about a case"[5] as a "very important objective." Of the other nineteen respondents, eighteen ranked this objective "important" and only one as "not very important." Thus, 234 out of 235 respondents regarded "explicating the truth" as either important or very important, thereby rendering this goal one of two "cardinal objectives."[6]

Though "discovering the truth" was also important to prosecutors in the Seattle survey, the nature and depth of their commitment to truth-finding differs consider-

---

3. I borrow the labels for these roles from James Q. Wilson's (1989) study of bureaucracy, but prosecutors in Japan use similar terms to make analogous distinctions: *hira kenji*, or "ordinary prosecutors," are the main operators; *jōshi*, or "superiors," are the managers; and *kanbu* translates literally as "executives."

4. There actually are three types of operators: administrative officials (*jimukan*), assistant prosecutors (*fuku kenji*), and frontline, rank-and-file, or "ordinary" prosecutors (*hira kenji* or *ippan no kenji*). In the assistant and frontline categories there are four main subtypes — investigative prosecutors (*sōsa kenji*), trial prosecutors (*kōhan kenji*), public security prosecutors (*kōan kenji*), and special investigation prosecutors (*tokusōbu no kenji*). I do not elaborate these distinctions because they are not central to this analysis. For a more detailed discussion, see Nomura (1988).

5. The Japanese reads "*jiken no shinsō o kaimei suru koto*," which means "to make clear the facts of a case." As explained in the text, prosecutors have extensive power to package and arrange the facts, and thereby construct the truth, as they deem proper.

6. Achieving the other "cardinal objective" ("not prosecuting the innocent and prosecuting and convicting only those who have really committed crimes") depends on clarifying the truth, so the latter is more fundamental.

ably (Rayment 1999). Put simply, prosecutors in Japan define their core task differently than American prosecutors do. Among the latter, many define their mission less in terms of truth than in terms of trial success (Heilbroner 1990). This different task definition is reflected in training courses, where there is little instruction on investigating, charging, or plea-bargaining (even though in most American jurisdictions plea deals account for about 90 percent of all dispositions). The focus is on trials. As one prosecutor put it, "that is what we do here." Similarly, when Lief Carter conducted his seminal study of prosecutors in California, he asked them to rate the importance of nine office goals. "Clarifying the truth" was not among them (Carter 1974:178). When I was constructing the analogous part of my own survey, I borrowed liberally from Carter's questionnaire in order to make comparison possible. Having read other research, mostly about American prosecutors, I added to Carter's list several other objectives. Still, "clarifying the truth" was not among them. Only when I showed a draft of the survey to a Japanese prosecutor did I realize a glaring omission. The survey inquired about many prosecutor objectives, even some — like "keeping the cases moving" — that were utterly mysterious to prosecutors in Japan, but it did not ask about the one goal they consider central. After listening to a brief lecture on the importance of "clarifying the truth," I included the survey item that taps into their core task.

Mission statements from the two countries further reveal the different task definitions. For example, the Hennepin County Prosecutors Office in Minneapolis declares that "the mission of the Adult Prosecution Division is to promote a fair, just, and orderly society by prosecuting adults who commit felony and other crimes in Hennepin County through the equitable application of criminal law." Though this mandate presupposes some determination of the facts, neither the statement of purpose nor individual prosecutors pay that imperative much direct attention. In contrast, publications by Japan's procuracy baldly stress that "a prosecutor's first role is to explicate the truth about cases."

Many American scholars and legal professionals doubt that investigations or trials *can* determine the truth about past acts.[7] This skepticism predates the arrival of postmodern incredulity toward truth claims, for Western societies have long been losing faith in the reality of truth and interest in the search for it (Fernandez-Armesto 1997). In one of the most influential books of the American "legal realism" movement, Jerome Frank argued that "facts are guesses" (Frank 1949:14). Quoting Frank, Lief Carter contended likewise, that "the prosecutor's 'facts' are guesses" (Carter 1974:14). Other researchers concur (Littrell 1979; Utz 1978; Frohmann 1992; F. Miller 1969). This epistemological skepticism is shared by many American prosecutors. One stated his view as follows: "Our criminal justice system is not designed to find the truth. I am nervous talking about the truth. If we wanted to find the truth we would not have the Fifth Amendment [guaranteeing the right against self-incrimination]. What we want is justice, not truth. The Constitution teaches that truth is not para-

---

7. However, some commentators, dissatisfied with the American criminal justice system's seemingly low regard for truth, argue that "the goal of discovering the truth should play a dominant role in designing the rules that govern criminal procedure" (Grano 1993; see also Pizzi 1999; Amar 1997; McCoy 1996; Frankel 1978).

mount." Another laconically, if not Socratically, rejoined, "What is truth?" A third was asked how important it is that prosecutors be certain the defendants they charge really committed crimes. He retorted "Who is ever 'certain'? The standard is 'beyond a reasonable doubt.' "

After stumbling across the importance of truth-seeking to Japanese prosecutors, I confronted them with Frank's claim that "facts are guesses" and with the like-minded skepticism of American prosecutors. The details of their responses varied, but the main themes are sufficiently similar to reveal consistent agreement among themselves and disagreement with the Frankians. One prosecutor, a thirty-five-year veteran, related the common Japanese themes in uncommonly eloquent English:

> I would say two things to Mr. Frank. First, he is right; we cannot know the truth. What we treat as truths really are guesses. Only God knows the truth. In that sense you and Mr. Frank are correct as a matter of philosophy. But if we try hard, we can come closer to the truth, even if we are never able to see it perfectly. Furthermore, I think the degree of such effort differs a lot between the U.S. and Japan. There are many reasons for that of course. You have juries that simply convict or acquit, without elaborating reasons or particular findings of fact. That makes it possible, even logical, for prosecutors to present rough facts. Your investigators also have relatively little time to find the facts or be precise. But whatever the reasons, it seems that more than you Americans, we Japanese believe in the possibility of discovering the truth. And we have constructed a system of prosecution that makes finding the truth our first priority.

Japanese prosecutors agree not only about what their core task is but also about how to perform it. In brief, prosecutors clarify the truth by preparing written documents, or dossiers, during the pre-indictment investigation. The most crucial part of these dossiers is the suspect's confession, for prosecutors, judges, and defense lawyers agree that it "continue[s] to play an extremely important role in the criminal justice process" (Foote 1991:455). As it has long been, a confession is still the queen of evidence, "the decisive element of proof sought by every prosecutor before he takes a case into court and the single most important item determining the reception his efforts are likely to receive from most Japanese judges when he gets there" (C. Johnson 1972:149).

Prosecutors and police do not record confessions verbatim. They instead prepare a summary statement abridging and organizing the suspect's testimony. These summaries synthesize statements the suspect has given over several sessions (or days) of interrogation. Though lengthy and detailed, they are also *the prosecutor's construction of the truth* — or, as many defense lawyers see it and say it, "the prosecutor's essay." Prosecutors filter the raw materials that suspects provide, using the parts deemed most relevant to assemble the confession. Sometimes they allow suspects to read the dossier before asking them to sign it, but more often they (or their assistants) read the dossier aloud to the suspect, ask if any revisions are requested, and then seek the suspect's signature. In the dozens of interrogations I observed in Japan, only a handful of suspects requested revisions. Prosecutors read the dossier to the suspect very rapidly, even when the confession continues for twenty or more pages. This makes it difficult for suspects to digest the details in the dossier. Critics contend this method of constructing "truth" enables prosecutors to generate "closely-knit and logically consistent accounts which judges may find difficult to resist" (Foote 1991:454). Some prosecutors unwittingly lend credibility to that criticism, as do the troubling cases described in chapter 8. "In major cases," one veteran said, "I would question for two or three days, taking notes on the confession in my notebook, and then prepare a statement covering that two or three days' worth of material. If you don't do that you can't get an organized statement and you run the risk of getting a statement that contradicts earlier or later statements of the same suspect or statements of other suspects" (quoted in Foote 1991:454).

Prosecutors obtain some confessions directly, by interrogating suspects and composing the results in dossiers. More commonly, however, they use these interviews to confirm the details of confessions gained by the police, filling in holes, "painting over" problems, and, in the argot insiders employ, "wiping police butts" as necessary (H. Yamaguchi 1999:49).[8] If the prosecutor files charges the case goes to trial, where large, liberally interpreted exceptions to the hearsay rule allow most dossiers to be entered as evidence (Hirano 1989:138). The judge's role is then, in fact if not in principle, to review the results of the investigation as recorded in the police and prosecutor dossiers. As a former judge of the Osaka High Court put it, "Criminal trials — and in particular the fact-finding that lies at the heart of trials — are conducted in closed rooms by the investigators." Many court proceedings are merely "formal ceremony" and "empty ritual" (Ishimatsu 1989:143). This does not mean judges allow the prosecutor and defense to stipulate to facts that are brazenly untrue, as often happens in American plea bargains (Langbein 1978) and Japanese civil cases (Ramseyer and Nakazato 1999:143). It does mean that serious judicial scrutiny of the prosecutor's case tends to occur in the judge's chambers or living room, where the dossiers are inspected. The truth that typically prevails — the truth that judges authoritatively pronounce — is the truth that prosecutors have uncovered and constructed. In the end, of course, claims about the status of "truth" in particular cases depend on perceptions about the legitimacy of the process — and the actors in the process, especially prosecutors — for construing and constructing the truth (Bracey 2000).

Managers: Cultivating Mission and Controlling Operators

If Japanese prosecutors unite in agreeing that uncovering and constructing the truth is their core task, then how is that sense of mission inculcated, and how are operators coordinated and controlled so as to accomplish that task? In large part the answer is managers, who perform two key functions. First, managers cultivate in operators a sense of mission, or widespread agreement about and endorsement of the way their critical task is defined. Second, managers coordinate and control operators in order to attain organizational objectives such as consistency and correction.[9] In both respects managers try to gain operators' compliance with the organization's goals. They usually succeed.

---

8. In the survey, 180 out of 235 prosecutors (77 percent) agreed or strongly agreed that "police do the important investigative work in almost all cases." Responses to a related question reveal part of prosecutors' motivation for seeking confessions so single-mindedly: 217 (93 percent) agreed or strongly agreed that "when a suspect does not confess, disposing of the case is much more difficult and time-consuming."

9. Managers are found in a variety of positions in the procuracy: as assistant division chiefs, division chiefs, branch chiefs, deputy district chiefs, and district chiefs, and in various posts in the High and Supreme Prosecutors Offices as well. In this book, the distinctions between types of managers are less central than their functional similarities.

MANAGERS CULTIVATE MISSION

From the start of their careers as legal professionals, prosecutors are educated to be-lieve in the crucial importance of truth through confessions. The lectures that man-agers and other veteran prosecutors gave to the legal apprentices (*shūshūsei*) during the apprentices' four-month stay in the Kobe office repeatedly stressed that seeking "truth through confession" should be every prosecutor's main mission. In the two dozen lectures I attended while doing field research, the pursuit of truth through the inducement of confession was by far the most prominent theme. Sometimes the mes-sage was explicit, as when a manager stated that "since only the suspect knows what really happened, the only way for you to find out is by taking his confession." The metaphor is revealing: because the suspect alone possesses the truth, the prosecutor must "take" it from him. Usually, however, the point was driven home more subtly and powerfully through illustration, anecdote, and the sheer volume of words used to describe cases in which confessions were essential to obtain but hard to elicit. Like the Japanese detectives studied by Miyazawa Setsuo, prosecutors believe "procuring con-fessions is primary" and "the first priority in an investigation" (Miyazawa 1992:81, 158).

Managers recite, elaborate, and emphasize this tenet to operators on numerous other occasions. Formal training programs help inculcate a shared sense of mission (Ando 1995), but the most important settings for instruction about how to be a good prosecutor are restaurants, bars, karaoke clubs, and, after hours, the prosecutors of-fice itself. Prosecutors are not especially busy, but like Japanese working in other large organizations, whether business or bureaucracy, they spend a great deal of time together. Indeed, the organization so envelops prosecutors that it sometimes resem-bles a "total institution"—a place where the usual barriers between play and work (and to a lesser extent sleep) break down (Goffman 1961:5). In urban offices most prosecutors spend at least ten and often twelve or more hours in the same place, under the same authorities, and in the company of the same group of significant (prosecutor) others. In this setting young prosecutors are regularly instructed in the organization's traditions and implored to carry them on.

When I first visited the Kobe office I drank little of the tea I was served for fear that the caffeine would exacerbate my stomachache. At the conclusion of our chat my prosecutor host, with evident concern in his voice, startled me with a question: "You are not a Mormon, are you?" He asked, of course, because Mormons do not drink caffeine—or alcohol—while prosecutors do, often in prodigious amounts. In-deed, prosecutors spend significant time, together, in the presence of open bottles of alcohol. On these occasions the conversation frequently turns to one of their two fa-vorite topics: transfers and personnel changes, on the one hand, and interactions with suspects, on the other. Prosecutors express considerable anxiety and dissatisfac-tion about the former, but they relish discussing strategies they have used to extract confessions from recalcitrant suspects. Sometimes their stories seem stranger than fiction, or even apocryphal,[10] but the text and subtext are always clear to the audi-

---

10. One of the most memorable confession stories was related by a veteran prosecutor who had in-terrogated a suspect about an attempted rape. For two days of interrogation the suspect, a *yakuza* gang mem-ber, denied any sexual contact with the victim. *Yakuza* normally confess quickly, the prosecutor explained,

ence: a prosecutor's job is to determine the truth, and the best way to do that is by obtaining a full, detailed confession. The cumulative effect of these countless conversations is a strongly shared sense of occupational mission.

MANAGERS COORDINATE AND CONTROL OPERATORS

In addition to cultivating agreement about how the core task is defined, managers coordinate and control operators' activities to an extent unseen in American prosecution offices (Tōjō 1968:55). It may seem axiomatic that "any large, bureaucratic organization must have some means of insuring that policy formulated by higher-ups will be applied by subordinates in the field," but such policies tend to be rare and primitive in the United States. In fact, many American prosecutor organizations have "virtually no instruments by which to enforce" office policies (Abrams 1971:53; see also Feeley 1973:422). Japan's procuracy is different.[11]

First of all, in order to direct subordinates' exercise of discretion, managers articulate and communicate specific criteria in written manuals, guidelines, and standards. The importance of policy in Japan's procuracy has been overlooked by most other commentators. Setō Shūzō (1983:1), a highly respected reporter who for years covered prosecutors for one of Japan's largest newspapers, claims that apart from doing justice the procuracy has no policy, but in fact Japanese prosecutors work in an organization saturated with policy directives. More important, these criteria are not dead letters, as guidelines in the United States often are (Abrams 1971; Vorenberg 1981; Burnham 1996). Instead, operators in Japan regard them as indispensable guides to action. In my survey, 232 out of 234 prosecutors (99.1 percent) agreed or strongly agreed that "formal manuals and rules are very important sources of information on how to do our job." Manuals and rules are always within arm's reach of Japanese prosecutors, and they frequently refer to them.

The "standards for case dispositions and recommended sentences" (*shori kyūkei kijunshū*) are compiled by Supreme, High, and District Prosecutors Offices and are distributed to all offices in their jurisdictions. The main book of standards in a typical District Office is 130 pages long and is divided into twenty-two offense types, ranging from traffic crimes to fishing offenses and from drug possession to murder. Though the guidelines are bound together in loose-leaf form so that additions and replacements can easily be made, such changes are uncommon. In my survey, only 9 out of 235 prosecutors (less than 4 percent) agreed or strongly agreed that "policies in the office seem to change frequently" (Appendix, part 2:74). The guidelines instruct prosecutors about presumptive charge decisions and sentence recommendations.

---

but this one was stubborn. After trying a number of strategies that failed to elicit an admission of guilt, the prosecutor finally hit on a technique that worked. He told the suspect that since the victim had described certain "distinguishing marks" on the suspect's penis, he would call in a medical expert to examine the gangster's member so as to test the veracity of the victim's account. The gangster immediately confessed.

11. This feature of Japan's procuracy is not sui generis. In France, for example, the managing powers of top prosecutors "are very strong," and frontline prosecutors are "in large part controlled" by their superiors (Guarnieri 1997:185).

Prosecutors sometimes deviate from the guidelines, though seldom very far, and must orally justify any departures at *kessai* consultations with their superiors and, in important cases, in writing as well.

The standards for traffic and drug offenses encourage mechanical decision-making, unlike the highly individualized decision-making that occurs in most other cases. Traffic offenses are disposed of in an especially machinelike manner. Since they constitute nearly 85 percent of all cases disposed of and 90 percent of all cases charged, nearly half of the main book of standards is devoted to them. One major principle is that traffic offenders should not be charged unless the victim's injury is above a precisely defined threshold level. (The prosecutors who showed me the standards did so on the condition that I promise not to publish their contents.) Thus, the extent of the victim's injury forms the first of two axes in the traffic offenses grid. The other axis expresses "demerit points," which are calculated from other variables such as the type of crime, the number of prior offenses, and the type of vehicle. About 95 percent of all traffic cases are prosecuted using a simple summary procedure that allows offenders to pay a fine through the mail and thereby avoid the process and reputational costs of an appearance in court. The standards for drug offenses, especially possession, use, and sale of methamphetamine (*kakuseizai*), promote similarly standardized decision-making.

The standards for violent crimes such as murder, rape, and extortion come in two forms, one simple and the other more elaborate. Prosecutors first consult a chart (if they have not already memorized it) which distinguishes the presumptive sentence recommendations for gangsters (*bōryokudan*) and the general public (*ippanjin*). Then, in order to fine-tune their decisions, prosecutors extract from data banks (in the office and at court) lists of like cases that have been charged and sentenced in the past. These cases are selected to resemble the current case along a number of dimensions, including the nature of the offense, the offender's prior record, whether and how the offender repented, the extent of the victim's injuries, and whether restitution was made. Application of these standards is decidedly unmechanical. Indeed, prosecutors go to great lengths in gathering prior cases, collating them along appropriate dimensions, and reasoning by analogy in order to discern how like or unlike the present case is to past ones. Throughout the process the dominant but tacit assumption is that, whenever possible, prior case dispositions should govern present ones.

Charging and sentencing standards are important to Japanese prosecutors and, of course, to the people they process. Many Americans argue that "a bureaucratic, rule-oriented, administrative model of management does not fit the nature of the job of criminal prosecution" (Carter 1974:117), but in Japan it surely does. Indeed, the vast majority of Japanese prosecutors believe that manuals and rules are important sources of job information.

In contrast, when a case crosses the desk of an American prosecutor, especially a "minor" case in a busy urban district, it is disposed of in minutes if not seconds, and with far less regard for standards or prior practice (Heilbroner 1990:58). When an American scholar asked thirty-six prosecutors in a California office if formal manuals and rules are important, only one agreed and all but six strongly disagreed (Carter 1974:198). Likewise, in a review titled "Guides to the Exercise of Discretion: The Present State of the Art," Norman Abrams (1971:8) noted that even though the Department of Justice — the U.S. leader in this respect — "has articulated a great deal of policy," most of it is unsystematic and "difficult to describe as much advanced beyond the primitive." In other large American prosecution offices, one usually finds an office manual or handbook of some sort, but "in most instances it is difficult to say that these materials set forth prosecutorial policy." Most often, Abrams says, "they amount to elementary instruction books for junior prosecutors which describe the procedures to be followed in particular types of cases and the applicable rules of law. If they occasionally lapse into statements of policy designed to guide discretion, that policy is usually of the most general and unsophisticated sort." In federal prosecution offices in the 1990s, the situation had improved so little that one commentator calls the system an "adhocracy" (Burnham 1996:83).

Managers in Japan further specify rules for performance by requiring operators to clear decisions with supervisors, chiefly through the *kessai* system of consultation and approval. In order to make charge and sentence recommendation decisions, operators must consult with and obtain the approval of two or three managers, depending on the seriousness of the case. This is known as *shobun kessai*, or "disposition approval." In serious cases operators must obtain approval to arrest (*taiho kessai*), detain (*kōryū kessai*), and extend detention (*enchō kessai*) of suspects. In all of these cases, operators go to the office of the supervising manager, with dossiers and other supporting documentation in hand, and describe the content of the case and the desired decision. Many prosecutors telephone the manager's secretary before going to *kessai* in order to avoid logjams at the manager's office. *Kessai* interactions vary in length, from five minutes or less in simple cases to an hour or more in complicated ones. *Kessai* styles also differ markedly. Some managers allow the operator to talk freely before asking any questions, while others pepper the operator with queries from the outset of the interaction. In cases where the pre-charge investigation lasts several days or weeks, operators interact many times with managers to discuss how to proceed. In cases of special importance (involving, say, a politician or prominent businessman), managers at the District Office level consult with executives at levels higher in the hierarchy — from the High Prosecutors Office, to the chief of the Ministry of Justice's Criminal Affairs Bureau, to the Prosecutor General. These are called "specially designated cases." Even simple cases like traffic violations or petty larcenies require *kessai*, though often it is done more on paper than in person. In these minor cases the operator simply sends the relevant records and draft decision to the supervising manager, who either stamps the documents, indicating approval, or asks the operator for further clarification.[12]

In sum, the managing prosecutor (or *kessaikan*) performs at least four functions. As judge he reviews the adequacy of evidence. As teammate he provides aid and moral support in difficult cases. As teacher the veteran prosecutor helps educate young operators about how to perform their work. And as manager he ensures that like cases are treated alike.

12. In significant respects the *kessai* system for prosecutor decision-making resembles decision-making in other large Japanese organizations. See, for example, the discussions of *nemawashi* (negotiating beforehand) in bureaucratic agencies (Vogel 1975:xxii; Craig 1975:17) and *ringisei* (drafting and preparing proposals in order to obtain approval) in business companies (Clark 1979:125).

Some commentators stress the political control function of the *kessai* system, especially in high-profile cases. One analyst contends that "Japanese prosecutors have a highly selective approach to corruption in the political world," in part because of the *kessai* system.

> Individual prosecutors operate, in theory, on their own, but in practice they are expected, before taking action against influential officials, ministers, Diet members or local government leaders, to write preliminary reports for their superiors all the way up to the minister of justice, and to wait for their consent. This controversial *shobun seikun* (request for instructions as to steps to be taken) system of responsibility within the procuracy has led to the dismissal of many political corruption cases. Even when such corruption cases are not dismissed, the politicians involved will usually be allowed to emerge unscathed, and bureaucrats-turned-politicians need not at all fear being publicly tainted." (van Wolferen 1989:223)[13]

Although this view correctly depicts the hierarchical control function of *kessai* and its correlates, this system of coordination and control plays an equally significant but salutary function in the far more numerous cases which do not rise to the level of a *shobun seikun* requirement. In short, *kessai* helps prosecutors in Japan achieve consistency across similar cases, a goal many American prosecutors regard as peripheral, elusive, or even irrelevant (see chapter 5). Managers routinely stress the crucial role *kessai* plays in treating like cases alike and different cases differently. As one put it, "*Kessai* helps even out unwanted disparities between cases. The most important purpose of *kessai* is fairness."

Kessai's order-enhancing effect is evident in manager and operator behavior. In form, *kessai* is fundamentally an interaction between an operator and a manager. Since such interaction is regularly required, operators and managers are highly interdependent. Indeed, the task definition of each depends on the nature of the interaction, or expected interaction, with the other. At *kessai*, for example, managers compare the current case with others that have come before it, reasoning by analogy across a number of dimensions to determine which cases from the past can guide decision-making in the present. Sometimes, of course, a well-established principle or guideline expresses the earlier decisions and so disposes of the present case without much need for analysis. At other times, however, the governing rule is discovered in the process of determining the similarity or difference between present and prior cases. In either event, managers attend closely to the problem of treating like cases alike. Further, since managers must do *kessai* on many cases brought by other operators, they cannot gather by themselves all the information needed to make good decisions. They are, in other words, dependent on operators for much of the informa-

---

13. A senior prosecutor distinguished three modes of supervising case dispositions. *Kessai* is "approval by a senior prosecutor in charge of supervising each frontline prosecutor." *Shobun seikun* (request for instructions as to steps to be taken) is, in effect if not name, a stronger form of *kessai*. When these requests are made, a superintending prosecutor — what I call an executive — unilaterally decides how to dispose of the case. Thus, *shobun seikun* is less a form of consultation and approval than a complete "takeover" of the case by prosecutor executives. Because of the sensitive nature of the cases in which *shobun seikun* is used, prosecutors are reluctant to discuss this form of strong supervision. The third form of supervision, known as *hōkoku* or "report," is a weak form of *kessai*. Prosecutors simply notify executives of their disposition decision after the decision has been made (Tōjō 1968:66).

tion they use to identify relevant similarities and differences across cases. At the same time, operators learn to anticipate what questions managers are likely to ask at *kessai*. In preparation, operators conduct careful comparisons between past and present cases so as to avoid being vexed or embarrassed by a manager's "What about this case?" query. I have seen poor performance at *kessai* ruin a prosecutor's day, and repeated poor performance can cause significant damage to one's career. Thus, to both operators and managers, consistency is a primary work objective, and *kessai* consultations express and reinforce that aim.

In addition to standards and the *kessai* system, a third internal control on prosecutor discretion is the audit, or *kansa*. Once a year managers in each District Office sample case dispositions to see if they have been properly and consistently decided. Every two or three years the eight High Offices do the same for the District Offices in their jurisdictions. (The Supreme Prosecutors Office does likewise, albeit less often.) In an audit, managers and executives review cases that have not been charged. When they find a case which should have been prosecuted but was not, auditors seek written or oral explanations from the responsible prosecutors. Though cases are seldom deemed inappropriately dropped, the audit's importance should not be dismissed. Like audits in the business world, they are one more check to ensure that the organization's accounts are in order.

In sum, managers not only cultivate a shared sense of mission in the organization's operators, they wield strong controls over their subordinates' behavior. Managers specify rules, standards, and procedures, orally and in writing, to guide operator discretion. In principle and in fact, those guidelines constrain and channel operator behavior. Similarly, through *kessai* consultations, managers detect and discourage deviation from the principle of consistency while maintaining an equally strong commitment to the ideal that case dispositions should be individualized and offenders should be corrected. Most important, managers recruit, train, and socialize operators so as to ensure conformity to the organization's norms. In these ways, direct and indirect, managers exercise more influence over disposition decisions than do their American counterparts.

Executives: Securing Autonomy and Maintaining the Organization

Executive prosecutors create space for operators and managers to conduct their jobs. Their chief concern is acquiring sufficient freedom of action and external political support so that operators can perform their critical task and so that managers can infuse the definition of that task with a sense of mission. Executives also "maintain" the organization by acquiring the resources it needs to survive and prosper. As we shall see, both tasks are easier to accomplish in Japan than in the United States.[14]

---

14. The executive class can be defined broadly or narrowly. Narrowly construed, the class includes only the Prosecutor General, the Deputy Prosecutor General, the Superintending Prosecutors of the eight High Offices, and the Administrative Vice Minister of Justice. Since other veteran prosecutors perform similar functions, I adopt a broader definition that incorporates all District Office chiefs, Supreme

ORGANIZATIONAL AUTONOMY

The main focus of executive prosecutors is organizational autonomy. Autonomy has two dimensions, external and internal (Selznick 1957:121). Externally, executives try to minimize rivals and secure freedom from political constraints. As we have seen, prosecutors in Japan monopolize the decision to charge. Furthermore, politicians grant them substantial independence to pursue crime control and criminal justice objectives, at least with respect to ordinary street crimes (van Wolferen 1994:110). In this regard prosecutors resemble bureaucrats in other Japanese agencies (such as the Ministry of Foreign Affairs) that possess few divisible benefits for politicians to acquire and return to their constituencies. As a result, executives need to devote little attention and few resources to achieve the external aspect of autonomy. Occasionally, of course, some aspect of prosecutor behavior, or misbehavior, becomes a public and political concern, as when death row inmates are acquitted on retrial or prosecutors hide exculpatory evidence from defendants (Foote 1993b; C. Johnson 1972). At these times, executives concentrate on managing the crisis, much as do their counterparts in the United States. The key difference, however, is that executives in Japan face few such crises because crime and criminal justice have not been politicized as they have in the United States. Thus, instead of struggling to maintain external independence, executives are free to focus on the second, internal aspect of autonomy—cultivating a widely shared and approved sense of the procuracy's central tasks. With managers, executives have forged a strong consensus about what the procuracy's main tasks are and how they should be performed. The consequence is a high level of internal autonomy as well.

Though their chief task is securing and protecting organizational autonomy, prosecutor executives are not as imperialistic as many theorists of bureaucracy predict they must be—always seeking to grow by taking on new functions and gobbling up bureaucratic rivals. Even James Q. Wilson (1989:189), a sharp critic of such theorists, contends that an important rule of thumb for achieving organizational autonomy is that agencies should, and successful agencies do, "fight organizations that seek to perform your tasks." In fact, from the late 1950s through the 1960s, several elite Japanese prosecutors advocated narrowing the scope of two key prosecutor powers—the authority to investigate any case and the monopoly power to charge—by expanding police authority accordingly. In 1963, Itoh Shigeki recommended precisely these two reforms. He was no loose cannon. At the time, Itoh was Councillor in the Ministry of Justice's Criminal Affairs Bureau, and later became postwar Japan's best-known Prosecutor General. Itoh argued that the procuracy should delegate more investigative responsibilities to police, because that was the best way to improve police abilities and because prosecutors should concentrate more of their

Office prosecutors, and Ministry of Justice prosecutors at the level of bureau chief or higher. Prosecutors within the broader definition attend "executive meetings" at least occasionally (Kubo 1989:120; Mukaidani 1993a:18). Executives also play the manager roles described above, such as cultivating mission and coordinating and controlling frontline operators, but in this section I emphasize their distinctive functions.

resources on charging and trying cases. What is more, Itoh advocated giving police the authority to prosecute certain minor crimes. As we have seen, since the Occupation's legal reforms, police have possessed power to dispose of minor cases (*bizai shobun*) by simply dropping them from the criminal process without consulting prosecutors. Itoh, however, wanted to expand police power so they could not only drop minor cases but also charge them, thus reducing the scope of prosecutors' power proportionately (Itoh 1963:118). Police naturally welcomed these proposals, which seemed stimulated in part by acquittals in the conspiracy at Matsukawa case and other high-profile, public order trials. In the end, however, neither reform was implemented. Itoh met resistance from prosecutors more concerned about protecting their turf and from lawyers and citizens who opposed expanding the powers of a police force whose repressive prewar activities were still fresh in their minds. Thus, after considerable debate inside and outside the procuracy, the organization preserved its autonomy.

ORGANIZATIONAL MAINTENANCE

The second major concern for executive prosecutors is organizational maintenance, or assuring the necessary flow of resources to the organization. Maintaining the organization means obtaining sufficient amounts of three crucial inputs: capital, labor, and political support (Wilson 1989:181).

Obtaining adequate financial appropriations has seldom been a major problem for prosecutor executives. The "rite of budget revision" reveals what a former bureaucrat has called "the village mentality of the Japanese bureaucracy," but in the Ministry of Justice, as in many other Japanese ministries, "no plan marking a significant break with established ways of thinking has the slightest chance of seeing the light of day" (Miyamoto 1994:79). Competition between different sections, departments, and bureaus in the ministry is sometimes fierce, but actual appropriations change little. In fact, the procuracy's share of the national budget has hardly changed since 1980, when its budget was approximately 62 billion yen ($50 million), about 0.132 percent of the national budget. By 1990 it had grown to nearly 80 billion yen ($64 million), though the larger figure constituted a slightly smaller share — 0.120 percent — of the national budget. Throughout the 1980s the procuracy's share of the national budget was never more than 0.134 percent or less than 0.120 percent. As a percentage of GNP the procuracy's budget remained steady at about 0.020 percent, about one-third the size of the budget for Japan's courts. About 90 percent of the procuracy's budget goes to pay personnel expenses, mostly salaries and bonuses. As of December 1997, salaries ranged from about $2,000 to $14,000 a month, or (including bonuses) from $30,000 to $200,000 a year. A thirty-year veteran made over $160,000 a year. By comparison, rookie prosecutors in the U.S. Department of Justice made about $40,000 a year, and battle-hardened litigators earned around $125,000.

Acquiring an adequate supply of operator labor has been a more difficult task for executives, but they have always managed to do so satisfactorily. Recruiting enough able operators was a perennial concern for much of the postwar era. Shortly after the Pacific War ended in 1945, SCAP, the occupying power, purged hundreds of "thought prosecutors" (*shisō kenji*) for their repressive prewar practices. This prompted executives to create the new position of "assistant prosecutor" (*fuku kenji*) to help investigate, charge, and try cases. When the purged prosecutors were depurged three years later, the procuracy's size far exceeded its prewar scale, yet personnel worries soon re-emerged (Nomura 1994:17). By 1963, executives realized the need to better respond to the problem (Itoh 1963). By the early 1970s, executives were arguing that the organization needed a "new vision" in order to increase the number of new recruits, decrease the number of prosecutors leaving the office in midcareer, and stem the "salaryman-ization" of those who remained (Mitsui 1979:218). By the mid-1980s, the mass media and bar associations were proclaiming a full-fledged "prosecutor crisis," allegedly caused by the organization's inability to recruit and retain a sufficient number of able, frontline operators.

The personnel problems were especially serious from the mid-1980s through the early 1990s. Indeed, in the decade before 1993, no cause concerned executives more. Journalists have interviewed scores of "prosecutor-quitters" (*yameken*) who express antipathy for the ubiquitous bureaucratic controls inside the organization and for the transfers to new office and job assignments that occur every two to three years. In 1989, when the procuracy was lobbying for an increase in the number of people who could pass the annual bar exam, the Tokyo Bar Association published the results of a survey of 144 "prosecutor-quitters" (56, or 39 percent, responded). The survey reveals strong dissatisfaction, at least among the quitters, with the organization's bureaucratic controls. Respondents could select more than one answer, though only the most frequent replies are listed here.

1. Why did you quit the procuracy?
   — disliked transfers (14)
   — fairness in personnel matters is lacking (11)
   — stopped feeling meaning in the prosecutor's job (11)
   — cannot do the work independently (10)
2. Why is the number of prosecutor recruits decreasing in recent years?
   — problems in the prosecutor organization (30)
   — the prosecutor's job has no appeal (25)
   — the trend of the times is "separation from public officials" (18)
3. Why is the number of prosecutors who quit in midcareer increasing?
   — problems in the prosecutor organization (35)
   — the prosecutor's job has no appeal (26)
4. What do you think about the following statements?
   a. Young prosecutors "cower" because hierarchical relations are severe.
      — agree (12)
      — disagree (22)
      — cannot say (21)
   b. The application of the *kessai* system must be reformed, and individual prosecutors should be given wider authority and responsibility.
      — agree (29)
      — disagree (8)
      — cannot say (18)

c. The procuracy's sense of mission has weakened, and it has bureaucra-
tized and abandoned itself to a "peace-at-any-price" principle.
   —agree (32)
   —disagree (14)
   —cannot say (9)
d. Family life is unstable because transfers are frequent.
   —agree (41)
   —disagree (4)
   —cannot say (9)

In short, the survey reveals that many prosecutors quit the organization out of discontent with its thoroughly bureaucratic character, especially the hierarchical controls such as *kessai* and transfers.

In response to the perceived crisis, executive prosecutors have taken a number of steps to ensure an adequate supply of operator labor. For example, prosecutors in Japan are notoriously reluctant to grant public interviews, but under these circumstances several executives appealed in the mass media and in specialist journals for public support and proclaimed a "new age" for the procuracy. The Secretariat and the Criminal Affairs Bureau of the Ministry of Justice even produced glossy brochures to explain the organization to prospective prosecutors and to persuade them to join it. Most notably, executives lobbied for, and obtained, significant increases in the number of persons permitted to pass the bar exam. In 1990 the quota of bar-passers was fixed at five hundred. That figure increased to six hundred in 1991 and to seven hundred in 1993. By 1998 the number had risen to eight hundred. In 1994, executives in the Ministry of Justice called for more than doubling the number of bar-passers, to fifteen hundred, while the Bar advocated an increase of only one hundred, to eight hundred. In response, prosecutors, judges, and lawyers in the Reform Council of the System for Training Legal Professionals presented a "proposal to investigate" the ministry's recommendation in exchange for imposing a limit on the number of times aspiring legal professionals could take the bar exam. In August 1995, the Japan Federation of Bar Associations approved lowering the threshold for passing the exam to permit one thousand successful applicants annually, up from what was then a quota of seven hundred. In April 2001, an advisory council to the government proposed increasing the annual number of bar-passers to three thousand and the total number of prosecutors by one thousand. Whether those levels are reached or not, both the bar and the procuracy seem certain to grow in the years to come.

Prosecutor executives have tried to increase the total number of bar-passers in order to produce more new recruits for the organization. Since the reforms were passed, the number of recruits has increased markedly. In 1995, eighty-six new prosecutors were appointed, the largest number ever, and in 1996 recruits had to be turned away in order to avoid surpassing the organization's legal capacity, which was fixed at 1,173 prosecutors and 919 assistant prosecutors. Executives attribute much of the increase to the economic recession that followed the collapse of the bubble economy in 1991. When times are bad, executives argue, legal apprentices are more likely to seek the security of jobs with government, either in the judiciary or in the procuracy. Executives still worry, however, that personnel problems will recur when the economy recovers. Indeed, in one of my last interviews of a Kobe executive, I was told that the personnel problem is still one of the three main challenges facing the procuracy.[15]

In summary, executives have had some difficulty acquiring and keeping enough personnel to maintain the organization, in large part because many potential recruits dislike the procuracy's pervasive bureaucratic controls. Still, the personnel problem has never been as extreme as critics of the organization allege. Indeed, even when the number of prosecutors falls below official capacity, prosecutor caseloads have remained comparatively light. While executives have sometimes struggled to maintain personnel, they have done at least an adequate job. If the personnel problem is an illness, the procuracy has seldom had worse than a common cold.

The third way executives maintain the organization is by *securing sufficient political support* to enable operators and managers to perform their jobs effectively. In general, executives are successful when they find and maintain the support of some key external constituency, that is, a group whose interests their organization represents (Wilson 1989:203). The key constituency for prosecutors is the public, with whom executives quietly but consistently cultivate good relations.

Executives care about, and therefore manage, their relationship with the public for several reasons. First, executives need to recruit qualified personnel to fill the organization's ranks. The legal apprentices whom the organization recruits participate in the wider culture and thus are influenced by popular perceptions of the procuracy. Hence, executives must care about how the public perceives them. Compared to the police, however, prosecutors devote little attention to currying public favor or placating critics. The mass media often report on issues or reforms important to the police, largely because police executives invest substantial resources in shaping and managing public opinion (Ames 1981:226). Many prosecutors admit that police are adept at explaining their behavior or reforms to the public, and lament that in comparison the prosecutors office is "inept at public relations." Curiously, some executives boast about the procuracy's long-standing custom of not defending or explaining itself to outsiders. The phrase they use (*benkai shinai*) connotes a range of meanings, from explanation to excuse to apology, and the norm which it expresses proclaims that explaining or apologizing for one's behavior besmirches the reputation of both the prosecutor and the procuracy (Nomura 1994; Kubo 1989). For example, executives publicize Japan's high conviction rates in order to cultivate constituency support, yet they do so in a low-key manner because, at least to the uninitiated, convictions seem to speak for themselves. The organization's version of *res ipsa loquitur* — that prosecutors should let their acts speak for themselves — also makes it difficult for researchers to acquire information. Not only executives but almost all Japanese prosecutors are less forthcoming than their American counterparts (D. Johnson forthcoming). Nonetheless, some prosecutors, especially young ones, believe silence is not always golden. Once, when two novice prosecutors learned I was about to inter-

---

15. The other two "big problems" were crimes committed by foreigners and the "imbalance of advantage" in criminal procedure. The latter, this executive believed, wrongly confers too many rights on criminal suspects.

view an executive, they urged me to pose a question they themselves could not ask directly: Why don't executives try harder to explain prosecutor practice to the public, as police elites do?

Prosecutors also care about their relationship with the public because Article 4 of the Public Prosecutors Office Law imposes a duty to be "representatives of the public interest." They take this obligation seriously. Whether lecturing legal apprentices, consulting with each other about case dispositions, or explaining themselves to outsiders like myself, prosecutors often refer to this duty to act in the public interest. Of course, discerning that interest is sometimes difficult, and other imperatives sometimes deflect behavior away from it, but prosecutors do feel bound to be responsive to the public (Uematsu 1981; Kawakami 1981). Mitsui Makoto, a legal scholar and leading expert on Japan's procuracy, has summarized the most salient themes in prosecutor culture between 1950 and 1980. To discern those themes Mitsui reviewed hundreds of publications written by and for prosecutors. He notes that throughout this thirty-year period, executives stressed their connection to the public and the need to continuously seek the public's understanding, cooperation, and trust (Mitsui 1979:220). If anything, this theme has only increased in importance. Indeed, public trust is essential to prosecutors, not only as an end in its own right but also as a means of maintaining independence from political intervention (Haley 1998:58,122). In this way, public support serves the executives' aim of securing autonomy for the organization.

An internalized obligation to the public and the organizational need to recruit new members are not the only forces that motivate executives to heed public opinion. More fundamentally, in order for prosecutors to clarify the truth about cases and thereby perform the organization's critical task, they must secure the public's cooperation — as victims, complainants, witnesses, suspects, and defendants in the criminal process, and as citizens interested in the quality of criminal justice. As we will now see, this is the most basic reason executives seek public support.

The Kanemaru Case: The Day Support Sank

When public support for prosecutors is stable it is difficult to perceive, but when public support erodes it becomes clear how dependent on it prosecutors are.[16] Support sank in September 1992, when prosecutors charged Kanemaru Shin — then the most powerful politician in the ruling Liberal Democratic Party — with violating the Political Funds Control Law by accepting a 500 million yen ($4 million) cash contribution from the Sagawa Kyūbin Company, a sum far in excess of the maximum contribution allowed by law. Tokyo prosecutors did not require Kanemaru to suffer

16. The Kanemaru case shows that a lack of public support can make it difficult for prosecutors to perform their tasks. At the other extreme, in the investigations of the Aum Shinrikyō religious group following the poison gas attacks of 1995, strong public support facilitated some of the most aggressive policing and charging practices in postwar Japanese history (Kaplan and Marshall 1996; Sayle 1996). The two extremes display what often is hidden: prosecutors' dependence on public support.

the indignity of appearing at the prosecutors office for an interview, as they often do in lower-profile cases. Instead, through a process known as summary procedure that enabled Kanemaru to pay his penalty through the mail, prosecutors fined Kanemaru 200,000 yen (about $1,600), the legal maximum.

The public was outraged. In a premeditated act of civil disobedience, the forty-five-year-old president of a corporation defaced the sign in front of the Tokyo District Prosecutors Office with five bottles of yellow paint. Newspapers throughout the country printed editorials harshly rebuking prosecutors for giving Kanemaru "special treatment." Satoh Michio, a prosecutor executive in Sapporo, penned a harsh critique that was published on the front page of the *Asahi Shimbun,* Japan's second largest national newspaper. Thousands of other citizens sent letters of protest to executive prosecutors in Tokyo (Mukaidani 1993b).

After these incidents I asked several executives about the public reaction to the Kanemaru case and what effect, if any, it had on the procuracy. Why, I inquired, do prosecutors even care what the public thinks? After all, no one has to worry about getting re-elected, and in many respects the procuracy seems impervious to public pressures and demands. I expected vague replies, perhaps emphasizing the duty to represent the public interest or the need to preserve organizational legitimacy, but their response was surprisingly concrete. In the weeks following Kanemaru's summary indictment, prosecutors throughout the country confronted a massive increase in uncooperative witnesses and suspects. In more harmonious times prosecutors rely heavily on the public's "voluntary" cooperation to get their work done. However, after this disposition, countless citizens simply refused to come to the prosecutors office for interviews and interrogations, or came but refused to talk, or chided prosecutors about the Kanemaru case instead of responding directly to the investigators' questions. Other citizens refused to pay fines, arguing that if Kanemaru had to pay only $1,600 for his flagrant violation, then their own fines were unfairly severe. To prosecutors accustomed to receiving a level of deference and compliance that few American prosecutors can imagine, this backlash of noncooperation was a shock. It reminded prosecutors (and their observers) that the organization's ability to get its work done is deeply rooted in the soil of public consent. When the soil erodes, the roots give way and the organization shakes (Y. Yamamoto 1998).

Finally, while executives do attend to the organizational need to innovate, this concern is less pressing in Japan than in the United States. The well-known bureaucratic adage to "never do anything for the first time" reflects the fact that all organizations tend to resist innovation. Indeed, since organizations exist in large part to "replace the uncertain expectations and haphazard activities of voluntary activities with the stability and routine of organized relationships," standard operating procedures are indispensable (Wilson 1989:221). However, if innovation means creating new programs or technologies to perform new tasks or to alter the way existing tasks are performed, then Japan's procuracy has innovated little. To be sure, since 1980 executives have increased the proportion of women prosecutors and have automated much office work. Similarly, in 1987 the procuracy changed its long-standing policy for charging traffic offenders. In response to recent increases in the number of crimes committed by foreigners, the organization has created new positions and procedures. In the mid-1990s executives modestly increased the number of prosecutors assigned to investigate white-collar crimes. Nonetheless, unlike executives in many large American prosecution offices,[17] executives in Japan have not multiplied new organizational units to attend to crimes of special concern. Given the low levels of crime and public concern about crime, they have not needed to. Furthermore, executives rarely alter internal guidelines or other controls that channel operators' decisions. In my survey, less than 4 percent of prosecutors agreed or strongly agreed that "policies in the office seem to change frequently," and in interviews, prosecutors of all ranks said that regardless of the executive or issue, innovation is as rare as it is unnecessary.

Conclusion

Outwardly, prosecutor offices in Japan and the United States look a lot alike: they are organized bureaucratically; they distinguish operator, manager, and executive roles; they function as gatekeepers in the criminal process; they promote workers on the basis of merit tempered by seniority; and they confront analogous problems of compliance, resources, and autonomy. This chapter has argued that these external resemblances should not be allowed to obscure deep differences in how core tasks are defined, mission is cultivated, operators are controlled, and autonomy is gained. This conclusion expands the argument by highlighting several additional ways in which the organization of prosecution varies between Japan and the United States. It shows that prosecution in Japan is more collective, pervasive, hierarchical, secretive, and cohesive.

At the outset of this book, former U.S. Attorney General and Supreme Court Justice Robert Jackson (1940:18) rightly noted that "*the prosecutor* has more control over life, liberty, and reputation than any other person in America" (italics added). While Japanese prosecutors also have tremendous discretion, Jackson's statement must be revised to fit the Japan case, for it is not so much the individual prosecutor who exercises discretion in Japan as it is *prosecutors collectively.* Indeed, from arrest to detention, investigation, charge, and trial, almost all major discretionary decisions are made collectively, after thorough consultation among at least several prosecutors.[18] *Kessai,* in its various manifestations, is the primary form the consultation

---

17. In 1995, Arlo Smith, the longtime District Attorney of San Francisco, was the subject of a critical four-part series in the *San Francisco Examiner* (Winokur 1995). The articles appeared two months before Smith ran for re-election (and lost). Smith's response stressed that he "continually innovated" and pushed his staff to "design programs specifically tailored to San Francisco's crime problems." More particularly, Smith emphasized several new organizational units he had created to address hate crimes, deadbeat dads, juvenile gangs, bad check restitution, and child abduction. Because these problems are not public issues in Japan, Japanese executives have seen little need to innovate as Smith and other American chief prosecutors have (Taylor 1996). In 2001, however, Justice Ministry officials did propose the establishment of teams of "specialist prosecutors" in Japan's major cities, primarily to deal with white-collar crimes (*Mainichi Shimbun* 4/19/01).

18. The *collective* nature of prosecutorial discretion in Japan illustrates a critical point, that comparative criminal justice research "is not just about explaining variation in similar phenomena amongst different cultures but is also about appreciating the variation in what each [culture] takes to be the phenom-

takes. Prosecutors in Japan, like workers in many large Japanese organizations, take collective decision-making for granted. "This is the way it is done," they say, "and this is the way it should be. Of course. We are deciding important matters. Better decisions get made when people with different perspectives participate in the process. We check each other, we test each other, and we control each other's excesses. We believe the result is sounder decisions than those arrived at individually."

Ironically, this faith in collective decision-making is shared by Americans who justify the institution of the jury on the grounds that twelve heads are better than one, but it is dismissed and even scorned by many American prosecutors, including some managers and executives. I once asked an executive prosecutor in California if his large urban office had any analogues to Japan's *kessai* system for reviewing and checking operators' decisions. It is difficult to capture the incredulous tone of his response. "This is a people business," he averred. "If you get good people you don't have to hover over their shoulders." Good people make good decisions. This was his assumption, a premise shared by many Americans, prosecutors and not, who maintain that "it is not the organization that matters, it is the people in it." While there is truth in this position, it is a truth recognized in Japan too, where legal professionals compare favorably with the best and brightest in any country, including the United States. In Japan, however, the truth that people matter does not crowd out the parallel reality that checks and reviews promote sound decision-making. More to the point, there are two obvious errors in the view that "only people matter." First, people are in large measure composites of their positions and roles. If sociology has established anything in the last one hundred years, surely this is it. And second, what people are able to accomplish in and through an organization depends greatly on having "the authority and resources with which to act" (Wilson 1989:23). Which is to say, people matter, but so do the contexts within which they work.

Japan's procuracy is also more "pervasive" than prosecutor organizations in the United States, for it attempts to control more of the activities carried out inside the organization. In general, the more pervasive an organization tries to be, the greater the effort required to maintain effective control (Etzioni 1964:71). For prosecutors in Japan, the collective exercise of discretion does not naturally emerge from some peculiar cultural propensity to act as a group or to prefer hierarchical relations. Those cultural propensities do exist, and in various ways they justify and support practices like *kessai*, but in the end discretion is exercised collectively because prosecutors have consciously decided to coordinate activities that way. They have done so for decades. Most operators accept and approve managerial efforts to control their behavior, but some chafe at the restrictions on their autonomy and resist or evade attempts at control. Even so, the controls are ubiquitous, and prosecutors who cannot make peace with them become "prosecutor-quitters" of the sort surveyed by Japan's bar association. To the quitters, and to many who remain in the procuracy, the or-

---

enon" (Nelken 1996). Japan contrasts sharply with the individualistic nature of prosecution in the United States, but the starkest contrast is Italy, where prosecutorial discretion is extremely decentralized, individualistic, and nonhierarchical (Di Federico 1998).

ganization is both ally and enemy. I interviewed an ex-prosecutor a few years after he left the organization in order to begin private practice as an attorney. He had been on the procuracy's "elite course" for thirteen years, including several years in Tokyo's Special Investigation Division, home to many of the most sought-after posts in the organization.

> I quit the prosecutors office because I wanted to experience a wider world. As a pros-
> ecutor, you come in contact only with suspects, defendants, witnesses, and other
> prosecutors. Your world is very limited. As a prosecutor I was involved in enough or-
> ganizational wars; I wanted to fight more personal battles. In the prosecutors office,
> comments as an individual are forbidden. One always speaks as a member of the
> group and one always speaks carefully, with an ear tuned to what the group will feel
> about what you say. And you know, the world never knows exactly who handled a
> particular case. The media simply report that "the Special Investigation Division"
> did it, or they occasionally mention a manager's name, but frontline prosecutors
> don't get any public recognition. In this sense, individuals do not exist in the procu-
> racy. Individual prosecutors exist only as cogs in the organizational wheel. This, of
> course, has its own satisfactions. The organization looks out for you, and you make
> friends with lots of other prosecutors. Above all, the organization can fight battles
> that individuals acting alone cannot. Still, sometimes these satisfactions just aren't
> enough. I wanted to do more on my own, to be more autonomous, to be perceived
> as an individual. As a prosecutor that's not how I felt. That's why I quit.

This man's yearning for autonomy and individual identity poignantly illustrates the hierarchical character of collective discretion. I know what he means. As described in this book's introduction, nowhere did I experience more hierarchical control, or more difficulty, than in my efforts to administer the survey. The determination to permit the survey had to be made, like all discretionary decisions, collectively and hierarchically. My survey was therefore thoroughly *kessai*-ed. I never learned the details of the review process. Indeed, until I stumbled across it, the review itself, not to mention its exactitude, was meant to be secret. The secrecy derived, at least in part, from the bright line the procuracy draws between insiders and outsiders, and from the corollary belief that inside information should be kept hidden from outside scrutiny. Bureaucracies everywhere are secretive, of course — that is one of their defining qualities — but they are not uniformly so. Neither are prosecutor organizations.

The organization of prosecution in Japan is also cohesive to an extent matched by few, if any, American prosecutor organizations. Indeed, its members manifest a commitment to the organization and to each other that I have seldom seen elsewhere. Even when the organization stifles individuality (as it did for the prosecutor quoted above), the stifled continue to conform to the standard operating procedures. For the vast majority of Japanese prosecutors the only real options are exit and loyalty; voice is not a viable choice. The inability to speak out and against can be costly. In 1995, for example, a Sapporo prosecutor killed himself in his office, probably, his peers say, because he felt impotent to resist a manager whose authoritarian directives he could not abide. Nevertheless, for the vast majority of Japanese prosecutors, hierarchical relations, solidarity with colleagues, and commitment to the organization's mission are job characteristics they welcome more than they deplore.

The high levels of cohesion and commitment reflect the procuracy's broad "scope." That is, prosecutors in Japan *jointly* conduct a wider variety of activities, from the occupational to the social, than do American prosecutors. Of course, all organizations confront the problem of compliance, the challenge of getting members to conform to regulations and expectations (Etzioni 1964:58). Wide scope, as in Japan's procuracy, promotes compliance, chiefly because it increases the effectiveness of nonutilitarian, normative controls by separating prosecutors from other social groups and by increasing their involvement in and commitment to the organization. More specifically, wide scope increases the salience of nonmaterial rewards, such as the meaning derived from acting out of a sense of duty, purpose, or calling; it raises regard for the status rewards bestowed by other prosecutors; and it enhances the associational benefits that accrue to those who work in the highly cohesive organization. Although these rewards are difficult to measure, they are critical sources of control and compliance and therefore constitute another principal distinctive of the Japanese way of justice.

Finally, the Japanese way of organizing prosecution enables prosecutors to effectively manage the strain between two imperatives of justice that Americans regard as often incompatible and always in tension: the need to individualize case dispositions, and the need to treat like cases alike so as to achieve a tolerable level of consistency. As the following two chapters show, the conscious pursuit of consistency, and the ability to achieve high levels of it without sacrificing the imperative to correct offenders by individualizing charge decisions, are qualities of Japanese prosecution that merit both examination and commendation.

PART II

THE CONTENT OF
JAPANESE JUSTICE

5

Consistency

Comparative law, especially the study of legal institutions and procedures, should be ranked among the most illuminating branches of legal science. When teaching a course that emphasizes comparative procedure, I remind students of the justification that was given them when they were asked to learn Latin in school: We study Latin to learn English. So with comparative law. . . . The purpose of comparative study is to help understand what is distinctive (and problematic) about domestic law.

John H. Langbein, "The Influence of Comparative Procedure
in the United States"

Scenes from Home and Abroad

Oakland, California

I met Larry for the first time in July 1993. At the time, he was an eighteen-year veteran in the Oakland County District Attorney's Office, one of 142 prosecutors in what may be the most highly respected local prosecutors office in California. Nearly two decades earlier Larry had graduated from a prestigious public law school in the same state. A former classmate, now a public defender in the Oakland County Superior Court, regards Larry as "a good guy," "an able prosecutor," and a more-or-less "typical" senior deputy district attorney.

Larry was a manager. As one of four "trial team leaders" in the Oakland office, he was the captain of a group of eight prosecutors, or deputy district attorneys, who handled trials and related hearings in Superior Court. Nonetheless, within ten minutes of our first meeting Larry told me he consults little with other team members and wants them to consult him only in "extraordinary" circumstances. "My pet peeve," Larry explained, "is when other deputies send me stuff [cases] that they should decide on their own." Larry said he consults with his superiors only on serious cases which are likely to attract significant media attention. He said that the best part of his job is doing jury trials — "they're a real rush" — but that since becoming a team leader, he had become more occupied with other activities, like plea-bargaining. At least two days a week Larry went to the chambers of one of the fourteen criminal court judges in Oakland to plea-bargain cases which had not been settled in Municipal Court. Since this was an important part of his job, I asked if I could observe.

Larry consented. Compared with Japanese prosecutors, Larry was remarkably open to outsiders. He obviously felt there was little to hide.

The next morning when I arrived at Larry's office I spent a few minutes skimming the stack of blue three-by-five cards on his desk. Larry explained that the cards summarized the cases he would plea-bargain. Each card had space for information about bail, prior prosecutor and court actions in the current case, current charges pending, criminal record, the names of police and other prosecutors who had handled the current case, and a brief summary of the case facts — seldom more than a sentence or two, usually less.

While Larry acquainted himself with the contents of the cards, I asked him to explain how he and the other prosecutors plea-bargain. Larry said that for some offenses, especially drug crimes, the office tries to standardize offers. In other cases, however, "offers vary a lot because reasonable people differ and because we [prosecutors] have different values." According to Larry, the hardest part about making offers is the prosecutor's feelings about the defense attorney. "Whether he's a friend or an asshole matters a lot," Larry explained. "Friends tend to get better deals." Larry also averred that problems in his personal life, such as fights with his wife, had little influence on the offers he made. He then described two styles of plea-bargaining, both common in Oakland. Some prosecutors make high offers ("overcharge") and then negotiate when the defense attorney counters. This strategy gives a prosecutor more leverage over the defense. Other prosecutors make "rock-bottom" offers right away, leaving little room for negotiation. Larry said he prefers the second style because "it saves time and monkey business."

I followed Larry to Judge Lancaster's chambers in order to see his style for myself. By the time we arrived the judge and several defense lawyers were already present. Judge Lancaster sat in a chair behind his desk, feet propped up on the desk's edge. Like the others in the room, he drank coffee from a Styrofoam cup and munched on doughnuts while waiting for the remaining participants to arrive. Larry and I sat on a big, overstuffed black couch directly across from the judge. Soon we were joined by more coffee-consuming, doughnut-devouring defense lawyers, most of whom appeared to know each other well. The group chatted amiably about baseball and movies and vacation plans for another several minutes before the morning's business began.

From 10:10 to 11:10 A.M., Larry plea-bargained with eight or nine defense lawyers (it was impossible to keep an exact count). During that period he disposed of six cases and tried to reach plea agreements in four or five more. At several points during the hour Larry was negotiating simultaneously with two, three, or even four defense lawyers about their clients' cases. It was like juggling: while one offer was in the air another offer was on its way up so that still another could be caught and sent up yet again. I will not (and cannot) capture the simultaneity here. Instead, consider these scenes from two of the cases I observed that morning.

> In one case the defendant was accused of stabbing a friend in the chest with a knife, causing death. The defendant was charged with voluntary manslaughter. The victim had a blood-alcohol content of .32 (.10 made one legally drunk in California). The victim and defendant had been best friends. The defense lawyer claimed the victim

was a notoriously violent man who, in a drunken rage, backed the defendant into a corner. At least that is what his client told him. Larry, relying on the two-sentence description of case facts on his blue card, said the defendant took a "roundhouse swing" at the victim, without provocation. Larry offered six years for a plea of guilty. The defense lawyer, soon to become a judge, countered with an offer of three years. Another lawyer in the room tried to convince the defense lawyer that there is not much difference between three and six years because "actual time served won't vary much anyway." The defense lawyer was unconvinced, however, and instead of accepting the six-year offer asked Larry again for a more lenient deal. "Look," he said, "the victim and my client were best friends and the victim was a very violent guy. It's a tragedy." Larry was unmoved. "Look man," he said, "*I don't know what the truth actually is. I'm just going by the card.*" Judge Lancaster tried to pressure the defense lawyer into taking the six-year offer, hinting that he would make up part of the difference at sentencing. The defense lawyer left the room to ask his client if six years was acceptable, but quickly returned to report it was not. He sought and obtained a three-week continuance. Later Larry criticized the defense lawyer for being unable to persuade his client to take "a good offer." In Larry's view the defense lawyer lacked adequate "client control." He said a better lawyer—someone like Bill—would have gotten a better deal.

Bill was the defense attorney in the second case. His client was accused of raping a woman in the kitchen of her home after she had tried to end a long-term relationship. Larry initially offered fourteen years. Bill replied with a stream of colorful invective ending with the imperative to "go fuck yourself." After another look at the appropriate blue card, Larry followed up with an offer of six years. A deal soon was struck.

Kobe, Japan

In the summer of 1993 I had the opportunity to watch Yoshio, a ten-year veteran of Japan's procuracy, decide what to do about a man accused of stealing eleven mushrooms from private property on a remote hillside on the outskirts of Kobe, a large city in western Japan. Mushroom thieves are not especially common in Japan, even though they can make a good profit by selling their ill-gotten fungi to shops and restaurants.

Since the offender had fully confessed, the question for Yoshio was what punishment to seek. The court would make the final decision, but as the investigating prosecutor Yoshio had to decide whether to charge the offender and, if he charged him, what to recommend as a sentence. Yoshio telephoned the victim, who owned the land on which the mushrooms grew, and asked what he would like done with the offender. The victim wanted the offender punished severely, though he stressed that above all he did not want his name mentioned in connection with the case. The victim recently had received several harassing phone calls, possibly from the mushroom thief, and he feared additional trouble if he openly pushed for a harsh punishment.

The mushroom thief had no prior criminal record, other than a few traffic offenses which Yoshio said would not influence the present disposition. In the most serious such case, decided eight years earlier, the offender paid a fine of 20,000 yen ($160) for speeding. In the present case the offender had violated the Forest Law, which provided for no more than three years' imprisonment and/or a 300,000 yen ($2,400) fine. The offender was not detained in jail during the period his case was investigated and decided.

Yoshio had a problem: in the absence of precedents to guide him, how could he tell what punishment, precisely, the mushroom thief deserved? Yoshio first had his assistant check the Kobe office records to see if any other mushroom thieves had been prosecuted in recent years. Nothing was found. Reasoning by analogy, Yoshio next figured that since stealing eleven mushrooms is less serious than breaking into someone's residence but more serious than shoplifting, the offender should get something in between the going rates for these two crimes. Further, Yoshio reasoned, shoplifters almost always get a suspended sentence for the first offense. Since this case was more like shoplifting than burglary, perhaps the mushroom thief should be forgiven too. But after further discussion with his assistant Yoshio determined that "if we forgive him he'll probably just do it again." A 50,000 yen ($400) fine seemed about right, but without guidelines to rely on, Yoshio was reluctant to follow his instincts.

So Yoshio conducted further research. A newspaper search using an electronic database uncovered no cases sufficiently similar to provide the guidance Yoshio sought. Next he had his assistant call the police to find out if they had disposed of any mushroom cases by using their powers to "dispose of trivial crimes." Still no help. Then Yoshio had his assistant call two prosecutor branch offices in rural areas well known for the production of mushrooms. Two days later the branches called back to report that no precedents could be found. Determined to find something to go on, Yoshio then conducted, this time personally, another search of the Kobe office records. Bingo. Two years earlier a prosecutor had charged another mushroom thief and imposed a fine. Since the prosecutor-in-charge was still working in Kobe, Yoshio telephoned him to ask for more details about the prior case. With this standard in hand, Yoshio decided to seek the same punishment he originally deemed proper: summary prosecution and a fine of 50,000 yen ($400). Before making the final disposition, he gained the approved of two of his superiors through *kessai* consultations, just as office policy requires.

The first point of these stories is that in prosecution, as in armies and schools, organization matters (Wilson 1989). As explained in chapter 4, Japanese prosecutors work in an organization — a system of consciously coordinated activities — that differs markedly from the organizations in which their American counterparts work. This fact has profound implications for how prosecutors define and perform their tasks and thus for the content and quality of Japanese criminal justice. It should have an equally profound influence on how Japanese criminal justice is studied but unfortunately it has not. The crucial significance of organizations has been sorely neglected in previous works, a peculiar dereliction considering the central importance scholars ascribe to organizations in Japanese society (Nakane 1970; Vogel 1975).

The second point of these stories is that the Japanese way of organizing prosecution regularly and effectively manages the tension between two imperatives of justice that Americans regard as often incompatible and always in tension — the need to individualize case dispositions, and the need to treat like cases alike so as to achieve consistency or "order."[1] This chapter begins by describing the "limits of order" in American prosecution systems and the "possibility of order" in Japan. Then it explains the differences. The chapter continues the story, begun in chapter 4, about the centrality of bureaucratic administration in Japanese criminal justice, an important but little-understood reality in the sociology of criminal justice. By presenting the structure, roles, and tasks of Japan's procuracy, the previous chapter provided a descriptive account of some of the proximate causes of consistency. All explanations must be bounded — one cannot explain everything — but the foregoing account is unsatisfactory insofar as it fails to connect the organization of prosecution to broader cultural and structural realities. This chapter tries to make those connections explicit. Because the story is comparative, it is also about inconsistency and disorder in American prosecution practices. This is, in other words, an account of how Larry and Yoshio came to be such different prosecutors. Their stories matter because consistency and justice do.

The Limits of Order in American Prosecution

> A bureaucratic, rule-oriented administrative model of management does not fit the nature of the job of criminal prosecution. Both theoretical literature and case studies . . . support this position.
>
> Lief H. Carter, *The Limits of Order*

In his seminal study of a large prosecutors office in "Vario County," California, Lief Carter (1974) argues that attempts to impose organizational control over individual prosecutors either fail or, to the extent they succeed, impair the quality of case dispositions. Prosecutors cannot develop structured procedures for disposing of cases, Carter contends, and the best offices do not even try to do so. The overlapping objectives of order, regularity, consistency, and uniformity of dispositions — of treating like cases alike — must be sacrificed in order to enable prosecutors to learn, adapt, innovate, and thereby individualize justice. In short, both prosecutors and their students must recognize "the limits of order."

Many American scholars agree that ordered, consistent justice either is impossible to achieve or else is purchased at the price of individualized decision-making — a cost most consider too high. Nearly two decades after Carter wrote *The Limits of Order*, a group of scholars summarized the 1950s American Bar Foundation Survey of the Administration of Criminal Justice, "the most extensive and, probably in constant dollars, most expensive empirical investigation of the criminal justice system ever undertaken" (Ohlin and Remington 1993:xiii). Their review focuses on the unavoidable "tension between individualization and uniformity" in criminal justice, and in a survey of "discretion by criminal justice decision makers" which introduces

---

1. The term "consistency" has several synonyms, including "regularity," "uniformity," and "order." In this chapter all these objectives refer to the imperative to "treat like cases alike." I use the words interchangeably.

the volume, Lloyd Ohlin (1993:17) laments that individualized justice has too often been sacrificed at the altar of uniformity:

> The current assault on discretion by criminal justice officials may be producing a system that is too rigid in application and likely to be unresponsive to the need to temper criminal justice with social justice. Most of the authors [of the chapters in this book] would endorse a position stated as follows: Complexity is a fundamental attribute of the variety of problems officials encounter at all major points of decision in the system of criminal justice. Responses to criminal offenders must address this fact if they are to be sufficiently flexible to take account of individual differences.

In another chapter in the same volume, Frank Remington (1993:113) reviews the research on prosecution practices, both before and after the ABF studies. He singles out Carter's work as "one of the most useful studies of prosecutorial practices," and argues, in complete accord with Carter, that "the clear message of the ABF research" and "the conclusion reached by those who, in the ensuing three decades, have studied prosecutor day-to-day practices" is that "we should prefer that [efforts to control discretion] fail." Instead of pursuing the specter of order, criminal justice reform must primarily seek to develop people and organizations that "change, innovate, and learn in sustained rather than haphazard fashion." Like Carter and many others, Remington is devoutly skeptical of efforts to pursue order in the prosecutors office: "We do not know what, if anything, should be done about the immense amount of discretion possessed by the prosecutor. . . . We lack the knowledge necessary to decide . . . how best to structure the charging decision so that it does focus on the substantive concern of how best to achieve the social control objectives of the criminal justice system" (Ohlin and Remington 1993).[2]

My own research in American prosecution offices reveals that many American prosecutors are similarly agnostic (or unconcerned) about how to control discretion and are pessimistic about the possibility of harmonizing the two imperatives of justice: individualization and consistency.[3] One of the first American prosecutors I in-

---

2. Remington (1993:113) notes that similar conclusions about the "limits of order" have been reached by Robert Weninger (1987) in his study of prosecution in El Paso, Texas; Pamela Utz (1978), who studied prosecutors in San Diego and Alameda counties in California; Arthur Rosett and Donald Cressey (1976) in their analysis of California prosecutors; and several other observers of American prosecutors. Similar assertions have been made by Davis (1969:230), LaFave (1970:538), Abrams (1971:7), Rabin (1972:1075), Abrams (1975), Vorenberg (1976), Weinreb (1977), Langbein and Weinreb (1978), Weigend (1980), Vorenberg (1981), Frase (1990), Feeley (1992b:285), Baumgartner (1992), Pizzi (1993:1346), Burnham (1996:83), and Uviller (1999:71).

3. Belief in the "limits of order" is not confined to prosecutors; other American enforcement officials seem to share it as well. For example, in 1994 the Internal Revenue Service sought criminal prosecution in 4,542 cases of alleged tax fraud, tax evasion, and money laundering. However, the chances of being recommended for prosecution were far higher in some areas of the country (such as Roanoke, Virginia, and Pittsburgh, Pennsylvania) than in others (such as New Mexico and Idaho). North Dakotans were nearly four times more likely to be referred for prosecution than South Dakotans. Critics charged that "the data raise the question of whether the American people are getting equal treatment under the law." In response, the deputy commissioners of the IRS said that although the agency "strives to treat taxpayers in similar situations the same way everywhere in the country," because IRS agents have discretion, "differences in how similar cases are handled are inevitable" (*New York Times* 4/14/96).

terviewed was the deputy chief of the Oakland County District Attorney's Office in California. Oakland is often regarded as one of the most professional, well-run prosecution offices in the United States, and the deputy chief is the number two post in it, beneath only the elected district attorney. Having just returned from a year of field research in Japan, I was especially interested in *kessai*, the Japanese system that requires frontline prosecutors to seek the approval of two or three superiors (or more in high-profile cases) before making any charge decision. Since I wanted to know if there was an American counterpart to Japanese *kessai*, I asked the deputy chief how he and other managers in the Oakland office reviewed and approved their subordinates' decisions. The response given by this twenty-three-year veteran completely rejected the premise of my question. "Every case is different," he declared. "You can't police everyone to make sure they do the right thing, and you can't regulate their decisions. It just doesn't work."

Of course, soon thereafter I learned that frontline prosecutors in Oakland are required to consult with the chief, the deputy chief, and other office superiors, although only in a small category of high-profile cases that are identified in an ad hoc manner as "likely to attract media attention or criticism." In high-stakes cases, *kessai*-like consultations and superior approvals also are required of federal prosecutors working in the ninety-four U.S. Attorneys offices and the Department of Justice (Stewart 1987; Nagel and Schulhofer 1992). Compared with Japan, however, hierarchical review in American offices is extraordinarily uncommon. What stands out is how infrequently and superficially superiors monitor their subordinates' decisions.[4]

Oversight in American offices is especially conspicuous by its absence in the great bulk of relatively "nonserious" cases—the American analogues to mushroom thefts. It is widely held that even if they wanted to, prosecutors in busy urban offices could not achieve the kind of consistency that Carter, for more principled reasons, says they should not seek anyway. David Heilbroner (1990), for example, in his insightful ethnography based on three years working in the Manhattan District Attorney's Office, describes prosecutors as "awash in petty crime" and "numbed by the numbers." In his first year Heilbroner and his fellow rookies were instructed by the deputy chief, "a reliable source of sage advice," not to fret over cases that, in Manhattan at least, were comparatively minor. "I don't know what you're all so worried about," the deputy chief counseled at the first training meeting. "For the first year nobody cares what you do. You're only dealing with misdemeanors" (p. 27). Before long, Heilbroner and his colleagues learned that their job "was to keep the wheels of the busiest and probably most chaotic court system in the world turning, or more appropriately, grinding" (p. 51). In order to "help free up the overburdened court system" the prosecutor's job was to "keep dispositions up" (p. 77). The real function of the DA's office, Heilbroner ultimately concludes, is "prosecuting serious cases" (p. 141).

4. Hierarchical review is more common in American federal prosecutors offices than in local ones, but compared with Japan it still is weak and infrequent. Most strikingly, in federal offices non-charge decisions are seldom subject to internal review. Federal drug enforcement is especially "erratic and unplanned." For example, drug dealers' chances of being prosecuted vary greatly depending on where they do business. For these and related reasons, David Burnham (1996:83) calls the organization of federal prosecution "an adhocracy."

With only slight modification, the statements of the Oakland and Manhattan deputy chiefs apply to prosecutor practice in the far more placid Minneapolis office, where I also conducted research. There, the elected chief asked that subordinates seek his approval only in "some" murder and rape cases. Probed about this practice, the captain of one of the Minneapolis crime divisions explained that "prosecutors learn by doing and by failing." Since "many cases are just not that important in the overall scheme of things," there is little need for prosecutors to consult about decisions or concern themselves with whether like cases are being treated alike. Indeed, the main imperative for frontline prosecutors is to "do the right thing," and they receive little coaching or control to reach that determination. This aspiration to do good, this impulse for flexibility and substantive justice, "gives rise to competing conceptions of justice. The freedom to pick and choose among these conceptions undercuts the morality of all of them, and ironically the impulse to provide justice seems to foster a sense of injustice" (Feeley 1992b:286). Which is to say, flexibility crowds out consistency, and deference to the discretion of individual prosecutors undercuts uniformity. Order has its limits, at least in American prosecution offices.[5]

The Possibility of Order in Japanese Prosecution

> Justice . . . is equality — not, however, for all, but only for equals. And inequality is thought to be, and is, justice; neither is this for all, but only for unequals.
>
> Aristotle, *Politics*, book 3, chapter 9

> Treating similar cases differently is not a good thing. It is wrong as a matter of justice, and it stirs up public dissatisfaction and criticism.
>
> Japanese prosecutor

Justice obliges prosecutors to take into account the "special needs and circumstances of individuals" — that is, to individualize decisions (Wilson 1989:326). This is

5. Some scholars contend that American prosecutors seek and achieve a high degree of consistency, but their arguments, which tend to be formalistic, are unconvincing (Silberman 1978:255; Mellon et al. 1981; Nardulli et al. 1988:245). William Pizzi (1993:1345), for example, argues that since "a scandal in the way prosecutorial power is exercised within the office could hurt the prosecutor's chances of re-election . . . internal controls over prosecutorial discretion aimed at assuring both fairness and consistency have obvious political advantages." From this electoral imperative and from the need to "process and resolve cases efficiently and expeditiously," Pizzi infers that "a prosecutor's office will usually find it wise to have some system of informal controls over charging decisions and plea bargaining decisions." American chief prosecutors do worry about scandals and re-election, and in busy jurisdictions they are pressed to be efficient. Moreover, most American offices do have some system of informal control. Compared with Japan, however, such concerns rarely get translated into the serious pursuit of consistency. In Los Angeles, for example, after the passage of California's three-strikes law, former District Attorney Gil Garcetti promulgated only the most rudimentary guidelines to direct prosecutors about when not to pursue a new felony as a third strike. Even under Garcetti's successor, Steve Cooley, prosecutors had so little guidance about when to "strike a strike" that one veteran in the office said reading the relevant policy "is like reading the Bible. Every time you read it, there is something new you get out of it" (*Los Angeles Times* 12/20/00 and 1/22/01).

an imperative many Americans stress, and Japanese prosecutors do it well. As Daniel Foote (1992a:321) has shown, "Japan's criminal justice system places great emphasis on the reintegration and rehabilitation of suspects in accordance with their individualized circumstances." But justice also means treating similar cases similarly — dispensing ordered, consistent justice — and Japanese prosecutors do this well, too.[6] Since the first fact has been well documented but the second has not, this section focuses on how prosecutors in Japan achieve a high level of consistency, much higher than most Americans think possible or even desirable (Tonry 1995:154).[7] If both of these claims are correct, if Japanese prosecutors make individualized and consistent decisions, then here lies one of the most noteworthy accomplishments in a half-century of Japanese history replete with remarkable achievements.

Hunting for Bias

The imperative to be consistent has received little attention in previous studies of Japanese criminal justice. Indeed, "the most important distinction" between Japan's system of "benevolent paternalism" and the ideal-typic "crime-control model" of the criminal process is said to be "uniformity." On this view, Japanese criminal justice

> does not seek simply to process cases as quickly as possible according to highly uniform standards and pursuant to routine, stereotyped procedure.... On the contrary, the Japanese system emphasizes the importance of individualized determinations, based on careful consideration of the individual's personal circumstances and other factors.... This emphasis on specific prevention does not simply come into play after conviction. Rather, it affects, if not pervades, every stage of the system. (Foote 1992a:341)

Other research also stresses the individualizing, correctional goals of Japanese criminal justice while maintaining that "neither the law nor its enforcers . . . insist on . . . equal treatment of different offenders for like offenses" (Haley 1998:79).

Japanese prosecutors reject the tenet that there is a necessary trade-off between individualized decision-making and ordered, consistent dispositions.[8] The presumption of tension must therefore be reconsidered in light of the Japanese case. Where prosecutors have sufficient time, resources, power, and information, they can apply a highly regularized set of standards that still take into account a broad range of fac-

---

6. Although the principle that like cases should be treated alike is not universal, it is considered imperative by most modern legal systems. Donald Black (1989) has argued that despite the normative commitment to consistency, discrimination is ubiquitous in the legal handling of cases. In his view, the quantity of discrimination varies across different legal systems depending on the social diversity of the society and the social information available to decision-makers.

7. As developed in chapter 6, there is widespread agreement that Japanese prosecutors, police, and judges individualize decisions about how to treat suspects, defendants, and offenders. See Haley (1999); Inagawa (1995); M. Satō (1993); Foote (1992a); Bayley (1991); Castberg (1990); Braithwaite (1989); Haley (1989); Aoyagi (1986); Wagatsuma and Rosett (1986); Goodman (1986); George (1984); Itoh (1982); Shikita (1982); Matsuo (1981); Mitsui (1970); Clifford (1976); Dandō (1970); and Hirano (1963).

8. The contradiction between "the twin promises of equality and individuation" has been called "the classic dilemma of legality" (Sarat 1989:782).

tors relating to the individual's circumstances. Where these conditions of prosecution prevail, and where prosecutor culture is committed to both individualization and consistency, the two imperatives of justice do not necessarily conflict. In Japan one finds both the conditions and the commitment that enable this to occur. As a result, consistency is not only possible, it is routinely aspired to and often achieved.

The procuracy's quest for consistency can be evaluated by hunting for its converse — inconsistency and bias — in the organization's decision-making. The hunt for bias is essentially an effort to document unjustly unequal treatment of like-situated offenders. Concretely, it is a search for discrimination in any of its three guises: evil motives, unfair outcomes, and uneven pressures on prosecutors (Katz 1999).

I can say little about how or how much prosecutors in Japan are consciously biased against specific categories of suspects, victims, or combinations thereof because I do not possess good evidence about prosecutors' attitudes regarding race, ethnicity, nationality, gender, and the like. I attempted to include questions on this subject in my survey but was not permitted to do so, and even if I had been able to ask, the questions would have been so freighted with emotional and ethical overtones — that, say, one should not regard Koreans or leftists as incorrigibly predisposed to commit crimes — that the responses would have merited little trust. My hunt for "evil motives" had to be qualitative, indirect, and impressionistic. A priori, one might suppose that intolerance and prejudice, toward other Asians especially, are as "rampant" among prosecutors as they are among Japanese more generally (Sugimoto 1997:170; Hicks 1997:vii). I found little evidence to support this view.[9] On the whole, prosecutors in Japan appeared to hold fewer and weaker racial biases than the American prosecutors I studied. That is merely an impression, however, and prosecutors' restraint and obliqueness in discussing racial and ethnic issues made it difficult to discern their real attitudes and motives. More generally, I cannot tell if Japanese prosecutors are significantly biased for or against certain social categories, with one major exception discussed in chapter 6. In sex crime cases, prosecutors often seem to discount the seriousness of the offense — on the basis, at least in part, of their reduced regard for the interests of female victims.

The inability to tell if much prosecutorial decision-making is contaminated by "evil motives" is less troublesome than it may seem, for studies show that inconsistency can be attributed less to conscious biases than to the cumulative and unwitting effects of class, race, and other social differentials on legal officials. In short, most inconsistency probably occurs "without intent or a plan of any kind" (Black 1989:110). The hunt for bias may therefore turn its attention away from evil motives and toward unfair outcomes.

The first target in this search must be prosecutors' treatment of foreigners. Daniel Foote (1992a:374) argues that Japan's homogeneity makes prosecutors likely

---

9. The most striking statement of prejudice I heard occurred when a veteran prosecutor told me America is a good "negative role model" for Japan because it teaches what does *not* work to maintain social order. If you want to control crime, he argued, do not do what America does: do not allow guns to proliferate, do not tolerate drug use or abuse, do not give women equal rights, and do not allow foreigners into the country.

to treat outsiders differently than Japanese. "The dominant role of prosecutors," he says, "and the extensive discretion vested in them increases [sic] the potential impact of official bias — whether conscious or not." This view predicts that prosecutors are likely to be most biased against leftists, Koreans, *burakumin* (descendants of outcast groups), indigents, day laborers, other "fringe groups," and especially foreigners. Criminal justice officials "have stepped up their surveillance and prosecution of [foreign workers]," and the influx of foreigners poses "the greatest external challenge" to the "benevolent paternalism" of Japanese criminal justice. Because of differences in language and values, prosecutors are unlikely to devote significant resources to the rehabilitation and reintegration of foreigners, instead concentrating simply on "processing such cases efficiently." Thus, Foote predicts, the criminal justice process is likely to follow "a separate track" for crimes by foreigners. "Some degree of bias — on regional, class, or other grounds — seems inevitable [and] . . . there are numerous points at which such bias — conscious or not — could and at least in some cases clearly does affect outcomes" (pp. 374–377).

If this view is right, then the order observed in Japanese criminal justice is a chimera caused by the relative homogeneity of inputs into the Japanese system (Black 1989:59). But order is no mirage. Assertions about inevitable bias are inconsistent with the best available studies of prosecutorial discrimination in Japan and the United States. Though more research is needed, it appears that compared with their American counterparts, Japanese prosecutors discriminate less, and less severely, against racial and ethnic minorities.

Consider American prosecutors first. Cassia Spohn and her colleagues have examined prosecutors' initial decision to charge and their subsequent decision to dismiss the charge in thirty-three thousand cases in the Los Angeles District Attorney's office from 1977 to 1980. After controlling for a wide range of potentially confounding factors, their data reveal a "pattern of discrimination" in favor of female defendants and against black and Hispanic defendants. Thus, L.A. prosecutors "do appear to take both gender and race into account in deciding whether to charge the defendant." Women benefit, while blacks and Hispanics suffer. This research concludes by noting that other studies of American criminal justice have found little evidence of racial discrimination in the formal trial process and the less formal guilty plea process, but "what happens before conviction may not be so reassuring" (Spohn et al. 1987:183). It is an apt conclusion. A recent review of charging and plea-bargaining decisions by American prosecutors finds "compelling evidence of racial disparity" that "frequently reflects racial discrimination" (Walker et al. 2000:139). Indeed, racially unfair outcomes are evident in a wide array of American prosecutor practices, from drug charges, which are systematically more severe for blacks than for whites (Mauer 1999:138; D. Cole 1999:132), to decisions to seek capital punishment, which reveal a clear pattern of privileging white victims that is "unexplainable on grounds other than race" (Gross and Mauro 1989:109).

In contrast, the Research and Training Institute (RTI) of Japan's Ministry of Justice has conducted two extensive studies of the treatment of foreign suspects and defendants (Kurata et al. 1992). The first study focused on larceny cases, the second on assaults. Since both studies were conducted by prosecutor insiders with an obvious interest in the research conclusions, one must interpret their results cautiously. Still, their findings contrast sharply with the results of the American research just described and with allegations that prosecutor discrimination against foreigners is egregiously widespread (Takahashi 1992; Herbert 1997). Neither RTI study finds evidence that foreign suspects or offenders are treated worse than Japanese. This hunt for bias — the most systematic so far — comes up empty. The hunt obviously should continue. Compared with America, Japan has few studies that systematically search for bias in the criminal process. Nonetheless, it is notable that even with respect to crimes committed by foreigners, the category of offender most expected to receive unjustly unequal treatment, consistency seems to prevail.[10]

"The punishment problem" discussed in chapter 2 further documents the commitment to consistency in Japan's procuracy. In that case prosecutors engaged in their own "hunt for bias" among Japanese judges. They found it. Sentences imposed by Kansai courts were more lenient than those imposed by courts in Tokyo and elsewhere in Japan. The Osaka episode reveals three core truths about consistency in Japanese criminal justice. First, although the sentencing disparities may surprise those who deduce from the unitary structure of Japan's judiciary that uniformity prevails (Ramseyer and Nakazato 1999:136), most disparities are minor. To take one example, Osaka courts suspended sentences 61 percent of the time, only 5 percent more often than courts elsewhere in Japan. Nevertheless, even these small inconsistencies greatly concerned prosecutors. Second, no prosecutor argued that the disparities were acceptable; the issue was never framed that way. The premise instead was that likes should be treated alike throughout the country, and the real issue was whether Kansai should become more like Kanto, or vice versa. Prosecutors pursued a two-pronged strategy to generate greater consistency in trial outcomes. Publicly, they rebuked judges in the media so as to generate pressure to move Kansai courts in a more punitive direction. Practically, they adopted policies for the Kansai area that aimed to "level up" the punishment disparities.[11] In the end, of course, they were unable to eliminate the inconsistency they stalked. Third and finally, the punishment problem disclosed the procuracy's commitment to achieving consistency not just between different prosecutors but between *different prosecutors offices*. In contrast, the American system of federalism, with its respect for local norms and regional differences, inhibits the pursuit of consistency between offices. In this respect, as in many others, Japanese prosecution shares more in common with prosecution in Civil Law countries than it does with the United States (Merryman 1985). The contrast, however, is not merely with America. Inconsistency across prosecutors offices appears to be a significant problem in Great Britain as well (Koyama 1991:1269).

10. One notable exception to this claim occurred in April 2000, when Govinda Prasad Mainali, a Nepalese man on trial for murdering a female office worker in Tokyo's Shibuya District, was acquitted by the Tokyo District Court. Prosecutors appealed the verdict and, despite the acquittal, Mainali remained in jail throughout his appellate trial. Critics charged that prosecutors sought Mainali's continued detention precisely because he was a foreigner, claiming that such treatment would have been "unthinkable for a Japanese suspect" (*Asahi Shimbun* 12/24/00). In December 2000, Mainali was convicted. The closest American analogue to this case may be the practice of refusing to release incarcerated defendants whose initial trial ends in a hung jury. Some such defendants remain in detention before and during their second trial.

11. When confronted with inconsistency, legal reformers usually "prefer equal severity to equal leniency" (Black 1989:73).

In addition to consistency across offices, Japan's procuracy also endeavors to ensure that *different prosecutors in the same office* treat similar cases similarly. This commitment is clearly manifested in the organization of prosecution, especially the *kessai* system of consultation and review and the charging and sentencing standards described in the last chapter. The stories about Yoshio and Larry that opened this chapter are only one reflection of the fact that Japan's commitment to consistency and its organizational routines for pursuing it contrast markedly with standard American operating procedures. Although no single story is ever representative, Yoshio's behavior is typical. Prosecutors in Japan routinely attend to the issue of consistency, just as Yoshio did (Kameyama 1999). They have to.

Kessai and standards aim to even out disparities that arise from the "uneven pressures" on prosecutors — the third incarnation of bias — that stem from their varying assessments of the legal and social differentials across cases. These internal controls seek to equalize what otherwise would be unjustly unequal treatment. The survey of factors influencing suspension of prosecution (table 3.2) revealed that prosecutors consider some social facts (such as the suspect's status or prior relationship to the victim) important when deciding whether to charge. In the abstract, there is widespread agreement between prosecutors about how and how much such factors matter, but in weighing their significance in particular cases discrepancies between prosecutors are bound to emerge. The hierarchical reviews and charging standards systematically search for such discrepancies and attempt to iron them out. Before deciding whether and what to charge, a prosecutor will take into account the managing prosecutor's probable response, and eventually she must confront the manager and explain her decision. This makes it difficult (though not impossible) for the prosecutor to pursue her own notion of justice if it differs from the organizational norm. Still, the two seldom differ, for most prosecutors internalize the norms enforced by the internal controls. The organization's commitment to consistency generates individual commitment too. In the end, uneven assessments of like-situated suspects get smoothed out by both the frontline operator's commitment to consistency and by the procuracy's organized hunt for bias.

A Summary and Two Qualifications

> Individuals . . . have no other way to make the big decisions except within
> the scope of institutions they build.
>
> Mary Douglas, *How Institutions Think*

Prosecutors make "big decisions" about justice within the context of an organization that is especially well suited to resolving the tension between consistency and flexibility, between order and individualization, between treating likes alike and unlikes differently. Previous studies have failed to recognize this crucial point. On the one hand, research on American prosecutors concludes that since we cannot realistically expect to achieve order from prosecutors, we should not demand it from them. On this view, prosecutors ought to accept in good faith the ambiguity of their tasks and strive to learn from experience in order to individualize justice (Carter 1974). On the other hand, research about prosecutors in Japan rightly concludes that they emphasize the importance of individualized determinations, but in its silence on the subject it overlooks the significance of consistency in Japanese criminal justice.

Consistency is not only possible in Japan's procuracy, it is routinely aspired to and often achieved.[12] The organization has engineered a strong consensus about its primary task—clarifying the truth—and operators in particular (with much help from the police) work diligently to uncover and construct the truth during precharge investigations. Managers, employing a wide range of carrots and sticks, coordinate and control operators so that equals are treated equally and unequals unequally. Executives secure and preserve the organization's autonomy so that operators and managers can attend to their main tasks. These are the roles and tasks—the prerequisites—of a highly consistent system of criminal justice. The claim that "a bureaucratic, rule-oriented administrative model of management does not fit the nature of the job of criminal prosecution" (Carter 1974:117) simply does not fit the Japanese case. To an extent inconceivable to some American researchers, the Japanese way of prosecution seeks and achieves concord, not discord, between individualization and consistency.

This claim may be misunderstood by those who recognize that Japanese criminal justice imperfectly realizes the consistency imperative, so I must clarify the claim by qualifying it in two ways. First, my focus is on prosecutors' decisions, not the police actions that precede them or the court determinations that follow. Chapter 2 showed that Japan's criminal justice system is a series of interlinked institutions and discretionary decisions. If the institutions linked to the procuracy do not seek or achieve consistency, then the Japanese way of justice may be less consistent than the Japanese way of prosecution. Nonetheless, since prosecutors play a pivotal role in the criminal process, their achievements in "order" likely translate, if imperfectly, into a significant measure of systemic consistency.

Second, we need more research, more systematic hunts for bias in Japan's procuracy and throughout its criminal justice system. This second qualification may seem a frustratingly monotonous refrain, but it needs to be heard and heeded by researchers and especially by the Japanese officials who control access to relevant research sites. The Japanese way of organizing prosecution irons out "uneven pressures" on prosecutors' decisions, but the data on "evil motives" and "unfair outcomes" are thin. Further research should target these domains.

The crimes of the powerful—police, politicians, bureaucrats, and businessmen—deserve special scrutiny. One of the best-known and most widely cited propositions in the sociology of law is that "downward law is greater than upward law" (Black 1976:21). This theorem holds that more law (or governmental social control) gets directed at low-ranking people than at high-ranking people. It appears to apply at all times and to all societies. Japan may be distinctive, however, in *the degree to which* downward law is greater than upward law, because the law's enforcers—police and prosecutors especially—work in a deeply dualistic environment (D. Johnson

---

12. As we saw in chapter 3, a primary prosecutor work objective is "treating like cases alike." My survey revealed that over 90 percent of Japanese prosecutors regard "treating like cases alike" as an "important" or "very important" work objective. Less than 1 percent said it was "not an objective."

1999). On the one hand, in "ordinary" cases of street crime, Japan's rules of criminal procedure confer so many powers on investigators that they are able to "make" cases far more easily than investigators in most other democracies (Miyazawa 1992). I have argued that prosecutors try to process these "normal crimes" consistently, and that they largely succeed. On the other hand, Japanese prosecutors lack many of the procedural powers, such as the authority to offer immunity or conduct undercover stings, that are routinely used in other countries to "make" cases against politicians and other white-collar offenders (Ugawa 1997). If this characterization of Japanese criminal justice is accurate, then Japanese law is like a cobweb, highly enabling of efforts to indict and convict small flies (the run-of-the-mill offenders) but simultaneously disabling of efforts to bring wasps and hornets to justice. In the context of this legal cobweb, some readers may regard the procuracy's achievements in order as insignificant, to which I must say: not when viewed in comparative perspective. Japanese prosecutors may imperfectly realize the ideal of consistency, but they come far closer to it than American prosecutors do. It is no mean feat.

Explaining Consistency

The previous sections described the different commitments to consistency in American and Japanese prosecution and set forth the proximate causes of that difference. All explanations must be bounded, but the preceding account is unsatisfactory insofar as it fails to connect the organizational causes of consistency to broader cultural and structural contexts. This section makes those connections explicit. A huge corpus of social science literature trumpets the causal importance of either culture or structure, but seldom of both. In the words of Mary Douglas (1986), this arbitrary separation of ideas from the institutions in which they work "creates a pernicious dichotomy, as if mind were out there, an existence, disembodied, supported by nothing, but somehow powerfully influencing the solidly physical institutions in curious ways. This perspective allows insoluble questions to fill the central forum of sociological debate." I want to avoid the harmful effects of creating such a dichotomy, but for ease of exposition I present my account in two installments — on culture and on structure. They clearly connect and influence one another in myriad ways. Most important, they are both critical causes of consistency in Japanese prosecution.

The Culture of Prosecution

> Instead of building on a foundation of our own cultural assumptions about organization, the anthropologist's task . . . is to seek first the architectural principles by which others build.
>
> Thomas Rohlen, *For Harmony and Strength*

In the study of Japanese criminal justice, as in the study of almost every other slice of social life, culture is often used as a "black box" to construct "circular" and "tautological" arguments (Steinhoff 1993:829). But invoking culture as cause need not be spurious. As David Bayley (1994:963) has said:

We must be careful not to go to the other extreme of making no provision in our explanations for behavioral propensities that people carry into different situations. . . . Legal culture is not . . . primordial but is created. At the same time, it would be naive indeed to think that socialization does not make different people behave differently in similar circumstances or predispose institutional actors to act in characteristic ways in different cultural settings. Appealing to legal culture is not always unintelligent reductionism.

In Japanese prosecution, culture promotes consistency in many ways, most importantly through its orientation to "facts" and its stress on the values of cohesion and control.

JUSTICE REQUIRES FACTS

> Justice is truth in action.
>
> Benjamin Disraeli

Truth is fundamental to everything else (Fernandez-Armesto 1997:3). One of the most important causes of consistency is prosecutors' belief that they must uncover the facts and construct the truth of a case before making a disposition decision. This widespread agreement about and endorsement of the way their critical task is defined — what I call the procuracy's "mission" — has been noted by other observers but has never been assigned the central significance it deserves. As emphasized throughout this chapter, justice implies two imperatives: treating different cases differently and treating likes alike. The crucial question is which suspects are different and which are alike. Japanese prosecutors believe they can deliver responsive, consistent justice in a case if and only if they know exactly what happened, for only then can they discern which suspects are "alike" and which are not. This is one key meaning of the phrase "precise justice," the label often used by prosecutors and others to describe Japan's system of criminal justice (Nomura 1994:143). Justice, they insist, cannot be done in the absence of facts. Before making ultimate decisions about who gets what, prosecutors must first decide who did what. They must, in other words, resolve issues of factual uncertainty. For Japanese prosecutors, as for the public they represent, justice is indeed truth in action.[13]

---

13. In this respect, Japan differs less from countries in the European Civil Law tradition than from the United States and other common law countries. Mirjan Damaska's (1986) classic comparative study of the legal process distinguishes two structures of state authority (hierarchical and coordinate) and two purposes of the legal process (conflict-solving and policy-implementing) in modern nation-states. These two axes determine four "faces of justice" or types of legal process. For hierarchical states committed to a policy-implementing process, "getting the facts right is normally one of the preconditions to realizing the goal of the legal process." In contrast, in coordinate states, which chiefly aim to solve conflicts, "truth seems elusive and reality, like the muses, seems always to have another veil." Clearly the "face" of Japanese criminal justice described in this chapter seems much closer to the former type than to the latter. It thus resembles the criminal processes of countries like Germany and France. However, there are at least two important differences between those countries and Japan. First, the commitment to "getting the facts right" seems stronger in Japanese criminal justice than in Damaska's activist states of western Europe (Damaska 1986:160; Frase 1990). Second, Japan's system places primary faith in prosecutors to discover the truth (Foote 1992a:372), whereas Damaska's "activist states" locate that responsibility in the hands of investigating magistrates and other state officials (Damaska 1986:162; Merryman 1985:48).

We have seen that American prosecutors define their tasks more ambiguously and that many reject truth construction through investigation as outside the scope of their duties (Carter 1974:195).[14] They do so not only because they consider truth a "by-product" that emerges after an adversarial clash with the defense (Feeley 1987:754), but also because even if they were to seek truth directly, they would be frustrated by numerous obstacles (Feeley 1992b:167). David Heilbroner (1990:336), for example, disconsolately describes the lesson he learned after three years as a prosecutor in the Manhattan District Attorney's Office: "Since starting work I had tried to use my discretion wisely, to do justice. But to be just, I had learned, you have to know the facts, and in the DA's office facts were a rarity. The true, the honestly mistaken, and the deliberately false stories of witnesses blurred indistinguishably into one another. I was doing the best I could under the circumstances, but the circumstances continued to wear me down."[15]

The conclusion Heilbroner eventually reached—that doing justice requires knowledge of the facts—is in Japan a taken-for-granted assumption that strongly influences almost everything prosecutors do. More important, the contexts of prosecution in Japan create circumstances that do not wear prosecutors down, as they did Heilbroner and his colleagues. As a result, facts are in fact anything but "a rarity." At the same time, it must be acknowledged that the "facts" of a case are hardly stable, objective realities (like palm trees or lizards) that can be directly apprehended through the senses. Rather, prosecutors start from a position of factual uncertainty and mobilize, construct, and compose facts in order to create "truth." Replacing uncertainty with something more solid requires prosecutors to rely on investigation, presumption, or some combination of the two. The nature of these options differs significantly between Japan and the United States.

In America, prosecutors draw on various sources for factual information. Defense lawyers, police, and probation officials all proffer data about the suspect's prior record, family history, and the instant case. However, the American prosecutor's search for facts is constrained in at least three ways that the Japanese prosecutor's search is not. First, American prosecutors, especially in urban settings, have heavier caseloads and thus face more significant resource limitations on discovering and clarifying the facts. Second, American prosecutors are more dependent on defense lawyers to provide information because they lack direct access to the defendant. Japanese prosecutors routinely interrogate suspects before making charge decisions, whereas American prosecutors rarely do. Several have told me that even if they could interrogate the accused they would not want to, because suspects "would just get in the way" of their effort to do justice. Similarly, in American offices the focus

14. Seattle prosecutors did express a strong commitment to "discovering the truth," but their capacity to capture the truth is undermined by several conditions of work: they have almost no contact with suspects; they work in an adversarial system in which no actor except the jury has responsibility for representing the truth; the legal regimes of evidence and procedure respect other values (like fairness) that rival truth in importance; and so on (Rayment 1999).

15. Though American commentators disagree about whether it is proper for a prosecutor to charge a suspect without personally believing in the suspect's guilt, "the prevailing view, at least in the world of practice, surely permits prosecutors to do so" (S. Fisher 1988:230; Stewart 1987:332). I know of no Japanese prosecutor who subscribes to this view.

of training programs is trial work, not investigations, charging, or plea-bargaining, because "that is what we do here," as one California prosecutor put it. Yet American defense lawyers often fail to provide prosecutors with relevant information, either because it is not in their client's interest to disclose or because they do not possess it themselves. This leaves many American prosecutors with vague, incomplete knowledge of case facts throughout the pretrial process. Third, in both the United States and Japan the prosecutor's investigation sometimes reveals conflicting accounts of the truth, but the problem is more pervasive in the United States because relationships in American criminal court communities are far more adversarial. American defense lawyers may believe that to "get along you must go along" with other criminal court actors, but they still go along far less than defense lawyers in Japan (S. Fisher 1988:228).

These constraints on the search for facts cause some American prosecutors to reject the fact-finding role, as when they proclaim that "whether the defendant did it is for the judge or jury to decide — it's not my job. . . . My job is to prosecute, not judge" (quoted in Alschuler 1968:63). However, even resolutely agnostic prosecutors cannot completely withdraw from the fact-finding role, for in sending a case to trial they simply pass judgment about "probable cause" instead of "reasonable doubt." Nonetheless, retreat from the fact-finding role is something Japanese prosecutors rarely even attempt. For them, retreat means surrender to inconsistency and injustice.

American prosecutors tend to resolve factual uncertainty by presuming facts that favor the suspect's guilt (Feeley 1992b:167). This, too, is something Japanese prosecutors try less often. Although some have argued that American prosecutors do not make guilt-favoring presumptions as often as they should (Uviller 1973), compared with Japanese, American prosecutors often do make presumptions — about the credibility of witnesses, the seriousness of the offense, and the character of the offender — against the suspect (S. Fisher 1988:230). In the typical American view, the prosecutor should "avoid deciding contested cases herself," for several reasons. First, many prosecutors are young, inexperienced, and therefore unable to make reliable judgments. At the same time, prosecutors have an obligation to ensure that victims and witnesses get their day in court, especially when their testimony supports conviction. Moreover, providing a forum for victims and witnesses helps "forestall public criticism of the district attorney's office." Since prosecutors work in an adversarial system as advocates for the public's interest, they fail to present the strongest case for the public if they do not press for conviction in "borderline" cases (Frohmann 1992). In short, in the United States uncertainty may not be resolved in favor of charging as often as some would like, but it is resolved in the pro-punishment direction more often than in Japan. This is one key reason that conviction rates are lower in Japan (see chapter 7).

Although prosecutors in Japan possess powerful legal levers for uncovering the truth, especially in ordinary street crime cases, when they fail to resolve factual uncertainty they tend to make different presumptions than their American counterparts. Most notably, prosecutors in Japan are more likely to resolve factual doubts — about credibility, seriousness, and character — in favor of the suspect's innocence. As a consequence, in many cases prosecutors do not charge suspects whom American prosecutors (in their own system) would. They do so for the converse of the reasons invoked to explain the American presumptions. First, since charge decisions are made collectively in Japan, it matters little if frontline operators are young and inexperienced. The pervasive system of controls and coordination mitigates the dangers of youth. Second, providing a forum for Japanese victims and witnesses is deemed less important than making a "correct" decision about whether to charge. Prosecutors, like just about everyone in Japan, believe that only the guilty should be charged and that the charged are almost certainly guilty. More than judges, prosecutors are the officials who actually try most suspects, and their careful screening is supported by public confidence in their "near infallibility" (Foote 1992a:373). Third, failing to provide a forum for victims or suspects is unlikely to result in public criticism, because of the public's confidence in prosecutors, because prosecutors are largely insulated from public criticism when it does occur, and because the public is unlikely to complain in the first place (Pharr 1990:207). Finally, as in the United States, prosecutors in Japan are advocates for the public interest, but in Japan's decidedly nonadversarial system of criminal justice, prosecutors do not interpret that duty to mean a primary commitment to victims and complaining witnesses. In the Japanese view, suspects are considered part of the public too, and whether critics like it or not, that public believes suspects should be charged only when there is sufficient evidence to support conviction (Hirano 1989:130).

In summary, doing justice by creating consistency requires detailed knowledge of the facts. This may sound like a universally valid maxim but it is invested with profoundly different meanings in different places. What is to American prosecutors an impossible or banal truism is a foundational principle for prosecutors in Japan. Their commitment to finding the facts — their shared sense of mission — is an important cause, and in important ways a cultural cause, of the consistent justice they dispense.

COHESION, CONTROL, AND CONSISTENCY

> Certainly no difference is more significant between Japanese and Americans, or Westerners in general, than the greater Japanese tendency to emphasize the group, somewhat at the expense of the individual.
>
> Edwin O. Reischauer, *The Japanese*

The social cohesion of Japan's procuracy and society helps further explain managers' control over operators and thus the high level of consistency in charging decisions. This cultural feature accounts in large part for something many American prosecutors would find baffling: Why do frontline operators, themselves prestigious legal professionals who have passed perhaps the most difficult credentialing examination in the world, tolerate such pervasive controls over their exercise of discretion? Don't they resent, resist, and escape the controls, as American prosecutors do in the face of far less intensive managerial efforts (Carter 1974:117)?

The Japanese who join the procuracy do not leave their values, norms, and cultural assumptions at the office entrance as they would their shoes upon entering a Japanese home. They do not cease being Japanese. While this fact is undeniable, its importance is too often discounted by "rational" and "moral" models of the relationship between an organization and the individuals who constitute it. In their shared stress on conscious reasons, whether preferences or norms, those models "neglect or marginalize the role of less overt, more taken-for-granted understandings" about, for example, the relationship between the group and the individual (Suchman and

Edelman 1996:903). Once this fact is recognized, it becomes clear that prosecutors enter the procuracy with many of the same cultural assumptions that other Japanese workers bring to their organizations (Lincoln and Kalleberg 1990).[16] Those predispositions help explain why prosecutors (for the most part) accept and expect controls rather than resist and resent them.

As the Reischauer quote suggests, chief among the Japanese predispositions is the tendency for individuals to emphasize and identify with the group, a quality that has been documented extensively not only in rural Japan but also in a wide variety of organizational contexts. Put simply, Japanese prosecutors accept and expect hierarchical control because, in part at least, they regard the self as a "contextual actor" whose identity is in large part defined by social relationships rather than as an "individual actor" whose identity and sense of self stand apart from the group (Hamilton and Sanders 1992:49). By diligent effort, Japanese prosecutors can be made to seem more and more like Americans, but the apparent convergence is not worth the sacrifice in sensitivity to real cultural differences. Thus, one key to accurate understanding, here as elsewhere in comparative research, is the will to "wrench ourselves out of well-worn ruts of assumption and expectation" (R. Smith 1983:6). Only then are we able to see Japanese prosecutors clearly rather than perceiving in them pale reflections of ourselves or of American prosecutors.

This cultural truth about Japanese — and Japanese prosecutors too — must be qualified to acknowledge that sometimes they do resist hierarchical controls. Indeed, a favorite topic of conversation among prosecutor operators is the alleged incompetence and unjustified intrusiveness of their superiors. Similarly, before going to *kessai*, operators sometimes scheme, individually or in pairs or groups, to make the encounter with superiors as trouble-free as possible. That may even mean shading presentations of fact or selectively withholding and disclosing information in order to achieve the disposition they desire. Few things ruin an operator's day so completely as a *kessai* that has gone badly, just as few things delight one more than smoothly navigating a *kessai* that was expected to be difficult or to demand further investigation. Nonetheless, these qualifications, each of which could be liberally illustrated, do not alter the fact that Japanese prosecutors accept and expect controls on their discretion to a degree seldom seen in the United States.

Because cultural arguments are frequently misunderstood, a few additional comments about the cultural causes of order are in order. I am not claiming that Japanese prosecutors do what they do because they are Japanese. That charge is often leveled at claims about culture, and when it sticks, it does so because the challenged argument forms a circle of unhelpfully small circumference. Culture is not the great uncaused cause, and saying culture shapes prosecutor behavior is not inconsistent with saying culture itself is shaped. What is more, saying culture counts is not the same as saying that only culture counts or that culture can be counted. If Japanese prosecutors regard themselves and their colleagues as "contextual actors" whose identities are largely defined by their relationship to the group, they do so because of cultural assumptions they bring to the group, but also because the group expects them

---

16. For example, one finds a similar "cultural commitment to consistency through control" in the activist efforts of Japanese judges to resolve traffic accident disputes in a highly uniform way (Foote 1995).

to and sanctions them if they do not. In this way, Japan's procuracy deals effectively with "the fundamental problem of all organizations, that of tying together the interests of the individuals that make up the organization with the interests of the organization as a whole" (Abegglen and Stalk 1985:182). In particular, managers and executives link individual and organizational interests by using office, job, and case assignments to reward prosecutors who seek consistency and punish those who do not.

If this is true, some will claim that self-interest and incentives, not culture, are the bottom line. Perhaps. But then what explains why managers and executives care about clarifying the truth and achieving ordered justice? They, after all, are the ones who create and implement the incentives. To recall Mary Douglas again, the arbitrary separation of structure and culture, and the tendency to privilege the causal force of only one side of that dichotomy, does little to advance understanding of criminal justice. One cannot escape the conclusion that both culture and structure count. The next section turns to the causal force of the second of these interconnected categories.

The Structure of Prosecution

> It is necessary to look at the totality of the interrelationships among institutional factors.
>
> Erhard von Blankenburg, "The Infrastructure for Avoiding
> Civil Litigation"

The "interrelationships among institutional factors" in Japanese prosecution are important structural causes of consistency. In this section, three such causes — the conditions of work, the structure of uncertainty, and the technologies and environments in which the organization operates — are identified and explained. In the process, the works of three American scholars — Michael Lipsky, W. Boyd Littrell, and Lief Carter — will be examined. Their accounts of the behavior of prosecutors and other "street-level bureaucrats" in the United States aid understanding of the determinants of consistency in Japan's very different context.

THE CONDITIONS OF PROSECUTOR WORK

> The determinants of street-level practice are deeply rooted in the structure of the work.
>
> Michael Lipsky, *Street-Level Bureaucracy*

In his classic account of "the dilemmas of the individual in public service," Michael Lipsky argues that several "conditions of work" prohibit street-level bureaucrats[17]

---

17. Lipsky defines street-level bureaucracies as "agencies whose workers interact with and have wide discretion over the dispensation of benefits or the allocation of public sanctions," and says that the concept of street-level bureaucrat includes teachers, social workers, health workers, police officers, judges, public lawyers, and other court officers. He demonstrates that the people who work in these seemingly diverse jobs "actually have much in common because they experience analytically similar work conditions" (Lipsky 1980:xi).

from providing their clients with either individualized or consistent services (Lipsky 1980:111). "The very nature of this work," Lipsky explains, "prevents [street-level bureaucrats] from coming even close to the ideal conception of their jobs." Lipsky points to five conditions of work that especially influence street-level bureaucrats:

1. *Resources* are chronically inadequate relative to the tasks workers are asked to perform.
2. The *demand for services* tends to increase to meet the supply.
3. *Goal expectations* for the agencies in which they work tend to be ambiguous, vague, or conflicting.
4. *Performance* oriented toward goal achievement tends to be difficult if not impossible to measure.
5. *Clients* are typically nonvoluntary; as a result, clients do not serve as the bureaucrats' primary reference group.

Then, in a passage which reads as if it were written with Japan's procuracy in mind, Lipsky notes that when a street-level bureaucracy faces different — that is, better — conditions of work, individualization and consistency can both be achieved: "*If for some reason these characteristics are not present*, the analysis is less likely to be appropriate, although it is instructive to understand why this is the case. If a legal services office encouraged its staff to take only four or five cases at a time in order to maximize the quality of preparation of each case, *the lawyers would behave differently* than if they worked in an office with much higher demands" (Lipsky 1980:28; emphasis added).

Because Lipsky's characteristics either are "not present" in Japan or else are present in highly attenuated form, Japanese prosecutors "behave differently" than American prosecutors do. Chapter 1 showed that with respect to the first two conditions of work — worker resources and client demands — Japan is paradise for a prosecutor. Claims of "institutional incapacity" notwithstanding, Japan's procuracy has adequate resources to fulfill the tasks it is asked to perform, and the "demand" for prosecutor services has not expanded to meet the available supply. The result is that prosecutors can devote careful attention to almost every case that enters their office — mushroom thefts included — an essential precondition to treating likes alike.

In addition, Lipsky's third and fourth conditions of work — goal expectations and goal measurement — are less problematic in Japan than in America. Although Japanese prosecutors pursue many goals simultaneously, they have forged an impressive consensus about how to define their critical task. Furthermore, while constructing the truth by pursuing confessions cannot be measured perfectly, achievement of that goal is more amenable to hierarchical evaluation than other, more ambiguous goals.

Finally, Japanese prosecutors are "benevolent" in significant respects, but suspects (Lipsky's "clients") certainly do not constitute a primary prosecutor reference group. As described above, that place is taken by other prosecutors in the organization. It is true, however, that prosecutors in Japan have more voluntary or quasi-voluntary clients than American prosecutors (Foote 1992a:343), a fact that further facilitates prosecutors' ability to construct the truth and achieve and measure their critical task. From there, it is a shorter step to consistent justice than from a position of greater uncertainty.

These benign conditions of work have at least two important consequences besides enabling Japanese prosecutors to achieve a high degree of consistency. Both concern crime control. First, Japanese prosecutors are not compelled to ration services as street-level bureaucrats must when their conditions of work are more severe. Lipsky calls such rationing processes "triage" because in circumstances where client demands exceed worker resources, bureaucrats must assign potential clients to different treatment priorities. The battlefield origin of the term is especially telling in light of the pressures many American prosecutors feel to triage cases for which they cannot afford to expend significant resources (Heilbroner 1990:26). American liberals often lament that their systems of criminal justice are too punitive (and in many respects they are), but the conditions of work that compel American prosecutors to triage cases also produce dispositions that are in many cases too lenient. Countless American offenders encounter a criminal justice system many times over without ever being taught the seriousness of their behavior (Braithwaite 1989:5). In fact, it seems likely that triage teaches many offenders precisely the opposite lesson: that their offenses do not rise to a level of gravity sufficient to warrant a careful look. The results of this triage are difficult to measure, but surely the United States pays a high cost in increased recidivism and victimization. Just as surely, the fact that Japanese police and prosecutors have fewer "casualties" to process, and thus less need to engage in triage, has salubrious crime control consequences.

Second, the benign conditions of prosecutor work in Japan retard development of the cynicism about work and clients that pervades less fortunate street-level bureaucracies, especially criminal justice agencies in America (Klinger 1997). American criminal justice officials, prosecutors included, are far more cynical about the work they perform than are Japanese judges, police, or prosecutors. Indeed, many American officials are contemptuous of the suspects and offenders with whom they deal. Prosecutors in Japan are markedly more respectful of their clients — not perfect of course, for there are significant exceptions, but the dissimilarity will be obvious to anyone who has spent time in both systems. I seldom heard Japanese prosecutors speak ill of the suspects whom they interrogated or tried, and even when they did the tones were closer to disapproval than disdain. This fact will be unsurprising to those who know something about Japan's culture more broadly, for the Japanese are often — and accurately — characterized as courteous and considerate. Even so, I do not believe that culture alone accounts for the vastly different levels of cynicism among Japanese and American prosecutors. Here, too, Lipsky (1980:140) helps explain why.

For American prosecutors, the difficult conditions of work confront them with a contradiction: they want, and are expected, to exercise discretion fairly and responsively, but in practice they must process people through stereotyped routines (like triage) in order to meet the demands on their time. American prosecutors "defend these patterns psychologically" in two ways, both of which breed cynicism (Feeley 1992b). First, they *modify their conceptions of work* in order to reduce the cognitive dissonance that arises from the contradiction between what they would like to do and what they can. Like street-level bureaucrats in similarly difficult work conditions, American prosecutors employ a number of strategies: they adopt private goal definitions in order to "close the psychological gap between capabilities and objectives," they specialize in order to "avoid seeing their work as a whole," they develop ideologies which legitimate lowered goal aspirations, they privately restrict the scope of their discretion, and so on. Modifying conceptions of work in these ways produces in many American prosecutors a pessimistic working personality — "there's not a helluva lot I can do" — rarely seen in Japan.

In addition, American prosecutors often *modify their conceptions of clients and offenders* by blaming, belittling, and bad-mouthing them. This aspect of their "client-processing mentality" further protects prosecutors from the intense dissatisfaction they would feel if they acknowledged how much working conditions force them to sacrifice aspirations to be fair and responsive. Such reactions, although psychologically functional for the prosecutors who employ them, can seldom be hidden from suspects and defendants. Here, too, the consequences for crime control are undesirable, for people obey the law mainly because they feel the legal authorities are legitimate and the legal procedures are fair. In particular, "people place great weight on being treated politely and having respect shown for their rights and for themselves as people" (Tyler 1990:164). Thus, defendants who are treated impolitely and disrespectfully are more likely to re-offend. Although cross-cultural differences in prosecutor respect for clients is difficult to measure — not all that counts can be counted — they are readily observed by anyone who spends time in various systems. Lipsky's framework reveals how the different conceptions of clients and the different levels of respect accorded them arise, at least in part, from the different conditions of prosecutor work in the United States and Japan. Courtesy not only has structural roots, it has crime-prevention consequences that often go unrecognized (Sherman 2000; Braithwaite 1989).

THE STRUCTURE OF UNCERTAINTY

> But why is the construction of crime uncertain? There are two reasons: some uncertainty arises from the special nature of the organization of prosecution and some uncertainty arises from the ambiguity that surrounds criminal circumstances.
>
> W. Boyd Littrell, *Bureaucratic Justice*

Consistency is easier to achieve where prosecutors face low levels of uncertainty. Littrell's analysis of "bureaucratic justice" helps illuminate the markedly different structures of uncertainty faced by prosecutors in the United States and Japan. It thus helps to further explain the different levels of consistency in the justice dispensed by each (Littrell 1979:29).

Littrell's account rests on two widely shared assumptions: that all crimes are constructed by officials, and that the organizational context in which officials work shapes the crimes they construct. An "adequate explanation of criminal dispositions must begin" with the basic fact that "bad acts are not automatically converted into crimes." The construction of crimes is not automatic because it results from "work that has some uncertainty," of which there are two main sources: the special nature of the organization of prosecution, and the ambiguity that surrounds criminal circumstances. Though both sources exist in Japan, they generate considerably less uncertainty than they do in the United States. Consider each in turn.

The first source of uncertainty in the construction of crimes is the fact that no one person makes the charge decision. In the United States the charge decision is usually the prosecutor's ultimate responsibility, but that decision is "shared" with more people than one might suppose: complaining victims and citizens, patrol officers who respond to complaints, detectives who investigate and gather evidence, witnesses, judges who conduct preliminary hearings, grand juries who decide whether or not to indict, and defendants who choose whether to end the case with a plea or a trial. Furthermore, in the United States the charge decision is "not made definitively at any single time," but is revised along the way (Littrell 1979:32) and "manufactured" in stages (Feeley 1992b:173). In contrast, Japanese prosecutors possess ultimate responsibility for all charge decisions, except in the rare case when judges permit private attorneys to "analogically institute" prosecution. Japanese prosecutors also "share" the decision to charge with fewer actors than American prosecutors do. Since they conduct investigations themselves, they rely less on police and detectives for information to make cases. Further, their charge decisions are not "shared" with judges (at preliminary hearings) or grand juries. Partly as a result, the charge decision is seldom revised once it is made (van Wolferen 1989:220). To be sure, Japanese prosecutors must interact with victims, complaining witnesses, and police in order to make cases. Even so, the organization of prosecution in Japan presents prosecutors with little uncertainty and thus more potential to construct cases in an orderly way.

The second source of uncertainty in the construction of crimes is the ambiguity of circumstances "surrounding the bad acts from which crimes are made" (Littrell 1979:47). Bad acts occur in the past and are stuck there. As a result, prosecutors face "the historian's problem" of discerning what happened, not immediately through direct observation but by interpreting evidence. The implications for consistency should be clear. Consistency (and thus justice) requires facts. In ways and for reasons discussed above, this premise is more central to Japanese prosecutors than to their American counterparts. At the same time, the laws of Japanese criminal procedure enable police and prosecutors to gather evidence and thereby to construct facts and build cases far more effectively than American police and prosecutors can (Miyazawa 1992). In short, "the historian's problem" is less foreboding for Japanese prosecutors than for American ones. So is the problem of consistency.

There is, for American prosecutors only, a third source of uncertainty: juries. To prosecutors in the United States, juries are perversely unpredictable (see chapter 1). When deciding whether and what to charge, American prosecutors have "a generalized preference for avoiding uncertainty," and usually assess the prosecutorial merit of a case in terms of the probability of conviction (Albonetti 1987:310; Frohmann 1992). It is difficult to make those assessments in an ordered way because different juries do not treat like cases alike. In this way, the limits of order created by the jury cast a shadow over prosecutor behavior at all earlier stages, further complicating efforts to achieve consistency even when it is a prosecutor goal. Take away the jury, as in Japan, and an important cause of the limits of order disappears. To put it in the converse, where judges write detailed opinions justifying verdicts and sentences, and where those decisions are themselves standardized by the judicial bureaucracy — as in Japan — prosecutors enjoy higher levels of predictability and produce higher levels of consistency. Here, too, the structure of uncertainty matters immensely.

ORGANIZATIONAL TECHNOLOGIES AND ENVIRONMENTS

> This book presented two arguments: first, we should not demand order
> and uniformity from those who do justice; second, we cannot realistically
> expect to achieve these goals. These arguments intertwine, since both de-
> rive from a body of organization theory dealing with consequences for or-
> ganizations of uncertain technologies and environments.
>
> Lief H. Carter, *The Limits of Order*

Since this chapter was stimulated by Lief Carter's claims about the "limits of order"
in American prosecution offices, it should come as no surprise that his causal account of those limits helps illuminate the Japanese case. Carter stresses two main
causes of American inconsistency, both borrowed from James Thompson's classic
study *Organizations in Action* (1967).

According to Carter, how people in an organization act depends mainly on what
they want and on what they believe about cause-effect relationships. Carter calls the
combination of desired outcomes and cause-effect beliefs *an organization's "technology."* Each dimension of organizational technology has two dichotomous aspects.
Standards of desirability — that is, goals or objectives — are either "crystallized" or
"ambiguous," and knowledge about cause-effect relationships is either "complete"
or "incomplete." Carter argues that "the degree to which organization members follow routinized or rule-ordered patterns of behavior" depends on their organizational
technology. He demonstrates that American prosecutors have ambiguous goals and
incomplete information; readers interested in the details of his argument are encouraged to consult the richly textured original.

In comparative perspective, what is most interesting is how different the technologies possessed by American and Japanese prosecutor organizations are. Japan's
procuracy has engineered widespread endorsement of the way its primary mission is
defined. At the same time, light caseloads and a wide array of investigative tools
make it possible for prosecutors to gather relatively complete information about
cases. In the Thompson-Carter jargon, Japan's procuracy has a substantially less "intensive" organizational technology than do prosecutor organizations in the United
States, and thus a higher potential for achieving consistency (Carter 1974:14).

Because Carter recognizes that organizations must deal with people and events
outside their formal boundaries, he also explores the influence of *organizational environments* on prosecutors. Environments may be either "homogeneous" (contain
people and institutions with similar interests and needs) or "heterogeneous" (make
competing and inconsistent demands on the organization), and either "stable"
(make predictable demands on the organization) or "shifting" (exert shifting demands and pressures). Organizations that confront heterogeneous, shifting environments "adopt flexible and decentralized operations which do not rely heavily on
rules" (Carter 1974:18). Carter shows, again convincingly, that American prosecution
offices face heterogeneous, unstable, and diverse environments that severely constrain their capacity to achieve order.

While Carter probably exaggerates the environmental obstacles to order in the
United States (Nardulli et al. 1988:85), the comparative differences between Japan

and the United States are clear. First, though Japan's homogeneity is often over-stated, Japanese society is less diverse than American society.[18] At the same time, the environments faced by Japanese prosecutors are more stable and predictable than those encountered by prosecutors in America. Finally, prosecutor organizations in both Japan and the United States are "open systems," but not equally so (Feeley 1992b:15). Indeed, Japanese prosecutors are well insulated from political pressures and public demands. As Carter's theory implies, these three differences give Japan's procuracy greater potential for consistency.[19] To an impressive extent it turns that potential into reality.

Conclusion

> I think we Americans should learn from other nations that the huge discretionary power of prosecutors need not be unconfined, unstructured, and unchecked.
>
> Kenneth Culp Davis, *Discretionary Justice*

> We should hold Japan up as a mirror, not a blueprint.
>
> Merry White, *The Japanese Educational Challenge*

So what? For Americans there are two bottom lines. As a mirror, Japan reflects an image of our own criminal justice system that, like the reflection of one's own face, partly pleases and partly disappoints. As a model, Japan suggests possibilities for reform of an aspect of our own system which, if it does not already disappoint, should.

Japan as Mirror

> It is impossible to understand a country without seeing how it varies from others. Those who know only one country know no country.
>
> Seymour Martin Lipset, *American Exceptionalism*

> American jurists are disinclined to interest themselves in foreign example for the same reason that scientists at American medical schools are disinclined to investigate the merits of medicine as it is practiced among the witch doctors of the Amazonian rain forest. They operate on the assumption that the foreigners have nothing to teach. But whereas the shortcomings of Amazonian medicine have been objectively verified, the disdain

---

18. It would be instructive to assess the importance of this cause by comparing prosecution practices in Japan with prosecution practices in homogeneous American jurisdictions such as Fargo, North Dakota or Portland, Maine.

19. Since Carter's work is not explicitly comparative, it says little about how prosecution offices vary on the "technology" and "environment" dimensions. Nonetheless, its conclusions about the "limits of order" depend heavily on circumstances more prevalent in the United States than in Japan. Where the relevant circumstances differ, Carter's theory predicts that more order is possible (Carter 1974:113,138).

for [foreign] law rests upon a witch's brew of ignorance, prejudice, and ve-
nality. Fortified in the lucrative fool's paradise that they inhabit, American
legal professionals have little incentive to open their eyes to the disturbing insights of comparative example.

John H. Langbein, "The Influence of Comparative
Procedure in the United States"

Organization matters. This is a fact that the Japanese — prosecutors and not — take
for granted. It is a reality too many Americans deny. Following the economists, some
Americans prefer to assume that organizations are like black boxes that, true to for-
mula, convert inputs into outputs. This substitution of assumption for observation
badly obstructs our ability to understand the central importance of bureaucracy in
criminal justice. It also helps to explain why so few American scholars have tried to
research the inner workings of the organizations that are home to prosecutors, the
most powerful actors in many criminal justice systems.

Organization matters because it can help create consistency. The hierarchical
controls and ubiquitous standards, guidelines, consultations, and audits described
above enable Japan's procuracy to confine, structure, and check discretion and thereby achieve "tolerable consistency" in prosecutorial decision-making (Abrams 1971:7).
As Aristotle said, "Justice . . . is equality — not, however, for all, but only for equals.
And inequality is thought to be, and is, justice; neither is this for all, but only for unequals." In short, this study matters because organization, order, and justice do.[20]

Yet when I ponder Japan's procuracy I also see things that concern me, especially
in how it reflects two values most Americans hold dear — autonomy and accountability. The capacity of Japanese prosecutors to treat like cases alike depends in no
small part on the fact that their criminal justice system "countenances substantial intrusions on personal autonomy" (Foote 1992a:368). Of course, American and Japanese conceptions of autonomy differ in pronounced ways, with the Japanese, in general, willing to accept conditions of criminal prosecution many Americans would
neither welcome nor tolerate (Foote 1991). When I say this, I do not mean that they
have got autonomy wrong (boo!) while we have got it right (hurrah!), but rather that
we think about the issue in fundamentally different ways (Fingleton 1995:25; Fallows
1994:9). The achievement of consistency comes at a cost in autonomy, a cost I probably reckon higher than most of my Japanese friends do but a cost nonetheless. If
Japan's procuracy produces a level and quality of consistency that I and other Americans find appealing, and if we would like American prosecutors to produce more of
that value here, then we must count the cost incurred in values like autonomy.

Because accountability links bureaucracy to democracy, one also needs to ask
how and to whom Japan's procuracy is accountable. Prosecutors are accountable if

---

20. Ironically, it is largely in the pursuit of more consistent justice that many American jurisdictions
have circumscribed the discretion of judges with sentencing guidelines and flat-time, mandatory, and de-
terminate sentencing requirements (Walker 1993:112). Unfortunately, the effect of these reform movements has been to greatly increase the discretion of American prosecutors without increasing external or
internal controls (Nagel and Schulhofer 1992). Considering that prosecutors are one of the chief conduits
of disorder to begin with, this seems an unwise direction in which to move if the aim is to make American criminal justice more consistent.

there is "a high probability that they will be responsive to legitimate authority or influence" (Lipsky 1980:160). As we have seen, prosecutors operating on Japan's frontlines are highly responsive to the managers and executives who supervise them. They are thus accountable to those legitimate authorities. But what about managers and executives, the pilots of the procuracy? Are they responsive to legitimate elected authorities and, through the latter, to the public?

Unfortunately, these questions admit few clear answers. Though I was given unprecedented access to frontline prosecutors working on ordinary cases, I had few opportunities to learn about how prosecutors connect with electoral politics. As in most Japanese bureaucracies, a norm of secrecy pervades the procuracy, especially concerning its connection to politics (Miyamoto 1994:126). At the same time, the Japanese non-prosecutors who should be most knowledgeable about this subject disagree among themselves about how accountable prosecutors are and about how they are accountable. For example, Hatano Akira, a Minister of Justice during the Nakasone administration and thus once the titular head of all prosecutors, argues that postwar prosecutors have changed little since the prewar era when they were accused of being "fascist" for trying to "change the world" (Hatano 1994b:65). Hatano, who until recently was also a Diet politician in the Liberal Democratic Party, laments what he considers the postwar procuracy's reckless, runaway attacks on fellow LDP politicians, especially former Prime Minister Tanaka Kakuei (Hatano's political mentor). He alleges that the root of the problem is prosecutors' lack of accountability to elected authority and their disregard for the public's welfare.

Yet the opposite argument is also made. Tachibana Takashi, for example, one of the most highly respected journalists in all of Japan, contends that the worst Japanese "bad guys" — politicians in the LDP — are "sleeping soundly" because prosecutors refuse to investigate or charge their crimes. According to Tachibana, prosecutor executives allow the bad guys to sleep precisely because they are bound too tightly to politicians. They are, he insists, too inclined to act in the interest of their political principals rather than in the interest of the public whom they ostensibly represent (Tachibana 1993; D. Johnson 1997).

When prosecutors in Japan are confronted with the intelligentsia's contradictory claims, they take solace in the contradictions, arguing that being attacked from both sides is evidence that they must be doing a pretty good job. Perhaps. But to an American living in a land where prosecutorial decision-making is more open to public inspection and potential criticism (Hagan 1994:139), the link between Japan's procuracy and democracy remains troublesomely opaque (Kawasaki 1991). In this regard Japan's procuracy — as mirror — reveals as much about myself as an American as about the subject of this study.

Japan as Model

> Our criminal justice procedures would seem as absurd to us as they do to foreigners if we were not so used to them. . . . Nothing could be healthier than for the American criminal bar to immerse itself in the study of comparative criminal procedure and thus discover that ours is not the only or even the best way of doing things.
>
> Phillip E. Johnson, "Importing Justice"

> I am afraid many Westerners do not want to acknowledge that we do
> things as well as, or better than, they do.
>
> Japanese prosecutor

This chapter shows that arguments about "inevitable" discrimination and "the limits of order" are untrue. The two imperatives of justice — individualization and consistency — are not locked in ineluctable tension, and more of one is not necessarily purchased at the price of the other.[21] Claims to the contrary will persist as long as Americans refuse to open their eyes to the disturbing insights the Japanese case presents. Claims to the contrary also perpetuate the pernicious myth that while the American criminal process may not *appear* to do justice, it *does* justice nonetheless (Silberman 1978:255). The comparison with Japan suggests that American criminal justice does neither satisfactorily. It thus provides a sorely needed perspective on American prosecution.

The first step to more tolerable consistency in American criminal justice is the recognition that things can be different — and better — than they are now. I have tried to suggest how looking at Japan as a mirror can spark that awareness. Unfortunately, considering the disdain most American legal professionals hold for all systems but their own, I am pessimistic about the chances for significant change in Americans' ethnocentric conviction that their system works, at worst, better than other systems do (Pizzi 1999). Nonetheless, if the first step were taken — if Americans awoke to the subversive insights of comparative example — the question arises: Can Japan serve as a model for American reform?

One must not regard Japan's procuracy as a blueprint for reform of unsatisfactory American prosecutorial practices. The two systems differ in too many fundamental respects. In ways, however, Japan can serve as something of a model for how to achieve more consistency in our own systems of prosecution. This suggestion will make some Americans uneasy and insecure; for a long time the thought disquieted me. But the facts are too clear and too numerous to deny: we have something to learn from Japan, if only we will listen. In some criminal justice respects Japan is just another country; with respect to consistency it is not.

The stakes are high. Criminal proceedings in which an individual may lose life, liberty, and reputation "constitute the principal indicator of the character of a society" (Skolnick 1975:v). Such proceedings reflect not only our ideals of justice but also how well we translate those ideals into reality. The prevailing tradition in Western philosophy "relates the core sense of 'justice' to the idea of equality" (Golding 1975:120). For the most part, we still agree with Aristotle that justice consists in treating equals equally and unequals unequally. Which is to say, the stakes are high because we care — or say we care — about consistency.

But the status quo is intolerable, and the problem is consistency, or rather the lack of it in American prosecution offices. Thirty years ago Professor Norman

---

21. This account also undermines one of the most widespread beliefs about Japanese legal culture: that universal standards of justice are "alien to the traditional habit of the Japanese people" (Kawashima 1979). For Japanese prosecutors, that claim could hardly be more baseless. For them, justice demands equal treatment of equals and unequal treatment of unequals.

Abrams, writing about how to guide the exercise of prosecutorial discretion through internal policy, concluded that "the present state of prosecutorial policy is primitive," leading to intolerable inconsistency instead of the "tolerable consistency" many claim to want (Abrams 1971:58). Today the level of inconsistency in American prosecution offices is still unacceptable. Of course, some scholars contend that in charging and plea-bargaining, two primary prosecutor practices, "consistency prevails to a surprising extent" (Nardulli et al. 1988:245). Their surprise, I surmise, arises from unawareness of the consistencies prevailing outside their national borders. After comparing the contours of American justice with those of Japan, the main thing which surprises me is how much inconsistency prevails on our side of the Pacific.

American prosecution can be moved farther along the road to tolerable consistency. In fact, since the late 1950s the dominant theme in American criminal justice has been "the attempt to control discretionary decision-making," and the best review of that period concludes that "discretion can be controlled." In some important areas it has been. Police use of lethal force has declined. Many municipalities have decreased the number of dangerous, high-speed police pursuits. And the Minnesota sentencing guidelines seem to have controlled the use of imprisonment in that state. In short, some things do work to control discretion. Meaningful change is difficult but not impossible (Walker 1993). Unfortunately, prosecutor discretion is not one of the success stories. This critical part of our system remains untamed. Years ago American scholars, concerned about prosecution inequities, frequently wrote about how to guide prosecutor discretion in order to achieve more tolerable consistency.[22] In recent years, however, such concern has slowed to a trickle, in part because many of the proposed reforms were neither politically feasible nor practically viable (Frase 1990). To be more successful we must build on what we have rather than supposing, wrongly, that we can import whole systems (Morris 1978:1369).

I have two modest suggestions. First, if consistency matters then so must organization. The connection is nonnegotiable. Prosecution will never be as coordinated or controlled in the United States as in Japan, and many Americans and almost all American prosecutors do not expect it to be. But American decisions about whether and what to charge are so important, and yet so unrestrained, that prosecutor managers and executives must take a greater interest in the routine decisions which, in the aggregate, constitute their office policies. At present, those decisions are made either too early or too late and, above all, with too little regard for treating likes alike (Frase 1990:616).

Second, managers and executives should make operators more accountable for their frontline decisions. Concretely, this could be done by implementing a modified form of *kessai*, so as to require at least one level of review for disposition decisions instead of the two or three levels customary in Japan (Uviller 1999:71). Or, if this seems impractical, prosecutor superiors could adopt and adapt methods from other systems (like France) for achieving more tolerable consistency (Frase 1990:617).

American prosecution offices are formidably resistant to change, in large part because prosecutors are reluctant to impose limits on their own discretion (Morris

22. See, for example, Davis (1969), Abrams (1971), Rabin (1972), Uviller (1973), Abrams (1975), Vorenberg (1976), Weinreb (1977), Langbein and Weinreb (1978), Weigend (1980), and Vorenberg (1981).

1978:1367; Feeley 1983). Legislative and judicial restraints may be part of the solution, but in the last analysis it is prosecutors themselves who must see the need for more "decent restraint" in the service of more "tolerable consistency" (Abrams 1971:58; Vorenberg 1981). Kenneth Culp Davis provided the first comprehensive discussion of discretion in American criminal justice. In the penultimate section titled "Philosophical Underpinnings" he eloquently set forth the heart of the matter:

> In an affluent country, I think the legal system's answers to such questions as these [about whom to prosecute and for what] should be based upon the most careful deliberation, not on considerations of convenience and economy, which gain support from habits and assumptions. Yet I doubt that our prevailing practices rest upon the best thinking of which our society is capable. *Our whole system of selective enforcement is built upon the assumption* — and I think it is no more than an assumption — *that justice does not require equal treatment* by police, prosecutors, and other enforcement officers of those who are equally deserving of prosecution or of other governmental initiative. *This assumption,* in my opinion, *is in need of profound reexamination.* (1969:230; emphasis added)

Davis titled his last section "The Unfinished Task." Japan, as mirror and model, shows that the task of producing more consistent criminal justice in America remains distressingly incomplete.

6

Corrections

> Japanese judges and procurators stress correction as a primary aim. . . .
> The restorative approach has become the predominant pattern in Japan
> because police, prosecutors, and judges recognize its success in correct-
> ing offenders and satisfying victim and public needs.
>
> John O. Haley, "Apology and Pardon"

> Contemporary rejection of the rehabilitation model . . . has prompted
> [American] states to impose increasingly repressive and punitive sanc-
> tions against those who commit crimes, with the claimed goals of pun-
> ishing and incapacitating criminals. This wave of "get tough" measures
> has been no more successful than the rehabilitation model in controlling
> crime, and by contributing to prison overcrowding it may be contributing
> to the breakdown of the criminal justice system itself.
>
> Daniel Van Ness and Karen Heetderks Strong,
> *Restoring Justice*

"Dear Prosecutor: Thanks!"

Gary was a blue-eyed, sandy-haired, twenty-five-year-old Australian resident of Japan.
At his arrest in late 1992 he was six feet, four inches tall and weighed 253 pounds. At
his release, after four months of detention and four weeks of interrogation, he was 55
pounds lighter and the toes of both feet were numb with frostbite caused by exposure to the air in his unheated cell. Gary detested the conditions of his confinement:
the solitude for all but half an hour per day; the rule requiring him to stay seated in
an upright position unless he gained explicit permission to lie down; the 10 percent
of guards who were "mean"; the lack of exercise; and the February cold. "Don't ever
commit a crime in Japan," he advised me during the first interrogation for which I
translated. "This place will kill anyone." Gary did not die in confinement, but by the
end of his encounter with the Japanese way of justice he was — on doctor's orders —
taking barbiturates to sedate his skittish nerves.

    Gary possessed a special fondness for three things: rugby; his Japanese girlfriend
Yūko; and mood-altering substances. It was the latter, in the form of 100 grams (3.5
ounces) of hashish, that led him to the office of Ms. Obayashi Keiko, the Japanese
prosecutor who charged Gary with the crime for which he was convicted, sentenced

(to eighteen months' imprisonment, suspended for three years), and deported. Gary wrote the following letter about two months after returning to Australia.

> Dear Obayashi *sama:*
>
> Hi. How are you? *Ogenki desu ka* [Are you well]? I hope so. How is your new neighborhood treating you? I hope that you are enjoying it there and settling in well, and I hope you can understand my letter OK. I want to tell you from the bottom of my heart that I like you very, very much and respect you very highly for what you taught me about life and about friends and about what good friends are. . . . I have, or had, a very strong body, but in my mind I am not as strong as I thought I was! I must say now that I enjoyed our meetings a lot even though I was roped and handcuffed. I promise you that next time we meet—and I hope we do—we can talk about better and happier things.
>
> Thank you for helping me get out of jail and spend some time with Yūko before I left Japan. Also, thank you for talking to [my lawyer] Mr. Matsuda and instructing him about how to deal with the judge so that I was able to get out. And thank you for talking to the police when I was rearrested in Kurayama.[1] I don't know how I can repay you. I just want you to know that I am very grateful to you for helping me out. Thanks!
>
> Well, my father's health is much better now and he is becoming very *genki* [well] again. When he first saw me he was a little bit shocked because I had lost so much weight. . . . I have almost stopped smoking. I haven't given up yet but I will soon I hope.
>
> I have your telephone number, and when I save enough money I will call you at your new office. I look forward to hearing from you in the near future. Take care of yourself, OK?
>
> Your forever friend. Love,
> Gary

Prosecutor Obayashi did not become Gary's pen pal. She did, however, write to me several times after Gary's deportation. When she mailed me a copy of the above letter she included her own seven-page, handwritten epistle, a portion of which follows.

> Today when I returned to my apartment I opened the postbox and found a letter from Gary. My heart began to pound, for fear that he might have changed the story he told when I charged him. But in the end Gary turned out to be a cute boy. I was most happy to hear his father has recovered from his heart attack. I enclose a copy of Gary's letter. I thought you'd like to know what happened to him since the last time you saw him.
>
> I am thankful Gary appeared before me. For me as a prosecutor it was a big gamble whether or not to believe his statements [about how he had acquired the hashish, and about his contrition and resolve to reform]. In deciding whether or not to believe a person, I wager my very existence. I mean, it is a test of all my abilities. For me, believing Gary came attached to a big risk, but I thought it was worth taking the challenge. For me, it was more important to discern how much I could be-

---

1. Shortly after being released on bail, Gary was arrested for an assault he had mentioned to police during his interrogation for the drug offense. The assault—a fight in a bar—had occurred months earlier. Gary paid the victim 20,000 yen ($160) in "compensation for damages" (*benshō*). The victim asked the prosecutor not to indict, and the prosecution was suspended.

lieve Gary, and to assess whether my judgment was mistaken, than to make sure Dennis Potter gets convicted.[2]

If Gary was telling the truth, I wanted to respond to him as a human being, not as a prosecutor. I believed that by doing that, Gary would come to possess in his own life the hope and desire to trust people. If I had refused to believe Gary's story in order to avoid the risk of an acquittal in the Potter case and thereby leave behind a "good record" as a prosecutor, Gary may have gone on to live his life with despair occupying some corner of his heart. So this was my anguish: to believe or not believe. I fought the fight. David *san*, do you suppose I won?

The outcome of Dennis Potter's trial is not the issue. When I read Gary's letter I gained assurance that I won the battle with myself. I am drinking wine right now, and making a toast (by myself). When I believe a person, I wager my entire existence. Gary has taught me that this way of thinking, risking, and acting is good. Therefore, I am thankful to Gary. . . .

Gary's path is clear. I am hoping he will go on to live well. In my position as a prosecutor, I can no longer have close contact with him. But Gary is a friend in my heart. From the bottom of my heart I pray for his happiness. . . .

On "Correction"

To correct is to "make or set right; to rectify; to reprove for faults." Gary's case exemplifies two faces of Japanese justice that generate starkly different interpretations of the place of "correction" in Japan's criminal justice system. On the one hand, the conditions of Gary's confinement and the length, intensity, and intrusiveness of his interrogations illustrate the sometimes "punitive and vexatious nature" of Japan's criminal process (Peters 1992:291).[3] On the other hand, the prosecutor's decision to "believe" Gary's expressions of remorse, and her attempts to reprove Gary's faults and "set right" his thinking, evoked Gary's profound gratitude for her benevolence.[4]

2. Dennis Potter was Gary's friend and twenty years his senior. During interrogation, Gary identified Potter as the source of the hashish. Potter denied the accusation but was prosecuted nonetheless, largely on the basis of Gary's statements. Prosecutor Obayashi was concerned that Gary would repudiate his statements if forced to testify in court in front of his friend. This is the "risk" to which she refers later in her letter. Potter was ultimately convicted.

3. The hardships Gary experienced in confinement are not unusual. A report by Amnesty International (1998) claims "prisoners in Japan suffer from systematic, inhuman or degrading treatment and are at high risk of being subjected to abusive forms of punishment." It further notes that frostbite of the kind Gary suffered "is a common complaint among detainees" because "almost all prison cells in Japan are unheated." Vivien Stern (1998:95) describes similar deprivations in Japanese prisons. Though not unusual, Gary's problems were aggravated by his status as a foreigner in a system that is "ill-equipped to handle different languages and cultures and may, at least to many Western prisoners, present much more serious restrictions on personal liberty than they would experience back home" (Horwich and Karasaki 2000). As of March 2000, fully 10 percent of all trials in Japan had foreign defendants. Ten years earlier the figure was just 1 percent. For an account of the punitive and vexatious features of Japan's pretrial process, see Miyazawa (1992).

4. Richard H. Mitchell's (1992) description of "Janus-faced justice" in Imperial Japan suggests that punitive and benevolent qualities have coexisted in Japanese criminal justice for decades. For a critical review of this view, see Haley (1992). Steinhoff (1991) also focuses on the tension between punishment and reform in prewar criminal justice. She argues that prosecutors and police aimed to "convert" (*tenkō*) Communists by reintegrating them into society so as to erode resistance to nationalism and thereby produce a dutiful nation supportive of the war effort.

While not all Japanese prosecutors are as committed to correction as Ms. Obayashi, she does embody a difference in central tendency that is impossible to ignore and unwise to discount: prosecutors in Japan are, on the whole, markedly more committed to "correction" than their American counterparts.

Scholars have painted contrasting portraits of Japanese criminal justice largely because they highlight these different features of the system. The prevailing portraits accentuate the propensity of police, prosecutors, and judges to correct suspects and offenders, to repair relationships between victims and offenders, and to heal the harms caused by crime (E. Johnson 1996; Bayley 1991; Haley 1989; Braithwaite 1989; Shikita 1982). I long resisted this interpretation because it seemed inconsistent with the baleful facts highlighted in the minority portraits of Japan's system (H. Yamaguchi 1999; Miyazawa 1995; Igarashi 1984). I now realize, however, that both portraits depict aspects of the truth. Japan's criminal justice officials — and prosecutors in particular — pursue "correction" in ways and to degrees that are seldom seen in American criminal justice. At the same time, the "setting right" that prosecutors attempt is selective, for they are neither lenient nor benevolent to all suspects; it is authoritarian, in that prosecutors help define the norms to which offenders are corrected and the stories which victims are permitted to voice; and it is problematic, as when prosecutors enable and even encourage money to influence their charging decisions.

This chapter depicts certain processes of prosecutorial "correction" without discounting either the cross-cultural differences in commitment to correction or the darker colors that must be added to the pleasant pastels of the majority portraits. It unfolds in two main parts. First I describe prosecutor efforts to determine which offenders are correctable and to "set right" those who are. After that, I focus on prosecutor attempts to repair the harms done to victims, especially in sexual molestation cases. The word "corrections" typically is associated with post-conviction stages of the criminal process. The Japanese case reveals that, for better and for worse, the desire to "set right" can animate parts of the criminal process long preceding prison and probation.

Judging Correctability

Chapter 3 showed that Japanese prosecutors believe in the importance of rehabilitating offenders by invoking remorse. This cultural commitment constitutes a necessary but insufficient condition for correction, for prosecutors neither seek to correct all offenders, nor try equally hard to correct those offenders whose reform they do seek. Thus, before attempting to set someone right, the prosecutor must first decide how correctable the offender is. This decision is not merely a choice between two binary options, correctable and not. Rather, prosecutors locate offenders along a continuum ranging from "not at all correctable" on one end to "highly correctable" on the other. Compared with American prosecutors, Japanese prosecutors construct a "distribution" of offenders that is centered markedly more on the "correctable" part of the continuum.

Prosecutors assess two main factors to determine correctability: the seriousness of the offense and the sinisterness of the offender's character.[5] As explained below, some bad acts, like gun crimes, are deemed so serious that the bad actor's correctability takes on distinctly secondary significance. Other offenses, including some sex crimes that fall on the heinous end of the American seriousness scale, are deemed less grave, and prosecutors devote much time and attention to the pursuit of correction.

In judging character prosecutors construe many gradations of good and bad, but three ideal types stand out. First, "the really bad person" is deeply, impudently, and remorselessly involved in serious or repeat offenses, especially against strangers. For the truly sinister, correction is at most a tertiary prosecutor objective (Hamilton and Sanders 1992:174). Second, "the person headed for trouble" will become "really bad" if his or her course is not corrected. Japanese prosecutors invest great effort in correcting these offenders who are near the character "tipping point." Finally, for "the basically good person in trouble" the encounter with the criminal justice system is itself sufficiently shameful or costly (or both) to motivate reform. For these offenders, prosecutors facilitate correction through lenient treatment (such as suspended prosecution) which is meant to minimize the criminogenic effects of stigmatization while simultaneously providing an opportunity to reintegrate into society (Braithwaite 1989:101).

As depicted in figure 6.1, these two dimensions — seriousness of offense and sinisterness of offender — define the variation in prosecutors' perceptions of correctability. The upper left-hand triangle of figure 6.1 represents the least correctable criminals. Bad guys accused of very serious offenses are considered either uncorrectable or else undeserving of correctional attempts. For these wrongdoers, desert trumps correction.[6] The lower right-hand triangle represents the other extreme: highly correctable offenders. For these law violators, correction is prosecutors' primary aim. In between, the slice running from lower left to upper right represents offenders deemed moderately correctable. For these people, seriousness and sinisterness are sufficiently grave that prosecutors must temper attempts at correction with considerations of desert. For these offenders, prosecutors tend to prefer the risk that an uncharged offender will reoffend to the risk that a charged offender will be acquitted.

---

5. On the use of "seriousness" and "sinisterness" to determine proper punishments in the American context, see Littrell (1979:133). On amenability to correction, see Haas and Alpert (1999:333).

6. Prosecutors permit considerations of character to influence punishment decisions even for some of the most heinous crimes on the seriousness scale. For example, in May 1998 the Tokyo District Court sentenced Hayashi Ikuo, the former "health minister" and chief doctor of Aum Shinrikyō, to life in prison for releasing nerve gas in the Tokyo subway system on March 20, 1995. Aum's multi-pronged attack killed twelve and sickened thousands. Hayashi was held responsible for the deaths of two subway officials and the poisoning of more than two hundred commuters. The sentencing judge said Hayashi's offense was "unprecedented in its viciousness," but nonetheless followed prosecutors' sentencing recommendation of life in prison. Hayashi had expressed deep remorse for his actions, apologized to the victims and their families, and cooperated with investigators when few other suspects or cultists were speaking. The widow of one of his victims, Takahashi Shizue, originally urged prosecutors to seek the same sentence for Hayashi — death — as for the other defendants accused in the attack. However, after hearing Hayashi repeatedly express remorse, Takahashi became convinced of his sincerity and supported the life sentence (*Asahi Shimbun* 5/26/98).

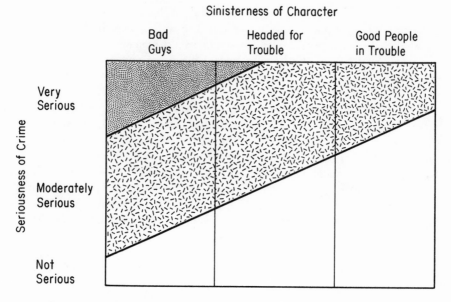

FIGURE 6.1 Determining desert and correctability

By attending to the variation portrayed in figure 6.1, it is possible to understand why observers of Japanese criminal justice disagree about the centrality of corrections in prosecuting crime. On the one hand, there is evidence that Japanese prosecutors often aim at "special prevention," that is, "the prevention of recidivism through the reformation and rehabilitation of the offender" (Foote 1992a:321). On the other hand, some analysts, stressing evidence that seems inconsistent with the claim that prosecutors care about correction, reach contrary conclusions (Miyazawa 1995; Igarashi 1984). These contrasting claims are in fact compatible once one limits their scope to the proper domain. The key to circumscribing these assertions is recognizing that prosecutors use the concepts of seriousness and sinisterness to assess desert and correctability. In my survey, for example, even while prosecutors expressed deep commitment to rehabilitation, over 92 percent agreed or strongly agreed that "the most important single consideration in determining the sentence to impose should be the nature and gravity of the offense" (Appendix, part 4:9). Less than 1 percent of prosecutors disagreed with this statement. Similarly, over three-fourths of prosecutors agreed or strongly agreed that "most people charged with serious crime should be punished whether or not the punishment benefits the criminal" (Appendix, part 4:1). This reality — that Japanese prosecutors are neither universally nor uniformly committed to correction — is also reflected in prosecutor appraisals of the factors influencing their charge decisions (see table 3.2). The two factors prosecutors deem most important in deciding whether to suspend prosecution — the damage done by the offense and the likelihood of reoffending — strongly correlate with, respectively, the seriousness and sinisterness considerations that prosecutors make when discerning desert and correctability. Indeed, all of the first eight suspension of prosecution "factors" shape the prosecutor's assessments of character and correctability.

Finally, the way prosecutors determine desert and correctability stands a cardinal jurisprudential principle on its head. For over two centuries criminologists have stressed the importance of "letting the punishment fit the crime" (Siegel 2000:6). This view, as enunciated by jurists as diverse as Beccaria, Bentham, and Kant, asserts that the severity of punishment should be commensurate with the seriousness of the wrong. The fact, however, is that when deciding how to charge an offender prosecutors routinely invert this principle. Instead of "making the punishment fit the crime," prosecutors assess culpability and character so as to select a charge that "makes the crime fit the punishment" (Littrell 1979:129). Indeed, after constructing "the truth" about an offense and offender, the prosecutor has discretion to choose from a number of crimes a charge that both "fits the facts" and "fits the punishment." The Japanese prosecutor normally selects a charge that reflects her appraisals of desert and correctability. Moreover, the procuracy's internal, organizational controls — standards and *kessai* especially — ensure that an organizational conception of correctability supersedes individual conceptions. In this regard correctability, like consistency, is collectively constructed.

Mechanisms of Correction

Japanese prosecutors employ two main mechanisms to try to correct offenders: instruction and leniency.[7] Through instruction, prosecutors appeal to an offender's self-interest and to social norms.[8] Through leniency, prosecutors provide offenders with time and opportunity to change, without stigmatizing them unduly or pushing them into criminal subcultures that reinforce criminal tendencies. Consider each mechanism in turn.

Instruction

Prosecutors in Japan "instruct" suspects and offenders, chiefly during interrogation. This distinguishes them from their American counterparts, who have little or no access to the accused prior to trial. Instruction presupposes a forum. Japanese prosecutors have one; American prosecutors do not.

Much instruction is informational: if you confess, the punishment will be X; if you persist in offending, and if you are rearrested, Y is likely to follow; if you use methamphetamine, you will harm yourself and your family; if significant others learn of your deviance, you will lose their social approval; and so on. This type of in-

---

7. A mechanism is an explanation in terms of interactions between individuals, or between individuals and some social aggregate. Two main mechanisms are rational choice, which is guided by a desire to reach the best overall outcome, and social norms, or expectations for behavior that are little concerned with outcomes (Elster 1989). While the idea of "mechanism" may conjure up images from physics, sociologists since Robert Merton have used it to refer to "the middle ground between social laws and description" (Hedstrom and Swedberg 1998:6).

8. Language is both the medium of instruction and "the essential mechanism" by which a prosecutor's power is applied, realized, reproduced, and challenged (Conley and O'Barr 1998:129).

struction adopts the teacher's approach, and the appeal is chiefly to the accused's self-interest.

In contrast, moral instruction appeals to norms, both as external realities in the accused's social world ("*we* believe drug use is wrong") and as internal realities in the accused's conscience ("*you* know drug use is wrong"). This is the approach of the parent or preacher. Its medium is the language of shame, disapproval, rebuke, and exhortation. Moral instruction works primarily by stimulating repentance (Etzioni 1999). It aims to build, or rebuild, consciences by catalyzing internal controls (Braithwaite 1989:79).[9]

Japanese prosecutors give instruction that is highly and distinctively moral. They routinely use the mechanism of moral instruction to activate self-control — the most powerful form of social control there is (Gottfredson and Hirschi 1990; Braithwaite 1989:81). The comparison with America is illuminating. While American prosecutors rarely interrogate, American detectives routinely do. When they do, their most common tactics involve appealing to the suspect's self-interest and confronting the suspect with evidence of guilt. In one study, each of these tactics was used in more than five out of six American interrogations. By contrast, appeal to the suspect's conscience was made in less than one-quarter of interrogations, and metaphors of guilt were invoked in only one out of ten (Leo 1996:278). I was unable to systematically sample prosecutor interrogations in Japan, so a careful comparison with these American data cannot be made. However, I did witness dozens of interrogations conducted by numerous prosecutors, and I asked many additional prosecutors to describe the interrogation techniques they use in various kinds of cases. Based on that research, I believe Japanese prosecutors — and probably detectives as well — rely more on moral instruction and normative appeals than do American interrogators. The following case not only illustrates that reliance, it shows that prosecutors in Japan sometimes enlist the support of "outsiders" to shame offenders and to facilitate reflection and correction.

The first case I encountered in my research involved a suspect — single, sixty-year-old Mr. Haneda — who employed a highly eccentric defense against the accusation that he used stimulant drugs. Haneda was watching television one evening when he heard a knock at his apartment door. On opening the door he was greeted by a team of police officers wielding a search warrant. Based on the word of an informer, police suspected Haneda of using and possessing methamphetamine, or speed (*kakuseizai*). Though the search uncovered no illicit drugs, police did persuade Haneda to provide a urine sample. It tested dirty, and Haneda was arrested and

---

9. The two types of instruction parallel John Braithwaite's (1989:75) description of the two levels at which shame operates to effect social control. However, instruction is a broader concept than shame because it includes acts of communication besides expressions of disapproval. I went to Japan skeptical of Braithwaite's (1989:79) claim that "Japanese police, prosecutors, and courts rely heavily on guilt-induction and shaming as alternatives to punishment." My research was in part motivated by his call to test his theory with ethnographic data. I came back convinced that guilt induction is a central objective and common practice for prosecutors in Japan. David Bayley (1991:142) has observed that Japanese police also act "with the aura of a teacher," not simply as agents of law. They often "deliver lectures on duty and morality" instead of making arrests or issuing citations.

detained in the same freezing jail that Gary would later deplore. Haneda denied knowingly ingesting the drug. He admitted, however, paying money to a prostitute on whom he performed cunnilingus. Since the prostitute did use speed, Haneda must have imbibed the drug during oral sex. This, at least, was the story he told and retold during hours of interrogation over the subsequent three weeks. Haneda confessed, finally, on day 21 of his detention.

In my view, this case seemed to involve an oddly improvident use of law enforcement resources. After all, Haneda had been convicted twice previously for drug offenses, and in the present case officials possessed compelling, objective evidence of guilt. Surely the prosecutor could convict without a confession, and just as surely he had better uses to which he could direct his own efforts, not to mention the efforts of the police detectives he was directing.

I was half right. The prosecutor was confident he could convict without a confession. He had scientific evidence of drug use, legally acquired by the police, and he was convinced the court would regard Haneda's defense as the preposterous tall tale he and his colleagues believed it to be. Still, the prosecutor did not consider the pursuit of a penitent confession a prodigal waste of time. Not at all. The goal of the interrogations was "to get the suspect to sincerely repent," and the means included both types of instruction, teaching and preaching. But the usual forms of persuasion failed. Haneda neither believed confessing was in his own interest nor felt sufficiently sorry to say so. On several occasions his resistance raised the prosecutor's ire, at which points he was browbeaten, but to no avail. Haneda was not intimidated. About two and a half weeks into his detention and interrogation, Haneda took a lie detector test. According to the prosecutor, he failed spectacularly. Haneda still did not confess.[10]

Two days later the prosecutor hit upon a strategy that finally elicited a confession. He telephoned Haneda's younger brother and Haneda's nephew (the son of Haneda's oldest brother), explained the circumstances of Haneda's arrest and detention, and invited them to his office to meet with Haneda and convince him to repent. Door-to-door the trip took over three hours. I could not attend the family reunion, but according to the prosecutor, Haneda's relatives rebuked him for using drugs and denying his transgressions, urged contrition, and offered to let Haneda live with them after his term of punishment ended. Haneda came clean, both to his relatives and, at subsequent interrogations, to the prosecutor and police. He was formally charged exactly three weeks after his arrest. The prosecutor sought a sentence of two and a half years' imprisonment, which the court subsequently imposed.

Haneda's case illustrates at least four truths about Japanese criminal justice. First, while the primary function of confessions is indeed evidentiary, this case shows that prosecutors go to great lengths pursuing correction through confession even when the confession would add little evidentiary value to the case being constructed (Foote 1991:471). Instruction, both instrumental and moral, is one main mechanism

10. Despite their scientific and technological trappings, lie detector tests are unreliable (though I doubt Haneda knew this when he was examined). Officials often use the test to deceive and intimidate suspects into confessing (Skolnick 1982).

in this approach, though when it fails to achieve "conversion," prosecutors may resort to practices like browbeating and the mobilization of peer pressure to effect at least external compliance, if not internal contrition (see chapter 8).

Second, issues of remorse — its presence or absence, depth, and authenticity — are critical in constructing an offender's character. Since constructing and construing character are themselves crucial criminal justice practices, issues of remorse are fundamentally important. In Japan it is primarily prosecutors who use remorse (or its absence) to make authoritative assessments of character.[11] As depicted in figure 6.1, the character thus constructed informs prosecutor decisions about what to charge and how to punish. Haneda's confession and concomitant displays of remorse shaved four months (or 12 percent) off the term of imprisonment prosecutors otherwise would have sought. In a sense, Haneda's confession pushed prosecutors' appraisal of his character one step in the "less sinister" direction — far enough, at least, to avoid the "denial tariff" prosecutors impose on more sinister, because less contrite, offenders. This determined pursuit of *a particular kind of confession* is one piece of a larger pattern of governance in Japan, whereby "the state has historically intervened to shape how ordinary Japanese thought and behaved — to an extent that would have been inconceivable in the United States and Britain, and would probably have strained the limits of statism in continental Europe" (Garon 1997:xiv).

Third, Haneda's case highlights the importance and the difficulty of distinguishing genuine remorse from its imposters. It took officials three weeks and thirty hours of interrogation to evoke a confession. In the end, did Haneda confess because he internalized the beliefs prosecutors had been pressing upon him, that stimulant drug use is wrong and deserving of disapprobation? Or was his confession an act of compliance, motivated more by the desire to gain reward (help from his relatives) and avoid punishment (the denial tariff) than by a new or reclaimed commitment to the immorality of illicit drug use? These different responses to social influence — internalization and compliance — have different motives and different correctional consequences. Since internalizing a belief is the most permanent, deeply rooted response to social influence, it is the response most likely to facilitate an offender's reform. In contrast, the central component in compliance is power. Since power shapes perceptions of self-interest, the compliant offender's behavior may be only as long-lived as the promise of reward or the threat of punishment (Aronson 1988:33).

It is difficult to say which response (or mix of responses) most accurately characterizes Haneda's confession. The U.S. Supreme Court has held confessions involuntary and impermissible as evidence if they are obtained after custodial questioning over a period of several days or even several hours on the same day (Foote 1991:469). Some observers of Japan question whether confessions induced after far longer interrogations can really be deemed voluntary, much less "remorseful" (Hamada 1992).

---

11. This discussion of remorse builds on Richard Weisman's (2001) insightful analysis of judicial efforts to detect remorse and its absence in Canadian criminal justice. Weisman notes that judge-made case law is merely one of many sites for constructing the official identity of an offender. In Japan, the pre-charge investigation stage is the primary site for constructing an offender's character, and the prosecutor is the primary builder.

Nonetheless, because feelings of remorse are inherently painful and therefore unwanted, remorse seems to have an essentially *involuntary* character (Weisman 2001;
Brooks 2000:32). If so, then even prolonged prosecutor pressure can elicit genuine
remorse. Moreover, the prosecutor tries not only to evoke remorse but also to validate
its authenticity. Since what Haneda showed — in tears, trembles, and tone — seemed
to correspond to what he said he felt, the prosecutor was sufficiently convinced of its
validity to reduce the punishment accordingly. In comparative perspective, the most
striking aspect of Japanese prosecutors' quest for correction is not the authenticity
of the remorse they evoke but their resolve to elicit remorse and ascertain its gen-
uineness, and their investment of substantial resources in pursuing those ends. These
are goals and practices that American prosecutors have all but abandoned.[12]

Finally, beneath the manifest functions — conviction and correction — of the
procuracy's pursuit of remorseful confessions lie latent functions that have little to
do with instrumental goals (like rehabilitation) and much to do with the symbolic
expression of core values and tacit assumptions in Japanese culture.[13] As Richard
Weisman (2001) has shown, remorse both reflects and reinforces the boundaries of a
moral community. In expecting remorse, prosecutors do not merely ask offenders to
fear the state's awesome power; they insist that offenders "feel from within" respect
for the values of the community as embodied in the criminal law. The absence of remorse is a form of rebellion; it is "inner treason" against the community and its collective conscience. The remorseful reveal their attachment to the official moral
order, or at least their desire to be readmitted to that order, whereas the remorseless
are deemed to be divested of the human qualities and commitments that members
of a community are presumed to share. Thus, remorse, or its absence, bears witness
to the community's hold over the offender. This expressive dimension of remorse
may be universal (Durkheim 1947), but it seems especially salient in Japan's "culture
of conformity," where individuality is routinely punished and where there is little en-
couragement to think and feel on one's own (Honda 1993:129; Miyamoto 1994:20;
Miyazawa 1994b:89; Inoue 1993:539; Field 1992:28; Miller and Kanazawa 2000). In
this respect, the role of remorse in Japanese criminal justice reveals as much about
the system's — and the nation's — intolerance for deviance as about its commitment
to correction (Murayama 1992).

Remorse reflects and reinforces not only the moral authority of the community
but also the official authority of prosecutors. When an offender regards his offense

---

12. Recall the lesson from Itoh Shigeki's "homily about risk," described in chapter 3. Itoh argued
that in pursuing correction, prosecutors must risk being "deceived" about the authenticity of an offender's
remorse.

13. Students of remorse raise two main questions about the subject. First, how does remorse affect
the conduct of the remorseful? Answers to this question come packaged in the language of recidivism.
Second, how does remorse affect official responses to criminality? Answers to this question engage issues
of social control. Though these are both important inquiries, they tend to crowd out a third query, about
what remorse says, not what it does. Attending to the symbolic significance of remorse requires one to ask
what the category of remorse reveals about underlying cultural values. In this approach, remorse is less
an independent variable shaping offender or official behavior than it is a window onto cultural beliefs
about authority and community (Weisman 2001).

as blameworthy, accepts moral responsibility, and resolves to restructure his life — that is, when an offender repents — he confirms the correctness of the prosecutor's judgment of guilt and the legitimacy of the prosecutor's power to evaluate character, assess culpability, and impose sanctions (Weisman 2001). Thus, the prosecutor's determination to see Haneda repent arose from at least two motivational springs: a desire to have Haneda *do the right thing* (correct his immoral behavior) and a desire to have Haneda *say the right thing* about prosecutor power. Remorse is thus doubly corrective: it helps correct offenders (or is believed to), and it conveys the "correct" messages about prosecutor power.

The symbolic, semiotic significance of remorse reflects and protects the central position of prosecutors in Japanese criminal justice. It has done so since at least the 1930s, when prosecutors sought to "change the direction and heart" (*tenkō*) of thousands of suspected Communists. Their systematic pursuit of *tenkō* not only helped Japan solve a "problem of integration" during the dual crises of political modernization and impending war, it strengthened the legitimacy of the Japanese state — and prosecutorial agents of the state — by impelling submission to it (Steinhoff 1991; Mitchell 1976). The Japanese prosecutor, then and now, "is an animal suspended in webs of significance" he himself has helped spin (Geertz 1973:5). Remorse is one of those webs, and analysis of it must attend as much to unraveling its meanings as to elaborating its effects.

Leniency

In addition to instruction, Japanese prosecutors use the mechanism of leniency to facilitate the correction of selected offenders. Among knowledgeable observers there is close to a consensus that criminal justice in Japan is "extraordinarily lenient" (Haley 1991:129). This is implicitly a comparative claim, and if the point of comparison is the United States it is correct, at least in the aggregate. Japanese criminal justice, and Japanese prosecutors, impose less severe sanctions than their American counterparts (Foote 1992a:317). Indeed, toward nonsinister offenders who have committed crimes of low-to-moderate seriousness, prosecutors, police, and courts act on their belief that mild treatment gives malefactors time and opportunity to change.[14]

Prosecutors recognize that criminal sanctions, especially severe ones like imprisonment, have the capacity to harm offenders, families, and communities. They realize, in other words, that harsh punishment is always costly, often ineffective, and sometimes criminogenic. As one prosecutor put it, "Formal punishment should be the last resort, not the first. For one thing, severe punishment often undermines rehabilitation. For another, informal sanctions are usually enough to control people. We [prosecutors] try not to overdo it." At the same time, prosecutors believe lenient

---

14. For arguments that Japanese criminal justice is lenient and that leniency facilitates correction, see Abe (1963:360); Bayley (1991:133); Braithwaite (1989:62); Dandō (1970:522); Foote (1992a:317); Goodman (1986:36); Haley (1998:79); Itoh (1987:3); E. Johnson (1996:1); Kawakami (1981:19); Mitsui (1974a: 1736); Murayama (1992:221); Nagashima (1963:299); Parker (1984:104); Ramseyer and Nakazato (1999:174); and Westermann and Burfeind (1991:109). Note also that if the point of comparison is the United States, virtually anyplace else looks lenient (Mauer 1999; Lynch 1995).

treatment, such as suspended prosecutions and sentences, promotes reform in many "correctable" offenders. As another prosecutor avowed, "When it comes to punishment, lighter may be better."

The sub-mechanisms are many. Leniency avoids unnecessary stigmatization and thereby reduces the likelihood that offenders will embrace deviance as a master status or join a deviant subculture (Chambliss 1973). Leniency enables offenders to maintain bonds — with work, family, friends, and community — that promote conformity by preserving the elements of informal control: attachment to conventional others; commitment to conventional norms; involvement in conventional activities; and belief in the legitimacy of legal rules (Hirschi 1969). For some offenders, leniency stimulates gratitude. When sanctions are delivered in a way that allows offenders to be heard and treated with respect, belief in the legitimacy of legal rules and authorities is bolstered (Tyler 1990). In the end, of course, prosecutors cannot change offenders, they can only provide them with the time and opportunity to consider (or reconsider) the benefits of conformity and the costs of crime. Japanese prosecutors believe that often this is enough.

Several social facts enable prosecutors to impose mild to moderate punishments. First, social norms about responsibility and punishment are more lenient, forgiving, and restorative in Japan than in the United States. For a wide range of misconduct the wrongdoer in Japan is considered a contextual actor who should be rehabilitated, reintegrated, and restored rather than, as in the United States, an individual actor who must be isolated and punished (Hamilton and Sanders 1992:179). These social norms appear to influence prosecutors' behavior, both through their own internalized commitments to the values the norms embody and through their deference to external standards (such as office *kijun* and *kessai*) that encode and express the norms. At the same time, legal controls tend to be weaker where other social controls are stronger (Black 1976:107). Informal controls are unusually strong and pervasive in Japan (Bayley 1991:175; Inoue 1993:539). Indeed, the strength of informal controls seems the key to understanding Japan's low crime rates (Komiya 1999:380; Braithwaite 1989:61). The lenity of Japan's formal sanctions both reflects and reinforces the power of informal controls (Haley 1991:199).

At the same time, Japan's stress on correction through leniency has not undermined the general deterrent effect of the criminal law, for general deterrence depends less on the severity of sanctions than on the probability of apprehension, or at least the perception of that probability. Clearance rates in Japan have dropped dramatically in recent years, but until recently they remained substantially higher (for most crime categories) than the corresponding rates in the United States and other democracies (Nakada et al. 2001). Since certainty of punishment affects potential offenders more than severity does, Japan's junction of high clearance rates and low severity likely generated more general deterrence than America's converse combination (Walker 1994:41). Time (and research) may tell if recent declines in clearance rates will motivate a "get tougher" movement by undermining the deterrent effect of Japan's traditional practices (Foote 1992a:389). Finally, the quiescent politics of criminal justice in Japan enables prosecutors to consider a fuller range of jurisprudential purposes (including correction) than can American prosecutors who are more constrained by punitive pressures outside their control.

Since the 1970s, American criminologists have produced numerous studies describing the harmful consequences of imprisonment — intended and unintended — and urging parsimony in the use of that sanction. Most such research has had a "voice crying in the wilderness" quality, winning few converts, especially among the politicians and practitioners whose actions, in the aggregate, constitute American criminal justice policy (Morris and Hawkins 1969:2; Mauer 1999:9). Indeed, among the fifty-nine nations in Europe, Asia, and North America for which data are available, the Unites States was "second only to Russia in its rate of incarceration," at a rate of 600 inmates per 100,000 population for the year 1995 (Mauer 1999:19). Japan's rate of 37 per 100,000 was sixteen times lower. By 2001, America's incarceration rate had increased to 700 inmates per 100,000 population. There is a wide gap in severity of sanctions between the United States and Japan, but even in Japan there are limits to leniency.

The Limits of Leniency

Japanese prosecutors are selectively lenient. As described above, their lenity depends on two main factors: the offender's character, as revealed in attitude and prior record, and the offense's seriousness, as indicated by harm caused and other perceptions of gravity. These factors interact with two secondary influences to determine severity of sanction: the victim's attitude, whether forgiving, retributive, or neutral, and the community's response, particularly its capacity and willingness to control released offenders. This section explores the circumstances in which the impulse to correct through leniency gets restrained or overridden by these limiting considerations. It argues that while Japanese prosecutors are lenient, they have not "abandoned the most coercive of all legitimate instruments of state control" (Haley 1991:138). Leniency is selective in that it is directed at people whom prosecutors consider correctable.

First of all, Japan's criminal justice system treats repeat offenders harshly. The severe treatment extends even to recidivists who commit seemingly trivial offenses. As the following example suggests, Japan has a counterpart of sorts to the American "Three Strikes" policy. One might call it "Four Dollars and You're Out."

On January 20, 1994, a Japanese prosecutor indicted a sixty-one-year-old man for violating the Theft with Habitual Recidivism Law. In his opening statement at trial, the prosecutor described the offender and offense as follows:

> The defendant was born in Kagoshima, completed primary education at a local school, and later worked as a forest laborer in various places around the country. . . .
> He has been imprisoned six times. Five of those times were for theft convictions. His most recent prison sentence was completed on March 25, 1993. . . . After being discharged from prison last March, the defendant led a vagabond life on a riverbank under a bridge in Kyoto. He survived by eating food discarded by supermarkets and drinking sake which he bought with money he found on the streets. . . . On January 8, 1994, the defendant spent his last 300 yen on sake. He tried to find additional money on the streets but failed. That evening the defendant wanted a drink but could not afford one, so he decided to steal coins from an offering box inside a pagoda at the Sōkokuji Temple [the money was donated by people visiting this

Buddhist temple]. On the way to the temple the defendant picked up a long nail to use for opening the offering box. When he arrived at the temple grounds, the defendant opened the unlocked pagoda door and, using the nail and a flashlight he possessed, took 411 yen [about $4] out of the offering box drawer. A police officer on duty near the pagoda witnessed the theft and arrested the defendant immediately after he put the money into his pocket.

The vagabond's trial was perfunctory. The prosecutor submitted twenty-one pieces of written evidence for the court to examine, including two full confessions taken from the defendant (one each by the police and the prosecutor), several police reports and victim statements, and records of the defendant's prior offenses. After the defense attorney consented to the prosecutor's proposal to admit these documents as evidence, there was little for anyone to say. The prosecutor called no witnesses, and the defense attorney asked his client just enough questions to elicit an oral admission of guilt and a brief expression of remorse. The entire proceeding took less than thirty minutes. In his closing statement the prosecutor summarized the state's case and made a sentence recommendation to the court:

> We believe that the facts stated in the indictment have been proven beyond a reasonable doubt.
>
> Regarding the circumstances of the offense, first, the defendant committed this crime because he wanted money to buy sake and continue his vagabond life. We cannot find a mitigating factor in his motivation. Second, the defendant has been imprisoned six times before, five times for stealing donated money from temples. His criminal habit is significant. Third, judging from the defendant's behavior and criminal habit, there is a strong probability he will commit more crimes. There also are many theft cases in which money is stolen from temples. Therefore, strict punishment is necessary in order to prevent such crimes generally. Finally, even if one takes into account mitigating factors such as the defendant's honest confession and the return of the stolen money to the victim, the defendant should be punished severely.
>
> Taking into account all of these factors, the prosecutor recommends that the court, after applying the necessary provisions of law, punish the defendant with three years' imprisonment at forced labor.

The judge, "after applying the necessary provisions of the law," sentenced the man to three years' imprisonment with forced labor, just as the prosecutor recommended.[15] Legally, of course, the prosecutor could have suspended prosecution in

---

15. The "necessary provisions of the law" to which the prosecutor referred were the Penal Code (Article 235) and the Law Concerning the Prevention and Punishment of Larceny, Burglary, Robbery, etc. (Article 3). The former law prescribes from one month to ten years' imprisonment with forced labor for "stealing the property of another." The latter prescribes from three to fifteen years' imprisonment with forced labor for the type of aggravated larceny known as "theft with habitual recidivism." Offenders (like the man in this case) are subject to enhanced punishment when two legal requirements are met: (1) the theft reflects the offender's criminal habit; and (2) the offender has been imprisoned for six months or more at least three times during the last ten-year period for convictions on theft or aggravated theft charges. In the present case, the offender had served eight months in prison in 1985–1986, two years and four months in prison in 1988–1990, and two years in prison in 1991–1993.

this case, as he can in any case, no matter how serious. Likewise, the judge could have found extenuating circumstances and reduced the penalty (*shakuryō genkei*) by imposing (and even suspending) a sentence as short as one month (or time already served). In many American jurisdictions this type of offense is either rejected by prosecutors as too trivial to pursue or, at the latest, is dismissed at arraignment by judges preoccupied with more serious cases. Not in Japan. Like their predecessors who judged this defendant the previous times he stole small sums from temples in order to buy food and drink, neither the prosecutor nor the court diverted the defendant onto the lenient "second track" of Japanese criminal justice (Haley 1991:125). Instead, the prosecutor disregarded several seemingly mitigating factors (the defendant's age, homelessness, alcoholism, confession, and return of the four ill-gotten dollars to the Buddhist priest/victim), and stressed specific and general deterrent rationales for the recommendation that the defendant "be punished severely." The court merely dotted the i and crossed the t in the prosecutor's proposed punishment.

As in many countries, one primary purpose of Japanese jails is to manage society's "rabble" — the "detached and disreputable riffraff and social junk" — who do not so much threaten the lives and property of ordinary citizens as prove irksome and offensive to the public and to the police, prosecutors, and judges charged with rabble management functions (Irwin 1985). Here lies a decidedly nonbenevolent, punitive side of Japanese criminal justice.

The vagrant in the preceding case is not a typical Japanese criminal — no single offender is — but he does represent the large category of repeat offenders who receive harsher treatment than first offenders. In 1993, for example, prosecutors suspended the prosecution of repeat offenders only half as often (24 percent) as they did for first offenders (48 percent). Similarly, police drop trivial cases and judges suspend sentences less frequently for repeaters than for first-timers. Of course in America, too, defendants with prior records are treated more severely than defendants without them (Gottfredson and Gottfredson 1988:259), but this is precisely the point. Since America has more serious crime and more hard-core offenders than Japan, it may seem predictable that, in the aggregate, American criminal justice treats offenders more severely. The severity gap is in part a function of the different "inputs" into the respective systems (Mukherjee 1994–1995). But only in part. If the attempts at correction work — and the available evidence suggests they do — then the system itself affects the inputs it receives (Haley 1998:85; Foote 1992a:366).

The treatment of gangsters (*yakuza* or *bōryokudan*), one of the most "sinister" types of offender Japan's criminal justice system encounters, further defines the confines of leniency. Prosecutors treat gangster offenders harshly, not just because their crimes are more serious but also because they are deemed depraved, dangerous people. Gangsters, in a word, have especially damnable character. Like repeat offenders more generally, they receive less lenient treatment because prosecutors locate them on the incorrigible end of the correctability continuum. This propensity is reflected in the procuracy's "standards for case dispositions and recommended sentences," which prescribe sentence recommendations that are 20 to 50 percent heavier for gangsters than for nongangsters. For instance, the presumptive sentence recommendation for extortion is two years for gangsters but just one year for nongangsters. Similarly, the instructions (written by executive prosecutors) which introduce the standards for stimulant drug offenses stress that "severe punishment" is the best policy for stimulant offenders because gangsters often engage in such crimes and because they obtain much of their money from the illicit manufacture, import, and sale of stimulants. Of course, it can be difficult for prosecutors to discern who is a gangster, for *yakuza* often deny membership in organized gangs. In such circumstances, prosecutors rely on the testimony of informants, group photographs of gang members obtained from gang headquarters, official membership lists, and the like.[16]

Drug crimes also circumscribe the limits of leniency in Japanese prosecution. To be sure, statutory penalties for drug use and drug dealing are less severe than in the United States. So are actual sentences. However, the United States is a notably prohibitionist society that relies on severe sanctions to condemn and control drug crimes (Mauer 1999). Moreover, Japan and the United States have incommensurable drug problems. The drugs that most concern Americans — heroin and cocaine especially — and that are the target of the harshest American punishments are almost unheard-of in Japan. American criminal justice is so punitive toward drug offenses that comparing it to criminal justice in other industrialized democracies (like Japan) will invariably make the latter look lenient (Lynch 1995). However, compared with nations like the Netherlands or Britain, Japan's drug enforcement looks punitive indeed (Vaughn et al. 1995:515). As one Japanese prosecutor explained, at least for some drug offenders, maximizing punishment is not a bad approximation of what prosecutors want:

> In drug offenses, it is difficult to arrest offenders and collect evidence for securing conviction, since they are perpetrated systematically and secretly. Regarding drug addicts, it is difficult for them to be rehabilitated by themselves, and even after being released from jail they are most likely to recommit the same offense. Therefore, the most important thing in handling drug offenses is to clear as many persons involved in the case as possible, collect as much evidence as possible, and prosecute as many suspects as possible, including simple users. (Kino 1994:1)

Compared with most Western democracies, drug offenses in Japan are conspicuously uncommon. Nonetheless, the nation has so little serious crime that drug offenses still account for about 20 percent of all formal trials. Four categories of drug offenses most concern prosecutors: stimulants, cannabis, narcotics (mostly cocaine and heroin), and opium. In 1992, prosecutors disposed of 22,977 suspects in these four categories. Stimulant suspects accounted for fully 92 percent of that total (21,135 suspects). Prosecutors, police, and judges agree that the use and abuse of stimulant drugs (especially methamphetamine, or "speed") is Japan's most serious drug problem (Ohbayashi 1995; Bayley 1991:117). Every year prosecutors dispose of few suspects in the other drug crime categories. In 1992, for example, prosecutors handled only 1,711 cannabis suspects, 455 narcotics suspects, and 86 opium suspects.

At each stage of the criminal justice system the response to drug suspects and offenders is stern. Generally, arrest is used less often to initiate criminal investiga-

16. Walter Ames (1981:105) describes relationships among gangsters, police, and other criminal justice officials. For other discussions of the role of *yakuza* in Japanese society, see Szymkowiak (2001), Whiting (1999), Seymour (1996), Mizoguchi (1993), Saga (1991), and Kaplan and Dubro (1986).

tions in Japan than in the United States (Foote 1992a:342). In 1992 only about 26 percent of all criminal suspects were arrested. The figure for stimulant suspects, however, was 65 percent, more than twice the overall rate. Prosecutors invariably request detention warrants of at least ten days for these suspects, doing so for nearly 99 percent of all arrestees, and judges almost always approve these requests. Once they detain a stimulant suspect, prosecutors are likely to file formal charges if there is sufficient evidence to convict at trial. In 1993 prosecutors suspended prosecution in only 7.7 percent of all stimulant drug cases, far lower than the nearly 50 percent suspension of prosecution rate in theft cases. Furthermore, since 1982 prosecutors have not employed the simpler summary prosecution procedure for even one stimulant suspect. This procedure would allow suspects who acknowledge guilt to pay a fine through the mail without appearing at trial, thereby saving substantial process costs. Instead, and without exception, prosecutors have sought formal trials for stimulant offenders. Virtually all stimulant defendants are convicted. In 1992 the conviction rate for stimulant offenders was 99.936 percent. Of those convicted, only 44 percent received suspended sentences, far lower than the rate of 64 percent for all cases ending in conviction. No stimulant offender was simply fined.

The severity documented in these statistics is further substantiated by prosecutor attitudes toward drug offenses and offenders. One prosecutor told me that America is a good "negative role model" for Japan because its unwisely lenient policies reveal what *not* to do in order to maintain social order. "Your country is far too lenient with drug offenders," he opined. "As a result, your drug problem is out of control. Our [Japanese] history shows that strict enforcement works. We don't try to rehabilitate them. You can't. Nobody can. Drug users are dangerous criminals, threats to the social order, and they ought to be treated as such. We do."

Setting aside his inaccurate description of what is really a harshly punitive set of American drug policies (Mauer 1999), this prosecutor's words reflect the severe attitude toward drug offenders that permeates the procuracy. The procuracy's internal "standards for case dispositions and sentence recommendations" for stimulant offenses are one example. The standards distinguish between the import, export, and manufacture of stimulants, on the one hand, and the possession and use of stimulants, on the other. The presumption is that prosecutors will charge. They do so in over 90 percent of cases with sufficient evidence to convict. Likewise, in order to determine the sentence recommendation for the import, export, and manufacture of stimulants, prosecutors merely discern whether the suspect committed the crime for profit or not, and then count the number of prior offenses and grams of stimulant drug. For possession and use of stimulants, prosecutors make a slightly finer distinction between "regular people," "addicts," and "people possessing for sale," in addition to counting prior offenses and grams of the drug. Whatever the case, fixing the sentence is mostly a matter of finding the appropriate coordinates on the standards "grid" and reading down and across to the proper cell. Remorse (or its absence) can marginally affect the sentence selected, as it did in Haneda's case, but even offenders like Haneda are sentenced to prison.

These charge and sentence decisions are only slightly more individualized than the mechanical sentencing decisions required of American judges under U.S. sentencing guidelines (Tonry 1996). And prosecutors in Japan seem only a little more likely to deviate from the presumptions than are their judicial counterparts in the United States. In many drug cases, prosecutor decisions differ markedly from the "lenient sanctions tailored to the offender's particular circumstances" which characterize Japan's criminal justice response to other types of offenses (Foote 1992a:317). Moreover, the response to drug crimes has grown increasingly harsh since the 1980s as the government has been "perpetually amending and improving drug control laws" and adopting ever more aggressive drug enforcement strategies (Vaughn et al. 1995:510).[17] Some prosecutors report that drug enforcement must be strict because detection is difficult, and that the increasing severity of enforcement helps compensate for the decline in general deterrence caused by falling clearance rates.[18]

Leniency is limited for gun crimes too. Japan "comes as close as any industrialized country to being a gun-free society" (Kristof 1996; Kopel 1992).[19] Indeed, only about 1 percent of all Japanese households have guns, about half the percentage of gun-possessing homes in Holland (the next most gun-free country) and one-fiftieth the percentage of gun-owning American households. The scarcity of guns means there are few gun crimes. In 1994, for example, there were only 249 shootings reported in the entire country. In all, thirty-eight people were shot dead and twenty-eight more were injured (*Asahi Evening News* 3/31/95). In 1995 there were only

---

17. While this section has focused on stimulant offenses, Japanese criminal justice treats other drug crimes harshly as well. A comparison with the United States is illustrative. In 1996 an American software executive wrote an op-ed piece in the *New York Times* (March 9) objecting that he recently had done "major time for a minor [marijuana] crime" and arguing that Mayor Rudolph Giuliani and the New York City criminal justice system should stop "dispensing a brutal experience to a seemingly random sample of pot smokers on the street." The author and his friend had been arrested for possessing about "two joints' worth" of marijuana, driven around in a police van for several hours while the police arrested other drug offenders, held in various holding cells for thirty-six hours, and then released after a ninety-second hearing in which the judge "essentially dismissed" their case. The author complained that the holding cells were "stifling" and "rancid," jailhouse guards were "needlessly abusive," the professional aftershocks were "catastrophic," legal bills were "absurd," and the punishment was entirely too severe "for such a low-grade misdemeanor."

This executive's experience was undoubtedly unpleasant. However, as Gary's case suggests, had he been arrested in Japan for a similar offense (next to stimulants, cannabis is the most frequently abused illegal drug in Japan), he almost certainly would have been detained for longer than thirty-six hours, and would likely have been charged rather than released. Once he was convicted, his sentence would probably have been suspended, yet the "process punishments" he experienced going through the Japanese system would have, in both duration and intensity, far exceeded the treatment he received in New York. In short, for many drug offenders in Japan, even minor ones like Gary, "the process is the punishment" to a greater extent than in the United States (Feeley 1992b).

18. I am grateful to Daniel Foote for alerting me to this possibility.

19. Guns were not always so scarce. The Portuguese introduced guns into Japan in 1543, and "the Japanese were keen users of firearms for nearly 100 years" thereafter. But in the period that followed Japan's enthusiastic embrace of the gun, the Tokugawa Shoguns, through "an extremely slow series of cutbacks," effectively disarmed the country except for the swords that remained in the hands of the samurai warrior class. Japan thus "gave up the gun" completely for about 250 years. Firearms were reintroduced to Japan only in the Meiji era, when the appearance of Commodore Perry's black ships in Tokyo Bay convinced Japan's leaders that in order to keep future Perrys out of Japan, and thus maintain the country's autonomy vis-à-vis Western colonial threats, they had to get guns of their own. They did. This time, however, the oligarchs' plan for making Japan a "rich nation and strong army" meant keeping firearms out of the hands of private citizens (Perrin 1979).

thirty-two gun murders. Most people killed with guns are gangsters shot by other gangsters. Only twelve people who were not linked to the *yakuza* were shot dead by guns in 1994 and 1995. That is only slightly higher than the number of Japanese — nine — who were killed or injured by lightning in 1995. Yearly averages for 1989–1994 reveal a similar picture. The average number of shootings each year was 254, of which over 80 percent were by members of recognized criminal gangs. Thirty-one shootings resulted in death (Tani 1995:5). By comparison, in the United States there were 15,456 gun murders in 1994 (*New York Times* 5/19/96). In 1996 the number of American handgun murders had declined to 9,390, but that was still 626 times as many as occurred in Japan (*New York Times* 1/1/01). Gun crimes and attitudes toward guns differ so markedly between the United States and Japan that any effort to compare punitiveness in the two countries must take these differences into account.

Gun crimes in Japan are so rare that in my fourteen months in Kobe I did not encounter a single case of gun violence. Office guidelines, however, instruct prosecutors to charge all violent crimes in which a gun is used. Prosecutors also follow the guidelines' directive to request a punishment "gun tariff" of two to three years' imprisonment on top of the ten to twelve years "going rate" for sentence requests in murder cases. The extra punishment applies to crimes of gun possession too. Japan has "the toughest laws on the ownership of firearms, especially handguns, of any democratic country in the world" (Bayley 1991:172), and prosecutors strictly enforce them. One law requires all firearms, swords, and knives over six inches long to be registered. Permits are difficult to acquire. In 1993 prosecutors charged 2,125 out of 3,233 violators of that law, or about two out of every three offenders. Since this crime category lumps gun ownership together with ownership of less lethal instruments of violence, it is clear that prosecutors respond severely to offenders who "merely" possess illegal firearms. In fact, the "merely" in the last sentence is a word few Japanese (prosecutors or not) would apply to illegal possession. Prosecutors seldom suspend charges in gun possession cases, and courts are similarly severe. In the six months between February and July of 1994, courts sentenced 140 offenders for illegal gun possession, of whom only 41 (29 percent) were given suspended sentences, a rate half the suspended sentence rate of nearly 60 percent for all Penal Code offenders. Of those 140 offenders, only four received sentences of less than one year. Of the remaining 136, about half received terms of imprisonment greater than three years (Tawada 1995:46).

Finally, the harshest of all criminal sanctions is death, and Japan employs this punishment as well. The pattern throughout the West is "so simple it is stunning. Every Western industrial nation has stopped executing criminals, except the United States." Beyond Europe, "abolition of the death penalty is the standard policy of most developed countries," including Canada, Australia, New Zealand, and Israel (Zimring and Hawkins 1986:3). Japan differs from all these countries. Except for the United States, it stands alone among advanced industrialized democracies in retaining capital punishment.[20] In the seventeen years from 1976 through 1992, Japanese courts imposed the death penalty on sixty-nine capital offenders (4.3 per year). In roughly the same period (1976–1993) forty-two persons were executed (2.5 per

---

20. Though Japan has never come close to abolishing the death penalty, a nascent abolitionist movement has emerged in recent years, led by former Supreme Court Justice Dandō Shigemitsu(1997).

year). In 1994 Japan had eighty-six inmates on death row, fifty-six with confirmed death sentences and another thirty who were appealing their sentences or applying for retrial. Since seven such inmates were put to death in 1993, about 7.5 percent of the death row total was executed (Dowling 1994:32). By comparison, in the United States about three thousand inmates were on death row in 1994, of whom thirty-one were executed (about 1 percent of the total). No more than about 2 percent of the American death row total has ever been executed in any one year.[21]

While Japan's use of the death penalty distinguishes it from all but one of the Western countries with which it is typically compared, other Asian countries remain regular users too. China executes more people each year than all other countries combined, but India, Indonesia, Malaysia, Pakistan, the Philippines, Singapore, South Korea, Sri Lanka, and Thailand also retain and use capital punishment. There may be more "family resemblances" between criminal justice in Japan and other Asian nations than scholars heretofore have recognized. The subject deserves more research attention than it has received.

One final comparison further illustrates the limits of Japanese leniency. Between 1976, when the U.S. Supreme Court's decision in *Gregg v. Georgia* reopened the door to death in America, and October 1994, 253 persons were executed in the United States. That is an average of 13.4 executions per year. Over roughly the same period (1976–1993) Japan executed forty-two persons, or about 2.5 executions per year. The average number of yearly executions in the United States was over five times higher than in Japan. Does this mean the United States is more likely to execute capital offenders? Perhaps not, for disparities in population and in the number of murderers in the two countries exceed the difference in yearly executions. For instance, in 1988 the U.S. homicide rate was 8.4 per 100,000 population, seven times higher than Japan's homicide rate of 1.2 per 100,000 (Westermann and Burfeind 1991:31). Once the difference in the number of potentially "deserving" or "eligible" offenders is taken into account (together with the difference in population), it is Japan, not America, which appears more likely to execute capital offenders. In short, what seems on the face a more punitive American practice may again reflect the markedly different inputs into the two criminal justice systems. Once the different inputs are taken into consideration, Japan seems about as likely to impose and carry out the death penalty as the United States, and more likely to do so than many individual American states.

Japan's Two Systems

The late Dutch sociologist Antonie Peters argued that claims about the "lenience" and "benevolence" of Japanese criminal justice use "the American system as [the] main frame of reference," give "too much credit to official [Japanese] ideology," and

21. Japan has carried out executions regularly, albeit in declining numbers, for well over a century. During the Meiji era (1868–1912) a total of 8,771 persons were executed, for an average of about 200 per year. During the Taisho period (1912–1925) 543 people were executed, about 39 per year, and in the Showa era (1925–1989) 950 were executed, for a rate of about 16 per year. During the postwar period (1945–1990), 585 persons were executed, an average of approximately 13 per year.

thus reflect "the same American bias which has characterized so much of the postwar comparative understanding of Japanese law." Peters believed that in comparison with the Dutch system, "Japanese criminal justice cannot possibly be called 'lenient' when the punitive and vexatious nature of the criminal process is taken into consideration" (Peters 1992:291).

The tendency to give "too much credit to [the] official ideology" of Japanese criminal justice has indeed distorted understandings of the contours of leniency.[22] Japanese criminal justice officials, of whom prosecutors have been most voluble, enable the distortions by speaking in two dissonant voices. To American academic and liberal audiences who rightly excoriate the excessive punitiveness of American criminal justice, a lenient Japan is a convenient tool for criticism. "Lenient Japan" is thus a message comfortably delivered and uncritically received. Prosecutors also are adept at justifying their powers (and attempts to expand those powers) with a rhetoric of lenient benevolence (Miyazawa 1995). The second voice, however, speaks a strikingly nonbenevolent language. We heard that voice in chapter 2, when Ishihara Kazuhiko, the head of the Osaka High Prosecutors Office, reproached judges in his region for punishing criminals more leniently than judges in Tokyo. In fact, prosecutors have for decades castigated judges for excessive leniency. In the early 1960s, for example, Abe Haruo (1963:338) rebuked judges by stating that "judicial cruelty in the feudal age and judicial leniency in modern times are nothing but the two extremes of the same pendulum of judicial sentimentalism." Absent from the rhetoric in these cases is any claim that more punishment means more correction. The reasons invoked were instead the need to achieve "consistency" across cases and the rationales of deterrence and retribution. Abe even asserted that "the retributive view of punishment, with its emphasis on a correlation between penalty and culpability, has predominant currency in theory and practice in the administration of criminal justice in Japan." The imposition of death sentences is justified in similarly retributive terms.

It may make sense to speak not only of two rhetorics of Japanese criminal justice but also, as in America, of two realities (Gottfredson and Gottfredson 1988; Walker

---

22. There is other, more indirect evidence of the limits of leniency. For example, prosecutors may not seek, nor may judges impose, indeterminate sentences. Such sentences are used in other countries to tailor specific treatment programs to offenders' needs. Moreover, offenders sentenced to Japanese prison find few educational or vocational programs, and the "guidance" offered by prison personnel is aimed more at discipline and control than at rehabilitation. Persons sentenced to probation or released on parole receive assistance not from professional probation and parole officers (who are in short supply) but from elderly, overworked volunteers who can do little to promote reintegration into the community. Further, even correctional officers who are committed to the rehabilitative ideal often lack the necessary resources to pursue it (Miyazawa 1991). One also observes several reform efforts aimed at moving farther away from the rehabilitative ideal. Since at least 1977, prosecutors have been trying to make juvenile proceedings more like adult proceedings, chiefly by seeking a more prominent role for themselves at juvenile hearings. At present, prosecutors are not permitted to attend juvenile hearings, nor are they allowed to appeal family court decisions. Prosecutors, supported by LDP and other conservative politicians, are trying to create legal room to do both (*Asahi Shimbun* 5/17/00). They seem likely to succeed. One sees similar departures from the rehabilitative ideal in the priority prosecutors have placed on punishing mentally disturbed offenders rather than treating them, and in the efforts of criminal justice officials to normalize the use of police cells (*daiyō kangoku*) as pretrial detention facilities.

1989:22). The "first criminal justice system" is characterized by consensually defined serious events, such as gun and drug crimes, capital offenses, stranger crimes, and crimes committed by gangsters or other incorrigibles (like the homeless thief). Toward these offenses the people of Japan have attitudes at least as punitive as those of the American public (Hamilton and Sanders 1992:174). Officials seem to hold less punitive attitudes than the general public when it comes to sentencing (Abe 1963:336, 360; D. Johnson and Miyazawa 1994:682), but not when determining guilt or innocence (Lempert 1992; Tanase 1986:18). In either event, it is clear that Japanese criminal justice responds aggressively, even harshly, to some offenders. Throughout this "first system" of criminal justice the empirical norm is full processing and reduced concern for correction. Even here, however, in comparison with the American system the commitment to correction sometimes seems conspicuous.

In contrast, the "second system of criminal justice" is characterized by offenses of low seriousness and offenders of high correctability. It responds much more leniently. For nonserious offenses (like larceny or simple assault) committed by first-time, non-stranger offenders, prosecutors individualize treatment in pursuit of rehabilitative and reintegrative ends, especially with offenders deemed "properly" remorseful. Competing claims about the relative leniency or severity of Japanese criminal justice derive, in considerable part, from a preoccupation with one or the other of these two systems of criminal justice. Both systems reflect the Japanese way of justice.

Finally, one major difference between Japan and the United States again deserves emphasis — the difference in inputs into their respective criminal justice systems. Since Japan has fewer serious offenses and offenders — a smaller "first system" of criminal justice — the aggregate picture may look more lenient than it really is (Mukherjee 1994–1995). Similarly, the scarcity of serious cases in the "first" Japanese system allows prosecutors to devote more resources to correcting offenders in the "second" system than can their more burdened American counterparts (Stone 2000; Jackall 1997). In short, while both the United States and Japan have "two faces of criminal justice," the prominence of each face differs because of their different orientations to correction and because of their markedly different crime mixes. Critically, Japan's commitment to correction probably reduces the salience of the first punitive face by limiting the supply of incorrigible offenders in which it traffics (Haley 1998:79).

Correcting Victims

The impulse to correct is also evident in prosecutors' treatment of victims. Here their aim is less to rehabilitate offenders than to rectify the injuries caused by crime.[23] Although correction of this kind has ancient roots in the West, dating at least to Aristotle's analysis of "rectificatory justice" in the fourth century B.C., today that tradition

---

23. Of course, many Japanese prosecutors believe the acts of seeking forgiveness and making restitution facilitate an offender's correction.

little informs American prosecutor practice (Van Ness and Strong 1997; Etzioni 1999). Efforts to "make victims right" are much more evident in the Japanese way of justice, suggesting that victim advocacy is not necessarily "rooted in, and dependent on, an overheated and fear-ridden political climate" (Scheingold et al. 1994:760; Roach 1999:706). In my survey, for example, more than two-thirds of Japanese prosecutors regarded "repairing relations between the offender and victim" as an important or very important objective. In contrast, not even one Seattle prosecutor (out of fifty-seven) treated such repair work as an important goal. Similarly, "the victim's feelings about punishment" and "whether the suspect compensates the victim" were deemed important factors in suspension of prosecution decisions by about three-quarters of Japanese prosecutors.

Indeed, both of these factors were considered more important than "prior record." When suspending prosecution, more than five out of six prosecutors "usually make the offender promise to observe some post-suspension condition, such as making restitution to the victim." And almost four out of five prosecutors say that "whether or not a suspect has made *jidan* [a type of restitution described below] with the victim has a big influence on how the suspect is treated." In short, prosecutors believe justice consists not only in correcting offenders but also in restoring victims and healing the injuries caused by crime.

From the offender's point of view, making restitution is a primary way of demonstrating remorse — to the victim or victim's family, of course, but also to the decisionmakers who hold his fate in their hands. As a result, offenders (and their defense lawyers) make settling with victims a first priority. Three kinds of settlement are considered "favorable" for an offender. First, payment of "compensation for damages" (*higai benshō*) or "solace money" (*isharyō* or *mimaikin*) is a one-way transaction, from offender to victim. Though this is the least favorable kind of settlement to make, it is far more advantageous than paying no compensation at all. The second type of settlement is *jidan*, a private agreement between the offender, who pays compensation, and the victim, who promises not to pursue additional legal action against the offender. A *jidan* is contractual, and a *jidansho* is simply a record of the agreement, addressed to neither prosecutor nor judge. Finally, the best settlement for an offender consists of a *jidan* promise plus a written petition (*tangansho*) from the victim to the prosecutor or court expressing forgiveness and appealing for leniency. In effect, *jidan* protects the offender against civil liability and a petition helps mitigate judgments of culpability with correctional considerations. When victims refuse to make *jidan* or accept compensation, offenders commonly demonstrate their sincerity to repair harms in still another way, by making an "atonement contribution" (*shokuzai kifu*) to some third party, such as a legal aid association or charity.

Settlements significantly shape what offenders get in the criminal process. In part this means that money buys leniency. In a gang rape case, for example, compensation of 1.5 million yen (about $12,500) reduced the prosecutor's recommended and the court's imposed sentence by about one year, from four to three. Or at least it did for each of the six offenders who paid that amount. Two offenders who did not (or could not) pay got longer sentences. The trial prosecutor said that in cases of this kind, 1.5 million yen is about the "exchange rate" for a one-year reduction in punishment. In a robbery case where the victim refused to accept compensation, the offender's 330,000 yen ($2,750) atonement contribution to the local legal aid association cut the court's sentence by two months. In murder cases, where terms of imprisonment range from three years to life (and capital punishment is a possibility), the desires of the victim's survivors have an effect that must be measured in years, if not in life itself.

When settlement is made before the prosecutor has reached a charge decision, the amount paid and the presence or absence of *jidan* and *tangansho* can decisively influence whether and what to charge.[24] In a 1993 *chikan* (molestation) case, for example, a forty-one-year-old salaryman was nabbed by a train employee who observed him fondling the buttocks and private parts of a sixteen-year-old high school girl on a crowded train.[25] The police were called and the offender was rebuked, advised to apologize, and informed that his case would be sent to the prosecutors office for "at home" (*zaitaku*) processing. He was not arrested, even though he had been convicted and fined twice previously (for a minor assault and a boat safety violation) and apprehended but released for molestation four years before when a different victim refused to file a complaint. On the same day the offender was apprehended in the instant case, he and his wife visited the victim's family to apologize. He apologized in person twice more, the second time seven months after the first, just ten days before his prosecution was suspended. On each visit the offender was accompanied by his wife and defense lawyer. They gang-bowed the victim with apologies, reached a *jidan*

24. Although the cases described in the text mainly concern sex crimes against females, settlement affects prosecutor decisions in other cases too. For example, in traffic offenses where blame is minor or mitigated, *jidan* is encouraged because prosecutors consider it a functional equivalent to civil proceedings. And in minor, nonrepeat larceny cases, *jidan* "makes the victim whole," so prosecutors may see little need to impose further punishment. In many assault cases (such as bar fights), the victim shares in the blame and knows the offender. If settlement is made, prosecutors often suspend prosecution in order to avoid damage to, and encourage repair of, the victim-offender relationship. Similarly, extortion crimes are frequently committed to collect debts from victims who are themselves blameworthy (think of a *yakuza* loan shark collecting money from a heavily indebted gambler). Here, too, prosecutors prefer to let the parties resolve the conflict on, or mostly on, their own. In many of these cases prosecutors perform the role of referee or bill collector (Blumberg 1979:133). At the same time, some prosecutors resent being pressured by private parties to perform these roles. A large percentage of cases filed directly with the prosecutors office (instead of with the police) involve people attempting to use prosecutors to gather information they can use in civil disputes. One prosecutor told me his "two happiest days" are when he obtains a confession and when he gets a citizen to withdraw a complaint that puts him in the "bill collector" or "private investigator" role. Nonetheless, Japan's civil process is so slow and ineffective that many victims use the criminal process as a substitute (H. Yamaguchi 1999). They are empowered when the threat of criminal sanction elevates offenders' efforts to settle.

25. Sexual molestation is common in Japan; reporting the crime is not. In 1995 a police survey of Osaka junior and senior high girls revealed that in the preceding year fully 76 percent had been molested, typically on trains. Only 2 percent complained to the police. The reasons for not reporting ranged from "It is too embarrassing" to "I do not want to be asked various questions by the police" and "The other passengers merely pretend not to see it. In the end, you must protect yourself" (*Yomiuri Shimbun* 5/10/95). In December 2000, the Keio Electric Railway Company decided to set aside a train car exclusively for women. Keio elected "to introduce the man-free carriages after a random poll of members of both sexes found a majority supported the idea." Before the new policy was implemented, about 80 percent of female respondents and a majority of men said they supported the set-aside policy. Afterward, Keio executives reported receiving "more jeers than cheers for the initiative" (*Asahi Shimbun* 12/17/00). Keio set aside

agreement for the sum of 60,000 yen ($500), and lobbied the victim's parents to sign a *tangansho* petition worded in the victim's voice but drafted by the defense lawyer. The petition concluded with the victim appealing to the prosecutor to be lenient with the offender "this time only," since the offender "promised not to do it again" and "knows what will happen if he does." The victim and both her parents signed the petition. It is unclear if they knew the offender had confessed to prosecutors that in the months preceding this assault he had molested girls on the train "two or three times a month" in order to "make up for the sexual discontent" of his marriage.

A few days after getting the petition signed, the defense lawyer and the offender's employer visited the prosecutor, bearing the petition and two other "written reports" (*jōshinsho*) — one from the employer (also the offender's uncle) and one from the offender's wife — urging leniency and promising to "supervise" (*kantoku*) the offender if prosecution was dropped. The wife's report also stated that she was "shocked" to hear of this crime; that if her husband ever repeated it, she would divorce him; and that prosecution would have deleterious effects on their three children, ages seven, five, and three. Both the employer and the defense lawyer made verbal appeals to the prosecutor. After they left, the prosecutor explained that without the *tangansho* he would have prosecuted and the offender probably would have been fined. This, anyway, was the decision suggested by the twenty-seven molestation precedents he had collected in order to inform the current disposition. But suspending prosecution, he concluded, "is the only thing to do when petitioned this much." His supervisors agreed.

I described these Japanese practices to several American prosecutors. Most asserted that getting restitution for the victim may be an objective in property (especially white-collar) crimes, but insisted that for crimes against persons, such as rob-

---

the special cars on some final trains leaving Shinjuku station on weekend nights during December (in Japan there is a significant increase in the number of late-night revelers during the end-of-year party season). Banning men from train cars is not a new concept. From 1947 to 1973, Japan National Railways set aside carriages for women and children "to protect them from the potentially lethal throngs using Chuo Line trains" (*Mainichi Daily News* 12/6/00).

Groping does not occur only on trains. According to another survey, two out of three women working in government offices said they had been sexually harassed by men touching their bodies at work (*New York Times* 11/1/98).

It appears that domestic violence is also common in Japan, though it, too, goes largely unreported. A 1996 study by Japan's Supreme Court found that one-third of the 37,395 marriage arbitration cases filed by women in Japan's family courts involved complaints of domestic abuse. Most ended in divorce. A study by the Tokyo Metropolitan Government (released in May 1998) revealed that one-third of the 1,183 women in its survey had been battered by their husbands or boyfriends. Battered women are reluctant to complain for a variety of reasons, not least because police and prosecutors tend to treat domestic abuse as a "private" family matter. Critics charge that when police and prosecutors do get involved, "they often ask the woman if she really wants to press charges and [thereby] bring shame on her family" (*Honolulu Star-Bulletin* 9/29/98).

Partly in response to this criticism, the National Police Agency has instituted a new policy, to take effect in June 2001, allowing citizens to file complaints with police officials or public safety commissions about police misconduct and "inappropriate attitudes" (*Asahi Shimbun* 4/14/01). If this is a step forward it is a small one. Investigations of the complaints will be conducted by the police, who remain almost completely unaccountable to external agents of authority (Ochiai 2000; Terasawa 1998; Walker 2001). For an overview of domestic violence in Japan, see Kaino et al. (1998). On the politics and prosecution of sexual assault in the United States, see Bevacqua (2000) and Frohmann (1997).

bery or rape, it is not merely irrelevant, it is improper. One senior California prosecutor exploded in anger when I explained to her the Japanese *jidan* practice in rape and molestation cases. "Their [Japanese prosecutors'] behavior is outrageous," she declared. "It discriminates against poor offenders and it allows rich ones to buy their way out. Besides, it is a well-known fact that sex offenders recidivate. Prosecutors need to protect the public against them. If I were the next victim, I would sue." Another California prosecutor protested for a different reason, perceiving that defense attorneys who approach victims must either be suborning perjury or otherwise tampering with a witness. A Minnesota prosecutor averred that, in stranger assaults especially, victims would be — and should be — afraid to make contact with offenders or their representatives.

Nonetheless, Japanese prosecutors routinely foster, and sometimes compel, *jidan* and its correlates. Though not a direct party to these ostensibly private agreements, prosecutors participate in the settlement process through their interactions with offenders and victims.

First, prosecutors encourage, even urge, offenders to pay reparations. To them, reparations not only reflect remorse, they help constitute it, by demonstrating that the offender is serious about restructuring his life and restoring the victim's. Prosecutors assume justice should promote healing, not merely locate blame so as to impose pain, and believe reparations help heal the injuries victims have suffered. As one Japanese prosecutor explained,

> Justice is not just about punishment. Our job is to help victims, even as we try to help offenders. It is natural to consider *jidan* and other forms of compensation as advantageous circumstances for the offender. Of course. The question is, how much should they count? That is impossible to answer abstractly. We do it on a case-by-case basis, relying on office standards and our own good sense.

The subject of restitution often arises in interrogation. It is usually agreed that the offender should attempt to make restitution (if he has not already), but where offenders have not considered this course prosecutors commonly instruct or hector them to do so. Although offenders are disproportionately poor, prosecutors seem unconcerned about the economics of *jidan*. As one put it, "No matter how poor, just about everyone can come up with some money. Everyone has connections. At the very least, even poor offenders can borrow money from relatives and friends." While this perception may appear Pollyannaish, in Japan strikingly few offenders — or defense attorneys — object to restitution on the grounds of its inegalitarian potential.

It is in prosecutors' interactions with victims that restitution creates the most vexing problems. Prosecutors say they should not obstruct *jidan* negotiations. In a rape case, for example, one prosecutor professed that

> The prosecutor cannot hinder the victim's side from negotiating with the suspect before charges are filed, or even from withdrawing the complaint. This is natural, because rape is an offense subject to prosecution only on complaint [*shinkokuzai*], and because the victim may want to avoid the mental suffering caused by revealing the facts at trial. In rape cases and the like, even if the offender's conduct is malicious, we must strictly respect the victim's will because we cannot cause additional pain to the victim.

This view is consistent with American norms that allow the parties themselves to determine the course of litigation, whether civil or criminal (Damaska 1986). The problems most often occur not when prosecutors let victims alone, as this one advocated, but when that norm is violated and they pressure victims to agree to settlements they do not want to make (Nader 1990).[26]

Pressure is applied most conspicuously on female victims in sex crime cases. In one representative case, a twenty-three-year-old woman was groped from behind on her buttocks as she descended the stairs at a train station. The offender, a man in his early thirties with no prior arrests, was tackled by the victim's boyfriend, who heard her cry for help. A struggle ensued but the groper escaped, leaving his bag at the foot of the stairs. The victim and her boyfriend called the police, who lay in wait for the offender to retrieve the bag. When he did, he was arrested for "indecency through compulsion," an offense punished by imprisonment for up to seven years. At the same time the victim's boyfriend was also arrested (on the groper's complaint) for assaulting the groper. When the groper and boyfriend settled by *jidan* (no money changed hands), the question which remained was what to do about the original indecent act.

The groper had connections, one of whom was a politician in the local prefectural assembly. The victim told me she believes the politician pressured prosecutors, successfully, to go lightly on the groper. I could not verify the veracity of that claim. I did confirm, however, that the victim was interviewed once by the police, over a nine-hour period, and twice by prosecutors, four hours each time. The victim said that in each interview the investigators asked numerous irrelevant questions, and that they did so in a disrespectfully lighthearted way: How many boyfriends have you had? How many sexual experiences? When did you lose your virginity? You're so young; aren't you embarrassed to be in this position? And so on. The victim told police she would like to proceed more quickly with the interview because she had an appointment to keep. She was informed the process would go faster if she withdrew her complaint. The victim refused to sign several police statements because they discounted the seriousness of the assault. Similarly, in interviews with the prosecutor she felt she "was not taken seriously" on either occasion.

On her last visit the prosecutor composed a statement and urged her to sign it. The last sentence read "I have heard from the prosecutor that the offender is deeply repentant, so I will withdraw the charges." When she declined to sign, the prosecu-

26. Victims are also pressured to settle by *yakuza* enforcers who rely more heavily on intimidation than prosecutors do (Haley 1991:183). In one case I examined a *yakuza* boss was arrested for assault and extortion against a former gang member. The boss's attorney advised him that without a *tangansho* (a petition of leniency from the victim), he was likely to do time in prison. The victim, fearing pressure to settle and retaliation from the boss for filing the complaint, fled to Tokyo, hundreds of miles away, even though police had provided him with shelter and (apparently inadequate) protection. One of the boss's subordinates then forged a *tangansho* and sent it to the boss's attorney. Because the prosecutor refused to allow it to be admitted as evidence at trial, the attorney had the subordinate testify in court as to the petition's authenticity. The strategy failed badly. The subordinate was arrested for perjury, confessed, and was sentenced to two years in prison. His boss got two years too. *Yakuza* also pressure offenders to settle, as vividly depicted in Itami Juzo's excellent film *Minbō no Onna* (Woman Mob Fighter). On the *yakuza*'s roles as lawyer substitute and fixer-breaker, see Milhaupt and West (2000), Seymour (1996), and Mizoguchi (1993).

tor yelled at her, threw his pen, crumpled up the statement, and threw it in the trash. Thereafter, and seconded by his assistant, the prosecutor persistently pressured the victim to drop her complaint. She refused. Two months later she received a postcard from the procuracy saying that her assailant would not be charged. There was no explanation. In the seven months between the assault and the disposition, the victim received three phone calls from the groper's attorney inviting her to make *jidan*. He offered 40,000 yen ($333) in compensation. Each time the woman replied that she did not want money, she wanted the offender punished.

Few victims are as able as this one to resist entreaties to settle, but more than a few get pressured from both sides, defense *and* prosecution, to accept payment, make *jidan*, and withdraw or moderate complaints. Most seem to accede. The motivations for settling are multiple and conjunctural. Some victims settle because they believe it fairly and justly resolves the case or restores their losses. Some settle out of the desire to minimize process costs or get on with their lives. Some settle out of deference to authority. Prosecutors are difficult to defy; so are parents, husbands, and employers. And so are offenders and defense lawyers who repeatedly contact victims to offer restitution, often reminding them, by the way, that if everything comes out in the open at trial, things could get "hard" for the victim and her family. Many victims of sex crimes cannot face having their cases tried in open court. Being raped or groped or molested sullies a woman's reputation — if people hear about it. Moreover, many victims of sex crimes abhor having to interact with offenders or their lawyers and relatives who approach for the purpose of settlement. Thus, victims of these crimes often settle out of self-interest, in order to protect their reputation through preserving their privacy. In a rape trial I observed where the victim chose not to settle, the head judge asked what effect the crime had on the victim's relationship with her boyfriend. "We broke up," the young lady plaintively replied. The judge nodded knowingly. No one I asked — prosecutor, professor, or friend — seemed at all surprised.

Prosecutors believe it is their duty to "advise" victims as well as cry with them, but in sexual assault cases the "guidance" they give reflects their perception — shared by many Japanese males — that groping and molestation are not serious crimes. Moreover, their "advice" is often dispensed in a manner difficult for victims to refuse. As the above case illustrates, prosecutors can be manipulative and even coercive. They pressure victims for a variety of reasons. "Molestation is not serious because it causes little harm," declared one prosecutor. Another said he is "cautious" because "adverse publicity may damage the offender's reputation and undermine reform and reintegration." Several prosecutors told me it is simply less work to drop a case than to prepare it — and the victim — for trial. Others noted that since courts rarely impose more than a fine or suspended sentence on molesters, there is little point in aggressively prosecuting such cases. Whatever their reasons, by trying to dissuade victims from deviating from the official definition of the situation, prosecutors give "correcting victims" a less laudable meaning than is generally supposed.

Though suspending prosecution is the usual disposition, prosecutors do charge molesters, in two main ways. If the offender used or threatened force, or if the victim was unable to escape (as on a crowded train), the prosecutor can charge "indecent assault" (*kyōsei waisetsu*), which carries a prison term of six months to seven years. This charge is seldom instituted, often because prosecutors believe the crime does not fit the (deserved) punishment. More commonly, prosecutors charge under local "nuisance prevention" ordinances that typically prescribe a small fine ($100 or so) as the maximum punishment. In either case, prosecutors prefer to indict through a "summary procedure" that bypasses public trial. Offenders simply consent to the charge and punishment and pay the requisite fine.

Even when prosecutors charge the more serious crime of "indecent assault," the punishment can seem surprisingly lenient. One man, a thirty-one-year-old married father with no prior record, was charged with indecent assault for molesting a nine-teen-year-old woman during the six-minute train ride between two stations. The man — a cook at a golf course restaurant — confessed to inserting his finger in the vic-tim's vagina and fondling her breasts and backside. He claimed never to have mo-lested before. He offended, he said, because a debt incurred to a loan shark had an-gered his wife and upset their relationship. During the investigation, police took numerous photographs of the offender reenacting his assault against a mannequin. The pictures were included in the dossier prosecutors reviewed. Throughout the investigation and pretrial period, the offender apologized often — to police, prose-cutors, his wife, and the victim. But the victim refused all *jidan* overtures, arguing that this was "a problem of the heart," not a money matter. Prosecutors urged the offender to do his utmost to settle. His inability to do so helps explain why he was charged. Prosecutors asked the court to impose ten months' imprisonment. It did, but suspended the sentence for three years. Since the offender had been prosecuted on an "at home basis," he spent no time in jail except for the two days between his arrest and release on bail.

Because I was surprised by this outcome I interviewed a number of prosecutors about it. One said that even though the public probably wants harsher enforcement of laws against indecency, the suspended sentence accurately reflects the gravity of this offense. His superior agreed, adding that the offender's remorse and clean prior record make him a prime candidate for correction. A third suggested that the most striking thing about this disposition was the fact that it was charged. Most such cases are not charged, he noted, and should not be charged, especially when *jidan* is con-cluded. "Women should resist more vigorously," he opined. "We [prosecutors] can-not easily charge cases in which the victim has not resisted to the point of showing visible evidence of resistance" such as scratches, bruises, or torn clothing. As for their views of the victim, one prosecutor avowed that she had been "polluted" (*yogoreta*) by the offense, though it was impossible to tell if this was his personal view or his reading of the likely reaction of the victim's family and friends. Another prosecutor noted that the victim must be "strong-minded" to have filed the complaint and per-sisted through trial. Several male legal apprentices (*shūshūsei*) shared that view, at the same time acknowledging they would be "bothered" if their girlfriends were mo-lested because the women's "purity" would then be defiled. Three out of four female legal apprentices confessed that they had been molested on trains. None cried out, much less reported the offense to the police. "It's embarrassing," one stated. "And be-sides, even if you cry out, no one will help you anyway."

As for my own view, I cannot escape the conclusion that for sex crimes against women and girls, leniency as a "mechanism of correction" reflects sexist attitudes as much as correctional considerations.[27] Prosecution, like law of other kinds, has a direction in vertical space. It moves downward, from higher-ranking complainants to lower-ranking offenders, and upward, from lower to higher ranks. Prosecution of every kind is more likely to have a downward direction than an upward one (Black 1976:21; D. Johnson 1999). Since gender stratification is arguably the most salient form of inequality in contemporary Japan (Sugimoto 1997:136), it may seem "natural" that upward prosecutions, from women against men, are so lenient. It is also unjust.

There appear to be analogous patterns in the areas of domestic violence and sexual harassment. The cases I observed — unsystematically but repeatedly — suggest that just as leniency has limits, so does the consistency described in chapter 5. By routinely discounting the injuries of female victims, and by trying to "correct" victims who resist the official definition of the situation, prosecutors exemplify social norms even while they transgress the principle of equality embodied in Article 14 of the Constitution — that "all the people are equal under the law." Critics of this kind of "correction" are beginning to challenge the assumptions that victims should try to reconcile with offenders and that prosecutors should facilitate the propitiation process. As one female scholar sees it, Japan should stop "veering in favor of accused parties." Of course, many Japanese believe that reconciliation with the attacker helps the victim too, but in her view "it is only natural for the bereaved family and those whose health has been damaged for good to condemn the accused as long as they live." Like a growing number of Japanese, she insists that "we should not blame the victim for his or her inability to make up with the accused" (Atarashi 2000; *Asahi Shimbun* 9/15/00).

Finally, in the correction of offenders and victims, class matters. Suspects who have enough money and connections to hire a defense lawyer before the charge decision is made can produce evidence of remorse and forgiveness — a *jidan* settlement

27. In 1994, Samu Yamamoto, a forty-two-year-old illustrator for a Japanese sports newspaper, wrote a book entitled *Chikan Nikki* (A Groper's Diary) which recounts his experiences molesting women on trains. Yamamoto admits molesting an average of twelve women and girls a day for the previous twenty-six years. If his estimates are reliable, then at the time Yamamoto's book was published he had molested more than a hundred thousand females. The number may have increased in subsequent years because Yamamoto seems to have written the book more to publicize his lifestyle than to renounce it. He even made a round of TV appearances to plug the book (which sold fifty thousand copies in the first six months). Yamamoto reports that he has "suffered few repercussions in his personal or professional life since going public about his groping." He also says he "counted on women being too embarrassed to cry out, or too fearful of accusing the wrong man" on a crowded train. "I wouldn't try groping in the United States because American women seem too tough," Yamamoto told an interviewer. "But Japanese women tolerate us — or I'd be in jail by now." Of the many forms of sexual harassment that women in Japan face, molestation seems to be one of the most pervasive and (for the men offenders) least stigmatized (Yamamoto 1994). As described in the conclusion to this chapter, however, five years after Yamamoto's book was released the governor of Osaka, Knock Yokoyama, was charged and convicted for groping, in large part because public opinion made it impossible for prosecutors not to indict. Yokoyama's case suggests that tolerance of groping may be approaching a "tipping point." In fact, according to National Police Agency statistics for 1999, 911 people were arrested on suspicion of violating local groping ordinances. This was almost a 70 percent increase over the 538 arrests for groping in 1995 (*Asahi Shimbun* 12/17/00).

or a victim's *tangansho* — that decisively shapes the charge decision.[28] Similarly, after being charged, defendants who pay for a private defense can more effectively influence their trial by producing partisan evidence in the form of statements of victim forgiveness, character testimony, and pledges of community cooperation (H. Yamaguchi 1999:45). Victims, too, can better protect their interests and ensure that prosecutors respect their preferences when they are assisted by counsel. That takes money. In Japan as elsewhere, "people with extensive social ties and people with elevated social status have advantages in attracting the evidence necessary to sustain their legal cases" (Cooney 1994:834). In short, class matters because it and its correlates — money, status, respectability, and the quantity and quality of social ties — facilitate the production of evidence. Prosecutors prefer to regard "evidence" as a strictly legal — and therefore legitimate — consideration, but evidentiary strength, offense seriousness, and offender character are at least partly explained by the *social* composition of the case. Criminal cases do not have an asocial — or ungendered — legal core (Cooney 1994:853). As a result, the evidence mobilized for correction can facilitate discrimination. The devices described in the preceding chapter reduce the potential for inconsistency (especially compared with the United States), but they do not eliminate it.

Conclusion

In recent years a "restorative justice" movement has emerged in many countries, encouraging criminal justice that promotes healing, not merely punishment, as the proper response to crime (Umbreit 1998). Some have argued that because Japanese criminal justice emphasizes the offender's rehabilitation and reintegration, and the victim's restoration and reparation, it exemplifies restorative justice (Haley 1999:117). Does it?

Answering this question requires an understanding of what "restorative justice" means. Although its advocates have constructed a variety of models for "justice that promotes healing," most visions of restorative justice embrace three fundamental propositions (Van Ness and Strong 1997:31). First, restorative justice regards crime as more than merely lawbreaking or an offense against the state. On this view, crime causes multiple injuries to victims, offenders, and communities, as well as to the state. Second, restorative justice insists that the criminal process help repair the injuries caused by crime. Third, restorative justice resists the tendency toward government monopoly over the response to crime. Instead, victims, offenders, and communities

---

28. Japan is often said to be a land without plea-bargaining (Aoyagi 1986). It is not (see chapter 8). In fact, several prosecutors told me they regard the settlement process described in this chapter as a type of tacit plea-bargain. One said that in molestation cases he frequently exhorts the offender to apologize and the victim to forgive, because then he can dispose of the case more efficiently (through summary procedure) and avoid the risk that the victim will protest a non-charge decision to a Prosecution Review Commission (West 1992). Some defense lawyers are also cognizant of parallels between American-style plea-bargaining and the Japanese pattern of confession-settlement-forgiveness-suspended prosecution (H. Yamaguchi 1999).

must be encouraged and enabled to participate in the processes of rehabilitation, recompense, and repair. The question, then, is how well the Japanese way of justice fulfills these three requisites.

In my view, criminal justice in Japan comes closer to realizing the vision of restorative justice than does American criminal justice but still falls short. Japanese criminal justice does attend to the harms caused by crime more than does American criminal justice, at least for most offenses. And, as we have seen, harms to victims are more central considerations throughout Japan's criminal process, and offenders are more likely to have their problems diagnosed and addressed. At the same time, prosecutors encourage restitution and remorse at least in part to help heal the injuries caused by crime. They also permit nongovernment actors — victims, offenders, and communities — to help define responses to crime in ways seldom seen in the United States. The rich vocabulary for types and means of repair — *jidan* agreements, compensation for damages, solace money, petitions, written reports, and atonement contributions — reveals how Japanese criminal justice lets "outsiders" participate in the criminal process. To be sure, defense lawyers do play more secondary roles in Japan than in many other countries, and the community still cannot participate in fact-finding forums such as juries or mixed tribunals. Nonetheless, there are channels through which victim, offender, and community voices can be heard, and those voices are often canvassed and considered.

Prosecutor practice in sex crime cases is the most conspicuous deviation from this pattern. It is here that the Japanese venture falls farthest short of the restorative justice vision. Prosecutors in Japan perform a more ramified role than their American counterparts. As a result, they possess power to impose their own "definition of the situation" on victims (as in sex crimes) and offenders (as when "co-producing" remorse). These impositions not only undermine respect for "dominion," a core value of restorative justice, they unwittingly breed defiance rather than compliance, and contumacy instead of correction.[29]

Prosecutors, like all criminal justice officials, must earn their claims to justice based on their own personal conduct, one human relationship at a time (Sherman 2000). When prosecutors inform, instruct, and respect offenders, the outcome may well be correction of the kind that Gary's "Dear Prosecutor" letter gratefully acknowledged. Redemption must also be earned, and earning implies both effort and desert (Bazemore 1999). Japanese prosecutors do believe that correction must be worked for and deserved. As Gary's case illustrates, they sometimes go to extraordinary lengths to assist offenders in the earning. However, when prosecutors silence victims by rejecting and repressing their stories, the outcome is likely to be unjust and is certain to be reduced regard for the law and its enforcers. Victims want to be restored and made whole, not authoritatively "corrected" by an authoritarian prosecutor. In at least one significant slice of criminal cases, female victims get precisely what they do not desire. In these ways, the Japanese way of justice is more restorative

---

29. Although a full description of the meaning of "dominion" is beyond the scope of this work, at its core this value requires that an individual enjoy "the absence of arbitrary power" on the part of other persons (such as prosecutors) to interfere in the individual's affairs (Braithwaite and Pettit 1994:765).

than criminal justice in New York or Seattle, but there remains much room for improvement.

One last case suggests that when the public insists on it, prosecutors may heed victims' voices, not merely correct them, in molestation cases too. On December 21, 1999, prosecutors indicted former Osaka governor Knock Yokoyama for indecent assault and recommended that he serve eighteen months in prison. Yokoyama, who was a celebrity comedian before twice being elected governor, was charged with molesting a twenty-one-year-old campaign volunteer eight months earlier, while they were covered by a blanket in the backseat of his campaign van. Police officers were in the same vehicle. The woman (a college student) overcame the objections of her family and filed a criminal complaint against the governor (French 2001). The sixty-eight-year-old Yokoyama originally denied the accusation, whereupon the woman filed a civil suit seeking 12 million yen in compensation. When Yokoyama publicly called her "an absolute liar" and filed his own criminal complaint against her for bringing false accusations, the victim amended her civil suit to ask for 15 million yen. Early in the civil trial Yokoyama reversed his stand and admitted the assault. "I cannot justify the deeds for which I am accused," the ex-governor told the court, claiming it was "arrogance" that stopped him from realizing that the woman found his behavior repulsive. Nevertheless, during the legal proceedings Yokoyama never showed remorse, never directly apologized to the victim, and never made an adequate offer to settle informally. His insolence influenced judges and prosecutors alike. On December 13, 1999, the Osaka District Court ordered Yokoyama to pay his victim 11 million yen ($107,000), the biggest award for a sexual harassment suit Japan had ever seen.[30]

One week later, prosecutors raided Yokoyama's home and office. They said they were looking for evidence but it is likely they were responding to the press of public opinion to "do something" in this highly publicized case. Following the raid, Yokoyama resigned the governorship and was admitted to an Osaka hospital, ostensibly for "heart problems." (Japanese politicians have long preferred hospital over jail accommodations.) He was indicted anyway. At trial, prosecutors offered proof that Yokoyama's acts were premeditated and that he had fondled another woman just two days prior to the instant assault. On August 10, 2000, the Osaka District Court found Yokoyama guilty of committing a "heinously" indecent assault, sentenced him to eighteen months' imprisonment, and suspended the sentence for three years. Yokoyama's post-sentence statements expressed a curious combination of remorse and excuse. "I would like to spend the rest of my life in a corner of society repenting for what I did," the former governor vowed. Yet to the very end Yokoyama maintained that his "accidental" conduct was "spur of the moment" and that the sexual assaults were "rash, impulsive, and impetuous" acts. His excuses diluted the sincerity of his remorse, and this outraged many. A front-page column in one of Japan's largest newspapers castigated the suspended sentence as unduly lenient, largely because Yokoyama's attitude seemed insufficiently repentant. But even it acknowledged that for this sort of case a suspended sentence is "the kind of punishment most judges

---

30. The six-figure judgment in Yokoyama's case dwarfs by three digits the informal settlements in the other molestation cases described in this chapter. For many sex crimes, settlements seem to track litigated outcomes loosely (contrast Ramseyer and Nakazato 1999:90).

would hand down" (*Asahi Shimbun* 8/11/00). For prosecutors, indictment of a first-time offender exceeded the organization's "going rate" for molestation cases.

Some believe Yokoyama's losses signal "Japan's tougher line" toward sexual harassment, molestation, and inequality (*New York Times* 12/21/99). Perhaps. But events following Yokoyama's resignation suggest real change may occur slowly. The next governor of Osaka was Ota Fusae, the first female to be elected governor of a prefecture in Japanese history. Upon assuming office, Ota encountered gender discrimination of another kind. It is customary for governors to present awards to winning wrestlers on the last day of sumo tournaments held in their prefectures. It is also customary for women to be denied entry to the sumo ring where the awards are presented. In the Shinto tradition that informs sumo, the earthen ring is considered holy, and women are deemed impure. When these customs clashed, Ota asserted her right to do what all previous governors had done — enter the ring and make the presentations — but in the face of vigorous opposition from sumo elders and other traditionalists, she eventually backed down. Opinion polls showed that more of the public supported the governor's initial stand than the sumo tradition that ultimately prevailed. Ota has vowed to renew the struggle for gender equality the next time a sumo tournament comes to town. Time will tell the outcome.

We have seen custom and principle collide in the procuracy too, and to women's disadvantage. The Yokoyama case suggests things could be otherwise. Does his case portend positive change?[31] Will prosecutors give female victims of sex crimes the same voice and respect they usually give victims in other cases?[32] Or will prosecutors continue permitting sexist premises — that molestation is not a serious crime, and that repeat molesters are not sinister characters — to guide their discretion? For Japanese criminal justice to become more consistently restorative, the procuracy — a "man's world" through and through — must face this formidable challenge. There are limits to leniency, and there should be.

31. One sign that Yokoyama's case may not presage change is the media backlash against molestation victims that began in the summer of 2000. Numerous stories have been published about "cunning" young women who allegedly make false accusations in order to extort settlement money from vulnerable male commuters. See, for example, two articles in the weekly magazine *Sande Mainichi*: "The Day You Are Suddenly Denounced as a Pervert" (May 28, 2000), and "To People Who Want to Prove 'I Am Not a Molester'" (June 25, 2000). On February 1, 2001, a one-hour Fuji Television show (*Kabachi-tare*) dramatized "groper frame-ups" by depicting three high school girls extorting tens of thousands of dollars from innocent male commuters. It appears that the frame-up problem is real (Natsuki 2000). On February 6, 2001, the Criminal Defense Center of the Japan Bar Federation held a symposium on the subject titled "A Meeting for the Exchange of Experiences about 'Defense Activities in Miscarriage Cases Involving Gropers'" ("Renzoku Suru Chikan Enzai Jiken no Bengo Katsudō" Keiken Kōryūkai). Participants at the symposium presented stories and statistics to document numerous frame-ups, some of which resulted in wrongful charges and convictions.

32. In January 2000, the Criminal Law Division of the Justice Ministry's Legislative Council compiled a proposal recommending the expansion of victims' rights. Several of the proposed revisions are aimed at giving victims of sex crimes greater voice and respect. For instance, all victims would be allowed to give statements in court if they wish (instead of merely answering questions if called to testify, as is currently the practice), and victims of sex crimes would be allowed to testify via video links (*Asahi Shimbun* 1/26/00). Although these proposals are commendable, they do not address the more significant problems that crime victims encounter during the pretrial investigation period (Atarashi 2000; B. Smith et al. 2000).

7

Convictions

Japan Conviction Rate Dazzles, Deceives: Prosecutors Are Said to Cherry-Pick Airtight Cases

Wall Street Journal headline

You can't be overly cautious in these [murder] cases; you'll never make one. At some point in time, you just have to go for it. If you feel you have enough to make a strong argument before the jury, you just have to go for it. . . . You have to let the jury decide.

American prosecutor Bruce Sackman

A courtroom loss, even if predictable, does not mean the case should not have been brought.

American law professor Stephen Gillers

Before beginning research for this book I asked a well-known professor of law and Japan scholar what question he would most like to see answered in a work on Japanese criminal justice. His response was unequivocal. "Find out," he urged, "why their conviction rates are so high."

My professor friend is hardly alone in finding Japan's conviction rates noteworthy. Claims about the country's "extremely high" conviction rates or, what is the same thing, its "astonishingly low" acquittal rates, are indeed widespread. But while Japan's conviction rates are often lauded and lamented, they remain poorly understood because their causes have seldom been seriously sought or studied. This chapter locates Japan's famous conviction rates within the broader contexts of comparative criminal justice research in order to assess the veracity and significance of conventional claims. I first summarize the orthodox views and inspect their foundations. The analysis reveals that the conviction rate "gap" between Japan and other countries is not as wide as commonly supposed but that there is a real difference that needs to be explained. I then show that the procuracy's conservative charging policy and bureaucratic controls—the same controls that produce high levels of "consistency"—are largely responsible for the high rates of conviction. The penultimate section examines the "long historical decline" in Japanese acquittal rates that began no later than 1908, and argues that cycles of "blunder and response" account for much of the apparent decrease since the end of the Pacific War. Finally, the conclusion explores the consequences of Japan's conservative charging policy beyond the high conviction rate which is its most obvious effect. For suspects, victims, defense lawyers, judges, the public, and prosecutors themselves, the consequences are decidedly mixed. Ironically, a system that convicts almost all defendants turns out to be quite protective of the interests of criminal suspects. Chapter 8 extends the arguments in this chapter by analyzing the links between Japan's conservative charging policy and its deep and accelerating reliance on confessions.

Calculating Conviction Rates

Japan's high conviction rates are heralded by journalists, scholars, and prosecutors and by Japanese and foreigners alike. The country is said to have "the world's highest conviction rate," "an astonishing conviction rate," a "dazzling" conviction rate, "an extremely high conviction rate," a conviction rate "well over 99%," "an incredibly high conviction rate" of 99.8%, "an almost 100% conviction rate," and "a conviction rate of close to 100%."[1] Just as frequently the point is put in the converse: Japan has "low acquittal rates," a "very low acquittal rate," "very few acquittals," and an acquittal rate "approaching absolute zero."[2] No matter where one looks in the literature on Japanese criminal justice, the percentages 0 and 100 are not far away. Japanese courts seem to "convict with a vengeance" (Ramseyer and Rasmusen 2001).

But commentators disagree about what these statistics mean. On the one hand, the ABC news show 20/20 (7/24/92) harshly criticized the near absence of acquittals in its feature on Japan's "Iron Hand" of criminal justice, arguing by innuendo that the entire criminal process must be defective if so few defendants are acquitted. Japanese newspapers regularly report that because prosecutors are inappropriately "obsessed" with maintaining high conviction rates, they often fail to charge offenders who deserve to be punished (*Asahi Evening News* 2/19/95). Similarly, Hirano Ryūichi, one of Japan's most respected legal scholars, contends that his country's conviction rate is "extremely, and abnormally, high" (Hirano 1989:130), and a former judge pointedly asks, "Are criminal defendants in Japan truly receiving trials by judges?" (Ishimatsu 1989:143).

Prosecutors put a contrary spin on conviction rates. In papers and presentations they unfailingly focus on Japan's "extremely high conviction rates," claiming that the figures result from their thorough investigations and prudent charge decisions.[3] Some foreign observers agree. Daniel Foote (1991:417), for example, asserts that "Japan's criminal justice system ranks as one of the best in the world," and offers as partial justification the fact that "Japanese prosecutors enjoy a conviction rate of 99.9%."

---

1. See *Asahi Evening News* (2/19/95); *New York Times* (11/21/88); *Wall Street Journal* (12/19/95); Kataoka (1993:11); Mukherjee (1994–1995:9); van Wolferen (1989:221); Peters (1992:280); Goodman (1986:18).
2. See Araki (1985:623); Aoyagi (1986:229); Nomura (1994:145); Murayama 1992:236).
3. See Inagawa (1995:21); Sasaki (1995:25); Kitada (1995:5): Yamashita (1996:12); Kataoka (1993:11).

Before assessing which interpretation is most discerning, one must first examine how conviction rates are calculated and compared. Because comparisons across countries routinely ignore basic differences in criminal procedure, the conviction rate gap is often miscalculated and misconstrued. Indeed, Japan's acquittal rate approaches "absolute zero" only in a narrow, technical sense. The standard procedure calculates the Japanese rate by dividing the total number of complete acquittals into the total number of court verdicts, compares that figure to the percentage of American jury trials resulting in acquittal, concludes that Japanese courts are far less inclined to acquit than American courts, and either lauds or laments the difference.

But the standard procedure takes several misleading steps. First, unlike the United States, Japan does not have an arraignment system in which defendants can plead guilty and be sentenced without trial. Instead, all formally prosecuted defendants receive a full (if sometimes perfunctory) trial, in either Summary or District Court. If one calculates the acquittal rate using all formally prosecuted cases as the denominator, then Japan's acquittal rate does seem "astonishingly low." Moreover, if one includes in the denominator the large proportion of cases disposed of by summary procedure (approximately 93 percent of all prosecuted cases), then the acquittal rate even approaches "absolute zero." However, both of these calculations include in the denominator a large number of cases in which defendants have confessed. In fact, even in the method which excludes summary prosecutions, almost 94 percent of the denominator consists of cases in which the defendant has fully confessed. So calculated, "overall acquittal rates" in table 7.1 hover barely above zero, ranging (in District Court) from 0.06 percent at the nadir of this ten-year period (in 1996), to 0.38 percent at the peak (in 1991). The yearly average for District Court is 0.13 percent. For Summary Court it is 0.25 percent, or about twice as high. The overall average (all years, District and Summary Courts combined) is 0.15 percent.

When one juxtaposes these percentages with the American figures most often cited in comparisons — the percentage of jury trials resulting in acquittal — the contrast is stark. For example, the U.S. Department of Justice (1988:84) reports that in the 1980s the median jury acquittal rate for twenty-six local American jurisdictions was 27 percent. By this method of comparison, American juries acquit 175 times more often than Japanese judges. Put differently, it would take Japanese judges 175 years to acquit as many defendants as American courts acquit in one year, even if Japan had as many serious crimes (and thus trials) as the United States.[4]

The chief problem with the standard procedure is its failure to compare parallel cases. Unlike Japanese defendants, American defendants can enter a plea of guilty at arraignment and thereby avoid a full-fledged trial. Since the vast majority of defendants do just that, only contested cases go to trial. Thus, the first methodological corrective is to calculate the number of contested cases in Japan, as has been done in column B of table 7.1. In addition, the standard procedure considers only

---

4. A second review found that over a five-year period (1980–1982 and 1986–1987), the average jury trial acquittal rate in twelve U.S. local jurisdictions was 26 percent. In U.S. federal courts, where prosecutors can select cases with more care, acquittal rates during the 1990s vacillated around 15 percent (Givelber 1997:1336).

TABLE 7.1 Acquittal rates in District and Summary Court trials, 1989–1998

Year	Court	Total judgments (A)	Of which, pled not guilty (B)[a]	Percent pled not guilty (B/A)	Not guilty judgments (C)	Partial not guilty judgments (D)	Overall acquittal rate (C/A)	Acquittal rate in contested cases (C+D)/B
1989	District	52,177	3,867	7.41	89	63	0.17	3.93
1990	District	49,184	3,553	7.22	61	38	0.12	2.79
1991	District	46,994	3,424	7.29	177	42	0.38	6.40
1992	District	46,409	3,378	7.28	53	54	0.11	3.17
1993	District	48,692	3,547	7.28	104	54	0.21	4.46
1994	District	49,856	3,648	7.32	45	40	0.09	2.33
1995	District	51,537	3,493	6.78	39	37	0.08	2.18
1996	District	54,880	3,694	6.73	35	42	0.06	2.08
1997	District	57,301	3,800	6.63	50	36	0.09	2.26
1998	District	58,257	3,833	6.58	39	33	0.07	1.88
1989	Summary	10,638	697	6.55	45	2	0.42	6.74
1990	Summary	9,688	618	6.38	40	1	0.41	6.63
1991	Summary	8,723	509	5.84	23	4	0.26	5.30
1992	Summary	9,078	508	5.60	22	2	0.24	4.72
1993	Summary	10,179	496	4.87	31	1	0.30	6.45
1994	Summary	10,430	450	4.31	15	3	0.14	4.00
1995	Summary	9,938	473	4.76	17	0	0.17	3.60
1996	Summary	9,541	448	4.70	19	2	0.20	4.69
1997	Summary	9,604	475	4.95	17	2	0.18	4.00
1998	Summary	10,696	471	4.40	22	1	0.21	4.89

Source: Shihō Tōkei Nempō (Annual Report of Judicial Statistics), Supreme Court of Japan.
[a]This column captures cases in which defendants denied some or all of the facts charged in the indictment. Japan does not have an arraignment system; even defendants who acknowledge all the charged facts receive a trial.

"complete acquittals" in Japan (column C), thereby ignoring what in some years is an almost equal number of "partial acquittals," or convictions on some or lesser charges (column D). When this corrective is made, the acquittal rate in contested cases appears as in the last column of table 7.1, ranging in District Courts from 1.88 percent in 1998 to 6.40 percent in 1991. Over the ten-year period the average acquittal rate in District Courts is 3.12 percent, in Summary Courts it is 5.23 percent, and in both courts combined it is 3.38 percent.[5] By this last measure, Japan's acquittal rate is 8 times lower than the average jury acquittal rate in the United States, not 200 times lower as the other method suggests.

5. A more personal measure of the frequency of acquittals can be calculated by dividing the number of acquittals in a year into the number of prosecutors who handled cases that year. For District Courts between 1987 and 1991, that ratio was 132.6/1740, or about 1 in 13. By this crude measure, each year in this five-year period, one in every thirteen prosecutors charged and/or tried a case that ended in acquittal. Put differently, the average Japanese prosecutor could expect to handle an acquittal case about once every thirteen years. A former Japanese judge estimates that some criminal judges participate in "fewer than ten acquittals during their entire careers" (Foote 1992b:81).

Thus, while there is a substantial "gap" between the propensity of American juries and Japanese judges to acquit, it is far narrower than most commentators have supposed. Moreover, when Japan is viewed in broader comparative perspective, the acquittal rate gap closes even further. For instance, South Korea's criminal justice system closely resembles Japan's, in part because Japan imposed it during forty years of colonial rule (1905–1945). As a result, in addition to their common Confucian heritage, the two countries share similar legal and institutional structures. From 1984 to 1992, the average "overall acquittal rate" in South Korea was 0.44 percent, just 2.5 times higher than the corresponding average of 0.15 percent for Japan (Moon 1995: 182).[6] In 1992 the "overall acquittal rate" in Thailand was 0.80 percent, or 4.7 times higher than the Japanese figure (Nanakorn and Kittayarak 1995:263). Conversely, countries such as Great Britain and Sri Lanka, which share a common legal heritage, have trial acquittal rates roughly similar to those in the United States (McConville et al. 1991; Dharmawardena 1995b:231).

Explaining the Gap

Japan's acquittal rates neither approach "absolute zero" nor are greatly surpassed by acquittal rates in some other Asian countries. Still, they *are* lower than the best available figures from countries as dissimilar as the United States and South Korea. In short, the acquittal rate "gap" yawns less widely than most observers have believed but it hardly disappears. Why? What explains Japan's low acquittal and high conviction rates?

Many believe the key cause can be found in an overly compliant judiciary. In a discussion titled "The [Japanese] Prosecutor as Judge" and subtitled "Infallible Guardians of the System," Karel van Wolferen (1989:221) contends that

> The incredibly high conviction rate is usually explained by Japan's judicial authorities as the result of police and prosecutors doing their homework extremely well. In fact, however, it amounts to official [judicial] endorsement of the prosecutor's infallibility. That they may have human failings is not recognised, for this would undermine the theory of the benevolent social order they represent.

This view, that judges adjudicate guilt in a pro-prosecutor manner, is shared by many members of the bar, particularly those who do criminal defense. For example, Shinomiya Satoru (2001), a lawyer in Chiba, believes judges play neither a neutral nor a passive role in Japan's ostensibly adversarial system. Routinely, he says, judges relax the rules of evidence by finding illegalities in official investigations insufficiently grave to exclude the evidence thereby gained. For Shinomiya, these "illegal but admissible" rulings amount to an "open sesame" for prosecutors to pursue conviction.

---

6. Unfortunately, the source for the South Korean statistics does not provide separate figures for contested and uncontested cases. However, Kwak Moo-Keun, a South Korean prosecutor, believes the proportion of contested cases and "partial not guilty judgments" is about the same in South Korea as in Japan (personal communication, February 1995). If so, then South Korea's acquittal rate in contested cases is also about 2.5 times higher than the corresponding Japanese rate.

He further notes that judges are hardly the passive players that adversarial logic prescribes them to be. Rather, judges actively question witnesses and defendants in systematically pro-prosecutor ways. Yamaguchi Hiroshi (1999:119), another well-known
lawyer, claims pro-prosecutor bias is especially conspicuous in cases where the public clamors for conviction.

These claims of pro-prosecutor bias are overstated. The most systematic study on
the subject examined all 455 District Court criminal case opinions published in 1976
and 1979 (Ramseyer and Rasmusen 2001).[7] This generated a sample of 321 judges,
whose career trajectories were then studied in order to determine whether judges who
acquitted were punished with undesirable job assignments. In general, judges who
acquitted were not so punished, but judges who acquitted cases by themselves (in
solo-judged cases) did seem to spend more time in undesirable posts. A close look at
the solo acquitters reveals that they are sanctioned for two types of conduct: siding
with opposition parties in politically charged cases, and misinterpreting the law. Notably, judges are not punished for concluding that prosecutors charged the wrong
person. If judges tilt toward the prosecution, they are not rewarded for the lean.

If judicial bias cannot explain Japan's high conviction rate, what does? In a word,
prosecutors, who make charge decisions cautiously, screening out before trial almost
all cases with even a remote risk of ending in acquittal. As many prosecutors put it,
"We do not take adventures." In response to claims that courts merely "endorse"
prosecutor decisions, as van Wolferen and others contend, one prosecutor has succinctly summarized the procuracy's position:

> Courts are not simply rubber-stamping our decisions. Rather, the high conviction
> rate is a result of several related prosecutor practices. We conduct investigations our-
> selves, carefully separating cases that should be charged from those that should not
> after thoroughly examining both the facts and the law. Further, our charging stan-
> dard is rigorous. We only prosecute cases that have a high probability of resulting in
> conviction. (Kataoka 1993:11)

Results from my survey reinforce this view. Fully 98 percent of prosecutor respondents believe "acquittals are rare because before charging the prosecutor clarifies the
truth and gathers sufficient evidence to convict." Not a single prosecutor disagreed
with this statement and only five (out of 235) said it depends on the case.

Most judges acknowledge that prosecutors' charging policy is the primary proximate cause of Japan's high conviction rates. Once a judge stopped by my office
while I was reading a report from the bar association on recently acquitted cases. The
report summarized the facts of the various cases and the judges' reasons for acquitting. It also listed the names of the participating prosecutors, lawyers, and judges.
Whenever my visitor recognized a judge's name he grumbled that he was "envious"
(*urayamashii*). "I want to acquit some cases, too," he wistfully sighed. He is not alone
(Foote 1992b:81). In October 1994 another judge told a prosecutor that "it is the
judge's job to ascertain guilt. Prosecutors have usurped that role." The prosecutor

7. At the time of this writing, Ramseyer and Rasmusen's (2001) incisive study was still unpublished.
I have relied on their working paper, obtained at http://Php.indiana.edu/~erasmuse.

agreed. A third judge has written extensively (and anonymously) about the subject of convictions. I quote him at length because many other judges share his views, and because collectively these judges substantiate the procuracy's claim that careful investigations and conservative charging standards are the main cause of the conviction rate "gap" between Japan and other countries.

> According to the latest statistics, the acquittal rate for 1990 was 0.2 percent. Since coming to this court I have handled criminal trials for two years and have presided over approximately 350 cases. Of these — and I feel a little sad about this fact — I have acquitted only two people, both in the same case last month. It is not that I have had especially few acquittals, but rather that the average for any individual judge is about one case a year. Why? We judges are criticized for many things: for mistaken evaluations of the evidence, for having a weak consciousness of human rights and a strong inclination to protect social order, and for lacking courage. I cannot claim that these criticisms are completely off the mark. For example, when I look at what Urawa District Court Judge Kitani has been doing [Kitani acquitted twelve cases in three years, to the furious dismay of many prosecutors], perhaps more cases should be acquitted.
>
> However, from my point of view as an average, frontline judge, I cannot necessarily agree with the most common criticisms of judges. Indeed, I have the feeling that such criticisms miss the mark. The truth is, if they could, criminal court judges would love to acquit more cases. *The problem is that cases which can be acquitted are almost never prosecuted. . . .* Because this is so, the low acquittal rate is a matter of course.
>
> Prosecutors value their authority a great deal. To prevent harm to their authority they investigate and filter cases very carefully. I think *this* is the cause of our country's high conviction rate. What in Japan is called "precise justice" [*seimitsu shihō*] is in fact a reflection of the careful, strict investigations which precede indictment. (emphasis added)[8]

"Precise justice" — and a high conviction rate — are facilitated by the absence of juries in Japan. Since Japanese prosecutors do not have to deal with this institution — one that American prosecutors find perversely unpredictable — they can more accurately assess the probability of conviction before making a charge decision. Foreseeing the likely outcome at trial, prosecutors can drop prosecution or change the charges in cases that risk acquittal.

Tanase Takao has reported the results of an experiment that helps demonstrate the influence juries could have on conviction rates if Japan reintroduced a jury system like the one it had from 1928 to 1943.[9] In the city of Kyoto, Tanase organized a mock jury trial based on a bank robbery case that had occurred in San Diego. The judge, prosecutor, defense attorney, and five witnesses were all Americans, but the

8. The judge's comments were prepared for a speech he made to a European audience of legal professionals. His comments to colleagues in Japan were markedly more circumspect.

9. Several important institutions — including the Supreme Court and the Bar Federation — are exploring the possibility of reintroducing juries (or some other form of lay participation) in criminal trials. There are many articles on the subject in *Shihō Kaikaku* (Journal of Judicial Reform in Japan), a periodical established in 1999 to articulate and examine reform proposals for Japan's legal system.

twelve jurors were Japanese. The mock trial was conducted in translation so that the jurors and the (mainly) Japanese audience could understand the proceedings. Ten legal professionals, twenty-three legal apprentices, and sixteen professors and graduate students — all Japanese — were in attendance. After the trial these forty-nine spectators were surveyed, together with the twelve Japanese jurors, about their "impressions of guilt or innocence." In the aggregate, responses were almost evenly divided between guilt and innocence, with thirty-one of the sixty-one respondents (51 percent) voting for guilt and 27 (44 percent) for innocence (three people were unsure). Broken down by occupation, however, the verdicts reveal a clear divide. All ten legal professionals believed the defendant was guilty, as did fourteen of the twenty-three (61 percent) legal trainees. In contrast, thirteen of the sixteen professors and graduate students (81 percent) voted to acquit, as did nine of the twelve jurors (75 percent). Three jurors were unsure.

In short, all of the legal professionals voted to convict the defendant but none of the lay jurors did (Tanase 1986:18). In February 2001, the Japan Federation of Bar Associations produced a similar mock jury trial that resulted in a similar split. A jury composed of general citizens acquitted the defendant, but students at the Legal Research and Training Institute — future lawyers, prosecutors, and judges — yielded a hung jury (*Asahi Shimbun* 2/11/01). And in real trials between 1928 and 1943, when Japan employed both bench and jury trials, defendants were much more likely to be acquitted by juries than by judges (Hayashi 1987:17; Saeki 1989:20). Indeed, almost 18 percent of defendants tried by jury were acquitted, while only 3 percent of defendants tried by judges were. Kalven and Zeisel's (1966) famous finding that American juries acquit more often than judges do seems not only to apply to the Japanese past but also would apply to the present if Japan reintroduced juries to adjudicate guilt. Which is to say, juries would produce more unpredictability and hence fewer convictions.

Besides the procuracy's conservative charging policy, the enabling Code of Criminal Procedure helps further explain Japan's high conviction rate. As described in chapter 1, Japanese law confers great power on police and prosecutors to control information and thereby build cases and "make" crimes. The most relevant legal benefits concern the files constructed by police and prosecutors during the pre-charge period. Investigators routinely take multiple statements from suspects and witnesses. These detailed dossiers are not verbatim transcripts of the interrogation or interview but summaries composed by the investigator. Prosecutors have up to twenty-three days to prepare these statements before making a charge decision. This extended period promotes prudence in prosecution.[10] What is more, the statements they take (and make) frequently are admitted into evidence at trial. Prosecutors select the evidence for trial from what is often a massive number of dossiers compiled during the investigation. They have no obligation to submit all dossiers to the court, nor to disclose the entire file to the defense. In a comparison of the Dutch and Japanese criminal processes, Antonie Peters (1992:283) has noted that "in this manner

---

10. Prosecutors in prewar Japan had up to ten days to decide whether and what to charge, while American prosecutors typically have less than two days.

of selectively producing, partly disclosing, partly concealing, checking and contesting documentary evidence, the Japanese criminal process reveals its *thoroughly bureaucratic nature.*" Moreover, Peters links prosecutor control over the "one-sided" dossier to Japan's high conviction rates:

> In Holland the trial is much less fixated on the assertion and contestation of a one-sidedly constructed documentary truth than in Japan. There is certainly more thoroughness and precision in the Japanese proceedings than in the Dutch, but this thoroughness and precision all go in the direction of a conviction, and, therefore, also add to the vexatious character which the criminal process has anywhere. (Peters 1992:283)

Peters wrongly concludes that the "thoroughness and precision" of Japan's criminal process "all go in the direction of a conviction," for as we saw in the last two chapters the precise nature of Japan's criminal process also facilitates high levels of consistency and correction. In hard cases, however, when suspects do not confess but prosecutors still feel obliged to charge, criminal investigations can be "vexatious" indeed. This is the subject of chapter 8. Peters does rightly stresses the "thoroughly bureaucratic" context from which Japan's high conviction rates arise. The next two sections elaborate that insight.

Checking the Prosecutors: External Controls

The argument so far is simple: conviction rates are high in Japan because prosecutors carefully screen cases before charging them. But this cause also calls for analysis. In particular, how are Japanese prosecutors able to screen so successfully? Don't prosecutors everywhere want to win—and more to the point, don't they all hate losing at trial? Indeed. However, prosecutors in different systems possess different capacities for controlling case outcomes, and prosecutors in Japan have more complete control over trial inputs—and therefore over trial outputs—than do prosecutors in countries with lower conviction rates. Hence, in order to account for Japan's high conviction rates we must examine the sources of that control. Internal, bureaucratic controls are especially consequential, but since checks on prosecutors are both internal and external, a brief summary of the role of external controls is first required. In principle, Prosecution Review Commissions, the Analogical Institution of Prosecution, civil lawsuits, and public opinion all serve as external checks on prosecutors' charge decisions. In fact, however, these controls seldom move prosecutors to charge cases they prefer to decline. As a result, the procuracy maintains almost complete control over the input of cases into the courts and thereby over the outputs—convictions and acquittals—that courts produce.

Prosecution Review Commissions

Prosecution Review Commissions (*kensatsu shinsakai*) are lay advisory bodies composed of eleven private citizens who review prosecutors' exercise of discretion in decisions not to prosecute. Throughout Japan there are 207 commissions, at least one for each of Japan's fifty District Court jurisdictions. A commission commences review of non-charge decisions in two ways: by responding to applications for review from victims or victim proxies, or by its own initiative. After conducting an investigation, a commission gives prosecutors one of three recommendations: non-indictment is proper ("you did the right thing"), non-indictment is improper ("you should reconsider"), or indictment is proper ("you did the wrong thing and should prosecute"). These recommendations are merely advisory. Prosecutors can ignore them, and usually they do. Over a five-year period (1982–1986), commissions reviewed an average of 1,992 non-charge decisions each year (about 0.35 percent of all non-indictments, or 1 in 286 non-charges). In only 71 cases per year (3.6 percent) did they recommend that prosecutors either reconsider or indict, and in only 10.4 cases per year did prosecutors actually change the original decision and file charges (0.5 percent of the total cases reviewed, and 14.6 percent of the recommended cases). In short, commissions are "obscure" and "underutilized" features of Japan's legal landscape, and even when they are used they have little effect on prosecutor control over trial inputs (West 1992).

Analogical Institution of Prosecution

The "analogical institution of prosecution" (fushimpan seikyū) has even less effect on prosecutors than the review commissions. Indeed, it constitutes "almost no check at all" (C. Johnson 1972:414). In the first place, this procedure can be applied to only a narrow range of offenses — mostly police brutality and other abuses of official authority. It is seldom used. Between 1949 and 1990, 10,800 complainants used the procedure to ask judges to file charges when prosecutors would not (about 257 requests per year). Judges charged in only sixteen cases — about 1 per 675 requests, or one charge every two and a half years. In the aggregate, analogical prosecution stands a short step away from utter irrelevance. It is notable, however, that when prosecutors lose control over trial inputs, conviction rates plummet. As of 1992, three of the sixteen judge-charged cases were still being tried. Of the other thirteen, four resulted in acquittal, for a conviction rate of 69.2 percent — a figure even lower than the jury conviction rate in many American jurisdictions.

Civil Suits

In theory, civil suits against the procuracy (kokka baishō seikyū jiken) should raise the conviction rate by discouraging prosecutions. However, since suits are rarely filed, they have only a slight damping effect on indictments. As one prosecutor put it, "the threat of a civil suit seldom enters my mind." For good reason. Between 1984 and 1993, 173 civil suits were filed (of which 89 were still pending as of 1995), about 17 per year. Of the total, the procuracy has lost or is appealing 19 civil verdicts, about 2 per year. Twelve of the losses were for obstructing meetings between defense lawyers and suspects or defendants, six were for wrongful prosecution, and one was for losing or destroying evidence. A longer view yields similar conclusions. Between 1955 and

1993 the procuracy lost a total of fifty-seven civil suits, about 1.5 per year. Liability in the losses is small. For obstructing meetings with defense lawyers, the state typically paid $2,000 to $10,00. For wrongful prosecutions the state paid an average of $2,500 per loss.[11]

Public Opinion

The final external control — public opinion — seldom prompts prosecutors to charge acquittal-risky cases except in a small, important, but statistically insignificant category of high-profile cases. As unelected, career bureaucrats working in a context where crime is not a serious problem, Japanese prosecutors are largely insulated from the public pressures and political exigencies that influence prosecutors elsewhere (see chapter 1). As a result, they are seldom compelled to indict cases that risk acquittal. The chief exception is scandals involving corporate elites and government officials, where public opinion can constrain prosecutors to charge cases they otherwise would not.[12] Such cases are "rather rare" in Japan (C. Johnson 1995:222). Moreover, between 1948 and 1992, prosecutors won only 55 percent of all corruption cases against Diet politicians (twenty-one convictions, seventeen acquittals). That rate is lower than the conviction rate for any other identifiable group of defendants, and it seems to reflect prosecutor responsiveness to public demands to indict "the big bad guys," even when the evidence is marginal. Here again, the low conviction rate for politicians, like the low rate for analogically prosecuted cases, reveals the tight coupling between control over trial inputs and control over trial outcomes. Nonetheless, the last "finalized acquittal" of a Diet politician occurred in 1959. Since then, ten current or former politicians have died while appealing guilty verdicts (an eleventh died while prosecutors were appealing his acquittal). Japan's lengthy appeals process is an ally of elderly — and wealthy — defendants. It also seems that prosecutors are more likely to charge "risky" cases when the suspect is a prominent politician but are less likely to do so today than in the past.[13]

11. As of this writing, a few cases for wrongful prosecution were still being appealed. The trial court awards in those cases were much higher, averaging almost $150,000 per verdict. However, if the past predicts the future, these awards are likely to be reduced or reversed on appeal. I am indebted to an anonymous Japanese prosecutor for sharing classified information from the procuracy's internal review of civil suits. Civil suits in the United States do little more to control prosecutor misconduct. Indeed, since American law generally immunizes prosecutors from civil liability, people who have been wrongly tried or convicted usually have no civil remedies, even in cases of grave misconduct (Kaminer 1999).

12. Depending on the year, conviction rates are low for election offenses too, in part because defendants are sometimes charged and tried en masse. In 1991, for example, 177 people were acquitted in District Courts, far more than in all recent years and more than triple the number of District Court acquittals for 1992. Of the 177 acquittals, 122 occurred in a single Osaka election offense case (Hirata 1992). See the extended discussion in chapter 8.

13. Nomura Jirō (1994:53), a Japanese journalist, has summarized postwar indictments of Diet politicians. Between 1948 and 1992, prosecutors charged fifty-five politicians, of whom twenty-one were convicted, seventeen were acquitted, twelve died during trial or appeal (ten while appealing guilty verdicts), and (as of 1994) three were on trial and two were on appeal (D. Johnson 1997). In 1994, two of the cases on trial were decided, both involving Diet politicians charged with accepting bribes in the form

Checking the Prosecutors: Internal Controls

External checks, such as review commissions and civil suits, leave prosecutors alone in the vast majority of cases; outside controls seldom compel them to charge. But institutional autonomy is an insufficient cause of Japan's high conviction rates, for it fails to address two key questions about how prosecutors convert their autonomy into convictions. First, why does the procuracy choose to enforce a conservative charging policy instead of some other kind? This is a question about the course executives and managers have chosen to steer. And second, how does the procuracy ensure that frontline operators follow the office's conservative charging policy? This is a question about mechanisms for achieving compliance.

Since it is simpler to answer the "how" than the "why," consider the question of mechanisms first. Internal controls on prosecutor discretion are far more important than the external controls just considered. Indeed, internal controls are as pervasive to Japanese prosecutors as water is to fish. Some prosecutors in the Ministry of Justice give lectures about how discretion is controlled in their system, but they routinely ignore bureaucratic controls because they are so taken for granted. To American onlookers, however, Japanese prosecutors swim in a different organizational medium indeed. As we have seen, hierarchical checks are uncommon in the United States, but are ubiquitous in Japan (Kameyama 1999:27). Because internal controls are the main mechanism by which office policy gets implemented, they are the primary proximate cause of Japan's high conviction rates.

The internal controls that most matter are, with one significant addition, the same ones that enable prosecutors to achieve consistency across cases: standards, audits, and *kessai* consultations (see chapter 4). Standards (*kijun*) provide the first level of guidance about whether and what to charge. Prosecutors rely heavily on standards and on the presumption which underlies them — that prior charge decisions should govern present ones. After-the-fact audits (*kansa*) review a sample of uncharged cases to ensure the propriety of non-charge decisions. Audits are an occasion when managers could push operators to risk more acquittals by charging more aggressively. Since they seldom do, this helps further explain how conservative policy gets executed.

Of the internal controls, *kessai* is most critical. As explained in previous chapters, in order to dispose of a case by making a charge decision and sentence recommendation, a prosecutor ordinarily must gain the approval of two or three superiors (*kessaikan*). The *kessaikan* performs four major functions. As manager he makes sure like cases are treated alike. As teacher he instructs operators about how to con-

---

of unlisted shares of a Recruit Company subsidiary. In return, the politicians purportedly promised to ensure that major employers would hire Recruit-sponsored college graduates. In one case, Ikeda Katsuya, a former member of the Clean Government Party, was convicted. In the other, Fujinami Takao, former Chief Cabinet Secretary of the Liberal Democratic Party, was acquitted. Prosecutors were furious at the judges who acquitted Fujinami. In a lecture which I attended at the Ministry of Justice, one prosecutor called the judges "stupid," and others said the acquittal would have a "big influence" on prosecutors, making them even more reluctant to charge "risky" cases in the future. Fujinami was convicted on appeal.

duct their work. As teammate he provides practical help and moral support in difficult cases. And as judge he reviews the adequacy of the evidence. This last function — *kessaikan* as judge — is especially important for explaining Japan's high conviction rates. Judges acquit few cases not because they "favor" the prosecution but because *kessai* prosecutors have already "acquitted" suspects who might have been acquitted at trial. This is what the anonymous Japanese judge meant when he disconsolately described how prosecutors "filter cases very carefully."

Kessai's capacity to screen acquittal-risky cases is evident in survey results as well.[14] Two-thirds of prosecutors agreed that "acquittals are rare at trials because the *kessai* system screens out most cases that might result in acquittal." An additional 21 percent said it depends on the case. Similarly, in interviews many prosecutors stressed that minimizing acquittals is the most important *kessai* function of all. One veteran manager put it this way:

> It is often said that Japan has a three-layered court system, made up of District Courts, High Courts, and the Supreme Court. Actually it has four, if you include the *kessai* review at the pre-charge stage. *Kessaikan* should allow cases to go to trial only if they are 100 percent sure they will result in conviction. If there is any doubt whatsoever, the *kessaikan* should not let it proceed further. Japan's acquittal rate is low not because judges fail to do their jobs or because trials are unfair to the accused, but because prosecutors act like judges at the *kessai* stage, and because front-line prosecutors have internalized the *kessai* standards themselves.

The Demerit Principle: Shittenshugi and Job Assignments

While these internal controls, and *kessai* especially, are important proximate causes of Japan's high conviction rates, one other organizational feature ought not to be neglected: the procuracy's hierarchical control over office, job, and case assignments. Unlike American prosecutors, who seldom are transferred against their will, Japanese prosecutors are routinely transferred from office to office and from job to job, typically every two years. Since office, job, and case assignments are the currency of status in Japan's procuracy, there is intense competition for the most desirable allotments. Managers and executives use their control over these assignments to reinforce, positively and negatively, the behavior of operators. Prosecutors found to be "negligently" responsible for acquittals pay heavy fines in this currency of status.[15]

---

14. For other survey questions about Japan's *kessai* system, see part 4 of the survey, questions 33–38, 72, and 96, in the appendix. There is one major exception to the *kessai* norm: prosecutors do not receive *kessai* in most traffic cases. In fact, most traffic cases are not handled by prosecutors at all, but by *jimukan*, their administrative assistants. I explained the Japanese system of hierarchical review and control to a senior prosecutor in a large California office. I asked if his office had anything similar. "Are you kidding?" he replied incredulously. "This is a people business. You can't regulate it like that. Besides, I have my own work to do. They [subordinates seeking advice or approval] just get in the way."

15. The structure of Japan's judiciary also permits wayward judges to be punished through office, job, and case assignments. For a concise review of research that documents the occasions, frequency, and severity of such punishments, see Ramseyer and Rasmusen (2000). I am indebted to Professor John Owen Haley for alerting me to the potential importance of office and job assignments, and for urging me to investigate their connection to Japan's high conviction rates.

Many prosecutors contend there is no career cost for acquittals. I asked four survey questions about the relationship between acquittals and careers (Appendix, part 4:31, 32, 40, 43). None revealed a strong link between the two. For example, only 19 percent of respondents agreed that "when a case results in acquittal, the charging prosecutor's career will suffer." An additional 42 percent said it depends on the circumstances of the case (Appendix, part 4:31). Similarly, only 10 percent agreed that "when a case results in acquittal, the trial prosecutor's career will suffer," and another 46 percent said it depends on the nature of the case (Appendix, part 4:32).

Nevertheless, persons outside the procuracy both predict and observe that acquittals hurt careers. Brian Woodall (1996:17), for example, has argued that in order to understand the behavior of government actors, one must identify "a critical institution" that most directly affects their purposive behavior. For prosecutors the critical institution is the civil service employment system, "particularly those aspects dealing with recruitment, promotion, and retirement." Empirically it appears that many prosecutors have severe acquittal anxiety "because of the perils they perceive to a bureaucratic career" if they lose a case. One scholar notes that prosecutors who lose are "very likely to find themselves sitting in Aomori or Okinawa," fine places to live if you like snowboarding or snorkeling, but a long way from the cultural, educational, political, and career centers of action where most prosecutors — like most Japanese — desire to live (C. Johnson 1972:150, 161, 411).

How, then, should we construe the contradiction between prosecutor assertions that acquittals do not harm careers and other claims that they do? Are job and case assignments used to control prosecutor behavior? I believe they are, for several reasons. First, these survey responses should not be accepted at face value. In the original draft of the survey I included several questions designed to probe the relationship between acquittals and careers. Unfortunately, those questions were cut by prosecutors during the "consultations" that were required before I could administer the survey.[16] In interviews, many prosecutors acknowledged that their sensitivity to acquittal-related questions reveals that they care more about the issue than their survey responses suggest. Some admitted the survey responses reflect official *tatemae* about "what should be ideally," namely, that charge decisions do not get made with an eye toward career repercussions. The *honne*, or actual reality, is to be discerned in the actual pattern of charging and in the organization's response to wayward charges. In place of the expurgated questions, prosecutors "strongly recommended" that I include item 69 in part 4 of the survey: "Acquittals are rare because before filing charges the prosecutor clarifies the truth and gathers sufficient evidence." Out of the 235 respondents, not one disagreed with this proposition and only five said it depends on the particular case. Put in the positive, nearly 98 percent of prosecutors agreed or strongly agreed. Prosecutors do consistently aim to "uncover and clarify the truth." That is, unmistakably, a "cardinal" work objective, and thorough investigations in the service of that end constitute one primary cause of Japan's low acquit-

16. Among other things, the suppressed survey questions asked how likely prosecutors are to file a charge in the absence of a confession, how (and how hard) prosecutors try to avoid acquittals, whether acquittals hurt the procuracy's reputation, and whether trials are merely "rubber stamps" and "empty rituals."

tal rates. But prosecutors regard another work objective as cardinally important, too: "not charging the innocent, and charging and convicting only those who have really committed crimes." Indeed, 98 percent of prosecutors consider this a primary purpose (see table 3.1).

Thus, the imperative to make "proper" charge decisions can be restated as follows: prosecutors assiduously aim to avoid making mistakes, of which one kind of acquittal — the so-called negligent acquittal — is the primary type. The organization inculcates and reinforces that desire by evaluating prosecutors on the "demerit principle" (*shittenshugi*), whereby the absence of demerits translates into desirable office, job, and case assignments. The best way to get ahead in one's career is not by performing one's assigned duties brilliantly — by winning big cases or making bold administrative or doctrinal innovations — but by scrupulously avoiding mistakes that might sully one's own or the procuracy's reputation. Newcomers quickly learn the importance of this principle and, more concretely, what mistakes most earnestly to avoid.

Simply "losing" a case is not always a demerit, for prosecutors distinguish between two kinds of acquittals, those which have been "negligently" charged and therefore are blameworthy (*kashitsu no aru muzai*), and those which "cannot be helped" (*shikata nai muzai*). Negligent acquittals hurt career prospects; unavoidable acquittals do not. In practice, of course, managers decide whether to hold a particular prosecutor responsible for an acquittal, but one rough rule of thumb used by many insiders is that acquittals the procuracy elects not to appeal have been, prima facie at least, negligently charged. In short, some acquittals are widely regarded as mistakes, are distinguished as such by the procuracy's appeals decisions, and lead to unwelcome job and case assignments for the prosecutors deemed responsible.

Two related top-down controls further guard against acquittals. First, prosecutors are condemned by their superiors and peers for "mistaken" indictments. Prosecutor Tōjō Shinichiro (1968:62) once noted that "when the defendant is acquitted because of insufficiency of evidence or other inadequate actions by the prosecutor who investigated and initiated the prosecution [the *sōsa kenji*], he is called to the Trial Section and criticized for his action or omission." Prosecutors today experience even stronger obloquy. One, an executive in Tokyo, told me his subordinates are "severely denounced" for negligent acquittals. Another said "there is hell to pay" for making mistaken charges. A third, whom colleagues considered an extremely able investigator, charged a fraud case that ended in acquittal during his fifth year on the job. "I heard a lot about that case after the fact" he explained, "more indirectly than directly. Some prosecutors try hard to avoid the subject when an acquittal occurs, but that only makes the prosecutor in charge uneasy because it feels so unnatural. At least it did for me. Many prosecutors lose confidence if they have an acquittal early in their careers. It makes them timid about charging cases in the future. But my acquittal caused me to study harder so as to avoid repeating the experience." Though this prosecutor did avoid repeating the acquittal experience, he never rose high in the managerial ranks. He averred that the early loss was a "wound" he "could never overcome."

The second form of control is the post-acquittal process. Japan's procuracy has its own version of a hospital's "morbidity and mortality conference," a closed-door session in which prosecutors, like surgeons, are required to review their mistakes and complications. Following an acquittal, the trial prosecutor must write a detailed report about the case, focusing in particular on the "problems" that caused the acquittal. Because these reports take days or even weeks to produce, they are widely considered one of the most unpleasant tasks a prosecutor has to perform.[17] What is more, the trial prosecutor and other "responsible" persons must attend a series of "appeal deliberation meetings" (*kōso shingi*) chaired by elite prosecutors from the District, High, and (in special cases) Supreme Prosecutors Offices. These meetings take still more time away from the prosecutor's regular duties. Because the audience is elite, the stakes are high, and the experience is infrequent, preparing and presenting the requisite reports is highly stressful. Most prosecutors regard the aftermath of an acquittal as "a real pain in the butt."

In the end, prosecutors in Japan do "cherry-pick airtight cases," as the quotation opening this chapter proclaims, but there is nothing necessary, natural, or nefarious about their behavior. Managers and executives use various levers to induce operators to charge winners and, with few exceptions, only winners. Informal office norms reflect and reinforce the hierarchical controls. Most prosecutors know a great deal about transfers and personnel changes: who wants what post, who got sent where, who is happy, who is upset, and who is likely to quit. Conversation on these subjects is so frequent that only confessions (and the interrogation techniques for eliciting them) rival personnel matters as the favorite topic of prosecutor talk.[18] Acquittals are much discussed too, albeit seldom as directly as transfers. Prosecutors adopt a "don't ask, don't tell" policy, rarely requesting or volunteering information straightaway. Nonetheless, informal grapevines transmit detailed information about cases that end in acquittal and who charged and tried them. When the acquittal is deemed negligent the tones are quite critical. Like formal controls through job and case assignments and official reprimands, these informal sanctions mold reputations and self-perceptions. Grapevine gossip has caused many prosecutors to feel "disgraced" and "wounded" by acquittals they have charged or tried. Since it is typically assumed that defense lawyers do not win cases as much as prosecutors lose them, lost cases usually mean lost status.

On a larger scale, the procuracy's reputation suffers analogous damage when the mass media (as they invariably do) publicize the procuracy's defeats (Hirano

17. Following the acquittal (3/31/94) of Okubo Yoshikuni in the "Los Angeles mystery" murder case, the responsible prosecutors spent months analyzing the causes of the acquittal and writing reports about their findings. Prosecutors appealed the verdict. I interviewed the prosecutor in charge of the appeal one year after the acquittal, by which time he already had produced several book-length reports on the case, including exhaustive (and exhausting) internal reviews of the causes of the acquittal. He said he frequently felt he was "drowning" in the acquittal's wake. Okubo's more notorious co-defendant, Kazuyoshi Miura, was convicted but then acquitted on appeal (7/2/98). For background on the case, see Marshall and Toyama (1994).

18. During transfer seasons, prosecutor offices are saturated with reports about personnel changes and reactions thereto. A few prosecutors specialize in producing informal newsletters about the changes, which are faxed or E-mailed to colleagues throughout the country. Prosecutors' preoccupation with personnel matters is hardly puzzling, for who is uninterested in residence or job issues? Prosecutors with children in school often feel extra pressure to obtain "good" transfers, because Japan's educational system, like its procuracy, can be unforgiving of failure (Rohlen 1983; Brinton 1993).

1989:130). In Japan almost all acquittals are noteworthy. They occur, on the average, about twice a week. If news is defined as "information about the world that stands out," it is understandable why acquittals get publicized. Still, some stand out more than others. Following the acquittal of Fujinami Takao, an LDP Diet member and former Chief Cabinet Secretary, the media went wild. Throughout the country, newspaper front pages declared "the total trouncing of the procuracy." According to the *Yomiuri Shimbun* (9/28/94), Japan's largest national daily,

> Observers said Fujinami's acquittal was a "total defeat" for prosecutors, noting that prosecutors had put in a tremendous amount of effort to win a conviction. They said the prestige of the procuracy was at stake. . . . [In court,] prosecutors seemed stunned by the verdict. They kept their heads down during the entire 1 hour and 45 minutes it took [Judge] Mikami to read the decision. Some sighed numerous times. At the special investigation [*tokusōbu*] headquarters of the Tokyo District Public Prosecutors Office, officials watched a TV screen in silence. Doors to the offices of high-level prosecutors were kept shut.

In sum, the procuracy's internal, hierarchical, and informal controls reflect the risks to which the organization is particularly averse. Managers monitor and sanction operators in order to minimize mistakes, especially mistaken charges, and they have instituted mechanisms for ensuring that the conservative charging policy gets faithfully implemented. The mechanisms work.

The Origins of Trial Sufficiency Policy

If Japan's procuracy obtains consistent compliance with its charging policy, why has it chosen to enforce a conservative policy instead of some other kind? Charging policies vary widely, both internationally (Fionda 1995; Tak 1986) and within individual countries or states (Flemming et al. 1992:41). Different policies aim at different outcomes. In the United States, for example, research has identified four distinct policies: legal sufficiency, system efficiency, defendant rehabilitation, and trial sufficiency (Jacoby 1980:15; Mellon et al. 1981). Some offices adopt a "legal sufficiency" policy to charge cases that satisfy the legal requirements of a crime. In this approach, evidentiary issues are not seriously reviewed until after a charge is instituted. Though many large American offices elect or accept this policy, it clearly does not describe the procuracy in Japan. Japan's conviction rates are incompatibly high with such weak screening. Other American offices adopt a "system efficiency" approach that mandates the speedy and early disposition of as many cases as possible. Pursuit of this policy usually indicates a backlogged court and an overworked prosecutors office with limited resources. Some analysts believe this policy characterizes Japan. I disagree. Though caseloads are not unrelated to Japan's charging policy, chapter 1 has shown that the procuracy is not nearly as understaffed as such arguments suppose. As a result, concerns about efficiency do not compel prosecutors to charge "only the most obviously and gruesomely guilty" (Ramseyer and Rasmusen 2001). A third policy — "defendant rehabilitation" — stresses early diversion of many defendants and vigorous prosecution of those cases that are criminally charged. As described in chapter 6, this policy is seldom seen in the United States[19] but it does shape (though not determine) Japan's charging policy. Finally, a "trial sufficiency" policy instructs prosecutors to charge only if a conviction at trial is highly likely. Effective implementation of this policy requires, above all, organization and discipline, which is to say, mechanisms for ensuring that frontline operators comply with office policy.

Japan has adopted a hybrid charging policy that pursues both rehabilitation and trial sufficiency. The origins of the commitment to rehabilitation have already been discussed. Prosecutors drop or divert many cases out of concern for correction, but they do not have to adopt such a rigorous standard for suspects outside the correctability continuum. If "trial sufficiency" is a policy choice, on what basis is it made?

One key to understanding the choice lies in the nature of the prosecutor function (Jacoby 1980). Prosecutors everywhere play three core roles — political, bureaucratic, and jurisprudential — but the salience of each role depends on the local context (Alschuler 1968). In Japan the political role is more secondary than in most American jurisdictions (Uviller 2000). Japanese prosecutors are not elected, and since crime is not much of a public problem they are seldom pressured to charge or punished for not charging. Consequently, it is not just individual prosecutors who face "trial sufficiency" incentives. Rather, prosecutors as an office face reduced incentives to charge hard cases and enhanced incentives to take the converse risk that uncharged suspects will reoffend. Similarly, the bureaucratic imperative to process cases efficiently — to "keep the cases moving" — is less compelling in Japan than in busier jurisdictions elsewhere. The low salience of the political and bureaucratic roles makes the jurisprudential role more prominent. Wearing that hat, as minister of justice, prosecutors can consider how the purposes of punishment should impinge on the decision to charge. In the absence of adversarial opposition, which is the customary context prior to charging, Japanese prosecutors do not feel compelled to overcharge, as many of their American counterparts do. Instead, prosecutors can choose the charge that best expresses their perceptions of desert, correctability, and convictability. Punishment, in other words, is constrained by the belief that the "gray guilty" should not be forced to undergo the stigmatization or process costs that criminal trials inflict. In this way, the procuracy's charging policy is shaped less by the demands of legal sufficiency or system efficiency and more by the purposes of punishment that are supposed to animate judicial sentencing. Of course, a version of the trial sufficiency standard governs prosecutors in some American jurisdictions

19. The exceptions suggest that in the American context it is difficult to combine rehabilitation and trial sufficiency policies as Japan's procuracy has done. For example, in 1994 San Francisco District Attorney Terence Hallinan adopted a rehabilitation charging policy, with decidedly mixed results. On the one hand, Hallinan's office sent many low-level drug offenders and other petty crooks to treatment instead of prison. Partly as a result, the number of people incarcerated from San Francisco dropped by two-thirds, from 2,136 in 1993, before Hallinan took office, to 703 in 1998. On the other hand, Hallinan was unable to pursue a trial sufficiency policy for offenders who were not diverted. In fact, in 1998 his office convicted a mere 27.7 percent of arrested felony suspects, by far the lowest conviction rate among California's fifty-eight district attorneys. The largest local newspaper, the *San Francisco Chronicle*, found Hallinan's conviction record so "abysmal" that it dubbed him "A Disgraceful D.A." (9/2/99).

too. Where it does, prosecutors adopt a "downstream" orientation, anticipating and considering how others will interpret and respond to particular cases (Frohmann 1997). However, the threshold of "convictability," defined as the probability of prevailing at trial, means something different in Japan, where prosecutors can better predict whether courts will convict, in part because trials are discontinuous, and in part because judges, unlike juries, have histories that prosecutors can study.

Thus, three forces interact to explain why a strong version of the trial sufficiency policy prevails in Japan: the institutional environment within which prosecutors work, especially the absence of juries and the nonadversarial nature of defense lawyering; the prominence of prosecutors' jurisprudential role, which itself reflects other features of their work environment; and prosecutors' beliefs about the purposes and limits of the criminal sanction. Together with the mechanisms the procuracy has implemented for securing conformity to its rigorous screening policy, these facts account for Japan's high conviction rates.[20] As we will see, the rates have not always been so high.

The Long Decline

The steady decline in acquittal rates since the end of the Meiji era raises a critical question: Has Japan's procuracy attempted to eliminate acquittals in a relentlessly purposeful pursuit of perfection? Saeki Chihirō (1989) has examined acquittal rates from 1908 to the present. Unfortunately, since longitudinal data on confessions are unavailable, Saeki was unable to investigate acquittal rate trends in contested cases as was done for table 7.1. Nevertheless, Saeki's analysis reveals such a steady decline in "overall acquittal rates" that, by this measure at least, the low percentage of "not

---

20. Though the features described in the text are the main sources of Japan's high conviction rates, a complete causal account is more complicated, and several additional (and interrelated) reasons also merit mention. First, Japanese judges often permit prosecutor dossiers to be used at trial and regularly refuse bail to defendants who do not consent to the admission of documents that prosecutors want introduced as evidence. This advantages the state (Igarashi 1984; Hirano 1989; Ishimatsu 1989). Second, unlike American juries, Japanese judges must justify their decisions in writing. It may be easier for judges to write sentences for conviction than for acquittal because the latter must be meticulously reasoned whereas the former can simply assert that the state has proved its case (personal interviews with Japanese judges). Third, some judges fear appeals of acquittals and appellate court reversals (Saeki 1989:19). Fourth, defense lawyers play a more restricted role during the investigation and trial than in countries like Holland and the United States. Some defense lawyers in Japan "inadvertently and indirectly contribute to the dramatization of the defendant's guilt" by endorsing the facts constructed by the prosecutor (Peters 1992:280). Finally, Japanese prosecutors rely on single-charge indictments (*kisojo ipponshugi*), unlike their Dutch counterparts, who "formulate subsidiary criminal charges with reference to the same incriminated facts." At trial, the single-charge indictment "has the effect of putting the [Japanese] prosecutor under undue pressure to prove that he is right in his legal qualification of the facts for which the defendant is prosecuted"—which is to say, prosecutors obstinately press for conviction on the facts in the indictment. The single-charge indictment "thereby produces a tension in the trial which may be considered dysfunctional from the perspective of searching for the truth" (Peters 1992:283; see also C. Johnson 1972:411; van Wolferen 1989:220).

guilty" cases does approach "absolute zero" (Murayama 1992:236).[21] Table 7.2 summarizes overall acquittal rates for the ninety-one-year period from 1908 through 1998. The long decline undermines claims that high conviction rates in postwar Japan arose out of a prewar system that discriminated against the ideologically motivated.[22] In fact, table 7.2 reveals that prewar judges were substantially more likely to acquit than their postwar successors. In historical perspective, change is more conspicuous than continuity.

Postwar Changes

Saeki explains the long decline by stressing changes in criminal justice that occurred since the late Meiji era.[23] He is especially interested in the decrease after 1948, when Japan's new Code of Criminal Procedure took effect, and he rightly acknowledges that officials' unfamiliarity with the new code led to numerous acquittals in the early postwar period. This is the causal story prosecutors and judges customarily tell, and Saeki accords it substantial weight as well.

However, Saeki stresses the causal importance of four other postwar changes that also fueled the acquittal rate decline. First, and most significantly, postwar judges admit more dossiers into evidence than did their prewar predecessors. Since the laws of criminal procedure confer substantial powers on prosecutors and police to make cases by constructing dossiers, Saeki regards this as "the biggest cause of the decline in acquittal rates." The increased reliance on dossiers is reflected in trial statistics (Murayama 1992:236). Over the last few decades the average trial length and the average number of sessions per trial have declined markedly. At present, over one-third of all defendants tried in District and Summary courts present no witnesses. Among defendants who do present witnesses, the average number is only 1.5.

21. The Soviet Union experienced a similar decline in acquittal rates, driven in part by the procuracy's desire to avoid charging risky cases (Solomon 1987). More precisely, the drop in acquittals, from 8.9 percent in 1945 to less than 1 percent in the 1970s and 1980s, has been explained by the "increasingly common practice of Soviet-style plea bargaining. Under this practice, judges and procurators avoid undesirable 'failures in court' (acquittals or overrulings on appeal), which would look bad on their respective performance records, by reducing charges to less serious offenses and by sentencing defendants to 'time served while awaiting trial,' in return for the defense's (express or implied) assurance not to appeal the decision. According to Solomon, Soviet defense counsel are 'keenly aware' of the opportunities offered by a criminal system that measures its officials' performance by chalking up good or bad marks, and often 'work hard' to arrange and achieve their deals. If all goes according to plan, these arrangements keep everyone happy: The procuracy gets its conviction, the judge avoids the threat of a possible appeal, and the defendant goes home" (Markovits 1989:1333).

22. Saeki's study contradicts Karel van Wolferen's (1989:221) claim that Japan's "incredibly high conviction rate" is "no different from what it was before the war, when judges rendered a guilty verdict on practically every suspect placed before their bench by the prosecutors."

23. In their study of the automobile — "the machine that changed the world" — Womack et al. (1990:13) claim that the Japanese system of "lean production" rejects the goal of "good enough" which characterizes systems of mass production. Instead, lean producers "set their sights explicitly on perfection," defined in part as "zero defects." One wonders if there may be a cultural connection between the drive for perfection in manufacturing and the procuracy's pursuit of a perfect conviction rate.

TABLE 7.2 Acquittal rates, 1908–1998

Era	Years	Acquittal rate (%)
Late Meiji	1908–1911	5.6
Taisho	1912–1925	4.7
Showa, prewar	1926–1940	2.5
Showa, Pacific War	1941–1945	no data available
Showa, postwar	1946–1959	1.0
Showa, 1960s	1960–1969	0.54
Showa, 1970s	1970–1979	0.48
Showa, 1980s	1980–1989	0.16
Heisei, 1990s	1990–1998	0.15

Sources: Saeki (1989); Shihō Tōkei Nempō (Supreme Court of Japan).
Notes: Data were unavailable for 1941–1945 and 1948. Figures represent overall acquittal rates for contested and uncontested cases in District and Summary Courts.

Moreover, in order to encourage efficient trials, judges use bail to pressure defendants into consenting to prosecutors' proposals to have dossiers admitted as evidence. In general, defendants who do not confess and consent do not get bail. As paper dossiers crowd out human witnesses, trials have become shorter, less adversarial affairs, and acquittals increasingly scarce.

Second, Saeki and others believe postwar judges find it easier to write sentences convicting defendants than acquitting them (Foote 1992b:82). Unlike convictions, acquittals must be "precisely" reasoned because they are certain to be carefully reviewed by prosecutors and may be appealed (H. Yamaguchi 1999). Third, Saeki notes that police and prosecutor powers have increased in the postwar years. The new Code of Criminal Procedure, promulgated in 1948, permits police and prosecutors to detain suspects for pre-charge investigation for as long as twenty-three days. In contrast, the prewar limit of ten days was strictly enforced. Conversely, postwar defense lawyers have less legal power than did their prewar predecessors, chiefly because prosecutors are no longer obligated to disclose results of the pre-charge investigation to either the defense or the court. Finally, Saeki observes, as we did earlier, that juries in Japan (1928–1943) were six to ten times more likely than judges to acquit. Suspension of the Jury Law in 1943 seems to have accelerated the decline in acquittal rates that was already under way. Like Hirano Ryūichi (1989:130), the legal scholar and former President of Tokyo University, Saeki believes Japan's overall acquittal rates are "extremely and abnormally high." To solve this problem, he advocates "the immediate resurrection and strengthening of jury trials" in Japan. Others agree (Shinomiya 2001).

This account of the postwar decline in acquittal rates is instructive but incomplete, in at least three ways. Most obviously, Saeki's explanation ignores the emergence of the automobile in Japanese society and the increased share of criminal cases that traffic offenses have come to constitute. Because traffic offenses are rarely contested, they seldom result in acquittal. Likewise, drug offenses have increased substantially since 1970 and, like traffic crimes, are seldom contested (Murayama 1992:235). Thus, the postwar decline in acquittal rates is in part an artifact of the different mix of cases in the postwar era.

In addition, acquittal rates have been declining since at least 1908, but the foregoing account does little to connect the prewar and postwar trends. This subject, and the reasons for the rise and decline of the jury, deserve more research attention than they have so far received. Masaharu Hino (1990:39) has argued that acquittal rates declined in prewar Japan because prosecutors began conducting thorough investigations. In 1872,

> just after the modern prosecutor system was introduced in Japan, the public prosecutor decided a case only based on the file submitted by the police. Thus the not guilty rate was very high. For instance, in 1902 the acquittal rate at the preliminary hearing (abolished after the second World War) was 27.2%, and the not-guilty rate was 10.0%. But the public at large was very critical of this practice by the public prosecutor. Consequently, public prosecutors conducted thorough investigations.

By 1912 the not-guilty rate had declined to 2.1 percent. It thus seems that acquittal rates in prewar Japan declined after — and because of — the advent of prosecutor investigations (Yamashita 1996:12; Nagashima 1963:298).

Finally, Saeki's account overlooks the effect high-profile acquittals have had on prosecutors in the postwar period, much as "big acquittals" have stimulated criminal justice change in other democracies. In the early 1990s, for example, the Royal Commission on Criminal Justice proposed far-reaching reforms in British criminal justice after several highly publicized miscarriages of justice. Many of the reforms have been implemented (Harding 1995). Sociologist W. G. Runciman (1994:8), the chairman of that commission, argues that the key agent of change was "blunders" or "unacceptable malpractices," and contends that the response to blunders is usually "a more potent source of what come to be hailed as 'reforms' than proposals emanating from high-minded commentators and hard-working lobbyists."

Blunder and Response

At least twice in the postwar period a similar pattern of "blunder and response" has prompted prosecutors to try to eliminate mistaken prosecutions. On both occasions prosecutors were condemned for charging cases that ended in acquittal and for "obstinacy in the face of error" (C. Johnson 1972:412).[24] In the first period, from the mid-1950s to the early 1960s, several "public order cases" involving political radicals ended in acquittal (Nomura 1994:23). The most famous acquittals occurred in the Matsukawa case, which has been described as the "the longest, most complex political-legal-economic cause celebre of postwar Japan." The case began in August 1949,

---

24. Long after Chalmers Johnson (1972:412) first made the charge, Karel van Wolferen (1989:222) elaborated the claim that prosecutors are obstinate, arguing that "in the extremely rare case of a not-guilty verdict, Japanese prosecutors forget all impulses to lenience and continue to appeal, fighting tenaciously to regain the 'dignity of the office.' The latter expression is common and has nothing to do with notions of the dignity of the law. Related to it is the expression 'dignity of fixed judgment' with which the prosecutors' office has long resisted retrials." In the cases described in the text, many people believed prosecutors blundered and obstinately refused to admit their mistakes. The resulting criticism caused prosecutors to screen cases even more carefully, further fueling the acquittal rate decline (Nomura 1994:23,145).

when a Japanese train was sabotaged in Matsukawa, a hamlet in northern Honshu. Three persons were killed: the engineer, his assistant, and the locomotive fireman. Of the twenty people arrested for the murders, nineteen were Communists, trade union leaders, or both. In 1950 the Fukushima District Court convicted all twenty and sentenced five to death by hanging. Thirteen years later, after four more trials, all the defendants were acquitted (C. Johnson 1972).

The Matsukawa case and the other public order trials that ended in acquittal had a major influence on Japanese criminal justice. Most crucially, the public's perception that prosecutors "blundered" caused the procuracy to buttress its trial sufficiency policy so as to require prosecutors to collect "all possible proof" (*banzen no risshō*) before instituting criminal charges. This is now standard operating procedure. Mere "evidence beyond a reasonable doubt" is considered inadequate to move forward. Nomura Jirō, a distinguished legal journalist, argues that Japan's "precise justice" (*seimitsu shihō*) and the high conviction rates which are its signal attribute "have been built on these bitter lessons from the past" (Nomura 1994:25).

The second period of "blunder and response" began in 1983 when the first of four "death penalty retrial cases" ended in the acquittal of Sakae Menda, a man who spent over thirty-three years wrongfully imprisoned on death row. Over the next five and a half years, three other death row inmates were acquitted at retrial. Each of the exonerated four was originally convicted in the 1950s, the same period when the public order cases had occurred, and each had spent at least twenty-nine years in confinement (Foote 1993c). These four death penalty cases were deemed "big losses" for the procuracy (Nomura 1994:146). They "generated much public (and private) self-examination and soul-searching" among prosecutors and judges (Foote 1993c:13). In a highly unusual move, the Minister of Justice and the Prosecutor General made public statements calling for prosecutors to exercise their powers more carefully. The Supreme Prosecutors office "prepared an extensive study of the cases and their lessons for the prosecution," chief of which was the need for "even more thorough interrogation of suspects to ensure more precise and complete confessions" (Foote 1993c:72). From the procuracy's perspective, if the problem was acquittals, the solution was still more precise justice, in manifold incarnations: more thorough investigations, more rigorous charging standards, and greater reliance on confessions.

A review of the death penalty retrials concludes that most commentary concerning the cases and most reform proposals aimed "at the total elimination of mistaken convictions" (Foote 1993c:102). This assertion must be modified. Proposals for reforming the procuracy aimed not only at "the total elimination of mistaken convictions" but also at the eradication of mistaken prosecutions — that is, acquittals — altogether. The blunder-inspired reform proposals resulted in few concrete changes, but public criticism and the consequent pressures for reform did cause prosecutors to gather evidence more thoroughly and screen cases more carefully than they had before the retrials (Nomura 1994:145). Most notably, prosecutors have become even more reluctant to charge contested cases. Between 1984 (just after the first retrial acquittal) and 1998, there was a steady decline in the percentage of persons tried who did not fully confess. In District Courts the proportion of non-confessors fell by almost a fifth, from 8.07 percent to 6.58 percent. In Summary Courts the proportion of non-confessors fell by over two-fifths, from 7.87 percent to 4.40 percent.[25] This evidence of an increase in prosecutor prudence is buttressed by interview data. Several executive prosecutors told me the retrial acquittals pushed investigations and charging policies in an increasingly conservative direction. Thus, prosecutor "blunders" have shaped the Japanese way of justice in two complementary ways: by reinforcing the justifications for a trial sufficiency charging policy and by strengthening the mechanisms of internal control that ensure compliance with that policy.

The Consequences of Conservatism

> There is a quantum leap between what is charged and what is provable.
>
> American prosecutor

> We require proof beyond an unreasonable doubt.
>
> Japanese prosecutor

Japan's conviction rate is higher than conviction rates in other countries. Moreover, it has increased continuously for at least ninety years. To explain these two facts—one comparative and the other historical—I have tried to weave together several interrelated features of the Japanese way of justice. The procuracy's conservative charging policy, its internal controls, and the steady strengthening of those controls over time are especially important strands in the explanation. Two questions remain to be addressed.

The first question concerns ultimate causes: What is the prime mover behind the increasingly precise Japanese way of justice? If the procuracy has instituted controls (guidelines, *kessai* consultations, and audits) and incentives (office, job, and case assignments) in order to minimize acquittals, why has it done so? Part of the answer is found in Japan's low crime rates and prosecutors' light caseloads. In comparative terms, prosecutors in Japan have light workloads and are insulated from the political pressures American prosecutors routinely face. These contexts of prosecution mean managers and executives can, as one prosecutor put it, "create work for themselves" by demanding that their subordinates thoroughly investigate and carefully screen cases.[26] The contexts of prosecution also enable prosecutors to attend to public expectations and guard the procuracy's reputation. The Public Prosecutors Office Law designates prosecutors as "representatives of the public interest," and they frequently invoke this duty when explaining or justifying the caution with which charge decisions are made (Kataoka 1993:12).

---

25. The declining percentage of defendants who plead not guilty does not appear to be generated by caseload pressure. To be sure, between 1993 and 1998 the percentage of non-confessors decreased as caseloads increased. However, for the previous nine years, from 1984 through 1992, the percentage of non-confessors decreased even though caseloads also decreased.

26. I once asked a retired Superintending Prosecutor (*kenjichō*) what kind of work occupied managers and executives. "Not much work," he replied. Other senior prosecutors echoed his remark. Indeed, among prosecutors entering the managerial ranks, a common complaint is boredom.

Acquittals are regarded as a "disgrace" for the procuracy, not only by prosecutors themselves but also "by the mass media and the great majority of the Japanese people." When acquittals occur, the media and public routinely condemn prosecutors because of "the huge stigma for defendants that results from the initial indictment." Prosecutor prudence reflects the social fact that "the stigma imposed by being indicted — even without being confined — is more serious than the burden resulting from being confined for several days" (Hirano 1989:131). It thus appears that prosecutors may be "responsive" to the public's aspiration to eliminate mistaken indictments (Nonet and Selznick 1978). If Americans demand "total justice" — a general expectation of recompense for injuries and loss — Japanese seem to desire "perfect justice," which is to say, a minimum of mistakes, and prosecutors try to produce it (Friedman 1985:5).[27] They aim above all to avoid mistaken charges.

With what effects? That is, who bears the burdens of Japan's conservative charging policy, and who benefits? This final question concerns the consequences of the procuracy's pursuit of "perfect justice." Many prosecutors think their approach works well to control crime and achieve justice (Shimizu 1998; Inagawa 1995; Sasaki 1995; Kitada 1995; Itoh 1986a). Many others believe the pursuit of perfect justice is ill-advised. In my survey, for example, prosecutors were almost evenly divided as to whether they "should screen cases less carefully . . . even if it means the acquittal rate increases substantially" (4:39). There were equally deep disagreements about whether to continue the current policy to charge only "cases that will definitely end in conviction" (4:80). Prosecutor Sugita Shu once was asked by a Canadian barrister if he worries that "out of these 99.8% of persons convicted, you might be convicting innocent persons within that large statistic." Sugita's reply shows that even within the procuracy there is significant opposition to the conservative charging policy. "The Japanese system," he said, "is not superior because of the 99.8% conviction rate. Personally, I feel this figure is too high. About 80% should be sufficient. Of course, we cannot say innocent people are never convicted" (Boyd and Layton 1991:57).

Since all criminal justice systems wrongly convict people, at least occasionally, Sugita's final remark is hardly a revelation (Radelet et al. 1992; Scheck et al. 2000). Japan's system does convict people who are actually innocent (Foote 1992b). However, I believe more innocent people are convicted in the United States than in

---

27. The legitimacy of both American and Japanese prosecution is rooted in public opinion, but there is also an important difference. In the United States, legitimacy is acquired largely through the election of office chiefs. In election campaigns, incumbent chief prosecutors sometimes advertise their performance by referring to conviction and acquittal rates, but other appeals also are made, to the chief's record of affirmative action hires, for example (*San Francisco Chronicle* 5/12/96), or to the implementation of new programs "specifically tailored" to the region's crime problems (*San Francisco Examiner* 9/17/95). Challengers may also run on (or against) the incumbent's conviction rates if they seem low (San Francisco Chronicle, 9/2/99). In comparison, the legitimacy of Japan's procuracy is rooted more deeply in performance measures, the most important of which is the overall acquittal (or conviction) rate. Peter Greenwood and his colleagues at the Rand Corporation (1976:135) suggest "there are six essential performance measures that must be examined to assess the effectiveness of a prosecutor's office." Neither American nor Japanese prosecutors do much to publicize the measures the Rand study prescribes.

Japan — probably many more.[28] I make this claim because (as described here and in chapter 3), Japan's system of prosecution prefers the risk that an uncharged offender will re-offend over the risk that a charged suspect will be acquitted. This preference, purposefully institutionalized and rigorously enforced, means many offenders who would be charged in other systems never face the threat of criminal sanction or stigma. At least in the crucially important charge decision, Japan's high conviction rates reflect less an "iron hand" of authoritarianism than a system more protective of suspects' rights than many foreign systems with lower conviction rates. At the same time, since plea-bargaining in Japan is less common and less coercive than in America, it is less likely to compel false admissions of guilt (Langbein 1978).

The criminal sanction — and prison in particular — has limited capacity to do good (Packer 1968). It is always expensive, seldom effective, and often criminogenic (Morris and Hawkins 1969:2). Japan's high conviction rate reflects prosecutors' prudence about punishment. They are more reluctant to use the criminal sanction than stereotypes of conviction-maximizing prosecutors assume (Landes 1971). The Hippocratic oath implores physicians to "first do no harm." Japan's high conviction rate, and the conservative charging policy on which it stands, are evidence that Japanese prosecutors subscribe to a corollary principle for criminal suspects.

However, Japan's conservative charging policy generates untoward consequences too. Consider victims. Japanese criminal justice is often considered victim-friendly, and in significant respects it is. Even so, the high conviction rate means many victims are never vindicated for the harms they have suffered, especially victims who are pressured by prosecutors to "forgive and forget" (recall the victims of sexual molestation described in chapter 6). More concretely, the high conviction rate means many victims never get their case tried in court. Just as criminal sanctions have limited capacity to do good, so criminal trials are little able to change society for the better (sorry, Bentham and Beccaria) or to rectify metaphysical imbalances in the moral order (contrast Hegel and Kant). A trial can, however, accomplish a less grandiose but still essential purpose: it can "stand by victims" and thereby refuse to abandon the innocent who suffer (Fletcher 1995:256).

---

28. Of course the "dark figures" of "actual innocence" are impossible to estimate reliably, much less know with certainty. The figure is especially difficult to gauge for Japan, because criminal justice officials (and prosecutors in particular) have so little external accountability. In the United States external adversaries (journalists, scholars, and lawyers) have been the main agents uncovering wrongful convictions. They have exposed "a system of law that has been far too complacent about its fairness and accuracy" (Scheck et al. 2000:xv). Indeed, "the steady accumulation of wrongful convictions and death sentences in the United States constitutes a prima facie case that we are dealing with widespread, systematic flaws in the administration of justice" (Berlow 1999:91). Researchers have estimated that the "wrong person" is convicted in 0.5 percent to 4 percent of all American convictions (Huff et al. 1996:61; Givelber 1997:1344). Even if the low estimate is ten times too high, at least 1,000 people would be wrongfully convicted of felonies in the United States each year. Wrongful convictions have been exposed in Japan, too, and more would surely surface if the system were more adversarial and accountable (Foote 1992a). Nonetheless, if reliable comparisons of the dark figures could be made, I believe Japan would have fewer, chiefly because the procuracy's hybrid charging policy — offender rehabilitation plus trial sufficiency — prescribes extreme charging caution, and punishes prosecutors who negligently charge cases that end in acquittal.

Japan's high conviction rate reflects the fact that many victims feel abandoned by prosecutors. They are voicing their dismay about the desertions with increasing volume (Morita 1994). Prosecutors maintain a contested conviction rate of around 97 percent because they are willing to sacrifice the victim's day in court if the charging policy so requires. Though it is impossible to say how often such sacrifices occur, it is notable that when Japanese are victimized by strangers, they seem to judge their offenders even more stringently than their American counterparts (Hamilton and Sanders 1992:174). Above all, it is these victims who bear the burden of the procuracy's charging policy. From their vantage point, the premise of the charging policy — to try only sure winners — is dubious indeed. As an American law professor noted when four New York City police officers were acquitted of shooting an unarmed black man nineteen times, "A courtroom loss, even if predictable, does not mean the case should not have been brought" (Gillers 2000).

Nor does it mean the trial had no value. Trials perform critical communicative functions by marking boundaries and making meanings (Joh 1999:913). Through judgments, condemnations, and classifications, trials "teach us (and persuade us) how to judge, what to condemn, and how to classify, and they provide a set of languages, idioms, and vocabularies with which to do so" (Garland 1990:252). In minimizing trials, Japan's conservative charging policy sacrifices many of these instructional opportunities. If Japan's discourse on norms and rights is as impoverished as many believe, it can be attributed in part to these pedagogical sacrifices (Inoue 1993). At the same time, victims in the criminal process care more about being treated with respect and having their views heard than they do about outcomes (Tyler 1990), and the public often benefits from an airing of facts in open court (Fletcher 1995). Trials thus bolster law's legitimacy and educate law's constituency.[29]

29. In 1835, Alexis de Tocqueville applauded the American jury for helping educate people about law, government, and the duties of citizenship (Hans and Vidmar 1986:249). Criminal trials perform analogous educative functions. Trials may also be seen as a kind of living theater in which "all of us are the audience; we learn morals and morality, right from wrong, wrong from right, through watching, hearing, and absorbing" (Friedman 1993:10). On June 28, 2000, Japan's Supreme Court taught a lesson about the meaning of acquittals that many commentators, including two dissenting justices, find difficult to digest. The Court upheld the detention of a Nepalese man, Govinda Prasad Mainali, despite his having been acquitted of murder and robbery. Prosecutors had appealed his acquittal and demanded that Mainali remain in jail, to prevent him from being deported on an earlier conviction for overstaying his visa. According to the Code of Criminal Procedure, Mainali could be detained only if there was reason to suspect his involvement in a crime, he had no fixed abode, and was thought likely to flee or destroy evidence. In a 3–2 ruling, the top court's First Petty Bench held that "in judging whether the accused is to be detained, the court can take into account the fact that procedures for deportation are being taken." Presiding Judge Fujii Masao's dissent argued that the majority decision empties the acquittal verdict of meaning. Fujii reasoned that if High Courts are authorized to permit detention of an acquitted accused after merely reading the record of the first trial, "that would make too light of the trial." However, if one accepts the fact that Japanese prosecutors have the right to appeal acquittals, then the Mainali decision may be little more grievous than the American practice of detaining defendants after hung verdicts, and is certainly more justifiable than the U.S. Supreme Court's (1997) decision in *United States v. Watts*, holding that judges may consider acquitted conduct when imposing sentence. The *Watts* ruling has rightly been excoriated for rendering acquittals "incoherent" (Joh 1999:909).

Prosecutors forsake these functions when they abandon victims by dropping hard but chargeable cases.[30]

The public loses not only opportunities to be educated by criminal trials but also the extra general deterrence that more aggressive charging policies generate. Deterrence works through the fear of being caught, convicted, and punished. For most of the postwar period Japan's high (now declining) clearance rates meant the probability of being caught was high. So, presumably, was the fear of being caught, at least for "rational" offenders. But the conservative charging policy and lenient punishments reduce the deterrent effect. That reduction may be offset by the rehabilitative effects of diverting offenders away from criminal sanctions and stigma, but it is impossible to say how much. The charging policy's sacrifice of deterrence may also have been enabled by Japan's high clearance rates. Indeed, research on deterrence generally finds that of the three determinants of the deterrent effect — certainty, celerity, and severity — certainty (and especially the probability of arrest) is most consequential (Siegel 2000:126). Thus, the crime control cost of Japan's trial sufficiency policy has been partly counterbalanced by the special prevention effects of the wide-scale diversion that the policy mandates (Foote 1992a) and by the high (but declining) clearance rates achieved by the police (Miyazawa 1992:32).

One of the most pernicious consequences of the charging policy is how it suppresses the supply of skilled, vigorous defense lawyering. A 97 percent contested conviction rate means defense lawyers almost always lose. Indeed, defense victories are so rare that Japan's criminal court community has adopted a distinctive discourse for interpreting the significance of acquittals. In the United States acquittals are widely regarded as "victories for the defense." In Japan they are more likely labeled "prosecutor losses." The paucity of acquittals, coupled with the fact that defense lawyers are largely disabled from participating in the critical pre-trial process, helps explain why many lawyers consider defense work "meaningless" (*yarigai ga nai*) and why the bar as an organization has had to resist the increasing "detachment from criminal defense work." These effects on defense lawyering perpetuate a vicious circle: the charging policy routinely results in defense losses; the likelihood of losing dissuades many defense lawyers from doing all they can to win ("why bother?"), and discour-

---

30. I have encountered two main criticisms of my claim that the costs of the conservative charging policy fall disproportionately on victims' shoulders. First, some argue that in comparative perspective, Japan's charging policy is not as bad for victims as it first appears to be. After all, the triumph of plea-bargaining in the United States means American prosecutors dispose of countless cases with little or no regard for victims' needs or desires (G. Fisher 2000). This point is true but incomplete. Plea-bargaining's triumph also means that American prosecutors can get some kind of conviction — and thus some victim vindication — even in cases that might not result in conviction at trial (Ugawa 1997; Langbein 1978). Second, some critics argue that because the "second track" of Japanese criminal justice stresses restitution and compensation, many victims are so satisfied with informal settlements that they do not want to go to trial. Restitution is important, and money and apology can help heal a victim's harms, "but they cannot so easily restore the dignity of those who have suffered arbitrary debasement" (Fletcher 1995:257). Furthermore, many settlements are less voluntary than they seem to be (see chapter 6 and, more generally, Nader (1990), on the coercion inherent in "harmony ideology"). Japan's burgeoning victims' rights movement has been spurred by the burdens many victims feel (*Asahi Shimbun* 4/29/98).

ages many of the best and brightest lawyers from doing any defense work at all; the lower quality of lawyering makes losing even more likely; and the circle is complete. Many Japanese lawyers have told me that at least some of the blame for Japan's high conviction rate must be laid at the lackadaisical feet of individual attorneys and the bar associations. Some prosecutors agree (Ōta 1999:281). I, however, am inclined to regard lawyers' causal contribution as minimal. Defense work pays poorly in the currencies of cash and meaning. It seems unfair and inaccurate to reprove lawyers for wanting to be rewarded for their work.

The charging policy seems to link prosecutors and judges in a different vicious circle, or possibly two. First, can judges remain neutral when they issue more than ninety-nine convictions for every acquittal? Or does the extreme imbalance in the numbers numb their capacity to detect reasonable doubt? In short, do judges tilt toward the prosecution? Many lawyers, and even some judges, believe they do. One former judge described "the typical judicial mind-set" by stating, "In general, there is a feeling from the outset that the defendant is guilty. . . . There's a psychological brake at work that leads judges to issue as few acquittals as possible" (Foote 1992b:83). This, to be sure, may be one harmful effect, but many prosecutors believe the converse consequence is more troubling still. In their view, the procuracy's propensity to charge only clear winners prompts judges to expand the meaning of reasonable doubt. Prosecutors raise their charging threshold accordingly. "To a Japanese judge," one veteran prosecutor told me, "any doubt is reasonable. Prosecutors are being precise because judges require them to be." Another elite prosecutor declared this pattern a "disgrace" and said it is getting worse over time:

> You asked me why we prosecutors do not take adventures. In one sense the answer is easy. *We require proof beyond an unreasonable doubt.* The fewer acquittals there are, the more attention and criticism each acquittal gets, and the more careful we become to avoid acquittals in the future. It's a vicious circle. Don't you see? In this way it is natural that the acquittal rate is declining over time. But it is not a good thing.

The reasonable doubt standard is "a prime instrument for reducing the risk of conviction resting on factual error."[31] Since it is also a social construction, the meaning of reasonable doubt varies from place to place, depending on the conceptions of "reasonable" and "doubt" that get formulated in different criminal justice contexts, and on the particular mix of values that different systems of criminal justice serve (Zander 2000). Japan's high conviction rate magnifies the meaning of every acquittal and thereby raises the resolve of prosecutors and judges to minimize mistakes. This has a double-ratchet effect: judges increase the quantum of evidence required to convict, and prosecutors increase the quantum of evidence required to charge. The arrows of influence are reciprocal. These evidentiary requirements generate an imperative to confess, for investigators and suspects alike. As the final chapter shows, for suspects unwilling to heed that imperative the pressures to confess can be immense.

31. Justice William Brennan, writing for the U.S. Supreme Court in *In re Winship* (1970) 397 U.S. 358.

8

Confessions

JUST SHUT UP.

> Full-page advertisement, Boston Yellow Pages,
> under "Attorneys"

The right to silence is a cancer. We must obtain confessions.

> Japanese prosecutor

If high conviction rates are the pride of Japan's procuracy, then confessions are its cornerstone. Indeed, many of the procuracy's major achievements have been built on the foundation of confessions. As we have seen, justice implies "consistency," and being consistent—treating like cases alike—requires detailed knowledge of case facts. Frontline prosecutors "uncover and construct" those facts chiefly by seeking thorough confessions. Similarly, the procuracy's stress on "correcting" offenders is based on the beliefs that remorse is a requisite step toward reform and that prosecutors can generate genuine repentance. The tie with convictions is equally tight. When suspects confess, prosecutors charge about two-thirds of the time. When suspects do not confess, prosecutors seldom charge. Only about one in fourteen defendants contest the charges against them. Thus, a confession is nearly a necessary condition for indictment, and the conservative charging policy—to charge only winners, and to gauge the probability of prevailing by the quality of the confession—is the primary proximate cause of Japan's high conviction rate.

It has often been said that confessions lie at the heart of Japanese criminal justice (Aoyagi 1986:170; Foote 1992b:86). Though the syntactic difference is slight, it may be more revealing to say confessions *are* the heart—the pump that keeps cases circulating in the system. Prosecutors do their utmost to preserve the system's pulse by keeping confessions coming. They seek admissions of guilt single-mindedly, by urging police to elicit them and by pursuing them firsthand through their own interrogations. They do so for a number of overlapping reasons.

First, prosecutors rely on confessions because they can. As chapter 1 described, Japanese investigators work in a legal environment that enables them to obtain confessions from the vast majority of suspects. They do so, or are supposed to do so, without engaging in plea-bargaining of the kind that dominates American criminal justice. Second, prosecutors (and police detectives) are evaluated in terms of their

244 The Content of Japanese Justice

investigative efficiency, which is measured chiefly by their success or failure in securing confessions. A prosecutor once said that "There is no greater thrill than breaking through a wall of denial and compelling your opponent to confess" (Shimizu 1998:78). I would only add that there is no greater boon to a prosecutor's reputation and career. Third, confessions save time. Prosecutors in Japan are not as understaffed or overworked as is commonly supposed, but they do maintain an interest in processing caseloads efficiently, not least because there is usually something else, and better, for them to do (Feeley 1992b:272). Fourth, confession is often the surest road to prosecutor purposes. Correction, for example, is a primary prosecutor aim, and confessions serve that end. Recall Mr. Haneda, the stimulant drug offender from chapter 6, whom prosecutors could have convicted solely on the basis of urinalysis but from whom they relentlessly pursued a remorseful confession anyway. More fundamentally, prosecutors consider confession the best route to their cardinal objective: "uncovering and clarifying the truth." Finally, prosecutors pursue admissions of guilt because confessions are considered the "king of evidence" by everyone in the system. In particular, confession remains the single most important item determining how judges regard cases at trial (C. Johnson 1972:149). Thus, if the first reason prosecutors rely on confessions is that they can, the last reason is that they have to. In the Japanese way of justice, judges have the final word about guilt and innocence. Most consider confessionless cases highly suspect.

This concluding chapter explores the nexus between confessions and several central problems in Japanese criminal justice. Japan is, in many respects, paradise for a prosecutor, but there are problems in this paradise. If the working personality of American prosecutors is flawed by a "conviction psychology" that prefers penal severity over other potential goals (S. Fisher 1988:200), then for Japanese prosecutors the corollary affliction can be called a "confession psychology" characterized by an almost paralyzing fear to charge in the absence of confession. We have seen that Japan's famously high conviction rate is a straightforward expression of prosecutors' reluctance to charge nonconfessing suspects and of the mechanisms they have created for screening out acquittal-risky cases. Nonetheless, many prosecutors believe the systems's biggest problem is the failure to charge offenders who should be tried. The result, many prosecutors lament, is "too many offenders escaping the punishment they deserve." Chapter 7's conclusion about "the consequences of conservatism" suggests the results are more mixed than these prosecutors perceive. Even so, one effect of the high conviction rate seems especially pernicious: everyone in the system — prosecutors, police, and judges — has become overly (and increasingly) reliant on confessions (Miyamoto and Sankei 2000:236).

Many prosecutors deplore their dependence on confessions, and even those who do not do seem to recognize the depth of their reliance on admissions of guilt. A suspect's silence or denial undermines the capacity to charge and convict. That is why some prosecutors regard the right to silence as a "cancer" capable of spreading throughout the criminal process. That is also why prosecutors cut questions from my survey about the extent, causes, and consequences of their reliance on confessions. As one prosecutor ironically admitted, "We know we depend too much on confessions, but we cannot make that big a confession."

The biggest problems occur when the case is serious, the level of suspicion is high, and the suspect refuses to confess. In this thin but important slice of cases, suspending prosecution — dropping the case — is not considered an option. Prosecutors believe they have to charge, and since judges expect prosecutors to obtain full confessions before instituting indictment, prosecutors believe they *have to* get a confession — one way or another. Extreme reliance on confessions leads to extreme efforts to obtain them. Much of the most disturbing prosecutor behavior springs directly or indirectly from the system's inordinate dependence on admissions of guilt.

Suspects who refuse to confess fall into three main (and overlapping) categories: those who believe the evidence against them is weak, those to whom the state offers insufficient "inducement" to confess, and those who are innocent (Givelber 1997: 1366). The first category of denier is large because the evidentiary centrality of confession means other forms of evidence are marginalized. Since the law forbids plea-bargaining, the second category — insufficient inducement — is bigger than many prosecutors would like. The next section shows that prosecutors have learned to evade restrictions on plea-bargaining in order to offer more compelling inducements to confess. Their evasions are problematic in two ways: they are illegal, and because they are illegal the defense cannot enforce bargains on which prosecutors renege. The subsequent sections demonstrate that when "necessary" — when the case is serious, suspicion is high, and the suspect does not confess — some prosecutors compensate for the problems in the first two categories by engaging (or permitting police to engage) in investigative techniques — like dossier "essays" and the "third degree" — that violate the law and taint the truth. In the process, they significantly increase the risk of indicting and convicting innocent suspects in the third nonconfessing category.

Plea-Bargaining

> In America, the guiding ideology that has caused "bargain justice" to grow is precisely American-style adversarialism, unsalted by the principle of the primacy of the actual truth.
>
> Satō Kinko, *Torihiki no Shakai*

> The Japanese prosecutor does not consult with the defendant or defense attorney and then institute a lesser charge in exchange for a confession.
>
> Former prosecutor Aoyagi Fumio, *Nihonjin no Hanzai Ishiki*

Prosecutors in Japan do plea-bargain. Claims to the contrary derive their force, illegitimately, from two normative claims: that prosecutors should not plea-bargain because "deals" are inconsistent with commitments to truth and consistency that ought to animate the criminal process, and that prosecutors should not plea-bargain because plea-bargaining is illegal. However compelling these normative claims, one cannot get to an "is" from an "ought," or even two. The fact is, Japanese prosecutors do plea-bargain (D. Johnson 2001). The interesting questions are how, why, and with what effects.

The threshold issue is conceptual: What is plea-bargaining? The modal American view is that "plea bargaining occurs when the prosecutor induces a criminal accused to confess guilt and waive his right to trial in exchange for more lenient crimi-

nal sanctions than would be imposed if the accused were adjudicated guilty following a trial" (Langbein 1978:8). By this definition, plea-bargaining cannot occur in
Japan because defendants can neither "plead guilty" (there is no arraignment) nor
waive their right to trial. But this conception truncates comparative research. A more
expansive definition, like the one used in other comparative studies, encourages the
search for functional equivalents (Weigend 1980).[1] On this view, plea-bargaining exists if suspects have a choice between complicated and simple models of case processing, and if suspects are pressured to "cooperate" by choosing the simple procedure. Japan in fact has two simple models for dealing with uncontested (confession)
cases: summary procedure, whereby guilt is determined in camera by a judge, and the
more or less uncontested trial, in which dossiers, not witnesses, comprise the bulk of
the evidence. At the same time, many suspects in Japan are pressured to choose one
of the streamlined procedures instead of the full range of rights and costs that come
with a contested trial where confession is absent or incomplete. In short, since Japan
has the two requisite elements of plea-bargaining, Japan has plea-bargaining.

I have documented elsewhere evidence of the pressure that prosecutors apply in
order to obtain pleas of guilt, evidence that is rooted in field observations and a wide
array of interviews with judges, journalists, lawyers, ex-offenders, police, and prosecutors (D. Johnson 2001). Let one example illustrate the more general pattern. In
1994, police found ten grams of stimulant drug in a Japanese man's apartment. The
prosecutor, fearing acquittal, was unwilling to charge without obtaining a confession, but the suspect insisted he knew neither the owner nor the origin of the drugs.
After sustained but fruitless interrogation, the prosecutor presented the suspect with
a choice: if he confessed the prosecutor would recommend release on bail and a sentence of two years' imprisonment, likely to be suspended; if he denied the prosecutor would seek a three-year term and continued detention throughout the pretrial
and trial processes. In effect, the prosecutor asked the suspect if he preferred more
punishment or less. Of course, the suspect could have continued refusing to confess
and tried for an acquittal at trial. To him, however, this felt like "the offer that cannot be refused." Predictably, the suspect confessed, the prosecutor did as promised,
and the court imposed a suspended sentence.

Plea-bargaining in Japan is unlike American plea-bargaining in several important respects. There are notable differences in quantity (plea-bargaining is less common in Japan), style (plea-bargaining in Japan is more tacit, more consensual, and
less concessionary), and attitude (the Japanese suspect's subjective experience of
plea-bargaining is more likely to combine self-interest with feelings of remorse).[2]
There is also a difference in the degree of pressure that prosecutors use to obtain
admissions of guilt. The "gap" between the complicated and simple models of case

1. This definition of plea-bargaining is consistent with common usage of the term in the United
States (Schulhofer 1984; Standen 1993; Maynard 1984; Littrell 1979) and Japan (Ugawa 1997; Satō 1974).
2. These differences lead some commentators to conclude that a more appropriate image than "plea-
bargaining" is of the defendant "throwing himself on the mercy of prosecutors, confessing to his transgressions, and imploring their forgiveness" (Foote 1986:100). Though there is an important element of truth
in this argument there is also a twofold problem. First, pleas for mercy occur in American criminal justice too. When they do, they routinely are called plea-bargains. Second, Japanese suspects do calculate
self-interest in response to cues, suggestions, and offers from prosecutors and police (D. Johnson 2001).

processing is wider in the United States, where jury trials are far more cumbersome than guilty pleas that eliminate the need for trial. Hence, in order to compel confessions, American prosecutors must impose a bigger "denial tariff" than their Japanese counterparts. In a study of criminal justice in New York City, for example, the denial tariff averaged 136 percent, which means that suspects who refused to plead guilty and later were convicted at trial received more than double the punishment they initially rejected (Zeisel 1980). To some analysts the denial tariff (or "sentencing differential") renders plea-bargaining inherently coercive, for it threatens the accused with a materially increased sanction if he avails himself of his rights and thereafter is convicted (Langbein 1978:12). To other observers plea-bargains reflect less the threat of extra punishment than the offer of concessions (Ugawa 1997). Japan's smaller denial tariffs may mean Japanese-style plea-bargaining is less coercive than plea-bargaining in the United States. Alternatively, Japan's smaller concessions may mean Japanese prosecutors are less often compelled to "sell at a discount." No matter how the inducements are perceived — as threats or concessions — prosecutors "deal" far less often in Japan than in America, where plea-bargaining so dominates criminal justice that "it can grow no more" (G. Fisher 2000:1075).

An American prosecutor told me he prefers "the Joe Stalin approach to plea-bargaining," in which concessions are unnecessary because "all the weapons" are on the prosecutor's side. Mixing his metaphors, however, this prosecutor said he seldom could use the Stalin style because "prosecutors always have to sell at a discount." Japanese prosecutors are less often pressured — by heavy caseloads, unwieldy, unpredictable jury trials, or adversarial lawyers — to sell low, but they sell nonetheless, illegally, in perhaps 10 percent of cases they handle. In some of those cases the defendant's "discount" disappears in a prosecutorial bait-and-switch. Since plea-bargaining is illegal, defendants do not enjoy the right to challenge the outcome of "deals" in which prosecutors fail to act in the promised manner. The biggest problems occur when prosecutors renege on promises to drop or reduce charges or to seek less severe sentences. It is difficult to discern how often such promises are broken; plea-bargaining's illegitimacy makes the topic taboo.[3] But the problem exceeds the hypothetical. Many defense lawyers can describe cases in which they or their clients reached agreement with prosecutors, only to have the bargain breached when prosecutors instituted more serious charges or sought heavier punishment than they earlier had assured. By then, of course, the confession bell cannot be unrung. Though one attorney told me "broken promises occur all the time," her formulation probably exaggerates the extent of the problem. As the next sections show, Japanese prosecutors benefit from a highly "enabling" legal environment that gives them almost complete control over the construction of case information and the "making" of crime. Even in hard cases, since complete confessions can ordinarily be obtained by wearing suspects down, manipulating voluntary compliance, and massaging facts in the dossiers, promises of leniency are less necessary than in less enabling systems. Occasionally, however, the imperative to compel confessions leads

3. In one thousand days of fieldwork in Japan I only once had a conversation with a prosecutor that left rancor in its wake. The topic was whether plea-bargaining occurs in Japan. The Japanese prosecutors who best understand plea-bargaining are most likely to acknowledge that they do it (Ugawa 1997).

prosecutors to make offers they cannot, or will not, and do not fulfill. The offers are themselves illegal. The failure to stand by them makes this brand of bargaining doubly troublesome.

Prosecutor Essays

> If the person who has committed the crime does not speak the truth from his own mouth, the truth of the case will never become clear.

Former prosecutor Sasaki Tomoko, Nihon no Shihō Bunka

> I do not mind lying but I hate inaccuracy.

Samuel Butler

Japanese law permits investigators to compose written summary statements of what suspects say during interrogations and interviews. As a result, the dossiers on which courts routinely rely to adjudicate guilt consist not of verbatim transcripts but of prosecutors' redacted versions of various conversations. Dossiers are thus "prosecutor essays" in a twofold sense: they are analytical and interpretive *compositions* written from a limited personal standpoint, and they are *efforts to persuade* judges of a particular point of view. Pressure to produce persuasive compositions can compel prosecutors (and police) to fabricate or distort the content of the essays.[4]

One illustrative invention occurred in a murder case in the early 1990s. The investigating prosecutor had three years' experience and only a handful of colleagues in his small, rural office. He was bound by law to make the charge decision by a certain Friday. His boss — the branch chief — demanded a punctiliously detailed dossier. A few days before the charging deadline the prosecutor got the suspect to sign a statement making incriminating but incomplete admissions of guilt. At *kessai*, the branch chief judged the statement inadequate. "What are you going to do if the case ends in acquittal?" bellowed the boss. "Or is that just fine with you?" After his harangue the

---

4. Although pressure to charge and win cases produces the most egregious abuses of the authority to compose dossiers, laziness and ineptitude can also corrupt the compositions (Matsuzawa 1992). An ironic illustration has been described by Murakami Haruki (Murakami and Anzai 1984:146), one of Japan's premier postwar novelists. Murakami reports that a police detective once needed his written statement (*chinjutsusho*) for a criminal case (Murakami provides no details about the alleged offense). The detective was an unskilled essayist, handicapped by every writing affliction except writer's block. Bad grammar, misplaced particles, mistaken Chinese characters, and "dreadful" descriptive abilities were just a few of his failings. Nonetheless, after the detective used pencil to compose a statement in his own hand, he made Murakami — the winner of numerous awards for literary excellence — trace the "horrible" prose in pen. Then the detective erased the pencil marks so as to make the statement look like Murakami's original composition. In interviews, some prosecutors admitted they make suspects and witnesses trace statements, or dictate statements to them, or give them written "models" to follow. They do so for a variety of reasons: because (unlike Murakami) some citizens cannot write well, because it is more efficient, and because judges may regard handwritten statements as having higher reliability than statements more obviously drafted by prosecutors or police. The late Itami Jūzō, one of Japan's foremost film directors and the author of several scripts about criminal investigation (including *Marusa no Onna* and *Minbō no Onna*), conducted extensive research for his films. Itami (1997:5) regarded police and prosecutor dossiers as extremely "unnatural" documents because the interrogator's agenda distorts the truth.

chief Xeroxed the dossier and edited his copy to read as desired. He then instructed his subordinate to remove the defective pages from the original and insert the designated changes. The prosecutor returned to his office and, with the aid of his assistant, did as instructed, reluctantly but illegally incorporating alterations in the text without gaining the consent of the suspect whose statement this ostensibly was. The prosecutors got their conviction. Some time later the branch chief pressured the same prosecutor to fabricate parts of another dossier. This time the prosecutor resigned, choosing to become a private attorney rather than face another discomfiting dilemma.

In an interview after these events, the ex-prosecutor observed that "a prosecutor is in a special position. As a lawyer he is committed to doing justice. As a bureaucrat in a large organization he is obligated to obey his superiors. When my conscience as a lawyer conflicted with my duty to obey my boss, I felt I either had to follow orders or quit." The man — a Christian and a graduate of one of Japan's most prestigious law faculties — said that when he quit the procuracy, none of his peers asked why, "perhaps because they had already heard through the grapevine." To him it was significant that neither his assistant nor his peers voiced resistance to the illegal directive to compose a counterfeit dossier. Their silent complicity reinforced his conviction that other prosecutors write fiction too. "Some of my former colleagues told me they have, although I think it is probably more common among the police. Police cannot quit and become lawyers, like I did, so they feel more pressure to comply with disagreeable directives."[5] The former prosecutor further surmised that judges know some dossiers have been illegally altered. "The darkness of the print varies, and the changed pages do not match the unchanged ones." Thus, he believed, in some cases judges "tacitly forgive" the forgery practices.

I asked a number of prosecutors to comment on this case. Their reactions are as revealing as the original sin. Some elite prosecutors insisted fabrications "absolutely

5. It is difficult to tell whether police or prosecutors are more inclined to compose deceptive dossiers. On the one hand, since prosecutor dossiers have extra evidentiary value, and since acquittals are a bigger concern to prosecutors than to police, prosecutors may be more motivated to deceive (Code of Criminal Procedure: Article 321). On the other hand, police have more opportunities to deceive because they compose more dossiers than prosecutors do, and police seem generally less concerned about due process violations (Miyazawa 1992:219). For the view that police forgeries are more common, see the study by the Three Tokyo Bar Associations (Tokyo Sanbengoshikai 1984). In 1994, Fukuoka police were discovered pressuring suspects and defendants to sign blank dossiers. "We don't have time to put your statements in written form right now," police told the accused. "After writing the dossier, we will bring it to jail and read it to you, so we want you to sign and fingerprint it beforehand" (*Yomiuri Shimbun* 12/16/94). When this scandal broke, the chief of police explained the misconduct as follows: "We questioned the woman [suspect] again after we sent her to jail, and we made her sign and fingerprint the blank pages beforehand, in order to apply psychological pressure so she would not lie [by changing her story]. The paper was not dossier paper, it was Western paper. It was an investigative technique." One month after making this statement, the chief of police committed suicide by hanging himself in his office. His suicide note said he aimed to take "managerial responsibility" for the scandal (*Yomiuri Shimbun* 12/28/94). More recently, police in Saitama forged a report about a man who died in police custody; they also faked a libel complaint from a female college student who had been murdered (*Asahi Shimbun* 8/8/00).

It is not just criminal suspects who have their statements forged. In September 2000, an assistant prosecutor in Tokushima composed a dossier detailing an interview with a victim he had never even met. Executive prosecutors elected not to indict the forger because the dossier was not submitted as courtroom evidence and because he confessed to forging it before it was discovered (*Yomiuri Shimbun* 1/28/01).

could not happen"; some of their equally elite colleagues disagreed just as vehemently. One said that in order to resist a superior's order a prosecutor needs support from others in the office. "Those who cannot resist tend to be young and isolated prosecutors who lack allies." Most prosecutors off the elite track were unsurprised by the tale of the doctored dossier. One dismissed the forgery as a personality problem. "There are idiots in every organization," he quipped, referring both to the boss who commanded the forgery and to the underling who complied. Other prosecutors were more analytical. "Unfortunately it happens" said one ten-year veteran. "It is almost impossible to charge denial [*hinin*] cases, and they are increasing in number. This puts great pressure on us to extract confessions, or to urge police to do so. . . . Since acquittals are disgraceful, sometimes we feel like we have to get a confession." Another prosecutor, considered something of a Luddite by his junior colleagues, believed the advent of computers has made it easier for investigators to taint the truth of dossiers:

> About 70 to 80 percent of prosecutors write statements with a computer. Some of us older guys oppose this because with a computer the suspect does not hear how the statement is being made. In the past we all dictated statements to our assistants and the suspect was right there to hear what was said. He could follow along. Now the suspect only hears the contents of the dossier once, after it has been written, and even then it is read to him very rapidly. . . . Although less common, a bigger problem is that with computers it is easier to substitute pages without gaining the suspect's consent. Does it happen? Well, I would rather not get into that too much. (See also Miyamoto and Sankei 2000:233.)

When the imperative to perform (by getting a confession) encounters the norm to conform (by heeding hierarchical mandates), the temptation to tamper with dossiers is especially intense. Indeed, the more inexperienced and ambitious the prosecutor, the more pressing the problem of forgeries seems to be. "Sure it happens," one second-year prosecutor acknowledged. "We are under a lot of pressure. It is hard to oppose your boss." For at least some prosecutors torn between the competing demands of law and loyalty, the most viable choice appears to be loyalty; exit and voice are less attractive options.

A more widespread problem than outright forgery is the selective presentation of evidence in prosecutor essays. This problem originates in Japanese law, wherein the opportunity to compose essays in the investigator's own words is exacerbated by limited disclosure requirements. Like essayists everywhere, prosecutors write drafts. Their readers — judges and defense lawyers — see only the end product. What they do not see is the reasonable doubt dross — the uncertainties, inconsistencies, and contradictions — that prosecutors have purged from the final product. I witnessed the refining process many times. The factual gap between first draft and last can be vast. In one normal case involving the sale of methamphetamine, a prosecutor composed at least six dossiers that neither judge nor defense lawyer ever saw. The draft dossiers contained countless contradictions — about the dealers' chain of command, the distribution of profits, and the drugs' source and destination — that would have been helpful to the defense and probative in court. Intentional efforts to suppress exculpatory evidence occur less commonly than omissions and additions that unconsciously but significantly validate the prosecutor's "expectations" (*mikomi*) and "predictions" (*yodan*) about how cases should come out. Most of the time prosecutors pursue "the truth," but when a confession "must be" obtained in order to charge a case that "must be" tried, and when the rules of law permit prosecutors to shape that confession through the successive production of drafts that are never disclosed to judges or defense lawyers, there is reason to doubt that the confession corresponds to either the defendant's narrative truth or the crime's historical truth.[6]

Ironically, the pressure to convict through confession not only corrupts the truth, it also degrades conviction rates. Table 7.1 revealed that in recent years the lowest District Court conviction rates occurred in 1991 and 1993. In each of these years a single massive acquittal accounts for the pronounced decline in the conviction rate, and in each instance the court acquitted because investigators had compelled defendants to sign dossiers they knew to be false. The two colossal acquittals comprise almost one-quarter of all complete acquittals during the ten-year period from 1989 through 1998.

In the 1993 case, forty-three defendants (over two-fifths of all the people acquitted that year) were simultaneously acquitted at a trial in Matsuyama on the island of Shikoku. The defendants (mainly women and the elderly) had been charged with violating the election law by receiving bribes from supporters of a political candidate. The court held that "because of inducements from investigators and the defendants' desires to please their interrogators, we cannot deny the possibility that their statements contradict the facts. . . . [Police and prosecutors] stubbornly concentrated their efforts on obtaining confessions. . . . We do not see any trace of evidence that they tried to examine the whole case from an alternative point of view." Other critics were less circumspect. One resident of Matsuyama summarized the defense position when he claimed that "the defendants were victimized by investigators who forcibly fabricated the confession statements." A journalist who covered the case from start to finish titled his post-acquittal editorial "Amazed That the Overreliance on Confessions Still Continues" (*Asahi Shimbun* 10/15/93). A defense lawyer explained how police and prosecutors erred: "Investigations into election violations involve the honor and 'face' of the officials in charge. Once they start investigating it is difficult to turn back. Prosecutors abandoned their duty to rectify overzealous investigations. Their responsibility is all the greater as a result" (*Asahi Shimbun* 10/12/93). Commentators have called the reluctance to turn back "procuratorial obstinacy in the face of error" (C. Johnson 1972:412). In some cases, like the Kabuto-

6. The "confession as second-hand essay" genre is not unique to Japan. In America, too, confessions of guilt are often " 'as told to,' indited by another hand and then presented to the suspect for signature" (Brooks 2000:78). But Japanese practice differs in several critical respects. First, nearly all Japanese confessions are secondhand essays, while far fewer American confessions are. (Many American confessions are recorded verbatim and tape- and video-recorded.) Second, the length of Japan's pre-charge process enables investigators to compose many more drafts than their American counterparts can. Third, prosecutors in Japan have far more limited obligations to disclose draft dossiers to the defense (see chapter 1). Plea-bargaining is the American practice that most resembles the Japanese prosecutor's "essay" in its potential to torture the truth, for much American plea-bargaining "involves a confession of guilt of an admittedly fictional sort" (Brooks 2000:84; Langbein 1978:15).

yama trials, which finally ended in acquittal twenty-five years after the defendant was arrested, the procuracy's obduracy lasts for decades.[7]

"Face" and the pressure to perform were also central features of the even more massive 1991 acquittal at Osaka District Court. In that trial, 122 defendants were simultaneously acquitted, accounting for almost 70 percent of the acquittals that year. Two-thirds of the acquitted were over age sixty; twenty-six were over seventy. As in the Matsuyama case, the defendants were charged with violating the election law by accepting bribes from agents of a candidate running for a seat in the Diet. The pressure to perform was intense because election law investigations operate under a time constraint: they begin the day after an election and by law must finish within a fixed number of days. This time limit fosters competition between and within investigators' offices, and it reduces the efficacy of internal controls such as *kessai*. One prosecutor, long familiar with such investigations, said "a special group consciousness emerges as the office takes on a festival-like atmosphere."

Similarly, there were fears about face because two prosecutors on loan from Tokyo were chiefly responsible for the Osaka investigation. In an effort to earn promotions back to the elite career track they were accustomed to riding, the prosecutors resolved to prove their mettle by proving criminal conduct on a grand scale. They so pressured suspects to confess that they produced (in collaboration with police) some 570 dossiers, many containing false confessions. In their compulsion to compel confessions the prosecutors overlooked and ignored much exculpatory evidence. The defendant charged with distributing the bribes was interrogated up to twelve hours a day for eight straight days — on a "voluntary" basis. Then he was arrested and interrogated even more intensely. This defendant grew so dismayed by the lead prosecutor's fictitious essays (thirty-five in all) that at trial he said, tongue partly in cheek, "I have heard that Mr. Y [the lead prosecutor] is now working as a lawyer, but he is so smart and so adept at making up stories I think he would probably make a lot more money as a novelist or playwright than as an attorney" (Hirata 1992:45).

The false confessions were extracted and composed through a variety of techniques documented in miscarriage of justice research (Ofshe and Leo 1997). Suspects were threatened, intimidated, worn down, led, induced, scolded, berated, manipulated, and deceived. Most important, statements contradicting the investigators' intuitions were rarely recorded, and protests about mistaken dossiers were ignored (Hirata 1992:123). The falsity of the confessions was discovered because of the conjuncture of two circumstances that seldom coincide in Japanese criminal justice: sustained, vigorous defense lawyering (by a team of six attorneys), and the court-ordered disclosure of draft dossiers to the defense. The lead defense lawyer perceived the false confessions early — enabled, he says, by twenty-four years of experience as a prosecutor. He devoted ten days a month to the case for the duration of the four-and-one-half-year trial.

---

7. In December 1996, a judge in the second District Court trial of Yamada Etsuko, the Kabutoyama defendant, wrote me a letter saying "It is probably unthinkable in America for a criminal trial to drag on for more than twenty years." I could not disagree. The judge also reported that Nostradamus, the sixteenth-century French astrologer, had predicted a catastrophe would strike the west coast of America on January 20, 1997, and he urged me to leave California a little before D-Day and go to Tokyo or some other "faraway" foreign country. I had already moved to Massachusetts by the time the well-meaning missive arrived. At the time of this writing, the predicted cataclysm has not yet occurred.

His major achievement was persuading the court to exhort prosecutors to disclose draft dossiers they had buried. The disclosure marked the turning point in the trial, since the defense could then show why the confessions were involuntary and unreliable. Prosecutors wisely decided not to appeal this loss, the biggest acquittal in postwar history. Neither did they apologize. But their boss, the Minister of Justice, did, at a Diet committee meeting where he said he was sorry for the grave mistakes prosecutors made and for the serious harm they caused the wrongly accused.[8]

Though the foregoing vignettes illustrate the troublesome link between the imperative to convict and the demand for confession, they are, nevertheless, selected stories. The best systematic research on "prosecutor essays" comes from a study conducted by the Three Tokyo Bar Associations (Tokyo Sanbengoshikai 1984), in which thirty-three former suspects were surveyed about the circumstances surrounding their false confessions. Thirty completed the survey, and ten of the thirty participated in a round-table discussion about the causes and consequences of false confessions. At the time of the study, fourteen of the thirty respondents had been acquitted, seven were fighting prosecutor appeals of acquittals, six were still on trial, and three had not been charged. In describing "how dossiers are made," seventeen respondents said they were compelled to sign statements that investigators had written in a "self-interested" way, thirteen said investigators did not listen to their requests to "correct" erroneous dossier content, and thirteen said they wanted dossiers corrected but "could not say so" because of interrogation pressures. The pressures can be intense. On the average, suspects in this study were interrogated for sixty-two days, and even the median suspect was interrogated for forty-four days. The longest day of interrogation per suspect averaged thirteen hours. Assuming that a typical day of interrogation lasted three hours instead of thirteen — a conservative conjecture indeed — the median suspect was interrogated for 132 hours, long enough for even the slowest writer to compose numerous dossier drafts.[9]

Prosecutor Brutality and the Third Degree

> To us Japanese, hitting in the head is not serious. Kicking is serious.
>
> Japanese prosecutor

> [The media] must maintain "sober eyes" by reporting from an objective perspective that looks squarely in the face of the actual circumstances of investigations.
>
> Japanese prosecutor

8. Both lead prosecutors in the Osaka case resigned from the procuracy after the case went to trial, and both claim they quit for reasons unrelated to the case. In an interview with the author, the former captain of the case's five-prosecutor team insisted the defendants really committed the crimes but acknowledged the investigations were "sloppy." Some of his former colleagues in the procuracy had less generous interpretations, calling the case "scandalous" and "shameful" and the investigative excesses "unpardonable." But other prosecutors empathized, noting that pressures to perform, fears about face, and the imperative to obtain confessions created a "very difficult work environment."

9. By comparison, one of the most comprehensive studies of American interrogation practices found that 92 percent of suspects were interrogated for two hours or less (Leo 1996:279).

The same study that found prosecutor essays to be a contributing cause of false confessions found that most false confessions are the product of an overborne will. Of the thirty former suspects in the survey, twenty were slapped, punched, kicked, or otherwise beaten by interrogators; twenty-three were not allowed to rest or sleep despite the fatigue caused by protracted interrogations; twenty-four were promised speedier release if they confessed; twenty-five were threatened with stiffer punishments if they refused to confess; and twenty-nine were persistently pressured to approve the investigators' false version of events. While police employed most of these third-degree tactics, prosecutors participated too, both indirectly, by demanding that police investigate aggressively and by overlooking the resultant police misconduct, and directly, through threats, promises, pressure, and brutality (Miyazawa 1992:223).

Three cases of outright brutality surfaced during my fieldwork.[10] Although I witnessed none of the three, I did extensive research into the circumstances, causes, and consequences of these eruptions of violence. I also heard yelling and pounding in prosecutors offices on several occasions, and I interviewed several prosecutors who described the techniques of intimidation they use to "facilitate candor." A few prosecutors make suspects stand on their heads, "to get more blood flowing into the brains of people who are not thinking clearly." Though that is one of the most unorthodox methods, it is not, by a long shot, the harshest.

The first act of brutality occurred on July 27, 1990, when prosecutor Matsuda Yasuo punched a fifty-four-year-old accountant in the jaw. The man had wanted to read a dossier before signing it. "Don't make light of me," Matsuda yelled just before delivering the blow. Matsuda acknowledged this assault. A witness at the scene said

---

10. Although their real names appeared in many media stories, I have decided to use pseudonyms for the first two "brutal prosecutors" (*bōkō kenji*), in part because they were never charged with crimes (both received suspended prosecution). Here is the background of my decision.

In December 2000, I showed a draft of this book manuscript to an executive prosecutor who gave helpful comments on several parts of the text. But one of his responses confused me. He advised that "even if their real names were previously reported by the media, as time passes the reputations (*meiyo*) of the uncharged prosecutors should be protected. This is what the law requires [here he cited the *Keiji Kakutei Soshō Kiroku Hō*], and in uncharged cases the demand is all the greater [here he cited article 47 of the Code of Criminal Procedure]... In publishing the real names of the uncharged prosecutors, the costs far outweigh the benefits." When I asked the prosecutor to explain what principle lay behind this seemingly self-serving argument, he said that offenders should be given a chance to rehabilitate, especially offenders who have not been indicted, and that reminding them and the public of previous misconduct undermines the correctional imperative.

One week later I participated in a roundtable discussion with thirteen Japanese judges who were working as instructors at the Legal Research and Training Institute in Saitama prefecture. All agreed with the counsel I had been given to not name the two prosecutors. Most cited the rehabilitation rationale. One said it would be just plain "mean" to use the real names. Several said it depends on my purpose in writing. When I argued that naming the prosecutors served the interests of truth and accountability, these judges reckoned that the rehabilitation value weighed more. Another judge opened a statute book to show what laws I might be violating; he cautioned that if I used the real names I could be liable for libel. In January 2001, Professor Ishizuka Shinichi of Ryūkoku University explained the libel problem in more detail. It seems that an author named Isa Chihirō (1987) wrote a book (first published in 1977) about a 1964 case in which four Okinawan youth allegedly assaulted two American soldiers stationed on their island (one of the soldiers was killed). The youth were indicted but acquitted. Isa used the defendants' real names in his book, which won a prestigious prize for literary excellence, but one of the ex-defendants sued Isa

Matsuda also elbowed the suspect and struck him in the head with the *roppōzensho,* Japan's 2,500-page compendium of laws. The victim suffered a broken jaw, for which he spent thirty-nine days receiving treatment. Matsuda, a sixth-year prosecutor two weeks shy of his thirtieth birthday, had been dispatched to the elite Special Investigation Division of the Tokyo Prosecutors Office in order to help investigate suspected stock manipulation by the Koshin group, an association of stock speculators. For a young prosecutor like Matsuda, this was a golden opportunity to demonstrate his investigative abilities, especially the capacity to compel confessions in high-profile cases.

Although officials in the procuracy learned of Matsuda's attack shortly after it occurred, they did nothing about it until almost four years later, when the victim filed a criminal complaint and sued Matsuda and the government for 6 million yen (about $50,000). In June 1994, after the government settled for half that amount, the victim withdrew the criminal complaint, the procuracy suspended prosecution and suspended Matsuda without pay for three months, and Matsuda resigned. The Prosecutor General—Japan's top prosecutor—was Yoshinaga Yūsuke. He had been chief prosecutor of the Tokyo office when Matsuda's assault occurred. In explaining the suspended prosecution to Japan's moderately interested press, a prosecutor executive said the violence, though "highly regrettable," was both "accidental" and "not so vicious." Another prosecutor, commenting on Matsuda's conduct, urged me to be sensitive to different cultural sensibilities about violence. "To us Japanese, hitting in the head is not serious," he explained. "Kicking is serious."[11]

---

for libel and won. The Supreme Court upheld the ruling against Isa, holding that the youth's interest in rehabilitating his reputation outweighed Isa's interest in writing the precise facts and the public's interest in knowing them.

In addition to the judges, I also asked a number of private attorneys about whether to write the prosecutors' real names. Though their views were divided, one did offer to defend me pro bono if I were sued for libel. Journalists' opinions were also split. Two of the most vocal insisted that the executive prosecutor was simply trying to bully me into self-censorship and that the judges were, as usual, tilting toward their friends in the procuracy. Perhaps. I suspect, however, that this controversy reflects major differences in Japanese and American beliefs about the proper balance to strike between truth, accountability, and rehabilitation when these values conflict.

This hunch was reinforced on April 24, 2001, when Japanese newspapers reported that the Tokyo District Court ordered a monthly magazine (*Uwasa no Shinsō*) to pay Prime Minister Mori Yoshiro over 3 million yen ($25,000) in compensation for defamation. In its June 2000 issue, the magazine had reported that Mori was arrested for hiring a prostitute during his university days. The court ruled that the article marred Mori's reputation by giving "the impression that his suitability as prime minister was questionable." At the time of the ruling, Mori's public approval ratings were in the single digits, the lowest level of support for a prime minister in Japanese history. As evidence in the defamation case, the magazine submitted Mori's fingerprint and criminal record numbers. The court asked police to look into that evidence, but law enforcers declined, saying their records could be used only in criminal cases. In the end, the court made no decision on Mori's criminal record, even though it found his refusal to cooperate with the court's investigation of his criminal record "incomprehensible." Magazine officials blasted the ruling as "politically biased," but it does seem consistent with the Supreme Court's decision in the Okinawa case.

Readers who want to know the names of the first two brutal prosecutors should consult the sources mentioned in notes 11 and 13.

11. For additional information about Matsuda's case, see the newspaper articles published on May 18, 1994 (describing the procuracy's settlement with the victim), and June 9, 1994 (describing Matsuda's suspended prosecution and suspension from the procuracy).

On March 1, 1994, three months before Matsuda's case was dropped, prosecutor Shimpachi Hitoshi, a ten-year veteran, sparked a similar chain reaction by slamming a desk into the arm of fifty-nine-year-old city assemblyman Toyoshima Kō, who was roped to a chair while being interrogated on suspicion of bribery. The case was part of an ongoing investigation of corruption in Tsukuba city's public works contracts. Frustrated by Toyoshima's refusal to confess, Shimpachi rose from his seat and, in the presence of a clerk and a police guard, lifted the end of his desk and drove it hard into Toyoshima's left forearm.[12] The blow resulted in severe bruises that took weeks to heal. Shimpachi hoped to scare the suspect into a more forthcoming demeanor, as he had attempted to do on several previous occasions. That night, Toyoshima tried to cool his wound with toilet paper soaked in water from the toilet in his cell. The next day he met his attorney, Nojima Tadashi, after Nojima threatened to sue the procuracy for denying access to his client. The lawyer photographed Toyoshima's arm in the interview room and promptly filed a criminal complaint and a lawsuit seeking 5 million yen ($41,666) in damages. Six months later, in October 1994, prosecutors admitted the assault, settled the case for 3 million yen (the same amount given Matsuda's victim), and convinced Toyoshima to withdraw his criminal complaint. They disposed of the case in the same manner they had Matsuda's assault, by suspending prosecution and suspending Shimpachi for three months without pay.

Shimpachi eventually resigned under pressure. After the criminal complaint was filed he had been transferred to a post with virtually no responsibilities. Several of his superiors wanted him to quit. Their reasoning reveals beliefs about brutality that seem less censorious than severe bruises warrant. The violence itself was "unacceptable," to be sure, but Shimpachi's other failings were equally important. One prosecutor said that "if Shimpachi had taken care of the victim after learning he was hurt, legal actions would not have been filed and the whole problem could have been avoided." Another believed that if Shimpachi had forged a good relationship with the suspect during interrogation, as prosecutors are supposed to do, the suspect never would have complained about the injuries.

The procuracy's public justification for the disposition closely tracked the reasons they gave in Matsuda's case. The settlement with the victim mitigated blame, a prosecutor spokesman said. Besides, the incident was "accidental," the injuries were

---

12. Shimpachi was well known among his colleagues as an intense, able prosecutor who "often lost his temper." Prior to working on the Tsukuba scandal with the Criminal Division of the Tokyo Prosecutors Office, Shimpachi spent three years as a judge in Tokyo District Court. At least one prosecutor believes his fuse on the bench was similarly short. A prosecutor who talked to Shimpachi during the period his disposition was being decided reported that Shimpachi admitted doing "indirect violence" but was frustrated that the procuracy publicly acknowledged the incident and was attempting to settle with the victim. Several of Shimpachi's colleagues tried to persuade him not to resign, since by quitting he would acknowledge that he did serious wrong when they deemed his behavior merely "negligent." As one prosecutor put it, "Shimpachi simply lifted up a desk and slammed it down. Many prosecutors do that during interrogation in order to scare and intimidate the suspect. It was a negligent mistake that could have happened to anyone. He should not be suspended or punished. If he is, other prosecutors will be quite upset." Shimpachi did quit the procuracy to become a private attorney in one of Tokyo's most prominent law offices.

"minor," and the behavior was "not intended to do physical harm." Justice Minister Maeda Isao did issue verbal warnings to Prosecutor General Yoshinaga and five other supervising prosecutors, urging them to strengthen managerial controls so that suspects' rights are better respected, but the minister's move actually was proposed by elite prosecutors, an intriguing reflection of the procuracy's autonomy, even in times of crisis, that the media never reported. One prosecutor told me that "the brutality cases drew so much unfavorable attention, we felt the need to solicit Maeda in order to show the public we are dealing with the problem seriously." Yoshinaga seemed reluctant to acknowledge that the organization shared culpability for the prosecutors' crime:

> The series of scandals has seriously damaged public trust and expectations regarding prosecutors. I would like to take this opportunity to renew our efforts to prevent a recurrence of such incidents and take every measure to regain public trust. . . . These incidents are extremely regrettable. There is nothing to be gained by using violence in interrogation. Denial cases are increasing in number, so investigations have become more difficult, but I am going to urge frontline prosecutors to investigate with a normal spirit. . . . These brutality cases are shocking, but they are entirely a problem of the individual prosecutor's temperament, not a problem of the character of the prosecutor organization. . . . The young prosecutors of recent years may not have the tenacity to interrogate patiently.[13]

Patient or not, some prosecutors do believe there is something to gain — a confession — and little to lose by utilizing third-degree methods. In the third and most severe case of brutality, Kanazawa Hitoshi, a thirty-three-year-old fifth-year prosecutor, beat two elderly witnesses (*sankōnin*) during a corruption investigation in Sendai that resulted in the indictment of former Miyagi governor Honma Shuntarō. Both "witnesses" were actually "gray suspects" whom prosecutors believed had committed crimes of corruption, but neither would confess or cooperate. Kanazawa's violence clearly exceeded the "kicking is serious" threshold I was asked to respect.

One victim was a sixty-five-year-old ex-official of the Miyagi prefectural government. Kanazawa yelled "fucking pig" (*butayarō*) and other obscenities at this senior citizen, forced him to kneel on the floor of the interrogation room, pressed his head to the floor with his foot, slapped him in the head and face numerous times, and kicked him in the chest and hips. The man's physical injuries took three weeks to heal.

The other victim was a fifty-seven-year-old executive of the Moriya Mokuzai lumber company. Kanazawa "interviewed" this "witness" twice, the first time for seven continuous hours, from 6 P.M. to 1 A.M., on October 13, 1993, and then again for six hours the next day, from 10 A.M. to 4 P.M. Since the interviews were done on a "voluntary" basis, the victim was not formally arrested or detained. Though the victim was never told of his right to remain silent, he did learn an agonizing lesson about the duty to endure questioning. In the first interview, Kanazawa resorted to the third degree out of frustration that the man's answers (such as his insistence that an envelope had been

---

13. For more details about Shimpachi's case, see the newspaper articles published on June 24, 1994 (describing the procuracy's efforts to settle with the victim), and October 6, 1994 (describing Shimpachi's suspended prosecution, suspension from work, and the warnings issued to his superiors).

white) did not conform to prosecutors' expectations for the case. Kanazawa shouted expletives, kicked the victim's chair numerous times, grabbed and shook his shirt collar, and threatened to send him home "half-murdered." Day one ended when Kanazawa instructed the witness to return the following morning at 10 o'clock sharp.

He did, and upon entering the interrogation room was greeted with the question that preoccupies prosecutors in Japan: "Have you recalled the truth?" Moments later the burly prosecutor spun out of control. First Kanazawa made the man, whom journalists described as "small of stature," stand facing a wall at a distance of six inches for forty minutes. When the victim swayed from dizziness and fatigue, Kanazawa warned him to keep his eyes open. Then the victim was made to kneel on the floor (*seiza*) and prostrate himself (*dogeza*). These positions of physical submission are believed to facilitate cooperation and compliance. As one prosecutor put it, "the mind follows the body." Kanazawa stepped on the back of the man's neck and banged his head to the floor. When the victim was returned to his chair, Kanazawa kicked him in the thighs and slapped the back of his head over and over again. The prosecutor's obscenity-laced tirade was peppered with remarks that may reveal his state of mind. "You asshole, I am doing this investigation with public tax dollars," he declaimed. "This is the authority of the state at work. Don't you get it?"

The abuse escalated that afternoon, when the victim was shoved against the wall and repeatedly kicked in the rear. Kanazawa noticed that the victim's belt buckle left a smudge on the white wall, so he made the man, now weeping profusely, erase it. "You've damaged state property," the prosecutor taunted. The kicks and slaps continued until the victim pleaded with the prosecutor to lay off his stomach because he had recently had surgery on his gall bladder and small intestine. Kanazawa quit kicking but increased the intensity of the slaps, hitting the man dozens of times until blood spurted from his right cheek onto the furniture and floor. "There's no way you could have AIDS, is there?" queried Kanazawa as he wiped the blood from the interrogation room table. He sent the victim to the rest room to clean his wound. A journalist who followed the case for one of Japan's largest newspapers told me (but not his readers) that Kanazawa ordered the man to wash his bloody face so that the prosecutor could beat him some more without soiling his suit. When the victim returned, Kanazawa concentrated his slaps on the man's unbloodied left cheek. The threats continued. "Maybe I'll throw you off the twelfth floor. Then what will you do?" Near the end of this session, Kanazawa made the victim write a pledge (*seiyakusho*) stating that "if I lie to the prosecutor, I will die." While his other "statements" were being composed on a computer, the victim was left sitting on his knees on the tile floor, "unable to stop crying because of the wretchedness of the situation." The victim signed the prosecutor's essay without reviewing it. "I did not have the strength to read," he recalled.

The victim's injuries were diagnosed as follows: cuts to the mouth requiring multiple stitches, bloody congestion of the left eardrum, contusions to the abdominal and genital regions, a sprain of the cervical vertebrae, and extensive bruising. The victim's lawyer, Matsuo Yoshikaze, called Kanazawa's conduct "plain old torture." A journalist writing (anonymously) for a weekly magazine averred that "when it comes to the terribleness of Kanazawa's interrogations, even the notorious Special Higher Police of the prewar period are put to shame."

Like almost all interrogations in Japan, Kanazawa's were witnessed by an administrative assistant (*jimukan*). The aide apparently found the prosecutor's behavior insufficiently serious to report to his superiors. Not so the victims. They filed civil suits against the government and criminal complaints against Kanazawa. On the morning of November 29, 1993, Kanazawa was fired. That afternoon prosecutors arrested him and subsequently charged him with "violence and cruelty by special public officials," a crime punishable by up to seven years' imprisonment. Prosecutors sought a two-year term, which the Tokyo District Court imposed but suspended for four years, just as they expected. Kanazawa never went to prison. This was the first time since at least 1952 that a prosecutor was found guilty of committing violent acts while executing public duties. The government paid each victim 3 million yen ($25,000) in restitution (which Kanazawa reimbursed), but even after Kanazawa was charged one victim continued to complain that prosecutors had not yet apologized. Following his conviction, Kanazawa became a tutor at a cram school for people preparing to take the bar exam. He was eligible to apply to practice private law in four years, after the suspended sentence expired, but one of his defense lawyers believed it would take longer to rejoin the legal profession because of opposition from members of the bar.

The Kanazawa case is a good venue for exploring the causes and consequences of "third-degree" abuses. Kanazawa was an unorthodox prosecutor in several respects. For one thing, he had Korean ancestors. Three prosecutors told me Kanazawa's brutality could be directly attributed to his "hot-blooded" Korean temperament; others seemed to think likewise. It is unclear how they would explain the brutality of their more indigenously "Japanese" peers. In addition, Kanazawa belonged to the Soka Gakkai religious organization, a controversial offshoot of Nichiren Buddhism that lays claim to being the largest lay organization in Japan. Kanazawa was a devoted follower, and even served as a bodyguard for the sect's leader, Ikeda Daisaku. Some prosecutors suspected his involvement in this new religion had corrupted his character, noting that before he was arrested Kanazawa had been the subject of several other brutality complaints. Finally, a prosecutor who knew Kanazawa told me his close relative had been murdered but the killer had never been found. As my informant saw it, "Kanazawa may have felt that for justice to be done, he had to go to extreme measures so the bad guys do not get away with it."

The appeal of these explanations to Japanese prosecutors is easy to fathom: the causes of misconduct are located inside particular people and therefore cannot affect other prosecutors and do not reflect the character of the organization. Two Prosecutors General, Okamura Yasutaka and Yoshinaga Yūsuke, argued as much during the course of Kanazawa's trial, claiming that the brutality bespeaks individual, not institutional, problems. "There is," they repeatedly insisted, "no problem as an organization." This is the same "bad apple" theory of brutality one often hears from American police executives, and it is no more compelling in Japan than in Los Angeles or New York City (Chevigny 1995).

The character-based accounts of brutality illustrate what social researchers call the "fundamental attribution error," which is "the tendency to attribute behavior exclusively to the actor's dispositions and to ignore powerful situational determinants of the behavior" (Reed 1993:25). In all three "third-degree" cases the "situational determinants" of brutality were powerful indeed. Like Matsuda, Kanazawa had been dispatched from a remote prosecutors office (Shizuoka) to the elite Special Investigation Division of the Tokyo office in order to help investigate a chain of bribery scandals involving major companies and politicians. This was the massive *zenekon* scandal, which commentators have called "the most notorious example of systematized political corruption" in Japan's long, odious history of structural corruption (Woodall 1996:13). Its importance was not lost on Kanazawa. Like Matsuda, he regarded this assignment as an opportunity to prove his ability to perform under pressure. Both Matsuda and Kanazawa were at a crucial stage in their careers, where good performance could assure plum job postings and average performance could bump them off the elite track for good.[14] Above all, a good performance meant a good confession. At trial, Kanazawa described his state of mind during the investigation:

> Before I went to Sendai, chief investigators at the Tokyo Prosecutors' Office told us that we [the "support prosecutors" (*ōen kenji*) sent to help investigate the *zenekon* scandal] were a group of prosecutors chosen from across the country, and that if we did only what we were told to do that would not be enough. . . . The witnesses refused to speak, so I was unable to obtain sufficient statements. . . . Because I was part of the historic probe into the general contractor scandal, I was desperate to get something out of it.

At sentencing, the presiding judge condemned Kanazawa for "greatly eroding people's trust in prosecutors," calling his conduct "vicious and despicable" and "a major shock" to those who administer justice. To many insiders the shock was less than major. Indeed, Kanazawa testified that his bosses complimented him on how smoothly his interrogations were going compared to those carried out by his colleagues. In an interview with the author, one of Kanazawa's defense lawyers emphasized the pressure that senior prosecutors placed on Kanazawa to extract confessions. The lawyer had underplayed this point at trial because Kanazawa wanted to become a private attorney and resistance from the procuracy could hurt that cause, and because the defense believed that if it did not implicate the prosecutor organization, then prosecutors would "end the trial quickly and lightly, without seeking to put Kanazawa in prison." It was a tacit bargain of sorts, though the attorney preferred to call it "a coincidence of interests." Whatever the label, it was certainly not in the procuracy's interest to have the court or public hear Kanazawa's defense lawyer say the following:

> Kanazawa's violence is not a problem peculiar to him. The procuracy also bears responsibility. There is a lot of pressure in the prosecutors office to obtain confessions, especially in the Special Investigation Division [where Kanazawa worked]. Yelling, making people stand against the wall or kneel on the floor, and other abuses occur

14. As one prosecutor said, if you are not assigned to Tokyo by your fourth or fifth year, "the probability is high that you will just keep making the rounds through the remote regional offices." At the time of their brutal interrogations, Matsuda had just finished his fifth year as a prosecutor and Kanazawa was in his fifth year. Shimpachi was in his tenth year, though he had spent the previous three years as a Tokyo District Court judge. According to a prosecutor well acquainted with his situation, Shimpachi was eager to stay in Tokyo and was determined to prove that his stint on the bench had not impaired his investigative abilities.

every day, though Kanazawa's level of aggression is more serious than most. But in Kanazawa's case, his superiors said he needed to get certain predetermined results by a fixed date, and said they expected him to do 200 percent of what he was asked. They urged him to make suspects and witnesses stand for long periods facing the wall and the like. . . . Moreover, Kanazawa made a lot of noise during interrogations, sometimes very loud noise, which other prosecutors heard when passing by his office. Far from criticizing Kanazawa, they praised his intensity. His bosses also made phone calls to Kanazawa's office during interrogations, commending his efforts and encouraging him to keep up the hard work. Thus, Kanazawa's superiors knew what he was doing but did nothing to stop him. . . . Kanazawa knew Matsuda too. In fact, he heard about Matsuda's violence directly from Matsuda. I think that may have served as an education for Kanazawa, or an incentive for him to use similarly rough techniques. The procuracy ignored Matsuda's case for over three years. They took it seriously for the first time only after Matsuda's victim filed a complaint. To me this means that despite widespread knowledge that violence is used, senior prosecutors tolerate and ignore it.

Senior prosecutors gamely tried to avoid admitting the obvious: that because the organization relies heavily on confessions it also bears blame for interrogation abuses. Instead, in interviews with the media, two anonymous former prosecutor executives misdirected attention to a number of implausible culprits. One explanation was architectural: as large, open, shared offices were replaced by small, closed, private ones, it had become increasingly difficult to monitor and control prosecutor conduct (never mind that bullpen-style offices disappeared from Tokyo in 1961). Another explanation was generational: young prosecutors had been trained to do everything, from dating women to passing the bar exam, by studying "manuals" of various kinds, but there are no "how to" manuals about interrogating (never mind that such manuals do exist and are consulted, or that interrogation tactics may be prosecutors' favorite topic of conversation, or that most prosecutors believe brutality is less common at present than in the past). The most insistent explanation was also the most spurious: "the brutality occurred because of problems in the individual prosecutors' sense of human rights," not because of problems (like the confession-conviction link) in the organization. This explanation fails to acknowledge the fundamental fact that the prosecutor's working personality is forged, first and foremost, *within and by the organization.*

Many of Kanazawa's colleagues decried the organization's efforts to evade responsibility. One prosecutor denounced her bosses for having "pilloried" Kanazawa by putting him "on public display" while allowing Matsuda's case to drag on so long that his disposition (a suspended prosecution) was decided after Kanazawa's conviction. "That was shrewd," she said. "This way the procuracy can discount the seriousness of Matsuda's behavior. He at least should have been fired and indicted." Other prosecutors deplored the different treatments Kanazawa and Matsuda received. "There was little difference in the degree of victimization," one said.

> Matsuda's actions were very violent too. He broke the victim's jaw, although the procuracy's expert witness [a doctor who examined the victim's medical records nearly four years after the assault] made the injury sound far less serious. . . . Kanazawa was thrown away by the organization. I think he was tossed aside because he is Korean and because he belongs to the Soka Gakkai religion. At any rate, he has no good connections in the organization. He is disposable.

Prosecutors who, like Kanazawa, had been dispatched to the Special Investigation Division in order to help investigate the *zenecon* scandal even submitted a letter of complaint to the Tokyo High Prosecutors Office. The letter stressed the features of the organization that encouraged Kanazawa's brutality and protested what they considered to be excessively harsh treatment of their erstwhile colleague.[15]

Media Lapdogs

During the period that these three instances of prosecutor brutality were exposed, from October 1993 to October 1994, Japan's mainstream media acted more like a lapdog than a watchdog (Freeman 2000). On a news broadcast after Kanazawa's case broke, Kume Hiroshi, Japan's premier news anchor, said that when he first heard the allegations of brutality he thought "No way! That's impossible." Few journalists even tried to explore the causes, consequences, or scope of third-degree tactics. I asked several reporters why they did not pursue these issues more diligently. Here is one representative response from a journalist for Japan's largest daily:

> I guess it didn't occur to us to ask those questions. Here in Japan, writing critical investigative articles is not a press custom. We know there are areas where we better not tread. . . . We don't make bold criticisms because if we did, we'd be shut off from information and unable to perform our jobs. . . . We have struck a kind of bargain: prosecutors give us information, and we give them good [uncritical] coverage. . . . Of course, prosecutors don't say directly that if we write so-and-so we'll get shut out of the loop, but everyone understands the deal. Prosecutors are our superiors and we are their supplicants. We have to be humble and play by the their rules.

Journalists in Japan may wonder how many criminal suspects have, or are compelled to have, a similarly deferent, "play by their rules" demeanor, and they may contemplate whether a suspect's compliant demeanor distorts the dossier "truth," but they seldom do so publicly. After the Kanazawa case broke, Yamaguchi Ichiomi (1994), a journalist for a major weekly magazine, received an anonymous letter from a Tokyo prosecutor rebuking the media for doing too much prosecutor cheerleading and too little analysis of prosecutor behavior, particularly in corruption investigations. The prosecutor wrote:

> On the one hand, the mass media frantically follow the special prosecutors who expose cases of corruption, even exalting prosecutors as "saviors of the nation." On the other hand, the media thoroughly denounce the big businessmen and government officials who are the targets of prosecutor investigations. I think you must not overlook the fact that the backdrop of the "Kanazawa case" is this kind of thoroughgo-

---

15. For further information about Kanazawa's case, see the newspaper articles published on November 30, 1993 (describing the firing and arrest of Kanazawa), February 24, 1994 (reporting the procuracy's opening statement at trial), and June 1, 1994 (recapping the case and describing Kanazawa's conviction and sentence). For media commentary on the "third-degree" cases, see the articles in *AERA* (12/12/93), *Shūkan Asahi* (1/28/94), *Asahi Shimbun* (2/2/94), and the *Daily Yomiuri* (6/10/94). For a graphic description of Kanazawa's brutality, see excerpts of a long interview with Kanazawa's second victim, published in *Shūkan Shinchō* (12/2/93). Japan's daily newspapers never published detailed accounts of Kanazawa's beatings.

ing media campaign which gives birth to adoration for special prosecutors and contempt for the people implicated in the scandals. In media images that chastise suspects as "immoral merchants" and "wicked politicians" there is unmistakably the message that prosecutors are "friends of justice" and "allies of the people." However, the prosecutor organization is itself a powerful state institution, and the media are supposed to play a power-checking role. I think it is important that the media do not merely follow investigations, or even lead them, by dramatically depicting exposures of corruption. They must also maintain "sober eyes" by reporting from an objective perspective that looks squarely in the face of the actual circumstances of investigations.

The journalist who received this letter endorsed the prosecutor's point, admitting that "it hurts our ears" to hear the truth told so plainly. In high-profile cases, public expectations, particularly of the media, encourage aggressive investigations while doing little to curb overzealous excesses. This kind of unbalanced coverage has been called "the crime of crime-reporting" in Japan (Asano 1987; Hatano 1994b:107). The problem is compounded because weak external controls overlap and reinforce one another: as the media do little to restrain prosecutors, so prosecutors do little to restrain police (Miyazawa 1992:219).

The major question not on the media's mind was the scale of the third-degree problem. Lawyers for a number of criminal suspects (including a former Minister of Construction and a former governor of Ibaraki prefecture) announced that their clients would refuse to cooperate in all interrogations because of the pressures and inducements prosecutors use to obtain confessions. Of course, since criminal suspects have a legal duty to endure questioning, refusing to cooperate did not end the interrogations. From the other side, prosecutors also weighed in on the subject of scale, most of them anonymously. Though some expressed surprise at Kanazawa's brutality, many acknowledged that prosecutors routinely use methods which inflict physical and mental distress in order to compel confessions.[16] For them, the most distinguishing characteristic of Kanazawa's case was the degree of distress inflicted. As one prosecutor put it, "We often slam desks, yell, and make suspects face the wall or kneel on the floor. That's how we get their attention." Hotta Tsutomu, a retired prosecutor renowned for helping convict ex-Prime Minister Tanaka Kakuei, explained that some "suspects and witnesses do not feel like they have to listen. In order to make them more interested, we've been making them stand against walls and using other aggressive tactics for years. Of course, that's no excuse for the violence Kanazawa committed." A prosecutor who, like Kanazawa and Matsuda, had been dispatched to Tokyo to assist in an investigation, asserted that violent investigations are caused by defects in "prosecutor consciousness," which are themselves a product of the organization's culture. Prosecutors tend to regard resistance as "unpardonably impudent," he explained, and his colleagues' frequent invocations of

---

16. In 1931 America's Wickersham Commission issued its famous *Report on Lawlessness in Law Enforcement*, in which it defined the "third degree" as "the employment of methods which inflict suffering, physical or mental, upon a person in order to obtain from that person information about a crime" (Leo 1994:13). By this definition, Kanazawa, Matsuda, and Shimpachi are hardly the only Japanese prosecutors to engage in third-degree tactics, though most commentators believe police use such tactics more often (International Bar Association 1994).

"the dignity of the procuracy" and "the reputation of the organization" embolden prosecutors to excess.

These instances of internal critiques could be multiplied further, but I close this section with a quote from a prosecutor who was brutally honest if not brutal in other ways. His statement exemplifies the attitude of other prosecutors I encountered. "Physical intimidation is a necessary tool," he declared. "We cannot just sit there and hope for a confession. This is not a church and I am not a priest."

Precise Justice and Problems in Paradise

> Taking a confession — that is an investigation's categorical imperative. All people who are on the front lines know the importance of obtaining confessions. The reason, of course, is because they want to clarify the truth of the case.
>
> Former prosecutor Sasaki Tomoko, *Nihon no Shihō Bunka*

> In Japan's system of precise justice we cannot help but rely on confessions.
>
> Japanese prosecutor

I began this book by arguing that Japan is paradise for a prosecutor. This chapter shows that paradise has problems. Japanese criminal justice relies so heavily on confessions that in some circumstances prosecutors use blatantly illegal tactics, like plea-bargaining, essay writing, and the third degree, in order to obtain them. They do so for many reasons, but chiefly because they can. Where investigators *can* do almost anything to get a confession, they *will* do almost anything to get the confession — if they "need" to. In this sense, Japan's confession problems are a price of paradise which arises, in significant part, from the enabling nature of Japanese law and from investigators' insulation from external oversight. Ironically, the enabling law that makes misconduct unnecessary in the vast majority of cases also makes it possible for investigators to abuse that law, when "necessary," to gain a confession. Similarly, insulation from public and political scrutiny renders prosecutor misconduct difficult to detect, if not downright invisible.

How often does such misconduct occur? I have made several imprecise, quantitative claims in the preceding pages: that plea-bargaining occurs in perhaps 10 percent of cases, that prosecutors routinely compose incomplete dossiers and occasionally even doctor them, and that interrogators often inflict physical or mental anguish in order to facilitate confessions from less forthcoming suspects. These are, I admit, rough judgments, but they are all that the available evidence allows. The comparative criminologist David Bayley (1994:963) has offered this advice for making reasoned and reasonable assessments about the quality of criminal justice in Japan:

> When James Thurber, the humorist, was asked "How's your wife," he replied "compared with what?" It is far more honest to make judgments about the normative quality of Japanese criminal justice by comparing it with the United States than to describe Japanese practices critically without a standard of judgment. Explicit com-

parative judgments can be tested; ungrounded criticisms cannot. . . . I put forward the following testable proposition: namely, that when the facts about Japanese criminal justice processing are carefully compared with American, Japanese institutions will be found to treat victims and suspects more humanely and equitably.

Though I believe Bayley's hunch is right — criminal justice in Japan generally is higher quality — we do not know enough of "the facts" about confessions in Japan to "carefully compare" this core criminal justice trait with analogous realities elsewhere. Most confessions occur inside an interrogation room, one of the most private spaces in any society and one that remains deeply shrouded in secrecy, especially in Japan. This book and one other (Miyazawa 1992) have partially penetrated that veil, but interrogation and confession remain more understudied, and therefore less understood, in Japan than in the United States (Leo 1996). I join Bayley and others in "urging the Japanese government to encourage study of criminal justice processes, especially by its own able scholars" (Bayley 1994:964). In the meantime, it is both necessary and possible to explore the significance of Japan's heavy and growing reliance on confessions. That is the purpose of the rest of this chapter.

Japanese criminal justice aspires to be "extremely precise" (Sasaki 2000:21). In many respects it succeeds. Prosecutors conduct thorough investigations and construct detailed dossiers, as do police. Prosecutors make charge decisions carefully and consistently, striving to harmonize the tensions between order and individualization, between treating like cases alike and different cases differently. And prosecutors prize accuracy and exactitude, qualities clearly reflected in the country's high conviction rates and the procuracy's low tolerance for "mistaken" charges that end in acquittal. In all these ways (and more) Japanese criminal justice differs greatly from the "rough justice" of the United States, where investigations are less thorough, dispositions are less consistent, charging standards are less rigorous, acquittals are less stigmatizing, and "truth" is a less primary pursuit.

There is one major way, however, in which Japan's "precise justice" is very "rough" indeed, and that is the reality of interrogation for many criminal suspects. Even if the third degree — the intentional infliction of physical or mental suffering in order to obtain information about a crime — is uncommon, there remains the ideal of "storytelling without fear" (as Chief Justice Earl Warren termed it) and the problem of "the overborne will" (Brooks 2000). In Japan, the conditions of interrogation — the duration and intensity of questioning, the duty to endure questioning even after the right to remain silent has been invoked, and the unavailability of defense lawyers to the vast majority of interrogated suspects — suggest that an "overborne will" is more than merely an occasional problem. Japanese courts rarely perceive the problem, seldom excluding confessions out of concern for "voluntariness" (Foote 1991:458). Comparison with American law is instructive. The milestone Miranda decision of 1966 aimed to dispel the compelling pressures inherent in custodial questioning. Thirty years later, a Boston police sergeant told me that Massachusetts law permits police to interrogate suspects only during the first three hours following arrest. In a 1944 case (*Ashcroft v. Tennessee*), the U.S. Supreme Court held that custody and interrogation of a criminal suspect for thirty- six hours is "inherently coercive." In the same case, dissenting Justice Robert Jackson articulated a position many Japanese prosecutors and judges espouse:

> To speak of any confessions of crime made after arrest as being "voluntary" or "un-coerced" is somewhat inaccurate, although traditional. A confession is wholly and uncontestably voluntary only if a guilty person gives himself up to the law and becomes his own accuser. The Court bases its decision [that the confession was coerced] on the premise that custody and examination of a prisoner for thirty-six hours is "inherently coercive." Of course it is. And so is custody and detention for one hour.

Jackson is right, of course: there is something involuntary about confessions that occur in the inherently compulsive atmosphere of an interrogation room. In criminal justice — and not just in Japan — it may well be that "the only true confessions are involuntary, somehow coerced" (Brooks 2000:32). But surely there are differences in degree, and surely the question is not just "is interrogation coercive?" but also "how coercive is it?" and "how is it coercive?"

We should also respect David Bayley's admonition to ask "compared with what?" In comparative perspective, interrogations in Japan are long, much longer than in the United States, where the vast majority of interrogations last less than one hour (Leo 1996). And interrogation in Japan is often grueling. As a Japanese detective sees it, "There aren't any confessions that are really voluntary. They're told that if they don't talk, they won't eat, won't smoke, won't meet with their families" (Miyazawa 1992:161). During the investigation of Obara Jōji, who ultimately was charged with the murder and dismemberment of Lucie Blackman, a twenty-two-year-old British bar hostess, interrogators acknowledged that "we go after him relentlessly until 11, 12 at night. We give him as little sleep as possible. We exhaust him physically and mentally. It's rough, but it's the only option remaining to us [because Obara refuses to confess]" (*Mainichi Daily News* 2/18/01).

United Nations committees on human rights have repeatedly rebuked the Japanese state for violating protocols about the length, location, and methods of interrogation; for excessive reliance on confessions for evidence; and for inadequate disclosure of evidence to the defense, leading many reformers to agree that Japan "cannot go on forever ignoring the counsel of the United Nations" (Hirano 1999:4). Even admirers of the Japanese way of justice acknowledge that "few suspects, innocent or not, have the fortitude to resist 23 days of interrogation" (Foote 1991:436).

Many Japanese prosecutors consider such critiques misleadingly Anglocentric. They are quick to counter that America and Great Britain are exceptional in their distrust of official authority and in their distaste for prolonged interrogation. Some dismiss critics' concerns as "nonsense" (Sasaki 2000:82), but the harshest critics tend to have decidedly non-Anglo origins (Hirano 1989; Ishimatsu 1989; H. Yamaguchi 1999). More to the point, comparative realities do not permit dismissal of Japan's confession issues. In addition to the United States, consider Holland, Germany, and France.

In Holland, dossiers play a central role throughout the criminal process, as they do in Japan, but with several significant differences. First, Dutch dossiers are less detailed, in part because investigators neglect many subjective aspects of the offense and offender that are considered cardinal in Japan's system of precise justice. This means Dutch interrogations can be — and are — shorter and less intrusive. At the same time, pretrial examinations are more open in Holland, to researchers and, more important, to the defense. Indeed, the investigative file is freely available to Dutch defendants and defense lawyers throughout the criminal process. The defense not only may examine the complete contents of the investigative record, they can even help construct it. As a result, dossiers in Holland are much less "one-sided" documents than they are in Japan (Peters 1992:281; Pizzi 1999:94).

With Germany, too, the comparative contrasts are stark. German prosecutors base their decisions almost exclusively on written information collected in dossiers, much as their Japanese and Dutch counterparts do (Blankenburg et al. 1978:350). But German prosecutors also exercise substantially more control over police investigations. More important, German law requires the prosecutor to investigate and prosecute every crime committed. Though this requirement has relaxed in recent years, even today it "gives the prosecutor no discretion in the most serious cases" (Feeney 1998:5). This principle of compulsory prosecution casts a long shadow over the pre-charge process. In particular, since German prosecutors need less evidence to charge, German investigators gather less evidence. Interrogations are, as a rule and a result, shorter, less intense, and less preoccupied with obtaining complete confessions. In one major study, German defendants "fully confessed" in only 41 percent of all trials and made a "partial confession" in another 26 percent (Frase 1990:637). We have seen that "full confession" rates at Japanese trials range around 93 percent. Not surprisingly, German acquittal rates are high, for most offenses even higher than those in the United States. At the same time, the defense's discovery rights are broader in Germany than in Japan, chiefly because the German defense lawyer's right to review dossiers extends to the entire investigative record, not (as in Japan) to the evidence prosecutors present at trial (Weigend 1999:195; Pizzi 1999:98). Access to the complete record enables German defendants to check, challenge, and change prosecutors' truth claims in ways Japanese defendants cannot.

The favorite country of comparison for Japanese prosecutors seems to be France (Fujinaga 1993:107), a democracy with "surprisingly little protection against police intrusions pursuant to an investigation" (Provine 1996:209). Even in France, however, there exist checks on investigators that are weak or absent in Japan. Internally, the French examining magistrate is supposed to supervise frontline investigators, though there is much disagreement about how effective the control is (Langbein and Weinreb 1978; Goldstein and Marcus 1978; Frase 1990). The clearer contrasts concern external control. France has been more willing than either Japan or the United States to "allow external review of their procedures for dealing with accused persons" (Provine 1996:219). The European Commission and Court on Human Rights has rendered several significant decisions stating that France must reform its highhanded investigative practices in order to better align itself with European standards. French judges have complied with such directives in numerous cases. So have French legislators. In 2001, for example, a new law took effect allowing lawyers to be present during the initial questioning of suspects (*Los Angeles Times* 1/1/01). At the same time, French defense lawyers have the right to review dossiers during the investigation, though the scope of that right has been subject to Ping-Pong-like expansions and contractions in recent years (Trouille 1994; A. West 2000). In short, even though France has one of the most intrusive, paternalistic criminal processes in Europe, in some respects even the French system employs more checks on investigators and interrogators than can be found in Japan.

It is difficult to generalize about five systems simultaneously. Nonetheless, the

comparative evidence from Holland, Germany, France, and the United States leads
to the conclusion that Japan stands out from these other democracies in the "precision" of its justice, in its reliance on confessions, and in the intensity and insularity
of its processes for obtaining admissions of guilt. The claim that rejects critiques of
Japan's reliance on confessions as "Anglocentric" must itself be rejected. In comparative perspective, Japan is exceptionally reliant on confessions and on the interrogations that produce them.

There is, however, a related claim that must be taken more seriously: to limit
the capacity of prosecutors and police to zealously seek confessions is to risk undermining the precondition for significant achievements in the Japanese way of justice.
The animating reality of "precise justice" is precisely the pursuit of confessions. Indeed, here is the procuracy's primary postulate: no confession, no truth, no consistency, no correction, no conviction, no justice. For the most part this premise has
served Japan well, as I have tried to describe in the preceding chapters. Criticizing
the system's reliance on confessions without considering the aims and attainments
that confessions serve is myopic, unfair, and inapt. This is not to condone the serious abuses described in this chapter; they cannot be excused and can be better pre-
vented (as I argue in the following section). In comparative research, however, elements selected for scrutiny must be examined within the context of the entire system
within which they operate (Frase 1990:664). As another comparativist noted, "A system for administering criminal justice is a detailed tapestry woven of many varied
threads. It is often difficult to understand the nature and significance of any particular fiber without at least a general appreciation of the function of the other threads,
and also a realization of the impact of the whole" (Pugh 1962:1).

Because the absence of a confession undermines other core commitments, especially the need to "uncover and clarify the truth" — the imperative presupposed by
all the other aims — prosecutors feel extreme pressure to obtain thorough admissions
of guilt. An ex-prosecutor has said, hyperbolically but tellingly, that "when indictment
looks impossible because a suspect refuses to confess even though the legal deadline
is fast approaching, the prosecutor feels like an inmate on death row counting the
hours to execution" (Sasaki 2000:38). The pressure to obtain confessions both reflects
and drives the demand for ever more detailed dossiers. Several prefectural police departments, including the Tokyo Metropolitan Police, have compared the amount of
paper that randomly selected police stations produced in burglary cases in 1978 and
1998. They "were stunned by what they learned" (*Asahi Shimbun* 8/22/00). In only
twenty years the number of documents increased fivefold and the number of pages
increased sevenfold. Other observers have noted the same trend in the procuracy and
judiciary, some calling it a "vicious circle" in which the production of more precision
begets demands for ever more detailed dossiers (Mitsui 1999:138).

Ironically, while criminal justice is becoming more precise and confessions
more important, confessions are getting harder to obtain (Sasaki 2000:123). Though
the change cannot be quantified, there is widespread agreement that "obtaining
statements through investigation has become more difficult" (Ugawa 1997:31; Ota
1999:276; Mitsui 1999:135). The causes are multiple. The public's "rights consciousness" has strengthened (Feldman 2000:39), and defense lawyers have become more
apt to advise their clients to exercise the right to remain silent (Takano 2001). This
"cancer" is greatly feared by investigators. One prominent prosecutor likens defense

lawyers' "inappropriate activities," such as advising clients to use their right to silence, to "a domino" which could cause the whole system to collapse (Ōta 1999:281).[17] At the same time, foreign suspects, who have long been less likely to confess than Japanese, constitute a far larger proportion of the criminal caseload than they did in 1990. Foreign suspects present prosecutors with a twofold problem: their confessions are harder to obtain, of course, but they also may "infect" Japanese suspects with alien, uncompliant attitudes.[18] Further, the significance of Japan's high conviction rate has sunk deeper into the country's collective consciousness. As one prosecutor has observed, suspects increasingly recognize that prosecutors "cannot charge without a confession" and that "if the evidence is not perfect, prosecutors will have extreme difficulty charging" (Ugawa 1997:31).

Whatever the causes, the increasing difficulty of obtaining confessions and the increasing "precision" of criminal justice have sounded an alarm. If confessions are the heart of Japanese justice, its pulse has started to slow. People — prosecutors, police, politicians, and the public — have noticed. Some believe the best response is to pursue confessions even more fervently because only this can preserve the system's considerable successes (Ōta 1999). Others think the system must ease its reliance on confessions by instituting reforms that make it legally possible to make cases through methods, such as plea-bargaining and immunity, that are anathema to many Japanese (Ugawa 1997). For the first time in a long time, Japan is confronting its capacity to do criminal justice differently.

Choices

> A legal system will do almost anything, tolerate almost anything, before it will admit the need for reform in its system of proof and trial.
>
> John Langbein, "Torture and Plea Bargaining"

> If there is not some kind of alternative to interrogation as a method for obtaining statements, it is greatly feared that in the future our country's criminal justice system may very well collapse.
>
> Prosecutor Ugawa Haruhiko, "Shihō Torihiki o Kangaeru"

17. There may be a corollary shift in the "rights consciousness" of prosecutors themselves, as younger prosecutors come to regard a suspect's right to remain silent as implying their own duty to leave the suspect alone. Although this is the view of some senior prosecutors, I find it implausible, in part because the abuses described in this chapter were committed by young prosecutors in the context of an organizational culture that compels and indulges aggressive interrogations. In fact, more prosecutors seem to agree with the senior colleague who told me "severe interrogations have become normal among young prosecutors. Many think the purpose of investigation is mainly to force confessions."

18. If Japan's most widely read newspaper column is an accurate index, many Japanese believe the country has already produced "a whole new breed of outsiders" who commit "acts of indiscriminate murder for the shakiest of motives" without seeming to feel "any guilt whatsoever" ("Vox Populi Vox Dei," *Asahi Shimbun* 9/20/99). In the late 1990s, a series of murders committed by Japanese youth helped generate a rhetoric reminiscent of American claims about youthful "superpredators" that led to reform of Japan's juvenile justice process.

One of the most articulate advocates for choosing change is prosecutor Ugawa Haruhiko (1997). Ugawa believes that unless significant reforms occur, the vicious circle of precise justice will implode, wreaking havoc on the criminal process. As he sees it,

> The most serious problem in our current system of criminal justice is rooted in the problem of criminal trials and investigations that have become immensely and un-necessarily precise. Prosecutors bear an extremely heavy burden of proof for estab-lishing the elements of a crime, including subjective elements. Not only that, the distinguishing characteristic of our country's criminal justice system is the demand for detailed proof. Until now, the method for satisfying this demand has been ob-taining statements through investigations [*torishirabe*]. . . . Prosecutors expend great energy on investigations. However, obtaining statements through investigation has recently become very difficult. . . . This is a matter of grave concern for traditional prosecutors who emphasize investigations, but because the environment around prosecutors is in the process of changing, it seems there is a need to take remedial measures that go beyond the merely psychological. . . . If there is not some kind of alternative to interrogation as a method for obtaining statements, it is greatly feared that in the future our country's criminal justice system may very well collapse.[19]

Thus, Ugawa believes criminal justice in Japan is both too precise and too re-liant on interrogation-induced confessions.[20] The system must change or break. It is easy to say "Stop relying on confessions so much" but it is difficult to do, Ugawa ob-serves, especially for the organized and organizational crimes that are hard to inves-tigate in the traditional, confession-centric way: corporate crimes, economic crimes, bribery, election law violations, and other white-collar offenses, and organized crimes by the *yakuza*, terrorist crimes by radical groups, and crimes of apocalyptic violence such as those committed by the Aum Shinrikyō religious organization. Citing Hi-rano Ryūichi, the dean of Japanese criminal justice scholars, Ugawa maintains that until alternatives to interrogation are introduced, many offenders who should be convicted will get off. His chosen reform? To legitimate the practice of plea-bargaining, so that prosecutors can practice it openly and often. Of course, Ugawa recognizes that many Japanese have "an allergic reaction" to plea-bargaining, but for them, and for critics who contend that bargains will undermine the system's com-mitment to truth and the procuracy's mission to construct it, Ugawa has an ironic re-

19. Ugawa has many supporters among his colleagues in the procuracy (Miyamoto and Sankei 2000). One executive said that "we need alternatives to confessions through interrogations, tools such as plea-bargaining and immunity. But in their absence we should not change the present system to make ob-taining confessions more difficult. That would be suicide" (personal interview, December 2000). Other prosecutors, including the man who believes the right to silence is a "cancer," regard plea-bargaining as anathema to the Japanese way of justice because it neglects and corrupts the truth (K. Satō 1974).

20. Ugawa's book-length analysis of plea-bargaining extends John Langbein's (1978) seminal argu-ment that the pursuit of too much truth and too many safeguards creates severe problems for a criminal justice system, as has occurred in the United States, which is dominated by coercive plea-bargaining, and in medieval Europe, where a sophisticated but gruesome law of torture was created in order to subvert laws of evidence that aimed to make wrongful convictions impossible. Viewed in the light of Langbein's analysis, the abuses described in this chapter may be considered "subterfuges" for dealing with problems of proof in Japanese criminal justice.

sponse. Plea-bargaining, he insists, especially offers of leniency to suspects whose co-operation will help solve other cases, is mainly a method for uncovering more truth in more cases. In the end, Ugawa feels compelled to clutch truth even as he tries to escape its too tight embrace. For this prosecutor as for many others, if the problem is too much truth, the solution must be justified in terms of its truth-telling capacity.

Ugawa identifies a major schism in Japanese criminal justice, a schism captured by satirist Jonathan Swift's quip that "laws are like cobwebs, which may catch small flies but let wasps and hornets break through." Swift's aphorism deftly depicts one of the hallmarks of the Japanese way of justice: that prosecutors work in a deeply dual-istic legal environment (Miyamoto and Sankei 2000). On the one hand, in "ordi-nary" cases of street crime the rules of criminal procedure confer so many powers on investigators that they are able to control the criminal process and "make" cases far more easily than investigators in the United States and elsewhere. On the other hand, investigators in Japan lack many of the procedural powers—such as the au-thority to plea-bargain, offer immunity, or conduct undercover operations—that are routinely used in the United States and elsewhere to "make" cases against elite of-fenders. This dualism renders Japan's Code of Criminal Procedure a cobweb, highly enabling of efforts to indict and convict run-of-the-mill offenders—Swift's "small flies"—but simultaneously disabling of efforts to bring certain "wasps and hornets" to justice (D. Johnson 1999).

As I noted in chapter 5, a central tenet in the sociology of law is that "downward law is greater than upward law" (Black 1976:21). This theorem asserts that more law gets directed at low-ranking people than at high-ranking ones. If the proposition ap-plies to all societies and at all times, as its proponents claim and as appears to be true, then one might suppose Japan is nothing special, since all societies are marked by the same legal schism. That conclusion is wrong; Japan does stand out. Downward law may everywhere be greater than upward law, but what is striking about Japan is just how much greater the downward law is. The fact of legal schizophrenia is not peculiar to Japan but the magnitude is.

Mending the cobweb is difficult because the dualism of Japanese law creates a dilemma for legal reform. To institutionalize more legal levers so that prosecutors and police can better investigate white-collar crimes is to exacerbate the already ex-treme imbalance of power between the state and the defense in the criminal process. Is that fair? Yet to leave the system alone, as has been done since the occupation, is to absolve many elites of accountability for their crimes (Hirano 1999). Forbidding particular investigative techniques (such as plea-bargaining, immunity, undercover stings, and wiretaps) is tantamount to sanctioning high levels of the types of of-fenses—white-collar especially—that those techniques are best able to control (Hey-mann 1985). Is that just?

These are difficult choices, and I leave it to Japan to determine whether its legal cobweb should be tolerated or mended (and if mended, how). I believe, however, that prosecutors could embrace three changes that would make their good system better. Prosecutors could, and should, relax the trial sufficiency charging policy; videotape interrogations and urge police to do likewise; and disclose more evidence to the defense prior to trial. These reforms would mitigate third-degree abuses and the problem of prosecutor essays. The last two, which empower the defense to uncover and clarify the truth, may also help diminish the schism that defines Japan's legal dualism.

Relaxing the charging standard is the most difficult proposal to defend. As chapter 7 explained, the policy to charge only "certain to convict" cases has a host of consequences, many (such as parsimony in the use of criminal sanctions) laudable. But the costs are large. Many victims do not get the day in court they desire, the "principle of trial-centered justice" gets swallowed by the reality of investigation-centered practice, and the infrequency of acquittals renders every acquittal significant and thereby stimulates the pursuit of ever-increasing precision through ever-increasing reliance on interrogation-induced confessions (Mitsui 1999:141). The conservative charging policy and the high conviction rate have long been a source of prosecutor pride, but even prosecutors recognize that they are a source of some of the system's biggest problems. An ex-prosecutor has summarized the misgivings of many of her former colleagues:

> As I have said repeatedly, the big objective of our code of criminal procedure is the clarification of truth. There are two aspects to the "principle of actual truth" [which forms the foundation of our system]: a passive face to not convict the innocent, and an active face to accurately punish the guilty. Screening that is too cautious tries so hard to achieve the passive aim that it slights the active one. . . Justice weeps when suspects who stubbornly refuse to confess go uncharged. Above all, courts should decide from the evidence whether or not to convict. Guilt and innocence are not matters that prosecutors should decide beforehand. I dare to offer this unpleasant advice because I love the procuracy. In this era when everything is undergoing bewildering change, I think the procuracy—which has been blessed with good human resources and a noble tradition—cannot help but change. (Sasaki 2000:152)

Relaxing the charging standard could satisfy more victims, invigorate defense attorneys, enliven the "empty rituals" that most criminal trials have become, educate the public, and reduce the incentives to compel confessions through questionable or illegal tactics. In short, a relaxed standard may make Japanese criminal justice less precise but more just.

My other two proposals — to videotape interrogations and to disclose more evidence to the defense — would create much-needed external checks on prosecutors and police by opening their investigations to outside scrutiny. In Japan, "transparency" has been to the 1990s what "internationalization" was to the 1980s: a real but unrealized aspiration. But even by Japanese standards the procuracy remains a singularly opaque agency. Ironically, it is less transparent now than it was before the Occupation, when prosecutors were required to disclose all dossiers to the defense, not just the statements they submitted as evidence at trial.

The procuracy has worked hard to delimit the defense's rights to discovery. Its justifications have been successful but self-serving. For an organization that trumpets truth-telling so much, it is ironic that the procuracy opposes disclosing to the defense more of the building blocks — the draft dossiers especially — that its operators use to construct the truth. We have seen that discovery rights are more restricted in Japan than in the United States, Holland, and Germany. Japan could do better and it did better in the prewar years. The proper scope of discovery rights and disclosure obligations has been discussed since the mid-1970s, with little improvement in defendants' actual access to draft dossiers. The present system relies inordinately on the goodwill of prosecutors to disclose relevant evidence (though occasionally they are spurred by "recommendations" from the bench). In many cases this leaves defense attorneys in the passive position of hoping that prosecutors do not withhold exonerating, mitigating, or otherwise relevant evidence. Though there are few worries for those who trust prosecutors to do the right thing, for those who fear that power tends to injure before it warns, prosecutors need to be better regulated (Mitsui 1999:152). Their fear is founded in fact. Many of the worst miscarriages in Japanese criminal justice occur when prosecutors withhold evidence from the defense and the bench (C. Johnson 1972; Foote 1993c). Reform will require legislative action, but since criminal justice legislation ordinarily originates in the Ministry of Justice, which is run by prosecutors, the procuracy must first recognize that fuller disclosure would serve the interests of truth and justice.

Finally, investigators in Japan—prosecutors and police—should tape-record custodial interrogations, as their counterparts must or commonly do in other democracies, such as England, Canada, Australia, and parts of America.[21] The need is all the greater in Japan, where interrogations are long and the right to silence is all but meaningless for many interrogated suspects. Some critics of the current system believe Japan can best confront its confession problems by creating its own Miranda rules (Takano 2001). The push for a Japanese Miranda is understandable but misplaced. In America, Miranda's home, interrogators routinely outsmart suspects by creatively evading the spirit, if not the letter, of the law, leading one expert to conclude that "even if Miranda-like requirements were implemented in Japan, they would not be likely to change the behavior of suspects under interrogation, police [or prosecutor] methods of questioning, or, more generally, the cultural significance of confession" (Leo 2001). In short, Miranda is unlikely to dispel the inherent coercion of sustained interrogation or to empower suspects to terminate interrogation by asserting their right to silence. Such aims will be realized only if other rules (such as the duty to endure questioning) are changed too. That seems unlikely.

Recording custodial interrogations would be more feasible and more effective than Mirandizing Japan.[22] As a medium for preserving the truth of interrogations

21. Videotaping became mandatory in England in 1986, in Alaska in 1985, and Minnesota in 1994. In Alaska and Minnesota, the state supreme courts mandated the requirement. In about a dozen other states, lawyers have tried to get state supreme courts to do the same but the courts have refused, saying it is the province of the legislature. The most serious legislative attempt to establish videotaping occurred in Illinois in 1999–2000. It failed. State legislatures in California, Florida, and Connecticut have had similar but smaller movements that also failed. As of 1990, about one-third of all American police departments serving populations of fifty thousand or greater videotaped at least some interrogations. In a nationwide survey, not a single American police department regretted the decision to videotape (Geller 1998:312). In Europe, at least six nations require the tape-recording of some or all interrogations (A. West 2000).

22. The benefits of taping interrogations are becoming increasingly apparent to people in Japan. In an argument for ensuring speedier trials, one major newspaper observed that "it always takes time to determine whether a confession has been made voluntarily and whether it is credible, so all such matters should be recorded on audiovisual equipment in order that defense lawyers can verify how their client was questioned" before being taken to court (*Asahi Shimbun* 10/15/00). For an argument about the feasibility and desirability of videotaping interrogations in Japan, see Leo (2001).

and confessions, video- and audiotaping serve the Japanese system's cardinal objective, a fact some observers are beginning to appreciate. Moreover, a recording requirement is a nonadversarial reform that would not structurally alter the balance of advantage between prosecution and defense. In fact, taping serves the interest of all parties in the criminal process. It obviously benefits suspects and defense attorneys, by deterring impermissible interrogation techniques and thereby affording suspects better protection against wrongful convictions based on false confessions. But interrogators — prosecutors and police — benefit too. Tapes protect them against false accusations of impropriety or abuse by creating a record they can use to demonstrate misrepresentations. Tapes also improve the quality of interrogations, by enabling investigators to spot inconsistencies or to show one offender's confession to an uncooperative co-offender. An impact study in America found that "the vast majority" of police departments that videotape interrogations believe "videotaping has led to improvements in police interrogations" (Geller 1998:307). It has been argued that recording costs too much time and money, but the opposite may be true since tapes obviate the need for a second person to be present to take notes and reduce the time interrogators must spend testifying in court.

Mandatory recording also benefits prosecutors and judges by giving them the information they need to assess the voluntariness and veracity of confessions. As a result, prosecutors could make more informed decisions about whom and what to charge, and judges could make more informed decisions about the admissibility of evidence and ultimate guilt. In the same American study, prosecutors were "in virtually unanimous agreement that videotaping helped them assess the state's case and prepare for trial." Ironically, defense attorneys' opinions of videotapes were more mixed, primarily because they believe tapes give the state "a strategic edge." Still, the weight of opinion among American criminal justice practitioners familiar with videotaping "seems clearly positive." Fully 97 percent of police departments that have ever videotaped find it, on balance, "useful" (Geller 1998:312). For Japan, too, electronically recorded interrogations would promote the goals of accuracy in fact-finding, procedural fairness, public respect for the system, and external accountability. These are compelling objectives. If Japan is to make its good system better, the last aim especially — accountability — must be pursued more seriously (Foote 1999).

The reasons for resisting recording are unconvincing. The number and duration of interrogations would create a large volume of information but not necessarily a large volume of physical material. Police departments in Japan and elsewhere have managed to monitor streets and traffic with video equipment, and without significant storage problems. In the age of cyberspace and in a country like Japan, the technological obstacles to taping are less formidable than the human ones. To opponents of recording who believe "busy defense lawyers" would not bother to view or listen to all of the tapes (Sasaki 2000:82), one can only reply: So what? Prosecutor Ōta Shigeru (1999:279), another advocate for maintaining the status quo, builds his argument on a foundation that consists of a rightful respect for the positive role confessions have played in Japanese criminal justice and a wrongful premise about how confessions are obtained. Ōta speaks for many of his peers when he says that in Japan's system of criminal justice police and prosecutors stand together on the principle of discovering the actual truth. They gather not only active evidence [of guilt] but also passive evidence [of mitigation and innocence], and they carefully scrutinize all of it before deciding whether or not to charge. Interrogators do not 'compel confessions'; they 'seek them in order to obtain the truth.'

In most cases, the "principle of discovering the actual truth" is important to Japanese prosecutors. Respect for this precept has helped them generate many of the achievements described in this book. Similarly, in most cases prosecutors do "carefully scrutinize" both inculpating and exculpating evidence. In these respects Ōta is right. However, the distinction between "compelling" and "seeking" confessions on which he and other prosecutors rely fails to reflect the reality of criminal interrogation. The Japanese expression for "let them talk" (*iwaseru*) is the same as the expression for "make them talk." Inside the interrogation room, however, the difference between the two realities must be maintained. Taping interrogations enables people outside the room to define and enforce this crucial distinction (Mitsui 1999:141). Making the distinction more openly could make the Japanese way of justice more distinguished than it already is.

Conclusion

Each time I work I am ready without a moment's hesitation to undo all
that I did the day before because each day I have the impression that I see
further.

David Williams, *Japan*

Reality is created out of confusion and contradiction, and if you exclude
those elements, you're no longer talking about reality.

Murakami Haruki, *The Tokyo Gas Attack*
and the Japanese Psyche

In writing this book I have often felt I should undo yesterday's work because today
I see farther. Indeed, if I were to begin this project anew, the result would no doubt
differ. I have also discovered that to know more is to become less capable of general-
ization. Criminal justice is complicated, and evidence often resists neat, summary
formulas. I have tried to include in this book some of the confusion and contradiction
that is prosecution in Japan. I fear, however, that the result is tidier than it should be.

The anthropologist Ruth Benedict (1946:1) once noted that "the Japanese have
been described in the most fantastic series of 'but also's' ever used for any nation in
the world."[1] In concluding this book I must speak in a different set of "but also's," less
provocative than those Benedict proposed but necessary qualifications nonetheless.
Japan is paradise for a prosecutor, but it also forbids powers — such as grants of immunity and undercover stings — that are taken for granted by prosecutors elsewhere.
Chapter 1 could have been called "*Almost* Paradise for a Prosecutor"; it nearly was.
Similarly, prosecutors play a more pivotal role in Japanese criminal justice than in
other criminal justice systems, but they also display deep interdependencies with

---

1. "The Japanese," Benedict (1946:1) argued, are "the most alien enemy the United States ever
fought in all-out struggle." They are, "to the highest degree, both aggressive and unaggressive, both mili-
taristic and aesthetic, both insolent and polite, rigid and adaptable, submissive and resentful of being
pushed around, loyal and treacherous, brave and timid, conservative and hospitable to new ways." Although Benedict overstated the "Japanese" differences and disregarded significant variation among
Japanese people, the core of her claim rings true: to understand Japan, it is necessary to take into account
"different habits of acting and thinking."

other members of the criminal court community—particularly police and judges. And Japan's prosecutor culture stresses the goals of invoking remorse, rehabilitating and reintegrating offenders, and repairing relations between offenders and their victims, but it also deems desert and deterrent values centrally important.

There is more complexity. The Japanese way of organizing prosecution enables like cases to be treated alike, but the mechanisms for doing so permit managers to control decisions in ways that favor friends, punish enemies, and undermine consistency. Prosecutors in Japan use other mechanisms—especially leniency and instruction—to correct offenders, but leniency is so limited that old, homeless men can be sentenced to three years in prison for stealing four dollars, and instruction is sometimes used to hector victims who want nothing more than their voices heard and their offenders called to account. Japan's high conviction rate is said to reflect a system that is badly biased against defendants, but the scarcity of acquittals is mainly a function of the procuracy's conservative charging policy, whereby many offenders who would be charged in other systems are not indicted at all. Although the high conviction rate is lauded and lamented, its consequences are, in fact, deeply ambiguous. Finally, confessions are in many ways the bedrock of Japanese criminal justice and the basis for its considerable achievements, whether consistency, corrections, or convictions, but some confessions are obtained in ways that belie the "truth through confession" premise which is supposed to animate the system.

In short, this portrait of Japanese justice includes much "confusion and contradiction" because that is what the available evidence requires. Like any portrait, this one is framed by assumptions about what does and does not matter. Unavoidably, much—and much that others consider important—has been omitted.[2] After six years of reflecting and writing about what I discovered during thirty-three months in the field, this portrait remains a pale reflection of reality. What it reflects, I hope, is that the Japanese way of justice seeks confessions, consistency, corrections, and convictions, and often obtains them, but also . . .

An eminent American scholar once told me that every comparativist is either a "lumper" predisposed to finding family resemblances across countries and cases, or else a "splitter" inclined to seek and stress differences. This dichotomy, unfortu-

2. One omission is the question of corruption in Japanese criminal justice. Foreign observers have failed to notice the problem (Bayley 1991; Parker 1984; Ames 1981), but the creation of slush funds (*uragane*) by cooking the books through illegal accounting (*fusei keiri*) has been practiced for decades by Japanese police (Ochiai 2000; Terasawa 1998; Matsuhashi 1994). It appears that prosecutors have done likewise, which helps explain why they overlook slush fund crimes committed in other parts of the bureaucracy. Between 1980 and 1999, prosecutors received eleven complaints about illegal accounting in various state agencies (these are just the complaints they accepted; prosecutors refused to receive many more). Of the nine cases they have decided, all ended in "no indictment" (*Asahi Shimbun* 2/24/99).

While this book was in press, investigative reporters revealed that the procuracy receives about $2 million each year for special "information gathering" and "investigative activities." Neither prosecutors nor their bosses in the Ministry of Justice are obligated to divulge how the money is spent. The reporters found that Kanō Shunsuke, chief prosecutor (*kenjisei*) of the Osaka District Prosecutors Office, embezzled $30 to $50 thousand from this account when he was chief prosecutor of the Kōchi District Prosecutors Office between July 1995 and July 1996. Kanō is said to have spent the money on meals at high-class restaurants, entertainment at bars and nightclubs, and golf. The misspent money was mobilized by

nately, is all too evident in social research about Japan. With few exceptions, accounts of Japan — and law in Japan — fall into two polarized camps. Either Japan is sui generis, a paradoxical enigma that cannot be understood using the customary tools of analysis (Haley 1991), or else it is a normal country for which there is no need to create a special category (Ramseyer and Nakazato 1999). The Japan I see is neither, or perhaps it is both. In comparative criminal justice research there is ample room for "splumpers."

When I began this research in the early 1990s, Japan was widely hailed as "number one" (Vogel 1979), poised, as one author put it, to "overtake the United States by the year 2000" (Fingleton 1995). Times have changed. During the "lost decade" of the 1990s, Japan failed to confront a host of problems, from high unemployment to high school exam hell and from bad debt to bad leadership. As I conclude this project, many commentators are cataloging "the dysfunctions that dominate an unhappy and declining country," and the American media routinely celebrate American exceptionalism by reveling in Japan's problems (Samuels 2001). In less than a decade, attention has shifted from explaining Japan's "miracles" to expounding how the country "went bonk" (Kerr 2001:5).

Japanese criminal justice does have problems. Investigations are highly intrusive and sometimes coercive. Truth is fabricated, corrupted, and concealed. Mistakes are made. Bias exists. Prosecutors are unaccountable and defense lawyers are all but impotent. Victims are sacrificed at the conviction rate altar. Most fundamentally, the system is so hostile to outside scrutiny that it remains impossible to see or say what many of the problems are.

Nevertheless, Japan as mirror reflects images of American criminal justice that prompt, in me at least, more deliberation than celebration. Many values in the Japanese way of justice — truth, individualization, consistency — are not peculiarly Japanese; they are shared, in the abstract at least, by thoughtful people everywhere, and they are served well, if imperfectly, by criminal justice in Japan. At a time when many Americans believe there is one right way — the American — and Japan is seen as the land of the setting sun, it is worth considering the possibility that American criminal justice works worse than criminal justice in Japan. If criminal justice is one of the principal indicators of the character of a society, this is no small matter.

---

subordinates who concealed the embezzlement in a second set of account books. It appears that this misconduct led to leniency toward other white-collar offenders. In May 2000, after a three-year investigation into alleged embezzlement by twenty-five officials in the Osaka prefectural government, prosecutors in Osaka found "insufficient evidence" to indict three of the twenty-five officials but adequate proof to charge the other twenty-two with crimes. None was indicted. "In consideration of extenuating circumstances" (the embezzlers returned the stolen loot during the course of the investigation), prosecutors suspended charges against all the wrongdoers. Frontline prosecutors wanted to proceed to trial, but their boss — the same Kanō — killed the cases at *kessai* (*Uwasa no Shinsō* 2/01).

During interviews I conducted in February 2001, three prosecutors admitted that some managers and executives "misuse money," though two insisted that the situation has "improved in the last few years." The Japanese media seldom touch this issue. For an exception, see the article in the weekly magazine *Shūkan Gendai* (5/22/99), disclosing statements by an anonymous whistleblower about slush fund abuses in the procuracy.

Finally, Japan-watchers often excoriate or extol that country without any comparative basis for their normative judgments. This comparison of prosecution in Japan and the United States suggests that Americans who care about the quality of criminal justice in their own country have cause for discomfort when they look in the Japanese mirror. If justice means taking into account the needs and circumstances of individuals, then Japanese prosecutors must receive higher marks than their American counterparts. If justice means treating equals equally, then the ability of Japan's procuracy to do so is impressive. If justice should promote healing, not just punishment, then Japanese prosecutors must be reckoned more restorative than prosecutors in Seattle, Minneapolis, or Oakland. And if doing justice requires clarifying facts, then readers will recognize how material this maxim is deemed to be in Japan.

Many liberals, American and Japanese, are unwilling to tolerate the powers invested in Japanese prosecutors and the intrusions on autonomy countenanced by criminal justice in Japan. I share similar concerns. My concerns, however, are not grave enough to change the normative bottom line: the Japanese way of justice is uncommonly just.

Appendix

The Survey: Prosecutors' Attitudes and Activities

Between January 1994 and May 1995, this survey was administered to 235 Japanese prosecutors. It was first given to 40 prosecutors (*kenji*) and assistant prosecutors (*fuku kenji*) in the Kobe District Prosecutors Office, after which a snowball sampling method generated an additional 195 responses from prosecutors in twenty-four other offices.

Part 1: Background Questions

Please answer the following questions.

1. Age? (as of 1/1/94 or 1/1/95, depending on date of survey)
2. Sex?
3. Birthplace? (city, prefecture, town, village, . . .)
4. In what cities or towns did you live most of your life before you turned eighteen?
5. College? Department? Specialization?
6. Year passed bar exam? Year became a prosecutor? Year entered this office?
7. Father's occupation?
   a. legal professional
   b. public official
   c. company employee
   d. self-employed
   e. other
8. Mother's occupation?
   a. legal professional
   b. public official

      c. company employee
      d. self-employed
      e. housewife
      f. other

9. Current position in this prosecutors office? Section (*bu*)? Position (*gakari*)? Special responsibilities (*tantō*)?
10. On the average, how many hours do you work each week?
11. What were your motivations for becoming a prosecutor?

Part 2: Prosecutor Work Objectives

Below are questions about prosecutor work objectives. Using the following answer scale, circle the answer you consider most appropriate.

Answer Scale.   Please use these four standards to indicate how important you believe it is to try to achieve the following objectives when disposing of cases:

4 — A very important objective
3 — Not as important as 4, but still an important objective
2 — A not very important objective
1 — Not an objective

1. Reducing the crime rate
2. Maximizing the punishment imposed on criminals
3. Discovering the truth about the case
4. Not prosecuting the innocent, and prosecuting and convicting only those who have really committed crimes
5. Treating like cases alike, and disposing of them equally
6. Disposing efficiently of as many cases as possible
7. Prosecuting and convicting as many cases as I can
8. Having the public understand that the prosecutors office is responding properly to crime
9. Rehabilitating and reintegrating offenders
10. Invoking remorse in the offender
11. Invoking condemnation in the public for the crime and/or criminal, in order to rehabilitate criminals and prevent crime
12. Repairing relationships between the offender and the victim and victim's family, by recommending restitution (*jidan*) and the like
13. Maintaining and improving the reputation and prestige of the prosecutors office
14. Maintaining good, cooperative relations with the police
15. Giving offenders the punishment they deserve
16. Respecting the rights of suspects
17. Protecting the public from criminals

Part 3: Suspension of Prosecution

Part A. This section asks questions about the suspension of prosecution (*kiso yūyo*). Please note that the questions in this section concern only the suspension of prosecution; they do not ask about other reasons for not prosecuting, such as insufficient evidence. Using the following scale, please circle the answer that best corresponds to your opinion.

Answer Scale:

> 5 — Strongly agree
> 4 — Mildly agree
> 3 — Cannot say either way
> 2 — Mildly disagree
> 1 — Strongly disagree

1. Deciding whether or not to suspend prosecution is a difficult decision.
2. Compared to prosecuting a case, suspending prosecution saves time and effort.
3. In some cases, suspending prosecution better helps to rehabilitate and reintegrate offenders than does prosecution.
4. I sometimes suspend prosecution in order to save my time and effort for other cases.
5. The decision whether or not to suspend prosecution is one of the most important judgments a prosecutor makes.
6. At *kessai*, the supervising prosecutor and the frontline prosecutor frequently talk about whether or not to suspend prosecution.
7. When I suspend prosecution, I usually make the offender promise to observe some conditions after non-prosecution, such us making restitution to the victim or the like.
8. After suspending prosecution, I obtain information about the suspect's behavior following the non-prosecution.
9. Deciding whether or not to suspend prosecution is one of the most rewarding, meaningful parts of my job.
10. Japan's prosecutors suspend prosecution too often in cases which should be prosecuted.

Part B. When you are investigating a case and think that suspending prosecution is a possible disposition, how important are the following factors in determining whether or not to suspend prosecution? Using the answer scale, please circle the answer that corresponds most closely to your opinion.

Answer Scale:

> 3 — Important factor
> 2 — Depending on the case, sometimes important and sometimes not
> 1 — Not an important factor

1. Suspect's prior criminal record
2. Suspect's age
3. Suspect's marital status
4. Suspect's family ties
5. Suspect's occupational and social status
6. Damage done by the offense
7. Suspect's motive
8. Likelihood of re-offending
9. Suspect's prior relationship with victim
10. Level of punishment prescribed by law
11. Whether suspect repents
12. Victim's feelings about punishment
13. Whether suspect compensates victim (*higai benshō, jidan,* etc.)
14. Opinion of police in charge of case
15. Effect prosecution would have on the suspect in the future — would suspect re-offend, lose job, etc. . . .
16. Public reaction and opinion about the offense
17. How much suspect cooperates with police and prosecutors during investigation
18. Suspect's demeanor during interrogation (is he polite, remorseful, etc.)

Part 4: Miscellaneous Questions

Using the answer scale below, please circle the answer to each question that best corresponds to your opinion.

Answer Scale:

5 — Strongly agree
4 — Mildly agree
3 — Neutral
2 — Mildly disagree
1 — Strongly disagree

1. Most people charged with serious crimes should be punished whether or not the punishment benefits the criminal.
2. It is important to sentence each offender on the basis of his individual needs and not on the basis of the crime he has committed.
3. The frequent use of suspended prosecutions and suspended sentences is wrong because it has the effect of minimizing the gravity of the offense committed.
4. Prisons should be places of punishment.
5. The failure to punish crimes amounts to giving a license to commit them.
6. Most people are deterred from crime by the threat of heavy penalties.

7. Most criminal behavior is the result of forces largely beyond the control of the offender.

8. Our present treatment of criminals is too harsh.

9. The most important single consideration in determining the sentence to impose should be the nature and gravity of the offense.

10. Cooperative defendants who confess, and thus save the state investigative and trial resources, should be given as lenient a disposition as possible.

11. Most people charged with serious crimes should be kept in jail until their trial, even if they have stable jobs and family lives.

12. People with stable jobs and family lives should not be detained prior to trial.

13. Because it is necessary to give suspects and defendants a taste of prison, bail should not be granted.

14. Because recent court decisions tend to place too much emphasis on protecting the rights of suspects, if they are allowed to continue, society will be endangered. Thus, the court decisions should be changed.

15. It is better to let ten guilty persons go free than to convict one innocent person.

16. Recent court decisions expanding the rights of defendants are basically sound.

17. Speeding up the criminal process will bring about unjust, inappropriate results.

18. Criminal procedure should be reformed so that it moves more quickly.

19. Handling the administrative challenges involved in my criminal court work is as satisfying as handling the legal challenges.

20. The criminal court should be run like a business.

21. In the handling of criminal cases, efficiency is important as an end in itself.

22. In deciding whether to charge a suspect with a crime, one of the most important factors I consider is the suspect's attitude: Does he repent of his crime and promise not to commit any more crimes?

23. In deciding whether to charge a suspect with a crime, one of the most important factors I consider is the victim's attitude: Does he forgive the offender and want him to be treated leniently, or does he want the offender severely punished?

24. Whether or not a suspect has made *jidan* (restitution) with a victim has a big influence on how the suspect's case is treated.

25. When a suspect does not confess, disposing of the case is much more difficult and time-consuming.

26. Suspects usually benefit by confessing; that is, suspects who confess get treated more leniently by prosecutors and judges.

27. My job would be more interesting and enjoyable if fewer suspects confessed.

28. The police do most of the important investigative work in almost all cases.

29. One of my most important responsibilities is to help rehabilitate offenders.
30. It is important to individualize the treatment of each suspect.
31. When a case that he has handled results in acquittal, the investigative (*sōsa*) prosecutor's career will suffer.
32. When a case that he has handled results in acquittal, the trial (*kōhan*) prosecutor's career will suffer.
33. I have learned a lot from *kessai* consultations.
34. I feel free to express my opinion candidly at *kessai*, regardless of whether it is popular or likely to be accepted by the *kessai* prosecutor.
35. *Kessai* is a pain in the butt.
36. At *kessai*, I rarely have disagreements with the *kessai* prosecutor.
37. When there is a disagreement at *kessai*, the *kessai* prosecutor's opinion usually prevails.
38. *Kessai* may be helpful for new, inexperienced prosecutors, but it is unnecessary for veteran prosecutors.
39. Prosecutors should screen cases less seriously, not prosecute only cases which are certain to result in conviction, and allow judges to make more of the important decisions, even if it means the acquittal rate increases substantially.
40. Acquittals are rare at trials because prosecutors are concerned that acquittals will hurt their reputations and careers.
41. Acquittals are rare at trials because prosecutors do not prosecute borderline cases in order to protect the rights of suspects.
42. Acquittals are rare at trials because the *kessai* system screens out most cases that might result in acquittal.
43. Generally, prosecutors who have prosecuted cases that result in acquittals do not get promoted very high.
44. Suspects should be permitted to have a defense attorney present during interrogation.
45. Defense attorneys should meet more often with their clients during the investigative period.
46. I feel very busy almost all of the time at work.
47. I have to process so many cases that I cannot devote as much attention to investigating each case as I would like.
48. Some prosecutors have much heavier caseloads than others.
49. Most of the time I am so busy that I do not have time to think about how to rehabilitate or reintegrate the offender.
50. A crucial part of my job is to keep the cases moving.
51. I am too busy to individualize treatment of each suspect, so I have to treat each suspect impersonally.
52. Generally, I have very good relationships with police and detectives.
53. Generally, police follow my instructions closely.
54. Police frequently ask me for advice about how to deal with cases and suspects.
55. I frequently talk to police about particular suspects and cases.

56. Defense attorneys generally do a good job of defending their clients.
57. Sometimes I engage in "plea-bargaining" (that is, tell a suspect I will treat him more leniently [suspend prosecution, seek only a fine, . . .] in exchange for a confession).
58. Suspects think that prosecutors will treat them more leniently if they confess and display remorse.
59. When I am deciding what to do with a particular suspect, I often think about what the Prosecution Review Commission (*kensatsu shinsakai*) might do if I do not prosecute.
60. The Prosecution Review Commission has almost no influence on the decision-making of prosecutors.
61. Prosecutors generally deal with suspects too leniently.
62. One of the major reasons Japan has a low crime rate is because prosecutors do their job very well.
63. Transfers are one of the things I least like about my job.
64. Prosecutor investigations usually simply check and supplement police investigations.
65. I like working as a *sōsa kenji* (investigating prosecutor) more than working as a *kōhan kenji* (trial prosecutor).
66. *Sōsa kenji* usually try hard to avoid saddling *kōhan kenji* with difficult cases.
67. *Sōsa kenji* should not prosecute cases that will be difficult for *kōhan kenji* to prove at trial.
68. *Sōsa kenji* and *kōhan kenji* frequently consult about cases that they both are handling.
69. Acquittals are rare because before prosecuting, the prosecutor clarifies what the truth is and gathers sufficient evidence to convict.
70. When trying to solve a problem concerning application of the law, and when deciding whether or not to prosecute, I depend on precedents and previous disposition records.
71. I often rely on trial precedents when deciding the *kyūkei* (recommended sentence).
72. Generally speaking, subordinates in this office feel completely free to discuss all aspects of their work with their superiors.
73. Formal manuals and rules are very important sources of information on how to do our job.
74. Policies in the office seem to change frequently.
75. Prosecutors have relatively complete and accurate information when they make most decisions in this office.
76. Due to differences in personality, philosophy, or religion, different people sometimes dispose of similar cases differently.
77. I usually do not consider public opinion when I decide what position to take on a case.
78. It is impossible to discover general rules about the job of prosecuting attorney, because each suspect and each crime are to some degree unique.

79. In most cases that go to trial, the defense attorney makes a vigorous defense of his client.
80. Prosecutors should charge only cases that will definitely end in conviction.
81. Swift and certain punishment is a key to solving the problem of crime in our society.
82. Generally speaking, criminals should be punished severely.
83. Generally speaking, suspended sentences are not effective for the rehabilitation of offenders.
84. The prosecutors office takes into sufficient consideration the rights of foreign suspects.
85. I usually try to convince the police of the appropriateness of a disposition before making that disposition.
86. Some people are so antisocial that they must be isolated in order to protect society.
87. There is really not much difference between the personality, values, and way of thinking of the average person we prosecute and the average person on the street.
88. In a case which will clearly result in conviction, if a suspect denies the facts and does not express remorse, this influences the sentence we recommend.
89. Japan has a serious crime problem.
90. I am very satisfied with my job as a prosecutor.
91. I feel that my workload is too heavy and that I cannot satisfactorily finish it in a normal workday.
92. I feel that I am not fully trained to handle my job.
93. I sacrifice my family because of my job.
94. The amount of work I have to do often cuts down on the quality of my work.
95. I feel unable to influence the decisions of superiors concerning matters like case dispositions and personnel changes.
96. I will remain a prosecutor until I retire.
97. I am glad I became a prosecutor.

References

Western-Language Publications

Abe, Haruo. 1963. "The Accused and Society: Therapeutic and Preventive Aspects of Criminal Justice in Japan." In Arthur von Mehren, ed. *Law in Japan: The Legal Order in a Changing Society*. Cambridge, Mass.: Harvard University Press.

Abegglen, James C., and George Stalk, Jr. 1985. *Kaisha: The Japanese Corporation*. New York: Basic Books.

Abel, Richard, and P. Lewis, eds. 1988. *Lawyers in Society*. 3 vols. Berkeley: University of California Press.

Abrams, Norman. 1975. "Prosecutorial Charge Decision Systems." *UCLA Law Review* 23: 1–56.

Abrams, Norman. 1971. "Internal Policy: Guiding the Exercise of Prosecutorial Discretion." *UCLA Law Review* 29:1–58.

Abramson, Jeffrey. 1994. *We, the Jury: The Jury System and the Ideal of Democracy*. New York: Basic Books.

Adler, Stephen J. 1994. *The Jury: Trial and Error in the American Courtroom*. New York: Times Books.

Albonetti, Celesta A. 1987. "Prosecutorial Discretion: The Effects of Uncertainty." *Law & Society Review* 21, no. 2:291–313.

Aldous, Christopher. 1997. *The Police in Occupation Japan: Control, Corruption and Resistance to Reform*. London: Routledge.

Allen, Francis A. 1996. *The Habits of Legality: Criminal Justice and the Rule of Law*. New York: Oxford University Press.

Allen, Francis A. 1981. *The Decline of the Rehabilitative Ideal: Penal Policy and Social Purpose*. New Haven, Conn.: Yale University Press.

Alschuler, Albert W. 1975. "The Defense Attorney's Role in Plea Bargaining." *Yale Law Journal* 84, no. 6 (May):1179–1314.

Alschuler, Albert W. 1968. "The Prosecutor's Role in Plea Bargaining." *University of Chicago Law Review* 36:50–112.

Amar, Akhil Reed. 1997. *The Constitution and Criminal Procedure: First Principles*. New Haven, Conn.: Yale University Press.

Ames, Walter L. 1981. *Police and Community in Japan*. Berkeley: University of California Press.

Amnesty International. 1998. *Japan: Abusive Punishments in Japanese Prisons*. Report ASA 22/04/98. New York: Amnesty International.

Anderson, David C. 1995. *Crime and the Politics of Hysteria: How the Willie Horton Story Changed American Justice*. New York: Times Books.

Ando, Miwako. 1995. *The Education and Training of Public Prosecutors in Japan*. Tokyo: Research and Training Institute of the Ministry of Justice.

Araki, Nobuyoshi. 1985. "The Flow of Criminal Cases in the Japanese Criminal Justice System." *Crime & Delinquency* 31 (October):601–629.

Archer, Dane, and Rosemary Gartner. 1984. *Violence and Crime in Cross-National Perspective*. New Haven, Conn.: Yale University Press.

Armstrong, Ken. 1999. "Trial and Error: A *Tribune* Investigation of Prosecutorial Misconduct." *Chicago Tribune*, January 8–14 (five parts).

Arnold, Thurman. 1935. *The Symbols of Government*. New Haven, Conn.: Yale University Press.

Aronson, Elliot. 1988. *The Social Animal*. 5th ed. New York: W. H. Freeman.

Baumgartner, M. P. 1992. "The Myth of Discretion." In Keith Hawkins, ed., *The Uses of Discretion*. Oxford: Clarendon Press.

Bayley, David H. 1994. "Review Essay Rejoinder" (to Patricia Steinhoff, 1993). *Law & Society Review* 28(4):963–964.

Bayley, David H. 1991. *Forces of Order: Policing Modern Japan*. Berkeley: University of California Press.

Bazemore, Gordon. 1999. "Communities, Victims, and Offender Reintegration: Restorative Justice and Earned Redemption." In Amitai Etzioni, ed., *Civic Repentance*. New York: Rowman and Littlefield.

Beer, Lawrence W. 1984. *Freedom of Expression in Japan: A Study in Comparative Law, Politics, and Society*. Tokyo: Kodansha International.

Benedict, Ruth. 1946. *Chrysanthemum and the Sword: Patterns of Japanese Culture*. Reprint, Boston: Houghton Mifflin, 1989.

Bennett, William J., John J. DiIulio, Jr., and John P. Walters. 1996. *Body Count*. New York: Simon & Schuster.

Berlow, Alan. 1999. "The Wrong Man." *The Atlantic Monthly*, November, pp. 66–91.

Bevacqua, Maria. 2000. *Rape on the Public Agenda: Feminism and the Politics of Sexual Assault*. Boston: Northeastern University Press.

Black, Donald. 1989. *Sociological Justice*. New York: Oxford University Press.

Black, Donald. 1976. *The Behavior of Law*. New York: Academic Press.

Blankenburg, Erhard von. 1994. "The Infrastructure for Avoiding Civil Litigation: Comparing Cultures of Legal Behavior in the Netherlands and West Germany." *Law & Society Review* 28(4):789–808.

Blankenburg, Erhard von, Klaus Sessar, and Wiebke Steffen. 1978. *Die Staatsanwaltschaft im Prozes strafrechtlicher Sozialkontrolle*. Berlin: Duncker & Humblot.

Blumberg, Abraham. 1979. *Criminal Justice: Issues and Ironies*. 2nd ed. New York: New Viewpoints Press.

Boerner, David. 1995. "Sentencing Guidelines and Prosecutorial Discretion." *Judicature* 8 (January–February):196–200.

Boyd, Neil, and Monique Layton. 1991. *Crime and Criminal Justice in Canada and Japan: Understanding Our Differences*. Vancouver, B.C.: Simon Fraser University School of Criminology.

Bracey, Christopher A. 2000. "Truth and Legitimacy in the American Criminal Process." *Journal of Criminal Law and Criminology* 90 (Winter):691–728.

Braithwaite, John. 1993. "Juvenile Offending: New Theory and Practice." In Lynn Atkinson and Sally-Anne Gerult, eds., *Proceedings of the National Conference on Juvenile Justice*, pp. 35–42. Canberra: Australian Institute of Criminology.

Braithwaite, John. *Crime, Shame and Reintegration*. 1989. Cambridge: Cambridge University Press.

Braithwaite, John, and Philip Pettit. 1994. "Republican Criminology and Victim Advocacy." *Law & Society Review* 28:765–776.

Brinton, Mary C. 1993. *Women and the Economic Miracle: Gender and Work in Postwar Japan*. Berkeley: University of California Press.

Brooks, Peter. 2000. *Troubling Confessions: Speaking Guilt in Law and Literature*. Chicago: University of Chicago Press.

Burnham, David. 1996. *Above the Law: Secret Deals, Political Fixes, and Other Misadventures of the U.S. Department of Justice*. New York: Scribner's.

Carbonneau, Tom. 1995. "Truth on Trial." *World & I* 10 (August):314–323.

Cardenas, Juan. 1986. "The Crime Victim in the Prosecutorial Process." *Harvard Journal of Law & Public Policy* 9(2):357–398.

Carter, Lief H. 1974. *The Limits of Order*. Lexington, Mass.: Lexington Books.

Castberg, A. Didrick. 1990. *Japanese Criminal Justice*. New York: Praeger.

Chambliss, William J. 1973. "The Saints and the Roughnecks." *Society* 11:24–31.

Chambliss, William J., and Robert B. Seidman. 1984. "The Use of Guilty Pleas in the Legal Process." In William J. Chambliss, ed., *Criminal Law in Action*. New York: John Wiley & Sons.

Chevigny, Paul. 1995. *Edge of the Knife: Police Violence in the Americas*. New York: The New Press.

Clark, Rodney. 1979. *The Japanese Company*. New Haven, Conn.: Yale University Press.

Cleary, William B. 1989. "Criminal Investigation in Japan." *California Western Law Review* 26(1):123–148.

Clifford, William. 1976. *Crime Control in Japan*. Lexington, Mass.: Lexington Books.

Cole, David. 1999. *No Equal Justice: Race and Class in the American Criminal Justice System*. New York: The New Press.

Cole, George F. 1970. "The Decision to Prosecute." *Law and Society Review* 4(3):331–343.

Coles, Catherine M., and George L. Kelling. 1999. "Prevention Through Community Prosecution." *The Public Interest*, no. 136 (Summer):69–84.

Conley, John M., and William M. O'Barr. 1998. *Just Words: Law, Language, and Power*. Chicago: University of Chicago Press.

Cooney, Mark. 1994. "Evidence as Partisanship." *Law & Society Review* 28:833–858.

Craig, Albert M. 1975. "Functional and Dysfunctional Aspects of Government Bureaucracy." In Ezra F. Vogel, ed., *Modern Japanese Organization and Decision-Making*. Tokyo: Charles E. Tuttle.

Crown Prosecution Service. 1994. *Code for Crown Prosecutors*. London: Crown Prosecution Service. Pp. 1–16.

Currie, Elliott. 1998. *Crime and Punishment in America*. New York: Metropolitan Books.

Curtis, Gerald. 1999. *The Logic of Japanese Politics*. New York: Columbia University Press.

Curtis, Gerald L. 1988. *The Japanese Way of Politics*. New York: Columbia University Press.

Damaska, Mirjan R. 1997. *Evidence Law Adrift*. New Haven, Conn.: Yale University Press.

Damaska, Mirjan R. 1986. *The Faces of Justice and State Authority: A Comparative Approach to the Legal Process*. New Haven, Conn.: Yale University Press.

Dandō, Shigemitsu. 1970. "System of Discretionary Prosecution in Japan." *American Journal of Comparative Law* 18:518–531.

Dandō, Shigemitsu. 1965. *Japanese Criminal Procedure*, trans. B. J. George, Jr. South Hackensack, N.J.: Fred B. Rothman.

Danelski, David J. 1973–1974. "The Political Impact of the Japanese Supreme Court." *Notre Dame Lawyer* 49:965–980.

Davis, Kenneth Culp. 1969. *Discretionary Justice: A Preliminary Inquiry*. Urbana and Chicago: University of Illinois Press.

del Frate, Anna Alvazzi, Ugliesa Zvekic, and Jan J. M. van Dijk. 1993. *Understanding Crime: Experiences of Crime and Crime Control*. Rome: United Nations.

Dershowitz, Alan M. 1982. *The Best Defense*. New York: Vintage Books.

Dharmawardena, Kolitha. 1995a. "Control of Crime and Criminal Justice in Japan: Ascertaining the Causes for Extraordinary Accomplishments," pp. 1–26. Unpublished paper.

Dharmawardena, Kolitha. 1995b. "A Criminal Justice Profile of Sri Lanka." In Kunihiro Horiuchi, ed., *Criminal Justice Profiles of Asia: Investigation, Prosecution, and Trial*. Tokyo: UNAFEI.

Di Federico, Giuseppe. 1998. "Prosecutorial Independence and the Democratic Requirement of Accountability in Italy." *British Journal of Criminology* 38, no. 3:371–387.

Donziger, Steven R. 1996. *The Real War on Crime: The Report of the National Criminal Justice Commission*. New York: HarperPerennial.

Douglas, Mary. 1986. *How Institutions Think*. Syracuse, N.Y.: Syracuse University Press.

Dowling, Peter. 1994. "Killing Time." *Tokyo Journal* (March):30–35.

Downes, David. 1988. *Contrasts in Tolerance: Postwar Penal Policy in the Netherlands and England and Wales*. Oxford: Clarendon Press.

Durkheim, Emile. 1947. *The Division of Labor in Society*. Glencoe, Ill.: Free Press.

Eisenstein, James. 1978. *Counsel for the United States: U.S. Attorneys in the Political and Legal Systems*. Baltimore: Johns Hopkins University Press.

Eisenstein, James, Roy B. Flemming, and Peter Nardulli. 1988. *The Contours of Justice: Communities and Their Courts*. Boston: Little, Brown.

Elster, John. 1989. *Nuts and Bolts for the Social Sciences*. Cambridge: Cambridge University Press.

Etzioni, Amitai. 1964. *Modern Organizations*. Englewood Cliffs, N.J.: Prentice-Hall.

Etzioni, Amitai, ed. *Civic Repentance*. 1999. New York: Rowman and Littlefield.

Fallows, James. 1994. *Looking at the Sun: The Rise of the New East Asian Economic and Political System*. New York: Pantheon Books.

Feeley, Malcolm M. 1996. "Comparative Criminal Law for Criminologists: Comparing for What Purpose?" In David Nelken, ed., *Comparing Legal Cultures*. London: Dartmouth Press.

Feeley, Malcolm M. 1992a. "Hollow Hopes, Flypaper, and Metaphors." *Law & Social Inquiry* 17 (Fall):745–760.

Feeley, Malcolm M. 1992b. *The Process Is the Punishment*. New York: Russell Sage Foundation.

Feeley, Malcolm M. 1987. "The Adversary System." In Robert J. Janosik, ed., *Encyclopedia of the American Judicial System: Studies of the Principal Institutions and Processes of Law*, pp. 753–766. New York: Scribner's.

Feeley, Malcolm M. 1985. "Foreword." *Crime & Delinquency* 31 (October):601–604.

Feeley, Malcolm M. 1973. "Two Models of the Criminal Justice System: An Organizational Perspective." *Law & Society Review* 7 (Spring):407–425.

Feeley, Malcolm. 1970. "Coercion and Compliance: A New Look at an Old Problem." *Law & Society Review* 4 (May):505–519.

Feeley, Malcolm M., and Mark H. Lazerson. 1983. "Police-Prosecutor Relationships: An

Interorganization Perspective." In Keith O. Boyum and Lynn Mather, eds., *Empirical Theories About Courts*, pp. 216–243. New York: Longman Press.

Feeley, Malcolm M., and Charles Lester. 1994. "Legal Complexity and the Transformation of the Criminal Process." In Andre Gorman, ed., *Subjektivierung des justiziellen Beweisverfahrens*, pp. 337–375. Frankfurt am Main: Klostermann.

Feeley, Malcolm M., and Jonathan Simon. 1992. "The New Penology: Notes on the Emerging Strategy of Corrections and Its Implications." *Criminology* 30 (November):449–474.

Feeney, Floyd. 1998. *German and American Prosecutors: An Approach to Statistical Comparison*. Washington, D.C.: U.S. Department of Justice.

Feldman, Eric A. 2000. *The Ritual of Rights in Japan: Law, Society, and Health Policy*. Cambridge: Cambridge University Press.

Feldman, Martha S. 1992. "Social Limits to Discretion: An Organizational Perspective." In Keith Hawkins, ed., *The Uses of Discretion*. Oxford: Clarendon Press.

Fernandez-Armesto, Felipe. 1997. *Truth: A History and a Guide for the Perplexed*. New York: St. Martin's Press.

Feuerverger, Andrey, and Clifford D. Shearing. 1982. "An Analysis of the Prosecution of Shoplifters." *Criminology* 20, no. 2 (August):273–289.

Field, Norma. 1992. *In the Realm of a Dying Emperor: A Portrait of Japan at Century's End*. New York: Pantheon Books.

Fingleton, Eamonn. 1995. *Blindside: Why Japan Is Still on Track to Overtake the U.S. by the Year 2000*. Boston: Houghton Mifflin.

Finkelstein, Michael O. 1975. "A Statistical Analysis of Guilty Plea Practices in the Federal Courts." *Harvard Law Review* 89 (December):293–315.

Fionda, Julia. 1995. *Public Prosecutors and Discretion: A Comparative Study*. New York: Oxford University Press. 1995.

Fisher, George. 2000. "Plea Bargaining's Triumph." *Yale Law Journal* 109 (March):857–1075.

Fisher, Stanley Z. 1988. "In Search of the Virtuous Prosecutor: A Conceptual Framework." *American Journal of Criminal Law* 15:197–261.

Flanagan, Timothy J., and Dennis R. Longmire, eds. 1996. *Americans View Crime and Justice: A National Public Opinion Survey*. Thousand Oaks, Calif.: Sage.

Flemming, Roy B., Peter F. Nardulli, and James Eisenstein. 1992. *The Craft of Justice: Politics and Work in Court Communities*. Philadelphia: University of Pennsylvania Press.

Fletcher, George P. 1995. *With Justice for Some: Victims' Rights in Criminal Trials*. Reading, Mass.: Addison-Wesley.

Flynn, Sean. 2000. *Boston D.A.* New York: TV Books Inc.

Foote, Daniel H. 1995. "Four Views of Japanese Attorneys." *Law in Japan* 25:102–103.

Foote, Daniel H. "Book Review: Policing in Japan." 1993a. *Journal of Criminal Law & Criminology* 84, no. 2:410–427.

Foote, Daniel H. 1993b. " 'The Door That Never Opens'?: Capital Punishment and Post-Conviction Review of Death Sentences in the United States and Japan." *Brooklyn Journal of International Law* 19, no. 2:367–521.

Foote, Daniel H. 1992a. "The Benevolent Paternalism of Japanese Criminal Justice." *California Law Review* 80, no. 2 (March):317–390.

Foote, Daniel H. 1992b. "From Japan's Death Row to Freedom." *Pacific Rim Law & Policy Journal* 1, no. 1:11–103.

Foote, Daniel H. 1991. "Confessions and the Right to Silence in Japan." *Georgia Journal of International and Comparative Law* 21:415–488.

Foote, Daniel H. 1986. "Prosecutorial Discretion: A Response (to Goodman)." *Pacific Basin Law Journal* 5:96–106.

Forst, Brian. 1995. "Prosecution and Sentencing." in James Q. Wilson and Joan Peterselia, eds., *Crime*, pp. 363–386. San Francisco: Institute for Contemporary Studies.

Forst, Brian, and Kathleen B. Brosi. 1977. "A Theoretical and Empirical Analysis of the Prosecutor." *Journal of Legal Studies* 6:177–191.

Fox, Michael H. 1999. "The Yasuda Arrest: Criminal and Political Considerations." *JPRI Critique* [Japan Policy Research Institute] (October).

Frank, Jerome. 1949. *Courts on Trial: Myth and Reality in American Justice*. Princeton, N.J.: Princeton University Press.

Frankel, Marvin E. 1978. *Partisan Justice: Too Much Fight? Too Little Truth? Equal Justice?* New York: Hill and Wang.

Frase, Richard S. 1990. "Comparative Criminal Justice as a Guide to American Law Reform: How Do the French Do It, How Can We Find Out, and Why Should We Care?" *California Law Review* 78, no. 3 (May):539–683.

Frase, Richard S. 1980. "The Decision to File Federal Criminal Charges: A Quantitative Study of Prosecutorial Discretion." *University of Chicago Law Review* 47(2):246–330.

Freeman, Laurie A. 2000. *Closing the Shop: Information Cartels and Japan's Mass Media*. Princeton, N.J.: Princeton University Press.

Freeman, Laurie A. 1996. *Japan's Press Clubs as Information Cartels*. Japan Policy Research Institute Working Paper no. 18. Cardiff, Calif.: JPRI.

French, Howard W. 2001. "Fighting Molestation, and a Stigma, in Japan." *New York Times*, July 15.

Friedman, Lawrence. 1994. *Crime and Punishment in American History*. New York: Basic Books.

Friedman, Lawrence. 1985. *Total Justice: What Americans Want from the Legal System and Why*. Boston: Beacon Press.

Friedman, Lawrence. 1975. *The Legal System: A Social Science Perspective*. New York: Russell Sage Foundation.

Frohmann, Lisa. 1997. "Convictability and Discordant Locales: Reproducing Race, Class, and Gender Ideologies in Prosecutorial Decisionmaking." *Law & Society Review* 31:531–556.

Frohmann, Lisa G. 1992. "Screening Sexual Assault Cases: Prosecutorial Decisions to File or Reject Rape Complaints." Ph.D. dissertation, University of California, Los Angeles.

Furuta, Yūki. 1995. *The Role of Public Prosecutors in Japanese Criminal Justice*. Tokyo: UNAFEI.

Gangloff, Joseph E. 1995. "Structure and Practice for the Investigation of Bribery of Public Officials in the United States." Paper presented at the Ministry of Justice, Tokyo, February 16.

Garland, David. 1990. *Punishment and Modern Society: A Study in Social Theory*. Chicago: University of Chicago Press.

Garon, Sheldon. 1997. *Molding Japanese Minds: The State in Everyday Life*. Princeton, N.J.: Princeton University Press.

Gawande, Atul. 2001. "Under Suspicion: The Fugitive Science of Criminal Justice." *New Yorker*, January 8:50–53.

Geertz, Clifford. 1973. *The Interpretation of Cultures*. New York: Basic Books.

Geller, William A. 1998. "Videotaping Interrogations and Confessions." In Richard A. Leo and George C. Thomas III, eds., *The Miranda Debate: Law, Justice, and Policing*. Boston: Northeastern University Press.

George, B. J., Jr. 1990. "Rights of the Criminally Accused." *Law and Contemporary Problems* 53, nos. 1 and 2 (Winter and Spring):71–107.

George, B. J., Jr. 1984. "Discretionary Authority of Public Prosecutors in Japan." *Law in Japan* 17:420–451.

Gerber, Jurg, and Susan L. Weeks. 1992. "Some Reflections on Doing Cross-Cultural Research: Interviewing Japanese Prison Inmates." *The Criminologist* (November–December): 7–13.

Gershman, Bennett L. 1992. "The New Prosecutors." *University of Pittsburgh Law Review* 53:393–458.

Gershman, Bennett L. 1991. "Abuse of Power in the Prosecutor's Office." *The World & I 6* (June):477–488.

Gillers, Stephen. 2000. "A Weak Case, but a Brave Prosecution." *New York Times*, March 1.

Givelber, Daniel. 1997. "Meaningless Acquittals, Meaningful Convictions: Do We Reliably Acquit the Innocent?" *Rutgers Law Review* 49:1317–1396.

Glazer, Elizabeth. 1999. "How Federal Prosecutors Can Reduce Crime." *The Public Interest* No. 13b (Summer):85–99.

Goffman, Erving. 1961. *Asylums: Essays on the Social Situation of Mental Patients and Other Inmates.* Garden City, N.Y.: Anchor Books.

Golding, Martin P. 1975. *Philosophy of Law.* Englewood Cliffs, N.J.: Prentice-Hall.

Goldstein, Abraham S. 1982. "Defining the Role of the Victim in Criminal Prosecution." *Mississippi Law Journal* 52:515–561.

Goldstein, Abraham S. 1981. *The Passive Judiciary: Prosecutorial Discretion and the Guilty Plea.* Baton Rouge: Louisiana State University Press.

Goldstein, Abraham S. 1974. "Reflections on Two Models: Inquisitorial Themes in American Criminal Procedure." *Stanford Law Review* 26:1009–1025.

Goldstein, Abraham S. 1960. "The State and the Accused: Balance of Advantage in Criminal Procedure." *Yale Law Journal* 69:1149–1199.

Goldstein, Abraham S., and Martin Marcus. 1978. "Comment on 'Continental Criminal Procedure.'" *Yale Law Journal* 87, no. 6:1570–1577.

Goldstein, Abraham S., and Martin Marcus. 1977. "The Myth of Judicial Supervision in Three 'Inquisitorial' Systems: France, Italy, and Germany." *Yale Law Journal* 87:240–283.

Goodman, Marcia E. 1986. "The Exercise and Control of Prosecutorial Discretion in Japan." *Pacific Basin Law Journal* 5:16–95.

Gottfredson, Michael R., and Don M. Gottfredson. 1988. *Decision-Making in Criminal Justice: Toward the Rational Exercise of Discretion.* New York: Plenum Press.

Gottfredson, Michael R., and Travis Hirschi. 1990. *A General Theory of Crime.* Stanford, Calif.: Stanford University Press.

Grano, Joseph D. 1993. *Confessions, Truth, and the Law.* Ann Arbor: University of Michigan Press.

Greenwood, Peter W., Sorrel Wildhorn, Eugene C. Poggio, Michael J. Strumwasser, and Peter De Leon. 1976. *Prosecution of Adult Felony Defendants: A Policy Perspective.* Lexington, Mass.: Lexington Books.

Griffiths, John. 1970. "Ideology in Criminal Procedure or a Third Model of the Criminal Process." *Yale Law Journal* 79, no. 3 (January):359–417.

Grosman, Brian A. 1969. *The Prosecutor: An Inquiry into the Exercise of Discretion.* Toronto: University of Toronto Press.

Gross, Samuel R., and Robert Mauro. 1989. *Death and Discrimination: Racial Disparities in Capital Sentencing.* Boston: Northeastern University Press.

Guarnieri, Carlo. 1997. "Prosecution in Two Civil Law Countries: France and Italy." In David Nelken, ed., *Comparing Legal Cultures*, pp. 183–194. Aldershot, U.K.: Dartmouth Press.

Guest, Robert. 1992. "Forced to Confess." *Japan Times Weekly*, October 31.

Haas, Kenneth C., and Geoffrey P. Alpert. 1999. *The Dilemmas of Correction: Contemporary Readings.* 4th ed. Prospect Heights, Ill.: Waveland Press.

Hagan, John. 1994. *Crime and Disrepute*. Thousand Oaks, Calif.: Pine Forge Press.

Haley, John O. 1999. "Apology and Pardon: Learning from Japan." In Amitai Etzioni, ed., *Civic Repentance*. New York: Rowman and Littlefield.

Haley, John O. 1998. *The Spirit of Japanese Law*. Athens: University of Georgia Press.

Haley, John O. 1997. Review of Richard H. Mitchell's *Janus-Faced Justice: Political Criminals in Imperial Japan. Monumenta Nipponica* 47, no. 4:557–559.

Haley, John O. 1992. "Criminal Justice in Japan." *Journal of Japanese Studies* 18:552–556.

Haley, John O. 1991. *Authority Without Power: Law and the Japanese Paradox*. New York: Oxford University Press.

Haley, John O. 1986. "Comment: The Implications of Apology." *Law & Society Review* 20, no. 4:499–507.

Haley, John O. 1989. "Confession, Repentance and Absolution." In M. Wright and B. Galway, eds., *Mediation and Criminal Justice: Victims, Offenders and Communities*, pp. 195–211. London: Sage Publications.

Hamilton, V. Lee, and Joseph Sanders. 1992. *Everyday Justice: Responsibility and the Individual in Japan and the United States*. New Haven, Conn.: Yale University Press.

Hans, Valerie P., and Neil Vidmar. 1986. *Judging the Jury*. New York: Plenum Press.

Harding, John. 1995. *The Changing Nature of Criminal Justice in England and Wales*. Tokyo: UNAFEI.

Hawkins, Keith, ed. 1992. *The Uses of Discretion*. Oxford: Clarendon Press.

Hedstrom, Peter, and Richard Swedberg, eds. 1998. *Social Mechanisms*. Cambridge: University Press.

Heilbroner, David. 1990. *Rough Justice: Days and Nights of a Young D.A.* New York: Dell.

Herbert, Wolfgang. 1997. *Foreign Workers and Law Enforcement in Japan*. New York: Kegan Paul International.

Heumann, Milton. 1981. *Plea Bargaining: The Experiences of Prosecutors, Judges, and Defense Attorneys*. Chicago: University of Chicago Press.

Heymann, Phillip B. 1985. "Understanding Criminal Investigation." *Harvard Journal on Legislation* 22 (Summer):314–334.

Hicks, George. 1997. *Japan's Hidden Apartheid: The Korean Minority and the Japanese*. Aldershot, U.K.: Ashgate.

Hino, Masaharu. 1990. "The Criminal Enforcement Process in Japan." In Valerie Kusuda-Smith, ed., *Crime Prevention and Control in the United States and Japan*. Dobbs Ferry, N.Y.: Transnational Juris Publications.

Hiramatsu, Yoshiro. 1989. "Summary of Tokugawa Criminal Justice," trans. Daniel H. Foote. *Law in Japan* 22:105–128.

Hirano, Ryūichi. 1989. "Diagnosis of the Current Code of Criminal Procedure," translated Daniel H. Foote. *Law in Japan* 22:129–142.

Hirano, Ryūichi. 1963. "The Accused and Society: Some Aspects of Japanese Criminal Law." In Arthur von Mehren, ed., *Law in Japan*. Cambridge, Mass.: Harvard University Press.

Hirschi, Travis. 1969. *Causes of Delinquency*. Berkeley: University of California Press.

Holmes, Malcolm D., Howard C. Daudistel, and William A. Taggart. 1992. "Plea Bargaining Policy and State District Court Caseloads: An Interrupted Time Series Analysis." *Law & Society Review* 26, no. 1:139–159.

Honda, Katsuichi. 1993. *The Impoverished Spirit in Contemporary Japan: Selected Essays*, ed. John Lie. New York: Monthly Review Press.

Horiuchi, Kunihiro. 1994. "Police Powers and Instructions to the Police in Respect of Police Detentions." Paper presented at the Congress of International Penal and Penitentiary Foundation, Macao, October 20.

Horwich, Jeff, and Tarō Karasaki. 2000. "Cultural Conflicts Intensify in Prison System." *Asahi Evening News*, June 20.

Huff, C. Ronald, Arye Rattner, and Edward Sagarin. 1996. *Convicted but Innocent: Wrongful Conviction and Public Policy*. Thousand Oaks, Calif.: Sage Publications.

Humes, Edward. 1999. *Mean Justice: A Town's Terror, a Prosecutor's Power, a Betrayal of Innocence*. New York: Simon & Schuster.

Humes, Edward. 1996. *No Matter How Loud I Shout: A Year in the Life of Juvenile Court*. New York: Simon & Schuster.

Igarashi, Futaba. 1989. "Coerced Confessions and Pretrial Detention in Japan." Paper presented at the 41st Annual Meeting of the American Society of Criminology, Reno, Nevada, November 11.

Igarashi, Futaba. 1984. "Crime, Confession and Control in Contemporary Japan." *Law in Context* 2:1–30. (Translated from *Sekai*, February 1984, and with an introduction and explanatory notes by Gavan McCormack.)

Inagawa, Tatsuya. 1995. *The Criminal Justice System in Japan: Investigation and Prosecution*. Tokyo: UNAFEI.

Inoue, Tatsuo. 1993. "The Poverty of Rights-Blind Communality: Looking Through the Window of Japan." *Brigham Young University Law Review* 1993(2):517–551.

International Bar Association. 1994. *The Daiyō Kangoku (Substitute Prison) System of Police Custody in Japan*. London: International Bar Association.

Irwin, John. 1985. *The Jail: Managing the Underclass in American Society*. Berkeley: University of California Press.

Ishimatsu, Takeo. 1989. "Are Criminal Defendants in Japan Truly Receiving Trials by Judges?," trans. Daniel H. Foote. *Law in Japan* 22:143–153.

Itoh, Osamu. 1995. *The Criminal Justice System in Japan: The Court*. Tokyo: UNAFEI.

Itoh, Shigeki. 1986a. *Characteristics and Roles of Japanese Public Prosecutors*. Tokyo: UNAFEI.

Jackall, Robert. 1997. *Wild Cowboys: Urban Marauders and the Forces of Order*. Cambridge, Mass.: Harvard University Press.

Jackson, Robert H. 1940. "The Federal Prosecutor." *Journal of the American Judicature Society*. Vol. 24 (June 1940), 18–20.

Jacoby, Joan E. 1980. *The American Prosecutor: A Search for Identity*. Lexington, Mass.: Lexington Books.

Jacoby, Joan E. 1972. *Snapshot—Spin Around: A Technique to Measure Capacity and Overload in a Prosecutor's Office*. Washington, D.C.: National Center for Prosecution Management.

Joh, Elizabeth E. 1999. " 'If It Suffices to Accuse': *United States v. Watts* and the Reassessment of Acquittals." *New York University Law Review* 74 (June):887–913.

Johnson, Chalmers. 1995. *Japan: Who Governs? The Rise of the Developmental State*. New York: W. W. Norton.

Johnson, Chalmers. 1972. *Conspiracy at Matsukawa*. Berkeley: University of California Press.

Johnson, David T. Forthcoming. "Getting In and Getting Along in the Prosecutors Office." In Theodore C. Bestor, Patricia G. Steinhoff, and Victoria Lyon Bestor, eds., *Doing Fieldwork in Japan*. Honolulu: University of Hawaii Press.

Johnson, David T. 2001. "Plea Bargaining in Japan." In Malcolm M. Feeley and Setsuo Miyazawa, eds., *The Japanese Adversary System in Context: Controversies and Comparisons*. London: Macmillan.

Johnson, David T. 2000. "Prosecutor Culture in Japan and the USA." In David Nelken, ed., *Contrasting Criminal Justice: Getting from Here to There*. Aldershot, U.K.: Dartmouth.

Johnson, David T. 1997. *Why the Wicked Sleep: The Prosecution of Political Corruption in Post-war Japan.* Working Paper no. 34. Cardiff, Calif.: Japan Policy Research Institute.

Johnson, David T. 1996. "The Japanese Way of Justice: Prosecuting Crime in Japan." Ph.D. dissertation, University of California at Berkeley.

Johnson, David T., and Setsuo Miyazawa. 1994. "Two Faces of Justice: A Milestone in Quantitative Cross-Cultural Research." *Law & Social Inquiry* 19 (Summer):667–685.

Johnson, Elmer H. 1997. *Criminalization and Prisoners in Japan: Six Contrary Cohorts.* Carbondale: Southern Illinois University Press.

Johnson, Elmer H. 1996. *Japanese Corrections: Managing Convicted Offenders in an Orderly Society.* Carbondale: Southern Illinois University Press.

Johnson, Elmer, and Masaharu Hino. 1985. "UNAFEI of Tokyo: A Descriptive Note." *International Journal of Comparative and Applied Criminal Justice* 9 (Winter):17–24.

Johnson, Phillip E. 1977. "Importing Justice." *Yale Law Journal* 87:406–414.

Kalven, Harry, Jr., and Hans Zeisel. 1966. *The American Jury.* Boston: Little, Brown.

Kaminer, Wendy. 1999. "Games Prosecutors Play." *The American Prospect* no. 46 (September–October):20–26.

Kaminer, Wendy. 1995. *It's All the Rage: Crime and Culture.* Reading, Mass.: Addison-Wesley.

Kamisar, Yale, Wayne R. LaFave, and Jerold H. Israel. 1994. *Modern Criminal Procedure: Cases — Comments — Questions.* 8th ed. St. Paul, Minn.: West.

Kanemoto, Toshinori. 1995. *Police Reforms of Japan After World War II.* Tokyo: UNAFEI.

Kaplan, David E., and Alec Dubro. 1986. *Yakuza: The Explosive Account of Japan's Criminal Underworld.* Reading, Mass.: Addison-Wesley.

Kaplan, David E., and Andrew Marshall. 1996. *The Cult at the End of the World.* New York: Crown.

Kaplan, John. 1965. "The Prosecutorial Discretion — A Comment." *Northwestern University Law Review* 60:174–193.

Kashimura, Takayuki. 1995. *Corruption in the Japanese Criminal Justice System.* Tokyo: UNAFEI.

Katz, Jack. 1999. "Hunting for Bias: On Evil Motives, Unfair Outcomes, and Uneven Pressures on Decision Makers as Targets for Documenting Unjustly Unequal Treatment, Especially in the Administration of Criminal Justice." In Patricia Ewick, Robert Kagan, and Austin Sarat, eds., *Social Science, Social Policy, and the Law.* New York: Russell Sage Foundation.

Katz, Jack. 1979. "Legality and Equality: Plea Bargaining in the Prosecution of White-Collar Crimes and Common Crimes." *Law & Society Review* 13:431–459.

Katzenstein, Peter J., and Yutaka Tsujinaka. 1991. *Defending the Japanese State: Structure, Norms, and Political Responses to Terrorism and Violent Social Protest in the 1970s and 1980s.* Ithaca, N.Y.: East Asia Program, Cornell University.

Katzmann, Gary S. 1991. *Inside the Criminal Process.* New York: W. W. Norton.

Kawashima, Takeyoshi. 1979. "Japanese Way of Legal Thinking." *International Journal of Law Libraries* 7:127–131.

Kawashima, Takeyoshi. 1963. "Dispute Resolution in Contemporary Japan" in Arthur T. von Mehren, ed., *Law in Japan.* Cambridge, Mass.: Harvard University Press.

Keehn, Edward B. 1990. "Managing Interests in the Japanese Bureaucracy: Informality and Discretion." *Asian Survey* 30:1021–1037.

Kerr, Alex. 2001. *Dogs and Demons: Tales from the Dark Side of Japan.* New York: Hill & Wang.

Kersten, Joachim. 1993. "Street Youths, *Bosozoku*, and *Yakuza*: Subculture Formation and Societal Reactions in Japan." *Crime & Delinquency* 39 (July):277–295.

Kerstetter, Wayne A. 1990. "Gateway to Justice: Police and Prosecutorial Response to Sexual Assaults Against Women." *Journal of Criminal Law and Criminology* 81, no. 2:267–313.

Kino, Hideki. 1994. *Effective Methods of Controlling Drug Offences.* Tokyo: UNAFEI.

Kitada, Mikinao. 1995. *The Role of Public Prosecutors in Japan.* Tokyo: UNAFEI.

Klinger, David A. 1997. "Negotiating Order in Patrol Work: An Ecological Theory of Police Response to Deviance." *Criminology* 35 (May):277–306.

Koh, B. C. 1989. *Japan's Administrative Elite.* Berkeley: University of California Press.

Komiya, Nobuo. 1999. "A Cultural Study of the Low Crime Rate in Japan." *British Journal of Criminology* 39 (Summer):369–390.

Kopel, David B. 1992. *The Samurai, the Mountie, and the Cowboy: Should America Adopt the Gun Controls of Other Democracies?* Buffalo, N.Y.: Prometheus Books.

Koyama, Masaki. 1991. "Prosecuting — Japanese Style." *New Law Journal,* September 20, pp. 1267–1269.

Kristof, Nicholas D. 1996. "Guns: One Nation Bars, the Other Requires." *New York Times,* March 10.

Kurata, Seiji. 1993. *The Criminal Justice System at Work.* Tokyo: Criminal Affairs Bureau, Ministry of Justice.

LaFave, Wayne R. 1970. "The Prosecutor's Discretion in the United States." *American Journal of Comparative Law* 18:532–548.

Landes, William M. 1971. "An Economic Analysis of the Courts." *Journal of Law and Economics* 14(1):61–107.

Langbein, John H. 1995. "The Influence of Comparative Procedure in the United States." *American Journal of Comparative Law* 43 (Fall):545–554.

Langbein, John H. 1978. "Torture and Plea Bargaining." *University of Chicago Law Review* 46:3–22.

Langbein, John H. 1974a. "Controlling Prosecutorial Discretion in Germany." *University of Chicago Law Review* 41, no. 3 (Spring):439–467.

Langbein, John H. 1974b. *Prosecuting Crime in the Renaissance: England, Germany, France.* Cambridge, Mass.: Harvard University Press.

Langbein, John H., and Lloyd L. Weinreb. 1978. "Continental Criminal Procedure: 'Myth' and Reality." *Yale Law Journal* 87, no. 6 (July):1549–1569.

Lempert, Richard. 1992. "A Jury For Japan?" *American Journal of Comparative Law* 40:37–71.

Lempres, Michael. 1995. "Crime and Culture in Japan." *The World & I* 10 (June):126–131.

Leo, Richard A. 2001. "Miranda, Confessions and Justice: Lessons for Japan?" In Malcolm M. Feeley and Setsuo Miyazawa, eds., *The Japanese Adversary System in Context: Controversies and Comparisons.* London: Macmillan.

Leo, Richard A. 1996. "Inside the Interrogation Room." *Journal of Criminal Law and Criminology* 86 (Winter):266–303.

Leo, Richard A. 1994. "Police Interrogation in America: A Study of Violence, Civility and Social Change." Ph.D. Dissertation, University of California at Berkeley.

Leo, Richard A., and Richard J. Ofshe. 1998. "The Consequences of False Confessions: Deprivations of Liberty and Miscarriages of Justice in the Age of Psychological Interrogation." *Journal of Criminal Law and Criminology* 88 (Winter):429–496.

Lincoln, James R., and Arne L. Kalleberg. 1990. *Culture, Control, and Commitment: A Study of Work Organization and Work Attitudes in the United States and Japan.* Cambridge: Cambridge University Press.

Lipset, Seymour Martin. 1996. *American Exceptionalism: A Double-Edged Sword.* New York: W. W. Norton.

Lipsky, Michael. 1980. *Street-Level Bureaucracy: Dilemmas of the Individual in Public Service.* New York: Russell Sage Foundation.

Littrell, W. Boyd. 1979. *Bureaucratic Justice: Police, Prosecutors, and Plea Bargaining*. Beverly Hills, Calif.: Sage.

Lofland, John, and Lyn H. Lofland. 1984. *Analyzing Social Settings: A Guide to Qualitative Observation and Analysis*. Belmont, Calif.: Wadsworth.

Luney, Percy R., Jr. 1990. "The Constitution of Japan: The Fifth Decade." *Law and Contemporary Problems* 53, nos. 1 and 2 (Winter and Spring). Special issue.

Lynch, James. 1995. "Crime in International Perspective." In James Q. Wilson and Joan Peterselia, eds., *Crime*, pp. 11–38. San Francisco: Institute for Contemporary Studies.

McConville, Mike, Andrew Sanders, and Roger Leng. 1991. *The Case for the Prosecution*. London: Routledge.

McCoy, Candace. 1996. "Police, Prosecutors, and Discretion in Investigation." In John Kleineg, ed., *Handled with Discretion: Ethical Issues in Police Decision Making*. New York: Rowman and Littlefield.

McCoy, Candace. 1993. *Politics and Plea Bargaining: Victims' Rights in California*. Philadelphia: University of Pennsylvania Press.

McDonald, William F. 1982. *Police-Prosecutor Relations in the United States*. Washington, D.C.: U.S. Department of Justice.

McDonald, William F., ed. 1979. *The Prosecutor*. Beverly Hills, Calif.: Sage.

McDonald, William F., and James A. Cramer. 1980. *Plea Bargaining*. Lexington, Mass.: Lexington Books.

McIntyre, Lisa J. 1987 *The Public Defender: The Practice of Law in the Shadows of Repute*. Chicago: University of Chicago Press.

Mann, Kenneth. 1985. *Defending White-Collar Crime: A Portrait of Attorneys at Work*. New Haven, Conn.: Yale University Press.

Manning, Peter K. 1992. "Big-Bang Decisions: Notes on a Naturalistic Approach." In Keith Hawkins, ed., *The Uses of Discretion*. Oxford: Clarendon Press.

Markovits, Inga. 1989. "Playing the Opposites Game: On Mirjan Damaska's *The Faces of Justice and State Authority*." *Stanford Law Review* 41 (May):1313–1341.

Marshall, Andrew, and Michiko Toyama. 1994. "Death in L.A." *Tokyo Journal*, May, pp. 32–37.

Mather, Lynn M. 1979. *Plea Bargaining or Trial? The Process of Criminal Case Disposition*. Lexington, Mass.: Lexington Books.

Mauer, Marc. 1999. *Race to Incarcerate*. New York: The New Press.

Maynard, Douglas W. 1984. *Inside Plea Bargaining: The Language of Negotiation*. New York: Plenum Press.

Mellon, Leonard R., Joan E. Jacoby, and Marion A. Brewer. 1981. "The Prosecutor Constrained by His Environment: A New Look at Discretionary Justice in the United States." *Journal of Criminal Law & Criminology* 72:52–81.

Merryman, John Henry. 1985. *The Civil Law Tradition: An Introduction to the Legal Systems of Western Europe and Latin America*. 2nd ed. Stanford, Calif.: Stanford University Press.

Milhaupt, Curtis J., and Mark D. West. 2000. "The Dark Side of Private Ordering: An Institutional and Organizational Analysis of Organized Crime." *University of Chicago Law Review* 67 (Winter):41–98.

Miller, Alan S., and Satoshi Kanazawa. 2000. *Order by Accident: The Origins and Consequences of Conformity in Japan*. Boulder, Colo.: Westview Press.

Miller, Frank W. 1969. *Prosecution: The Decision to Charge a Suspect with a Crime*. Boston: Little, Brown.

Miller, Frank W., Robert O. Dawson, George E. Dix, and Raymond I. Parnas. 1991. *Prosecution and Adjudication*. Westbury, N.Y.: Foundation Press.

Miller, Jeffrey J. 1990. "Plea Bargaining and Its Analogues Under the New Italian Criminal Procedure Code and in the United States: Towards a New Understanding of Comparative Criminal Procedure." *New York Journal of International Law and Politics* 22(2):215–251.

Mitchell, Richard H. 1996. *Political Bribery in Japan.* Honolulu: University of Hawaii Press.

Mitchell, Richard H. 1992. *Janus-Faced Justice: Political Criminals in Imperial Japan.* Honolulu: University of Hawaii Press.

Mitchell, Richard H. 1983. *Censorship in Imperial Japan.* Princeton, N.J.: Princeton University Press.

Mitchell, Richard H. 1976. *Thought Control in Prewar Japan.* Ithaca, N.Y.: Cornell University Press.

Miyamoto, Masao. 1994. *Straitjacket Society: An Insider's Irreverent View of Bureaucratic Japan.* Tokyo: Kodansha International.

Miyazawa, Setsuo. 1999. "The Politics of Judicial Reform in Japan: The Rule of Law at Last?" Paper presented at the Center for the Study of Law and Society, University of California, Berkeley.

Miyazawa, Setsuo. 1996. "For the Liberal Transformation of Japanese Legal Culture: A Review of Recent Scholarship and Practice." Unpublished paper.

Miyazawa, Setsuo. 1995. "Is Japanese Criminal Justice Reintegrative and Benevolent?" Paper presented at the Stanford Law School, Palo Alto, Calif., October 6.

Miyazawa, Setsuo. 1994a. "Administrative Control of Japanese Judges." In Philip S. C. Lewis, ed., *Law and Technology in the Pacific Community.* Boulder, Colo.: Westview Press.

Miyazawa, Setsuo. 1994b. "The Enigma of Japan as Testing Ground for Cross-Cultural Criminological Studies." In David Nelken, ed., *Comparing Legal Cultures.* Aldershot: Dartmouth Publishing.

Miyazawa, Setsuo. 1992. *Policing in Japan: A Study on Making Crime,* trans. Frank G. Bennett, Jr., with John O. Haley. Albany: State University of New York Press.

Miyazawa, Setsuo. 1991. "The Private Sector and Law Enforcement in Japan." In William T. Gormley, Jr., ed., *Privatization and Its Alternatives,* pp. 241–257. Madison: University of Wisconsin Press.

Miyazawa, Setsuo. 1990. "Learning Lessons from Japanese Experience in Policing and Crime: Challenge for Japanese Criminologists." *Kobe University Law Review* no. 24:29–61.

Miyazawa, Setsuo. 1989. "Scandal and Hard Reform: Implications of a Wiretapping Case to the Control of Organizational Police Crimes in Japan." *Kobe University Law Review* no. 23:13–27.

Moon, Young-Ho. 1995. "A Criminal Justice Profile of the Republic of Korea." In Horiuchi Kunihiro, ed., *Criminal Justice Profiles of Asia: Investigation, Prosecution, and Trial.* Tokyo: UNAFEI.

Morris, Norval. 1978. Book Review of Lloyd Weinreb's *Denial of Justice. Harvard Law Review* 91:1367ff.

Morris, Norval, and Gordon Hawkins. 1969. *The Honest Politician's Guide to Crime Control.* Chicago: University of Chicago Press.

Moskovitz, Myron. 1995. "The O.J. Inquisition: A United States Encounter with Continental Criminal Justice." *Vanderbilt Journal of Transnational Law* 28 (November):1121ff.

Moushey, Bill. 1998. "Win at All Costs: Government Misconduct in the Name of Expedient Justice." *Pittsburgh Post-Gazette,* November 22–December 13 (ten parts).

Mukherjee, Satyanshu. 1994–1995. "What Is So Good About the Low Crime Rate in Japan?" *The Australian Rationalist* (December–March):7–17.

Murakami, Haruki. 2001. *The Tokyo Gas Attack and the Japanese Psyche,* trans. Alfred Birnbaum and Philip Gabriel. New York: Vintage Books.

Murayama, Masayuki. 1992. "Postwar Trends in the Administration of Japanese Criminal Justice: Lenient but Intolerant or Something Else?" *Journal of the Japan-Netherlands Institute* 4:221–246.

Nader, Laura. 1990. *Harmony Ideology: Justice and Control in a Zapotec Mountain Village.* Stanford, Calif.: Stanford University Press.

Nagashima, Atsushi. 1963. "The Accused and Society: The Administration of Criminal Justice in Japan." In Arthur T. von Mehren, ed., *Law in Japan: The Legal Order in a Changing Society.* Cambridge, Mass.: Harvard University Press.

Nagel, Ilene H., and Stephen J. Schulhofer. 1992. "A Tale of Three Cities: An Empirical Study of Charging and Bargaining Practices Under the Federal Sentencing Guidelines." *Southern California Law Review* 66 (November):501–566.

Nakane, Chie. 1970. *Japanese Society.* Berkeley: University of California Press.

Nanakorn, Kanit, and Kittipong Kittayarak. 1995. "A Criminal Justice Profile of Thailand." In Kunihiro Horiuchi, ed., *Criminal Justice Profiles of Asia: Investigation, Prosecution, and Trial.* Tokyo: UNAFEI.

Nardulli, Peter F., James Eisenstein, and Roy B. Flemming. 1988. *The Tenor of Justice: Criminal Courts and the Guilty Plea Process.* Urbana and Chicago: University of Illinois Press.

Nelken, David. 1996. "Puzzling Out Legal Culture: A Comment on Blankenburg." In David Nelken, ed., *Comparing Legal Cultures.* London: Dartmouth Press.

Nelken, David, ed. 2000. *Contrasting Criminal Justice: Getting from Here to There.* Aldershot, U.K.: Dartmouth.

Nelken, David, ed. 1994. *The Futures of Criminology.* London: Sage.

Neubauer, David W. 1974. "After the Arrest: The Charging Decision in Prairie City." *Law & Society Review* 8 (Spring):495–517.

Newman, Donald J. 1966. *Conviction: The Determination of Guilt or Innocence Without Trial.* Boston: Little, Brown.

Nonet, Philippe, and Philip Selznick. 1978. *Law and Society in Transition: Toward Responsive Law.* New York: Harper Colophon.

Note. 1969. "Prosecutorial Discretion in the Initiation of Criminal Complaints." *Southern California Law Review* 42:519–545.

Ochiai, Hiromitsu. 2000. "Who Polices the Police?" *Japan Quarterly* (April–June):50–57.

Ofshe, Richard J., and Richard A. Leo. 1997. "The Social Psychology of Police Interrogation: The Theory and Classification of True and False Confessions." *Studies in Law, Politics and Society* 16:189–251.

Ohbayashi, Hiroshi. 1995. *Drug Crime in Japan: The Current Situation.* Tokyo: UNAFEI.

Ohbayashi, Hiroshi. 1994. *Economic Crime in Japan: The Current Situation.* Tokyo: UNAFEI.

Ohbayashi, Hiroshi. 1987. *The Discretionary Power of Prosecution and the Prevention of Its Abuse.* Tokyo: UNAFEI.

Ohlin, Lloyd E. 1993. "Surveying Discretion by Criminal Justice Decision Makers." In Lloyd E. Ohlin and Frank J. Remington, eds., *Discretion in Criminal Justice: The Tension Between Individualization and Uniformity*, pp. 1–22. Albany: State University of New York Press.

Ohlin, Lloyd E., and Frank J. Remington, eds. 1993. *Discretion in Criminal Justice: The Tension Between Individualization and Uniformity.* Albany: State University of New York Press.

Packer, Herbert L. 1968. *The Limits of the Criminal Sanction.* Stanford, Calif.: Stanford University Press.

Parker, L. Craig, Jr. 1984. *The Japanese Police System Today: An American Perspective.* Tokyo: Kodansha International.

Perrin, Noel. 1979. *Giving Up the Gun: Japan's Reversion to the Sword, 1543–1879.* Boston: David R. Godine.

Peters, Antonie. 1992. "Some Comparative Observations on the Criminal Justice Process in Holland and Japan." *Journal of the Japan-Netherlands Institute* 4:247–294.

Pharr, Susan. 1990. *Losing Face: Status Politics in Japan*. Berkeley: University of California Press.

Pizzi, William T. 1999. *Trials Without Truth: Why Our System of Criminal Trials Has Become an Expensive Failure and What We Need to Do to Rebuild It*. New York: New York University Press.

Pizzi, William T. 1993. "Understanding Prosecutorial Discretion in the United States: The Limits of Comparative Criminal Procedure as an Instrument of Reform." *Ohio State Law Journal* 54:1325–1373.

Provine, Doris Marie. 1996. "Courts in the Political Process in France." In Herbert Jacob et al., *Courts, Law, and Politics in Comparative Perspective*. New Haven, Conn.: Yale University Press.

Pugh, George. 1962. "The Administration of Criminal Justice in France: An Introductory Analysis." *Louisiana Law Review* 23:1ff.

Rabin, Robert L. 1972. "Agency Criminal Referrals in the Federal System: An Empirical Study of Prosecutorial Discretion." *Stanford Law Review* 24 (June):1036–1091.

Rabinowitz, Richard W. 1956. "The Historical Development of the Japanese Bar." *Harvard Law Review* 70:61–81.

Radelet, Michael L., Hugo Adam Bedau, and Constance E. Putnam. 1992. *In Spite of Innocence: The Ordeal of 400 Americans Wrongly Convicted of Crimes Punishable by Death*. Boston: Northeastern University Press.

Ragin, Charles C. 1994. *Constructing Social Research: The Unity and Diversity of Method*. Boston: Pine Forge Press.

Ragin, Charles C. 1987. *The Comparative Method: Moving Beyond Qualitative and Quantitative Strategies*. Berkeley: University of California Press.

Ramseyer, J. Mark, and Eric B. Rasmusen. 2001. "Why Is the Japanese Conviction Rate So High?" *Journal of Legal Studies* 30:53ff.

Ramseyer, J. Mark, and Eric B. Rasmusen. 2000. "Skewed Incentives: Paying for Politics as a Japanese Judge." *Judicature* 83, no. 4:190–195.

Ramseyer, J. Mark. 1986. "Foreword [on prosecutors in Japan]. *Pacific Basin Law Journal* 5: ii–iii.

Ramseyer, J. Mark, and Minoru Nakazato. 1999. *Japanese Law: An Economic Approach*. Chicago: University of Chicago Press.

Ramseyer, J. Mark, and Eric B. Rasmusen. 1999. "Why Is the Japanese Conviction Rate So High?" http://Php.indiana.edu/~erasmuse

Ramseyer, J. Mark, and Frances McCall Rosenbluth. 1996 .*The Politics of Oligarchy*. Cambridge: Cambridge University Press.

Ramseyer, J. Mark, and Frances McCall Rosenbluth. 1993. *Japan's Political Marketplace*. Cambridge, Mass.: Harvard University Press.

Rayment, Lauren. 1999. "Prosecutor Objectives in the United States and Japan." Unpublished paper, University of Washington School of Law.

Reed, Steven R. 1993. *Making Common Sense of Japan*. Pittsburgh, Pa.: University of Pittsburgh Press.

Reischauer, Edwin O. 1977. *The Japanese*. Tokyo: Charles E. Tuttle.

Reiss, Al. 1975. "Public Prosecutors and Criminal Prosecution in the United States of America." *Juridical Review* 20:1–21.

Remington, Frank J. 1993. "The Decision to Charge, the Decision to Convict on a Plea of Guilty, and the Impact of Sentence Structure on Prosecution Practices." In Lloyd E. Ohlin and Frank J. Remington, eds., *Discretion in Criminal Justice: The Tension Between*

Individualization and Uniformity, pp. 73–134. Albany: State University of New York Press.

Roach, Kent. 1999. "Four Models of the Criminal Process." *Journal of Criminal Law & Criminology* 89:671–716.

Roberts, Julian V. 1992. "Public Opinion, Crime, and Criminal Justice." In Michael Tonry, ed., *Crime and Justice: An Annual Review*. Chicago: University of Chicago Press.

Roberts, Julian V., and Loretta J. Stalans. 1997. *Public Opinion, Crime, and Criminal Justice*. Boulder, Colo.: Westview Press.

Roberts, Paul Craig, and Lawrence M. Stratton. 2000. *The Tyranny of Good Intentions: How Prosecutors and Bureaucrats Are Trampling the Constitution in the Name of Justice*. Roseville, Calif.: Prima Publishing.

Rohlen, Thomas P. 1983. *Japan's High Schools*. Berkeley: University of California Press.

Rohlen, Thomas P. 1974. *For Harmony and Strength: Japanese White-Collar Organization in Anthropological Perspective*. Berkeley: University of California Press.

Rokumoto, Kahei. 1988. "The Present State of Japanese Practicing Attorneys: On the Way to Full Professionalization." In R. Abel and P. Lewis, eds., *Lawyers in Society*, vol. 2. Berkeley: University of California Press.

Rosett, Arthur, and Donald R. Cressey. 1976. *Justice by Consent: Plea Bargains in the American Courthouse*. Philadelphia: J. B. Lippincott.

Rothwax, Harold J. 1996. *Guilty: The Collapse of Criminal Justice*. New York: Random House.

Runciman, W. G. 1994. "An Outsider's View of the Criminal Justice System." *Modern Law Review* 57 (January):1–9.

Rutherford, Andrew. 1993. *Criminal Justice and the Pursuit of Decency*. Oxford: Oxford University Press.

Saga, Junichi. 1991. *Confessions of a Yakuza*, trans. John Bester. Tokyo: Kodansha International.

Samuels, Richard J. 2001. "Land of the Setting Sun?" Review of Alex Kerr's *Dogs and Demons: Tales from the Dark Side of Japan* (New York: Hill & Wang, 2001). *New York Times Book Review*, April 15.

Sanchez-Jankowski, Martin. 1991. *Islands in the Street: Gangs and American Urban Society*. Berkeley: University of California Press.

Sarat, Austin. 1989. "Donald Black Discovers Legal Realism: From Pure Science to Policy Science in the Sociology of Law." *Law & Social Inquiry* 14:765–785.

Sasaki, Tomoko. 1995. *The Criminal Justice System in Japan: Investigation and Prosecution*. Tokyo: UNAFEI.

Satsumae, Takeshi. 1982. *The Bail System in Japan*. Tokyo: UNAFEI.

Satsumae, Takeshi. 1978. *Suspension of Prosecution: A Japanese Longstanding Practice Designed to Screen Out Offenders from Penal Process*. Tokyo: UNAFEI.

Sayle, Murray. 1996. "Nerve Gas and the Four Noble Truths." *The New Yorker*, April 1, pp. 56–71.

Scheingold, Stuart A. 1991. *The Politics of Street Crime: Criminal Process and Cultural Obsession*. Philadelphia: Temple University Press.

Scheingold, Stuart A. 1984. *The Politics of Law and Order: Street Crime and Public Policy*. New York: Longman.

Scheingold, Stuart A., Toska Olson, and Jana Pershing. 1994. "Sexual Violence, Victim Advocacy, and Republican Criminology: Washington State's Community Protection Act." *Law & Society Review* 28:729–763.

Scheck, Barry, Peter Neufeld, and Jim Dwyer. 2000. *Actual Innocence: Five Days to Execution, and Other Dispatches from the Wrongly Convicted*. New York: Doubleday.

Schulhofer, Stephen. 1984. "Is Plea Bargaining Inevitable?" *Harvard Law Review* 97:1037ff.

Schuyt, Kees. 1992. "Dutch Tolerance and the Criminal Justice System." *Journal of the Japan-Netherlands Institute* 4:206–220.

Selznick, Philip. 1957. *Leadership in Administration*. Evanston, Ill.: Row, Peterson.

Seymour, Christopher. 1996. *Yakuza Diary: Doing Time in the Japanese Underworld*. New York: Atlantic Monthly Press.

Sherman, Lawrence. 2000. "The Defiant Imagination: Consilience and the Science of Sanctions." The Albert M. Greenfield Chair Inaugural Lecture, Department of Sociology, University of Pennsylvania, February 24.

Sherman, Lawrence. 1993. "Defiance, Deterrence, and Irrelevance: A Theory of the Criminal Sanction." *Journal of Research in Crime and Delinquency* 30 (November):445–473.

Shikita, Minoru. 1982. "Integrated Approach to Effective Administration of Criminal and Juvenile Justice." In B. J. George, Jr., ed., *Criminal Justice in Asia: The Quest for an Integrated Approach*. Tokyo: UNAFEI.

Shikita, Minoru, and Shinichi Tsuchiya. 1992. *Crime and Criminal Policy in Japan: Analysis and Evaluation of the Showa Era, 1926–1988*. New York: Springer-Verlag.

Shinomiya, Satoru. 2001. "Adversarial Procedure Without Jury: Is the Japanese System Adversarial, Inquisitorial, or Other?" In Malcolm M. Feeley and Setsuo Miyazawa, eds., *The Japanese Adversary System in Context: Controversies and Comparisons*. London: Macmillan.

Siegel, Larry J. 2000. *Criminology*. 7th ed. Belmont, Calif.: Wadsworth.

Silberman, Charles E. 1978. *Criminal Violence, Criminal Justice*. New York: Random House.

Simon, David. 1991. *Homicide: A Year on the Killing Streets*. Boston: Houghton Mifflin.

Skolnick, Jerome H. 1982. "Deception by Police." *Criminal Justice Ethics*. 1 (Summer/Fall): 40–54.

Skolnick, Jerome H. 1975. *Justice Without Trial: Law Enforcement in Democratic Society*. New York: John Wiley & Sons.

Skolnick, Jerome H. 1967. "Social Control in the Adversary System." *Conflict Resolution* 11, no. 1:52–70.

Smith, Barbara E., Robert C. Davis, and Laura B. Nickles. 2000. "Impact Evaluation of Victim Services Programs: STOP Grants Funded by the Violence Against Women Act." Final Report submitted to the National Institute of Justice, Washington D.C.

Smith, Robert J. 1983. *Japanese Society: Tradition, Self and the Social Order*. Cambridge: Cambridge University Press.

Solomon, Peter H. 1987. "The Case of the Vanishing Acquittal: Informal Norms and the Practice of Soviet Criminal Justice." *Soviet Studies* 39:531ff.

Spencer, J. R. 1995. "Justice English Style." *The World & I.* 10 (August):314–323.

Spencer, J. R. 1987. "Do We Need a Prosecution Appeal Against Sentence?" *Criminal Law Review* (November):724–736.

Spohn, Cassie, John Gruhl, and Susan Welch. 1987. "The Impact of the Ethnicity and Gender of Defendants on the Decision to Reject or Dismiss Felony Charges." *Criminology* 25:175–191.

Standen, Jeffrey. 1993. "Plea Bargaining in the Shadow of the Guidelines." *California Law Review* 81:1471–1538.

Stanko, Elizabeth Anne. 1982. "Would You Believe This Woman: Prosecutorial Screening for 'Credible' Witnesses and a Problem of Justice." In Nicole Hahn Rafter and Elizabeth Anne Stanko, eds., *Judge, Lawyer, Victim, Thief: Women, Gender Roles, and Criminal Justice*. Boston: Northeastern University Press.

Stanko, Elizabeth Ann. 1981. "The Impact of Victim Assessment on Prosecutors' Screening Decisions: The Case of the New York County District Attorney's Office." *Law & Society Review* 16, no. 2:225–239.

Steinberg, Allen. 1984. "From Private Prosecution to Plea Bargaining: Criminal Prosecution, the District Attorney, and American Legal History." *Crime & Delinquency* 30, no. 4 (October):568–592.

Steinhoff, Patricia G. 1993. "Pursuing the Japanese Police." *Law & Society Review* 27:827–50.

Steinhoff, Patricia G. 1991. *Tenko: Ideology and Societal Integration in Prewar Japan.* New York: Garland.

Stern, Vivien. 1998. *A Sin Against the Future: Imprisonment in the World.* Boston: Northeastern University Press.

Stewart, James B. 1987. *The Prosecutors: Inside the Offices of the Government's Most Powerful Lawyers.* New York: Simon & Schuster.

Stone, Michael. 2000. *Gangbusters: How a Street-Tough, Elite Homicide Unit Took Down New York's Most Dangerous Gang.* New York: Doubleday.

Strier, Franklin. 1995. "Adversarial Justice." *World & I* 10 (August):288–303.

Suchman, Mark C., and Lauren B. Edelman. 1996. "Legal Rational Myths: The New Institutionalism and the Law and Society Tradition." *Law & Social Inquiry* 21:903–942.

Sudman, Seymour, and Norman M. Bradburn. 1982. *Asking Questions: A Practical Guide to Questionnaire Design.* San Francisco: Jossey-Bass.

Sugimoto, Yoshio. 1997. *An Introduction to Japanese Society.* Cambridge: Cambridge University Press.

Surette, Ray. 1992. *Media, Crime, and Criminal Justice: Images and Reality.* Belmont, Calif.: Wadsworth.

Sutherland, Edwin H., and Donald R. Cressey. 1978. *Criminology.* 10th ed. Philadelphia: J. B. Lippincott.

Suzuki, Yoshio. 1980. "Safeguards Against Abuse of Prosecutorial Powers." In *The Role of Public Prosecutors in Criminal Justice: Prosecutorial Discretion in Japan and the United States,* pp. 13–16. Tokyo: Japan Society Public Affairs Series, no. 14.

Szymkowiak, Kenneth. 2001. *Sokaiya: Extortion, Protection, and the Japanese Corporation.* Armonk, N.Y.: M.E. Sharpe.

Tak, Peter J. 1986. *The Legal Scope of Non-Prosecution in Europe.* Helsinki, Finland: Helsinki Institute for Crime Prevention and Control.

Takano, Takashi. 2001. "Miranda Experience in Japan." In Malcolm M. Feeley and Setsuo Miyazawa, eds., *The Japanese Adversary System in Context: Controversies and Comparisons.* London: Macmillan.

Tanaka, Hideo, assisted by Malcolm D. H. Smith. 1976. *The Japanese Legal System: Introductory Cases and Materials.* Tokyo: University of Tokyo Press.

Taylor, Lawrence. 1996. *The D.A.: A True Story.* New York: William Morrow.

Tevlin, Aidan. 1993. "Motives for Prosecution." *Journal of Criminal Law* 57 (August): 288–297.

Thompson, James D. 1967. *Organizations in Action.* New York: McGraw-Hill.

Thornton, Robert Y., with Katsuya Endo. 1992. *Preventing Crime in America and Japan: A Comparative Study.* Armonk, N.Y.: M. E. Sharpe.

Three Tokyo Bar Associations. 1989. *Torture and Unlawful or Unjust Treatment of Detainees in Daiyō-Kangoku (Substitute Prisons) in Japan: A Sampling of Recent Cases.* Tokyo: Three Tokyo Bar Associations.

Tipton, Elise. 1990. *Japanese Police State: Tokko in Interwar Japan.* Honolulu: University of Hawaii Press.

Tōjō, Shinichiro. 1968. "The Prosecutor's Discretion and Its Control in Japan and the United States." Master of Law Thesis, Boalt Hall School of Law, University of California at Berkeley.

Tonry, Michael. 1996. *Sentencing Matters.* New York: Oxford University Press.

Tonry, Michael. 1995. *Malign Neglect: Race, Crime, and Punishment in America.* New York: Oxford University Press.

Tonry, Michael. 1994. "Racial Politics, Racial Disparities, and the War on Crime." *Crime & Delinquency* 39 (October):475–494.

Trouille, Helen. 1994. "A Look at French Criminal Procedure." *Criminal Law Review* (October):735–744.

Tsuchimoto, Takeshi. 1992. "Comparative Observation of Criminal Procedure in Japan and the Netherlands." *Journal of the Japan-Netherlands Institute* 4:295–310.

Tyler, Tom R. 1990. *Why People Obey the Law*. New Haven, Conn.: Yale University Press.

Umbreit, Mark S. 1998. "Restorative Justice: Theory Meets Practice." *Western Criminology Review* 1 (June):1–29.

Upham, Frank K. 1987. *Law and Social Change in Postwar Japan*. Cambridge, Mass.: Harvard University Press.

Upham, Frank K. 1980. "*Japan v. Kawamoto*: Judicial Limits on the State's Power to Indict." *Law in Japan* 13:137–150.

U.S. Department of Justice, Bureau of Justice Statistics. *Report to the Nation on Crime and Justice*. 2nd ed. Washington, D.C.: United States Government Printing Office.

Utz, Pamela. 1984. "The Imperatives of Mass Processing." In William J. Chambliss, ed., *Criminal Law in Action*. New York: John Wiley & Sons.

Utz, Pamela J. 1978. *Settling the Facts: Discretion and Negotiation in Criminal Court*. Lexington, Mass.: Lexington Books.

Uviller, H. Richard. 2000. "The Neutral Prosecutor: The Obligation of Dispassion in a Passionate Pursuit." *Fordham Law Review* 68:1695–1718.

Uviller, H. Richard. 1999. *The Tilted Playing Field: Is Criminal Justice Unfair?* New Haven, Conn.: Yale University Press.

Uviller, H. Richard. 1996. *Virtual Justice: The Flawed Prosecution of Crime in America*. New Haven, Conn.: Yale University Press.

Uviller, H. Richard. 1973. "The Virtuous Prosecutor in Quest of an Ethical Standard: Guidance from the ABA." *Michigan Law Review* 71 (May):1145–1168.

Van Ness, Daniel W. 1993. "New Wine and Old Wineskins: Four Challenges of Restorative Justice." *Criminal Law Forum* 4:251–276.

Van Ness, Daniel, and Karen Heetderks Strong. 1997. *Restoring Justice*. Cincinnati, Ohio: Anderson.

Van Wolferen, Karel. 1989. *The Enigma of Japanese Power: People and Politics in a Stateless Nation*. New York: Alfred A. Knopf.

Vaughn, Michael S. 1991. "The Relationship Between Unemployment and Crime in Japan from 1926 to 1988: Trends During Emperor Hirohito's Reign." *International Journal of Comparative and Applied Criminal Justice* 15 (Fall):153–173.

Vaughn, Michael S., Frank F. Y. Huang, and Christine Rose Ramirez. 1995. "Drug Abuse and Anti-Drug Policy in Japan: Past History and Future Directions." *British Journal of Criminology* 35 (Autumn):491–524.

Vaughn, Michael S., and Nobuho Tomita. 1990. "A Longitudinal Analysis of Japanese Crime from 1926 to 1987: The Pre-War, War, and Post-War Eras." *International Journal of Applied and Comparative Criminal Justice* 14 (Winter):145–158.

Vera Institute of Justice. 1981. *Felony Arrests: Their Prosecution and Disposition in New York City's Courts*. New York: Longman.

Vogel, Ezra F. 1979. *Japan as Number One: Lessons for America*. Cambridge, Mass.: Harvard University Press.

Vogel, Ezra F. 1975. "Introduction: Toward More Accurate Concepts." In Ezra F. Vogel, ed., *Modern Japanese Organization and Decision-Making*. Tokyo: Charles E. Tuttle.

Vorenberg, James. 1981. "Decent Restraint of Prosecutorial Power." *Harvard Law Review* 94 (May):1521–1573.

Vorenberg, James. 1976. "Narrowing the Discretion of Criminal Justice Officials." *Duke Law Journal* 1976 (September):652–697.

Wagatsuma, Hiroshi, and Arthur Rosett. 1986. "The Implications of Apology: Law and Culture in Japan and the United States." *Law & Society Review* 20, no. 4:461–496.

Walker, Samuel. 2001. *Police Accountability: The Role of Citizen Oversight.* Belmont, Calif.: Wadsworth Thompson Learning.

Walker, Samuel. 1994. *Sense and Nonsense About Crime: A Policy Guide.* Pacific Grove, Calif.: Brooks/Cole.

Walker, Samuel. 1993. *Taming the System: The Control of Discretion in Criminal Justice, 1950–1990.* New York: Oxford University Press.

Walker, Samuel. 1980. *Popular Justice: A History of American Criminal Justice.* New York: Oxford University Press. 1980.

Walker, Samuel, Cassia Spohn, and Miriam DeLone. 2000. *The Color of Justice: Race, Ethnicity, and Crime in America.* Belmont, Calif.: Wadsworth.

Watanabe, Takashi. 1993. *Crime Control in Japan.* Tokyo: UNAFEI.

Weber, Robert Philip. 1985. *Basic Content Analysis.* Beverly Hills, Calif.: Sage.

Weigend, Thomas. 1993. "In Germany, Fines Often Imposed in Lieu of Prosecution." *Overcrowded Times: Solving the Prison Problem* 4, no. 1 (February):1ff.

Weigend, Thomas. 1980. "Continental Cures for American Ailments: European Criminal Procedure as a Model for Law Reform." In Norval Morris and Michael Tonry, eds., *Crime and Justice: An Annual Review of Research,* vol. 2, pp. 381–428. Chicago: University of Chicago Press.

Weinreb, Lloyd L. 1977. *Denial of Justice: Criminal Process in the United States.* New York: Free Press.

Weisberg, Robert. 1995. "Review Essay: Victims' Rights in Criminal Trials." *Criminal Justice Ethics* 14 (Summer/Fall):56–62.

Weisman, Richard. 2001. "Detecting Remorse and Its Absence in the Criminal Justice System." In Austin Sarat and Patricia Ewick, eds., *Studies in Law, Politics, and Society.* Stanford, Calif.: JAI Press.

Weninger, Robert A. 1987. "The Abolition of Plea Bargaining: A Case Study of El Paso County, Texas." *UCLA Law Review* 35:311ff.

West, Andrew. 2000. "Reform of French Criminal Justice." *New Law Journal.* Three parts: October 20:1542–1543; November 3:1630–1631; and November 10:1667–1668.

West, Mark D. 1992. "Note: Prosecution Review Commissions: Japan's Answer to the Problem of Prosecutorial Discretion." *Columbia Law Review* 92 (April):684–723.

Westermann, Ted D., and James W. Burfeind. 1991. *Crime and Justice in Two Societies: Japan and the United States.* Pacific Grove, Calif.: Brooks/Cole.

White, Merry. 1987. *The Japanese Educational Challenge: A Commitment to Children.* Tokyo: Kodansha.

Whiting, Robert. 1999. *Tokyo Underworld: The Fast Times and Hard Life of an American Gangster in Japan.* New York: Pantheon Books.

Williams, David. 1994. *Japan: Beyond the End of History.* London: Routledge.

Wilson, James Q. 1989. *Bureaucracy: What Government Agencies Do and Why They Do It.* New York: Basic Books.

Wilson, James Q. 1983. *Thinking About Crime.* Rev. ed. New York: Basic Books.

Winchell, Hilary. 1995. "Unanticipated Consequences: The Economic and Social Impact of 'Three Strikes' Legislation on California." *California Legal Studies Journal* 1:111–135.

Winokur, Scott. 1995. "Mr. District Attorney Arlo Smith: A Fixture for 15 Years, but What Does the Record Show?" *San Francisco Examiner,* September 10–13.

Womack, James P., Daniel T. Jones, and Daniel Roos. 1990. *The Machine That Changed the World: The Story of Lean Production.* New York: Harper Perennial.

Woodall, Brian. 1996. *Japan Under Construction: Corruption, Politics, and Public Works.* Berkeley: University of California Press.

Yamada, Shinji. 1994. *Tax Evasion and Corruption in Japan.* Tokyo: UNAFEI.

Yamashita, Terutoshi. 1996. *The Criminal Justice System in Japan: The Prosecution.* Tokyo: UNAFEI.

Zander, Michael. 2000. "The Criminal Standard of Proof: How Sure Is Sure?" *New Law Journal,* October 20:1517–1519.

Zeisel, Hans. 1982. *The Limits of Law Enforcement.* Chicago: University of Chicago Press.

Zeisel, Hans. 1980. "The Offer That Cannot Be Refused." In Franklin E. Zimring and Richard S. Frase, eds., *The Criminal Justice System: Materials on the Administration and Reform of the Criminal Law,* pp. 558–561. Boston: Little, Brown.

Zimring, Franklin E., and Richard S. Frase. 1980. *The Criminal Justice System: Materials on the Administration and Reform of the Criminal Law.* Boston: Little, Brown.

Zimring, Franklin E., and Gordon Hawkins. 1997. *Crime Is Not the Problem: Lethal Violence in America.* Oxford University Press.

Zimring, Franklin E., and Gordon Hawkins. 1995a. "Crime Is Not the Problem." Unpublished paper.

Zimring, Franklin E., and Gordon Hawkins. 1995b. *Incapacitation: Penal Confinement and the Restraint of Crime.* Oxford University Press.

Zimring, Franklin E., and Gordon Hawkins. 1986. *Capital Punishment and the American Agenda.* Cambridge University Press.

Japanese-Language Publications

Abe, Haruo. 1968. "Shinkensatsukanron." *Chūō Kōron* 83 (May):162–175.

Abe, S. 1992. "Watakushi dake ga Shitte Iru Kensatsu vs. Kanemaru, 'Torihiki' no Shinsō." *Shūkan Bunshū,* October 22, pp. 34–40.

Aoyagi, Fumio. 1986. *Nihonjin no Hanzai Ishiki.* 16. Tokyo: Chūō Kōronsha.

Aoyagi, Fumio. 1981. "Nihon no Kensatsu." *Hōgaku Seminā Zōkan* (August):29–36.

Aoyagi, Fumio. 1978. "Keiji Saiban to Jihaku." In Nomura Jirō, ed., *Hōsō Ano Koro,* vol. 1. Tokyo: Nihonhyōronsha.

Asano, Kenichi. 1987. *Hanzai Hōdō no Hanzai.* Tokyo: Kōdansha.

Atarashi, Eri. 2000. *Hanzai Higaisha Shien.* Tokyo: Komichi Shobō.

Bessho, Otarō. 1983. *Oni Kenji Oboegaki.* Tokyo: Yomiuri Shimbunsha.

Dandō, Shigemitsu. 1997. *Shikei Haishiron.* Tokyo: Yūhikaku.

Foote, Daniel H. 1999. "Nichibei Hikaku Keiji Shihō no Kōgi o Furikaette." *Jurisuto* no. 1148 (January 1–15):165–173.

Fujinaga, Yukiharu. 1993. *Gendai Kensatsu no Riron to Kadai: 21 Seiki no Kensatsu no tame ni.* Tokyo: Shinyamasha Shuppan Kabushikigaisha.

Furuta, Yūki. 1993. *Keihō to Iu Hōritsu.* Tokyo: Ōkurasho Insatsukyoku.

"Gendai no Bengoshi: Shihōhen." 1982. *Hōgaku Seminā Zōkan* 21 (December).

"Gendai no Kensatsu: Nihon Kensatsu no Jittai to Riron." 1981. *Hōgaku Seminā Zōkan* 16 (August).

George, B. J., Jr. 1981. "Nihon no Kensatsu Seido ni Kansuru Hito Hikaku Hōgakusha no Inshō." *Hōgaku Seminā Zōkan* 16 (August):204–210.

Hamada, Sumio. 1992. *Jihaku no Kenkyū.* Tokyo: 31 Shobō.

Hasegawa, Kiyoshi. 1978. *Watakushi to Kenji.* Hyōronsha.

Hata, Hiroto. 1998. "Keiji Bengo Katsudō no Nichijō to Keiji Bengoshiron no Tenkai: 'Keiji Senmon' Bengoshi no Kansatsu Kenkyū ni yotte." *Kobe Hōgaku Zasshi* 48 (September): 357–412.

Hata, Hiroto. 1993. "Keiji Bengo no Jitsuzō o Motomete: Kobe to Fukuoka ni okeru Hōtei Kansatsu to Mensetsu Chōsha kara." *Rokkaidō Ronshū* 40 (April):120–141.

Hatano, Akira. 1994a. "Kensatsu Fassho no Daitsumi o Tou." *Hōseki* (Feburary):61–79.

Hatano, Akira. 1994b. *Tsuno o Tamete Ushi o Korosu Koto Nakare: Kensatsu Kenryoku wa Kokumin no Teki ka.* Tokyo: Kobunsha.

Hayashi, Masahiro. 1987. "Sendai no Baishin Saiban ni Tsuite." *Hanrei Taimuzu* 17–24.

Hirano, Ryūichi. 1999. "Sanshinsei no Saiyō ni yoru 'Kakushin Shihō' o: Keiji Shihō Kaikaku no Ugoki to Hōkō." *Jurisuto* no. 1148 (January 1–15):2–15.

Hirata, Tomomi. 1992. *Zenin Muzai: 122nin Senkyo Ihan Jiken o Ou.* Tokyo: Gyōsei.

Hotta, Tsutomu. 1994. *Ogoru na Jōshi!: Jinji to Soshiki no Kanrigaku.* Tokyo: Nihon Keizai Shimbunsha.

Idei, Yoshio. 1986. *Kenji no Hikaeshitsu.* Tokyo: Chūō Kōronsha.

Idota, Akira. 1981. "Sōsa ni okeru Kensatsu no Yakuwari: Keisatsu to Kensatsu no Kankei." *Hōgaku Seminā Zōkan* 16 (August):88–95.

Igarashi, Futaba. 1995. "'Chōsho Saiban' no Kabe ni Ana Ga Hiraita: Gaikokujin no Kyōjutsu Chōsho wa Saiyō Sarenakatta." *Shūkan Kinyōbi*, March 10, pp. 35–37.

Igarashi, Futaba. 1994. "Nihongo o Bokokugo to Shinai Mono no Kyōjutsu Chōsho no Shōko Nōryoku ni tsuite." *Jiyū to Seigi* 45 (March):226–227.

Imai, Hidenori. 1999. *Zako Kenji no Jikenbo.* Tokyo: Kyōdō Tsūshinsha.

Inoue, Goro. 1989. *Aru Kenji no Kokoro to Tsubuyaki.* Tokyo: Shinyamasha Shuppan.

Isa, Chihirō. 1987. *Gyakuten: Amerika Shihaika, Okinawa no Baishin Saiban.* Tokyo: Bungei Shunjū.

Ishimatsu, Takeo. 1993. *Keiji Saiban no Kudōka: Kaikaku e no Dohyō.* Tokyo: Keisōshobō.

Itami, Jūzō. 1997. "Kyōjutsu Chōshotte Fushizen Da to Omoimasu." *Kikan Keiji Bengo*, no. 12: 4–7.

Itoh, Shigeki. 1992. *Kenji Sōchō no Kaisō.* Tokyo: Asahi Shimbunsha.

Itoh, Shigeki. 1988. "Watakushi no Ayunda Michi: Itoh Shigeki Kenji Sōchō ni Kiku." *Hōritsu no Hiroba* 39, no. 5:4–17.

Itoh, Shigeki. 1987. *Mata Damasareru Kenji.* Tokyo: Tachibana Shobō.

Itoh, Shigeki. 1986b. *Kensatsuchōhō Chikujo Kaisetsu.* Tokyo: Ryōshōfukyūkai.

Itoh, Shigeki. 1982. *Damasareru Kenji.* Tokyo: Tachibana Shobo.

Itoh, Shigeki. 1963. "Kensatsu Kanron." *Juristo* 265 (January 1):117–120.

Johnson, David T. 1999. "Kumo no Su ni Shōchō Sareru Nihonhō no Tokushoku." *Jurisuto* no. 1148 (January 1–15):185–189.

Kaino, Tamie, et al. (*Otto/Koibito kara no Bōryoku Chōsa Kenkyūkai*). 1998. *Domestic Violence: Otto/Koibito kara no Bōryoku o Nakusu Tame ni.* Tokyo: Yūhikaku.

Kameyama, Tsugio. 1999. "Keijisoshōhō 50 nen to Kensatsu no Kadai." *Jurisuto* no. 1148 (January 1–15):24–30.

Kataoka, N. 1993. "Wagakuni no Keiji Shihō ni okeru Kensatsukan no Yakuwari ni tsuite." Unpublished manuscript, Ministry of Justice.

Kawai, Nobutarō. 1979. *Kensatsu Tokuhon.* Tokyo: Shōji Hōmu Kenkyūkai.

Kawai, Nobutarō. 1954. "Giwaku no Maku wa Orosareta." *Bungei Shunjū* 32 (August):200–209.

Kawakami, Kazuo. 1981. "Shakai Seigi to Kensatsu: Gendai ni okeru Kensatsu no Yakuwari." *Hōgaku Seminā Zōkan* 16 (August):19–28.

Kawasaki, Hideaki. 1991. "Kensatsukanron no Kadai: Sengo no Kensatsu to Keiji Shihō." In Takuji Takada, ed., *Keiji Soshō no Gendai teki Dōkō*, pp. 1–24. Tokyo: Sanshodō.

Kensatsu Kōgian. 1991. Tokyo: Hōmushō Keijikyoku.

Kensatsu Tōkei Nempō. Tokyo: Hōmushō.

Kubo, Hiroshi. 1989. *Nippon no Kensatsu.* Tokyo: Kōdansha.

Kurata, Seiji, et al. 1992. *Iwayuru Rainichi Gaikokujin ni yoru Settō Jihan no Kenkyū.* Tokyo: Nihonkoku Hōmushō Hōmu Sōgō Kenkyūsho.

Maruta, Takashi. 1990. *Baishin Saiban o Kangaeru: Hōtei ni Miru Nichibei Bunka Hikaku.* Tokyo: Chūō Kōronsha.

Matsuhashi, Tadamitsu. 1994. *Wagatsumi wa Waga mae ni Ari: Kitai Sareru Shinkeisatsu Chōkan e no Tegami.* Tokyo: Shakai Shisosha.

Matsumoto, Ichirō. 1981. "Kensatsukan no Dokuritsu—Ittai no Gensoku." *Hōgaku Seminā Zōkan* 16 (August).

Matsumoto, Seicho. 1963a. "Kensatsukanryōron." *Bungei Shunjū* 41 (August):142–154.

Matsumoto, Seicho. 1963b. "Kensatsukanryō wa Kunan Suru." *Bungei Shunjū* 41 (September):118–142.

Matsuo, Koya. 1981. "Gendai Kensatsuron." *Hōgaku Seminā Zōkan* 16 (August):2–9.

Matsuzawa, Yasuo. 1992. "Watakushi no Chōsho wa Kenji no Sakubun Da." *Bungei Shunjū* 70 (November):168–174.

Mikami, Takashi, and Morishita Hiroshi. 1996. *Sabakareru Keisatsu: Hanshin Fan Bōkō Jiken to Fushimpan Jiken.* Tokyo: Nihon Hyōronsha.

Miranda no Kai. 1999. "Hōmushō 'Higisha Bengo o Meguru Shomondai' ni tai Suru Iken." Unpublished paper.

Miranda no Kai, ed. 1997. *"Miranda no Kai" to Bengo Katsudō.* Tokyo: Daigaku Tosho.

Mitsui, Makoto. 1979. "Sengo no Kensatsu: 'Kenshū'shi o Sozai toshite." *Jurisuto* 700 (September 15):214–220.

Mitsui, Makoto. 1971a. "Kensatsukan no Kiso Yūyo Sairyō (1): Sono Soshōhōteki oyobi Hikaku Hōseiteki Kōsatsu." *Kobe Hōgaku Zasshi* 21, no. 1–2 (June):31–96.

Mitsui, Makoto. 1971b. "'Ōura Jiken' no Nagekaketa Hamon: Naisō no Tokushoku to Kiso Yūyo Shobun no Tōhi." *Kobe Hōgaku Zasshi* 20, no. 3–4 (March):428–457.

Mitsui, Makoto, moderator. 1999. "Zadankai: Keiji Soshōhō no Genjitsu to Sono Mondaiten." *Jurisuto* no. 1148 (January 1–15):124–164.

Mitsui, Makoto, Nakayama Yoshifusa, Kawakami Kazuo, and Tamura Masayoshi, eds. 1988. *Keiji Tetsuzuki.* 2 vols. Tokyo: Chikuma Shobō.

Mitsui, Makoto. 1970, 1974a, 1974b, 1974c, 1977. "Kensatsukan no Kiso Yūyo Sairyō: Sono Rekishiteki oyobi Jisshōteki Kenkyū." *Hōgaku Kyōkai Zasshi* 87, nos. 9–10; 91, no. 7; 91, no. 9; 91, no. 12; 94, no. 6.

Miyamoto, Masafumi, and Sankei Shimbun Tokushūbu. 2000. *Kensatsu no Hirō.* Tokyo: Kadokawa Shoten.

Mizoguchi, Atsushi. 1993. *Gendai Yakuza no Ura Chishiki.* Tokyo: Nihon Purintekusu.

Mori, Isamu. 1981. "Nihon no Kensatsu: Nempyō [1868–1981]." *Hōgaku Seminā Zōkan* 16 (August):339–343.

Morita, Hisashi. 1994. *Fukiso no Giwaku: Chōnan no Kōtsū Jikoshi kara.* Tokyo: Nihon Toshokankōkai.

Mukaidani, Susumu. 1993a. *Chiken Tokusōbu.* Tokyo: Kodansha.

Mukaidani, Susumu. 1993b. "Kensatsu no 'Mihitsu no Koi.'" *Bungei Shunjū* 71 (May):147–150.

Mukaidani, Susumu. 1993c. "Yoshinaga Ryōsuke wa Nani o Kangaete Iru ka." *Bungei Shunjū* 71 (December):196–206.

Murai, K. 1990. "Kensatsukan wa Naze Yameru: Watakushi no Kensatsukan Inshōron." *Hōgaku Seminā* 35 (November):109–114.

Murakami, Haruki, and Anzai Mizumaru. 1984. *Murakami Asahidō.* Tokyo: Shinchōsha.

Murobushi, Tetsurō. 1981. "Kensatsu to Seiji: Kenryoku Chūkaku to no Kōbō." *Hōgaku Seminā Zōkan* 16 (1981):265–272.

Nakada, Kaoru, Horita Shinya, and Nagasawa Chiharu. 2001. "'Hanzai Kenkyoritsu 24.2%' ga Imi Suru Mono." *Spa*, January 31:20–23.

Narushima, Tadayoshi, and Uehara Shunsuke. 1989. *Tokyo Chiken Tokusōbu: Nihon Saikō no Sōsa Kikan wa Kyōaku ni Semareru ka.* Tokyo: Aipekku.

Natsuki, Eiji. 2000. *Detchiage: Chikan Enzai no Hassei Mekanīzumu.* Tokyo: Kadokawa Shoten.

Nihon Bengoshi Rengōkai. 1992. *Okinawa no Baishin Saiban.* Tokyo: Nihon Bengoshi Rengōkai.

Nihon Hyōronsha. 1983. "Nihon no Enzai." *Hōgaku Seminā* 27 (July).

Nomura, Jirō. 1994. *Nihon no Saibankan.* Tokyo: Kōdansha.

Nomura, Jirō. 1992a. *Nihon no Bengoshi.* Tokyo: Waseda Keiei Shuppan.

Nomura, Jirō. 1992b. *Nihon no Saibankan.* Tokyo: Waseda Keiei Shuppan.

Nomura, Jirō. 1991. *Nihon no Kensatsu.* Tokyo: Nihon Hyōronsha.

Nomura, Jirō. 1988. *Nihon no Kensatsu: Saikō no Kenryoku no Uchigawa.* Tokyo: Kōdansha.

Nomura, Jirō. 1984. *Kenji Sōchō no Sengoshi.* Tokyo: Bijinesusha.

Nomura, Jirō. 1980. *Nihon no Kensatsu.* Tokyo: Nihon Hyōronsha.

Nomura, Jirō. 1978a. *Kenji: Kenryoku to Jinken.* Tokyo: Kyōikusha.

Nomura, Jirō. 1971–1972. "Kensatsu to Chūritsusei." *Hōgaku Seminā Zōkan* Nos. 184–192 and 194 (May–February).

Nomura, Jirō, ed. 1978b. *Hōsō Ano Koro.* 2 vols. Tokyo: Nihon Hyōronsha.

Odanaka, Toshiki. 1981. "Kensatsu no Minshūka to Kensatsukan no Ryōshin." *Hōgaku Seminā Zōkan* 6 (August):37–45.

Odanaka, Toshiki. 1976. *Keiji Soshōhō no Rekishi teki Bunsetsu.* Tokyo: Nihon Hyōronsha.

Ogino, Fujio. 2000. *Shisō Kenji.* Tokyo: Iwanami Shoten.

Oki, Kazuhiro, et al. 1995. *Saibankan ni Narenai Riyū.* Tokyo: Aokishoten.

Omiya, Kenichirō. 1994. *Ji-Sha Renritsu Seiken: Seijika, Kanryō Jinmyaku Chizu.* Tokyo: Futabasha.

Ōno, Masao and Watanabe Yasuo. 1989. *Keiji Saiban no Hikari to Kage: Yūzairitsu 99% no Imi Suru Mono.* Tokyo: Yūhikaku.

Ōno, Tatsuzō. 1992. *Nihon no Kensatsu.* Tokyo: Shinnihon Shuppansha.

Osaka Bengoshikai. 1988. "Kenjichō Hatsugen Mondai ni kansuru Ikensho: Keijisaiban wa Dō Aru beki ka." Osaka: Osaka Bengoshikai.

Osaka Bengoshikai. 1987. "Kenjichō Hatsugen Mondai ni kansuru Ikensho: Ureu beki Keijisaiban no Genjō to Kongo no Kadai." Osaka: Osaka Bengoshikai.

Ota, Shigeru. 1999. "Kensatsu Jitsumu no Kadai." *Jurisuto* no. 1148 (January 1–15):276–281.

Saeki, Chihiro. 1989. "Keiji Soshōhō no Yonjūnen to Muzairitsu no Genshō." *Juristo* 930 (March 25):16–20.

Sasaki, Tomoko. 2000. *Nihon no Shihō Bunka.* Tokyo: Bungei Shunjū.

Satō, Kinko. 1974. *Torihiki no Shakai: Amerika no Keiji Shihō.* Tokyo: Chūō Kōronsha.

Satō, Michio. 1993. *Kenji Chōsho no Yohaku.* Tokyo: Asahi Shimbunsha.

Sawada, Tōyō. 1988. *Kensatsu o Kiru: Kensatsu Hyakunen no Habatsu to Jinmyaku.* Tokyo: Tosho Shuppansha.

Setō, Shūzō. 1983. *Hōmu-Kensatsu Ura no Ura: Sono Masei to Hokorobi.* Tokyo: Dōyūkan.

Shimizu, Isao. 1998. *Tokusōkenji no "Shōko to Shinjitsu."* Tokyo: Kōdansha.

Shinomiya, Satoru. 1999. *Baishin Tebiki.* Tokyo: Gendaijinbunsha.

Suzuki, Yoshio, Satō Fumiya, Nishigaki Michio, Nomura Jirō, and Mitsui Makoto. 1981. "Zadankai: Gendai Nihon no Kensatsu." *Hōgaku Seminā Zōkan* 16 (August):46–73.

Tachibana, Takashi. 1993. *Kyōaku vs. Genron.* Tokyo: Bungei Shunjū.

Tachibana, Takashi. 1992. "Kensatsu no kakumo Nagaki Nemuri." *Bungei Shunjū* 70 (December):94–109.

Takahashi, Hidemine. 1992. *Tokyo Gaikokujin Saiban.* Tokyo: Heibonsha.

Tanase, Takao. 1986. "Keiji Baishin to Jijitsu Nintei." *Hanrei Taimuzu* 603 (August 14):13–34.

Tani, N. 1995. "Wagakuni ni okeru Jūki Hanzai no Genjō." *Hōritsu no Hiroba* 48 (March):4–12.

Tashima, Yūko. 1998. *Onna Kenji hodo Omoshiroi Shigoto wa Nai.* Tokyo: Kōdansha.

Tawada, N. 1995. "Jūki Hanzai to Jūhō Tōken rui Shoji nado Torishimarihō no Bassoku Gōka." *Hōritsu no Hiroba* 48 (March):43–47.

Terasawa, Yū, ed. 1998. *Omawari san wa Zeikin Dorobō.* Tokyo: Media Works.

Tokyo Sanbengoshikai. 1984. *Nureginu: Kōshite Watakushi wa Jihaku Saserareta.* Tokyo: Seihōsha.

Uematsu, Tadashi. 1981. "Kōeki no Daihyōsha." *Hōgaku Seminā Zōkan* 16 (August):160–161.

Ugawa, Haruhiko. 1997. "Shihō Torihiki o Kangaeru." *Hanrei Jihō* nos. 1583:31–47; 1627:36–44.

van Wolferen, Karel. 1994. *Ningen o Kōfuku ni Shinai Nihon to Iu Shisutemu.* Tokyo: Mainichi Shimbunsha.

Wakamatsu, Yoshiya. 1992. *Hanzai Sōsa no Subete ga Wakaru Hon.* Tokyo: Sōgō Hōrei.

Wakamatsu, Yoshiya. 1990. *Sekken Kōtsū to Keiji Bengo.* Tokyo: Nihon Hyōronsha.

Weigend, Thomas. 1999. "Nihon no Keiji Bengo ni tai suru Dōitsuhō no Kanten kara no Komento." *Jurisuto* no. 1148 (January 1–15):193–197.

Yamaguchi, Hiroshi. 1999. *Shihō Fuhai.* Tokyo: PHP Kenkyūsho.

Yamaguchi, Ichiomi. 1994. "Tokusō Bōsō: Genshoku Kenji no Tegami ga Kataru." *Shūkan Asahi* (January 28):23–26.

Yamamoto, Samu. 1994. *Chikan Nikki.* Tokyo: KK Bestsellers.

Yamamoto, Yūji. 1998. *Kyōko to Gigoku: Tokyo Chiken Tokusōbu.* Tokyo: Ushio Shuppansha.

Yamamoto, Yūji. 1994. *Saikōsai Monogatari.* 2 vols. Tokyo: Nihon Hyoronsha.

Yamamoto, Yūji. 1989. *Tokyo Chiken Tokusōbu no Uchigawa.* Tokyo: Sekai Bunkasha.

Yamamoto, Yūji. 1988. *Kyōaku wa Nemurasenai.* Tokyo: Kadokawa.

Yamamoto, Yūji. 1983. *Tokyo Chiken Tokusōbu: Nihon Saikō no Sōsa Kikan.* Tokyo: Gendai Hyōronsha.

Yamamoto, Yūji. 1981. "Itoh Shigeki shi ni Miru Tokusō Kensatsu." *Hōgaku Seminā Zōkan* 16 (August):211–218.

Yamamoto, Yūji. 1980. *Tokyo Chiken Tokusōbu: Nihon Saikō no Sōsa Kikan: Sono Hikari to Kage.* Tokyo: Gendai Hyōronsha.

Yanagi, Toshio, Matsuda Akira, and Tatsuno Bunri. 1994. *Rainichi Gaikokujin ni yoru Shōgai Jihan no Shori-Kakei ni kansuru Kenkyū.* Tokyo: Nihonkoku Hōmushō Hōmu Sōgō Kenkyūsho.

Yasuhara, Yoshiho. 1985. *Kensatsu no Mado kara.* Tokyo: Kōbundō Shuppansha.

Yoshinaga, Ryōsuke. 1994. "Kenji Sōchō Yoshinaga Ryōsuke Dokusen Intabyū." *MarcoPolo* (July):34–39.

Zaikai Tenbō (Tokushū). 1979. "Hōmu-Kensatsu Kanryō no Jinji Kenkyū." (May):58–90.

Index